Shojo Beat

ORESAMA TEACHER

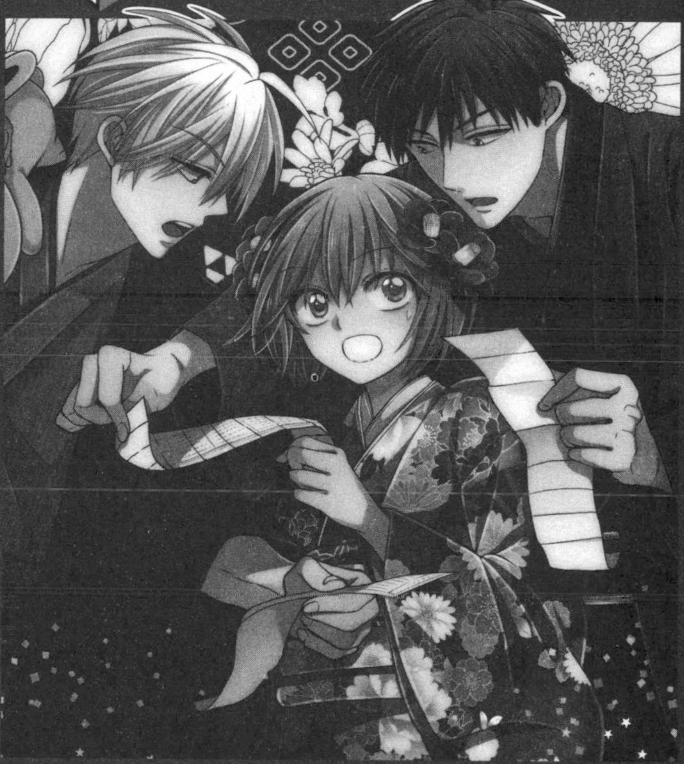

Vol. 23

Story & Art by

Izumi Tsubaki

ORESAMA TEACHER

CHARACTERS AND THE STORY THUS FAR

PUBLIC MORALS CLUB

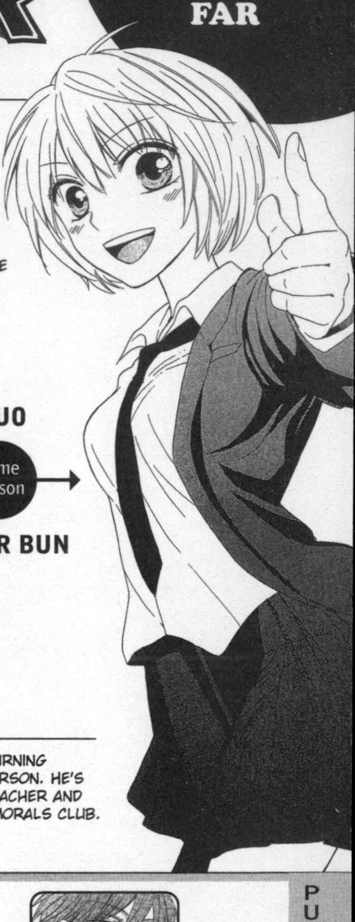

Mafuyu Kurosaki

THE FORMER BANCHO OF SAITAMA EAST HIGH. SHE TRANSFERED TO MIDORIGAOKA ACADEMY AND JOINED THE PUBLIC MORALS CLUB. SHE ALSO PLAYS THE PARTS OF NATSUO AND SUPER BUN. SHE IS CONCERNED BY THE FACT THAT SHE HAS NO FEMALE FRIENDS.

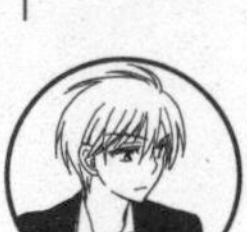

NATSUO

Same Person

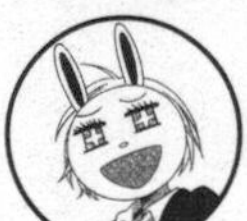

SUPER BUN

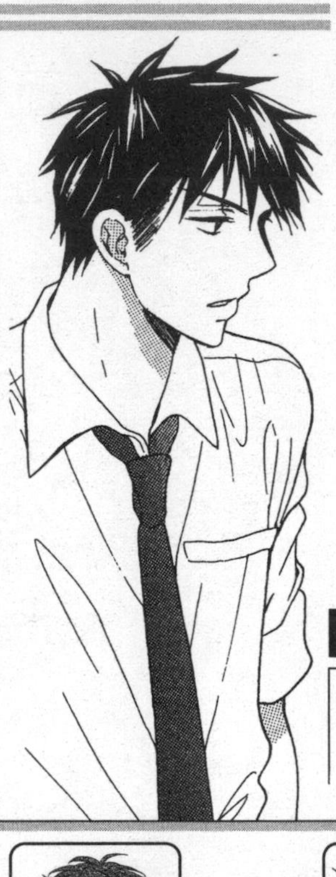

Takaomi Saeki

THE ONE RESPONSIBLE FOR TURNING MAFUYU INTO A TERRIFYING PERSON. HE'S NOW MAFUYU'S HOMEROOM TEACHER AND THE ADVISOR OF THE PUBLIC MORALS CLUB.

PUBLIC MORALS CLUB

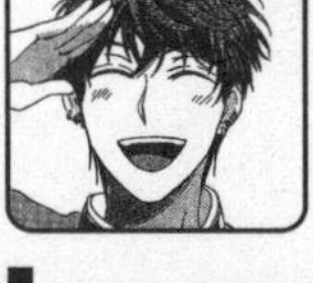

Aki Shibuya

A TALKATIVE AND WOMANIZING UNDERCLASSMAN. HIS NICKNAME IS AKKI. HE'S NOT GOOD AT FIGHTING.

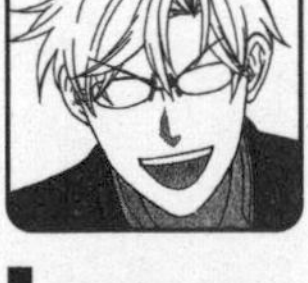

Shinobu Yui

HE WORSHIPS MIYABI, THE FORMER STUDENT COUNCIL PRESIDENT, BUT REJOINED THE PUBLIC MORALS CLUB. HE IS A SELF-PROCLAIMED NINJA.

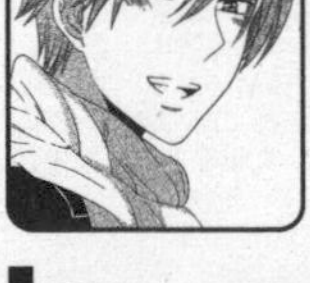

Hayasaka

MAFUYU'S CLASSMATE. HE ADMIRES SUPER BUN. HE IS A PLAIN AND SIMPLE DELINQUENT.

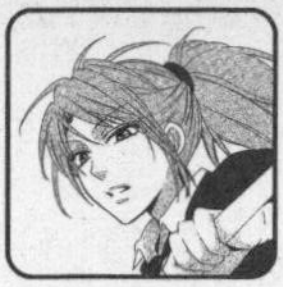

Wakana Hojo

SHE HAS A STOIC ATTITUDE AND WATCHES OVER HANABUSA, AND SHE HAS FEELINGS FOR YUI. SHE'S THE NEW STUDENT COUNCIL PRESIDENT.

THE STUDENT COUNCIL

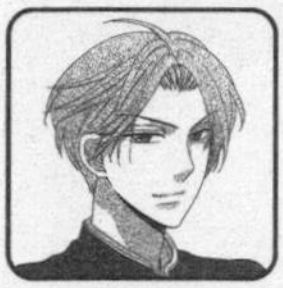

Shuntaro Kosaka

HE'S OBSESSED WITH DOING THINGS BY THE BOOK. HE DOES NOT HANDLE UNEXPECTED EVENTS WELL.

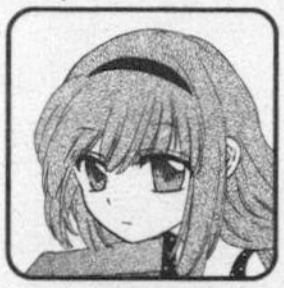

Komari Yukioka

USING HER CUTE LOOKS, SHE CONTROLS THOSE AROUND HER WITHOUT SAYING A WORD. INSIDE, SHE'S LIKE A DIRTY OLD MAN.

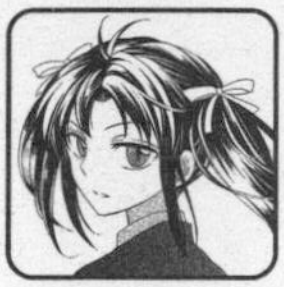

Kanon Nonoguchi

SHE HATES MEN. HER FAMILY RUNS A DOJO, SO SHE'S STRONG. SHE PLANNED TO DESTROY THE PUBLIC MORALS CLUB OUT OF GRATITUDE TOWARD MIYABI.

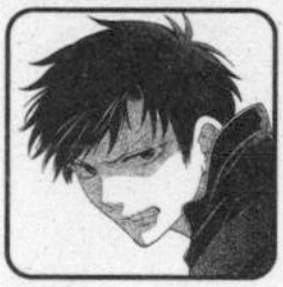

Reito Ayabe

HE LOVES CLEANING. HE GETS STRONGER IN DIRTY PLACES. HE IS A STUDENT COUNCIL OFFICER, BUT HE'S ALSO FRIENDS WITH MAFUYU.

KIYAMA HIGH SCHOOL

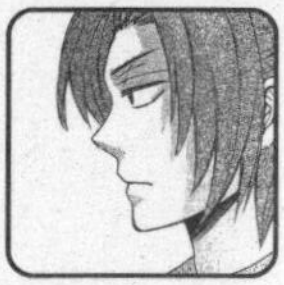

Nogami

THE BANCHO OF KIYAMA HIGH, A MIDORIGAOKA RIVAL. HE ONCE HAD A DISPUTE WITH KANON NONOGUCHI.

THE GRADUATES

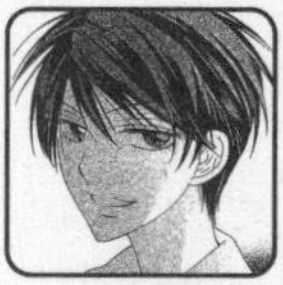

Miyabi Hanabusa

THE SCHOOL DIRECTOR'S SON AND THE FORMER PRESIDENT OF THE STUDENT COUNCIL. MADE SURE THE STUDENT COUNCIL HAD THEIR CHARACTER DEVELOPMENT ARC BEFORE HE GRADUATED. ATTENDING COLLEGE IN TOKYO.

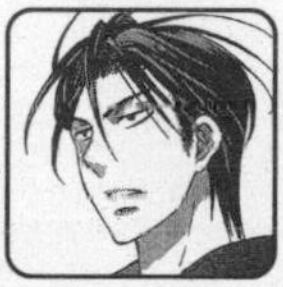

Kyotaro Okegawa

THE FORMER BANCHO OF EAST HIGH. DESPITE FLUNKING A YEAR, HE MANAGED TO GRADUATE AND IS ATTENDING A LOCAL COLLEGE. HE AND MAFUYU ARE ANONYMOUS PEN PALS.

story

★ MAFUYU KUROSAKI WAS A BANCHO WHO CONTROLLED ALL OF SAITAMA, BUT ONCE SHE TRANSFERRED TO MIDORIGAOKA ACADEMY, SHE COMPLETELY CHANGED AND BECAME A SPIRITED HIGH SCHOOL GIRL...OR AT LEAST SHE WAS SUPPOSED TO. TAKAOMI SAEKI, HER CHILDHOOD FRIEND AND HOMEROOM TEACHER, FORCED HER TO JOIN THE PUBLIC MORALS CLUB AND SHE HAS TO CONTINUE TO LIVE A LIFE THAT IS FAR FROM AVERAGE.

★ THE PUBLIC MORALS CLUB AND THE STUDENT COUNCIL ARE FIGHTING FOR OWNERSHIP OF THE SCHOOL. THE PUBLIC MORALS CLUB HAS THWARTED STUDENT COUNCIL OFFICERS LIKE KOSAKA, AYABE, NONOGUCHI AND KOMARI, AND ARE JOINED BY BANCHO OKEGAWA AND A FIRST-YEAR STUDENT BY THE NAME OF SHIBUYA. DESPITE THE CHAOS CAUSED BY YUI'S ART OF THE ECHO AND MOMOCHI'S HYPNOSIS OF HAYASAKA, THE PUBLIC MORALS CLUB IS MORE UNITED THAN EVER! MEANWHILE, A FAKE SUPER BUN HAS SHOWN UP AT SCHOOL AND THE MEMBERS OF THE STUDENT COUNCIL HAVE BECOME THE TARGETS OF VERY PERSONAL PRANKS. MAFUYU AND HER FRIENDS CHASE DOWN THE FAKE SUPER BUN, AND WHEN THEY FINALLY CATCH THE IMPOSTOR, THEY DISCOVER IT'S MIYABI HANABUSA. MIYABI IS GRADUATING SOON AND HAS BEEN USING SUPER BUN AS A MEANS TO SEE HOW WELL THE MEMBERS OF THE STUDENT COUNCIL HAVE OVERCOME THEIR ISSUES.

★ GRADUATION DAY FINALLY ARRIVES! ALTHOUGH MAFUYU HAS BEEN HIS ENEMY, MIYABI TELLS HER THAT SHE'S HIS HERO. MAFUYU SAYS FAREWELL TO THE GRADUATES AS THEY MAKE THE JOURNEY TO A NEW STAGE OF THEIR LIVES. NOW MAFUYU AND HER FRIENDS ARE ABOUT TO BEGIN THEIR FINAL YEAR IN HIGH SCHOOL...

ORESAMA TEACHER

Volume 23
CONTENTS

Chapter 129

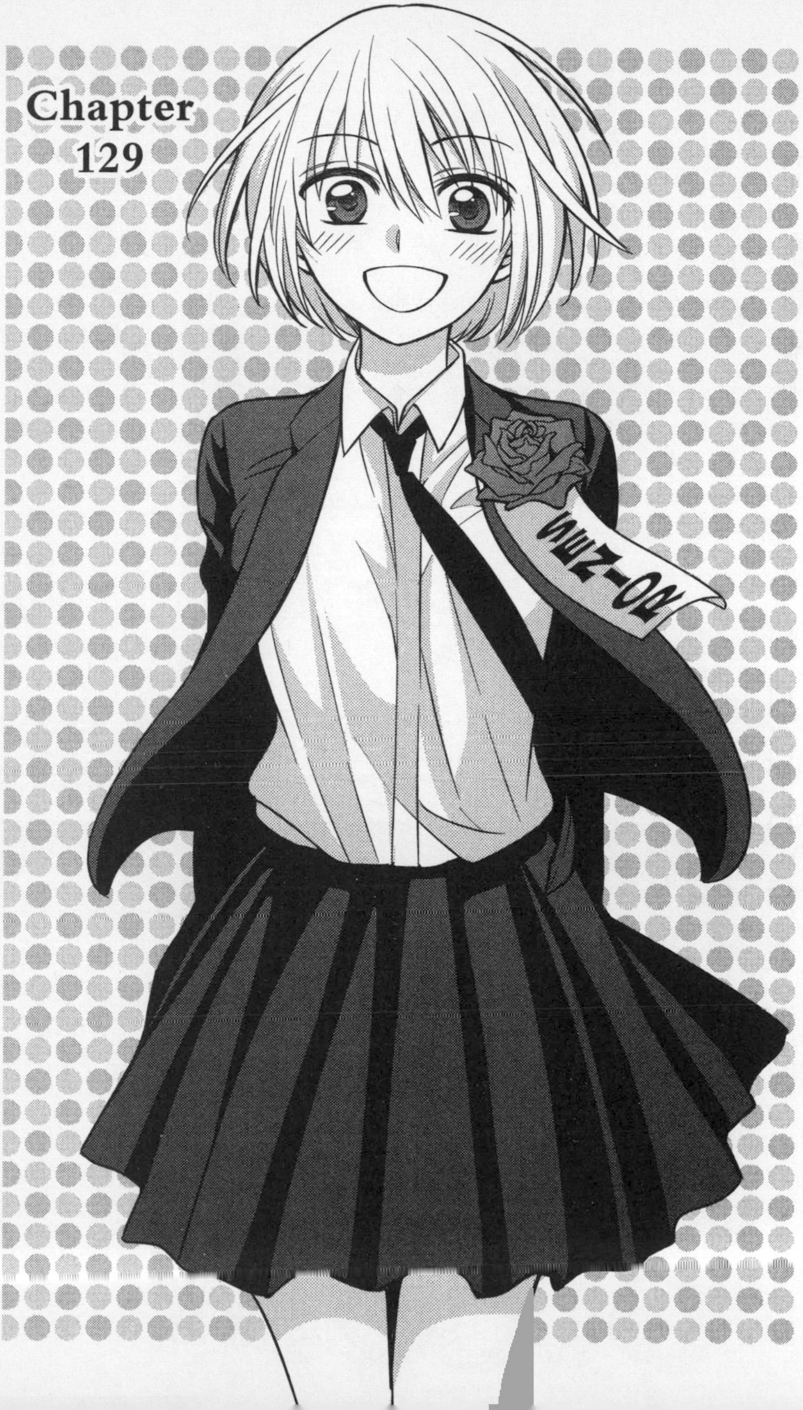

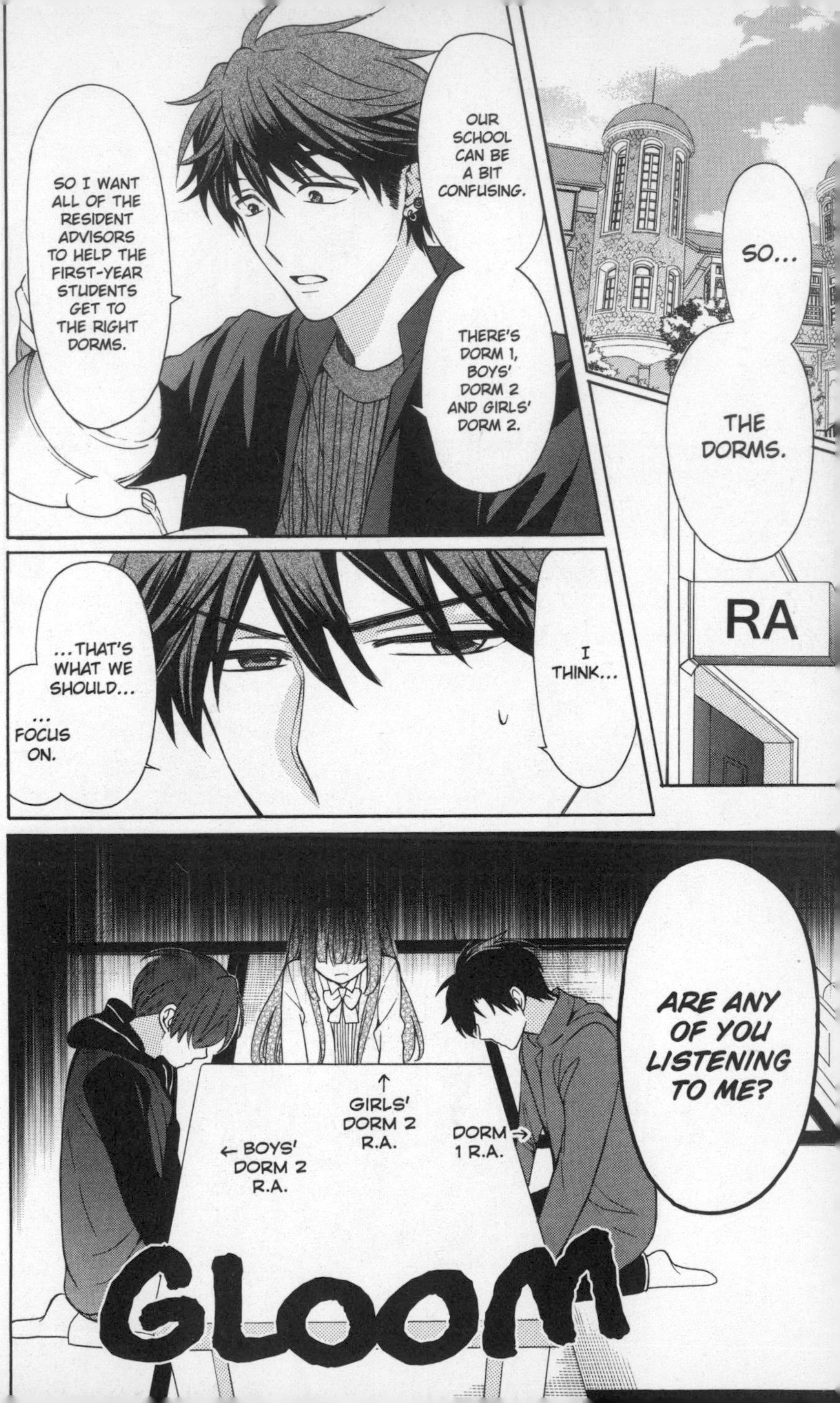
SO...
THE DORMS.
RA
OUR SCHOOL CAN BE A BIT CONFUSING.
THERE'S DORM 1, BOYS' DORM 2 AND GIRLS' DORM 2.
SO I WANT ALL OF THE RESIDENT ADVISORS TO HELP THE FIRST-YEAR STUDENTS GET TO THE RIGHT DORMS.
I THINK...
...THAT'S WHAT WE SHOULD...
... FOCUS ON.
ARE ANY OF YOU LISTENING TO ME?
DORM 1 R.A.
GIRLS' DORM 2 R.A.
BOYS' DORM 2 R.A.
GLOOM

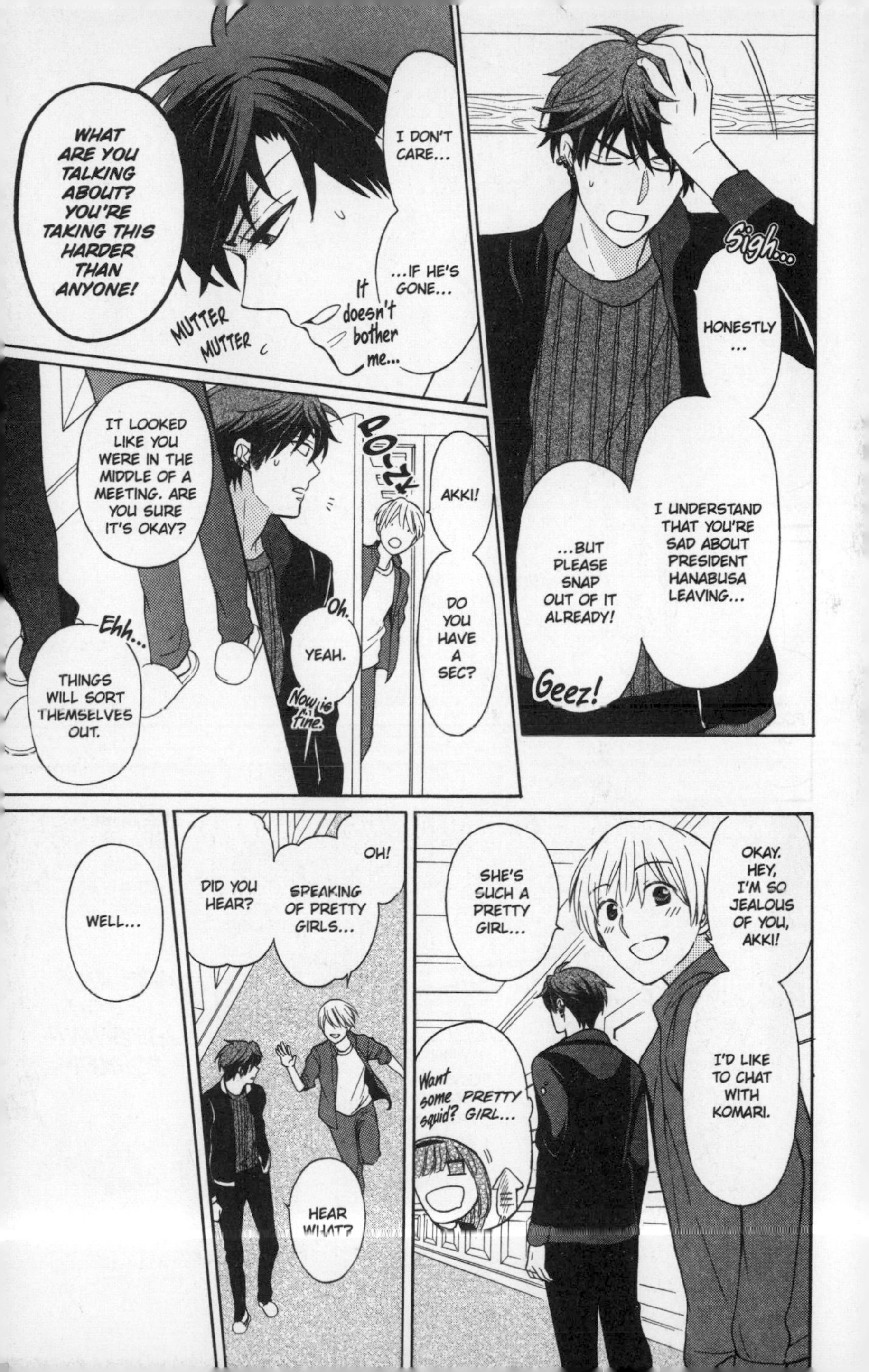
Sigh...
HONESTLY ...
I UNDERSTAND THAT YOU'RE SAD ABOUT PRESIDENT HANABUSA LEAVING...
...BUT PLEASE SNAP OUT OF IT ALREADY!
Geez!
I DON'T CARE...
...IF HE'S GONE...
It doesn't bother me...
MUTTER MUTTER
WHAT ARE YOU TALKING ABOUT? YOU'RE TAKING THIS HARDER THAN ANYONE!
AKKI!
DO YOU HAVE A SEC?
Oh.
YEAH.
Now is fine.
IT LOOKED LIKE YOU WERE IN THE MIDDLE OF A MEETING. ARE YOU SURE IT'S OKAY?
Ehh...
THINGS WILL SORT THEMSELVES OUT.
OKAY. HEY, I'M SO JEALOUS OF YOU, AKKI!
I'D LIKE TO CHAT WITH KOMARI.
SHE'S SUCH A PRETTY GIRL...
Want some squid?
PRETTY GIRL...
OH!
SPEAKING OF PRETTY GIRLS...
DID YOU HEAR?
HEAR WHAT?
WELL...

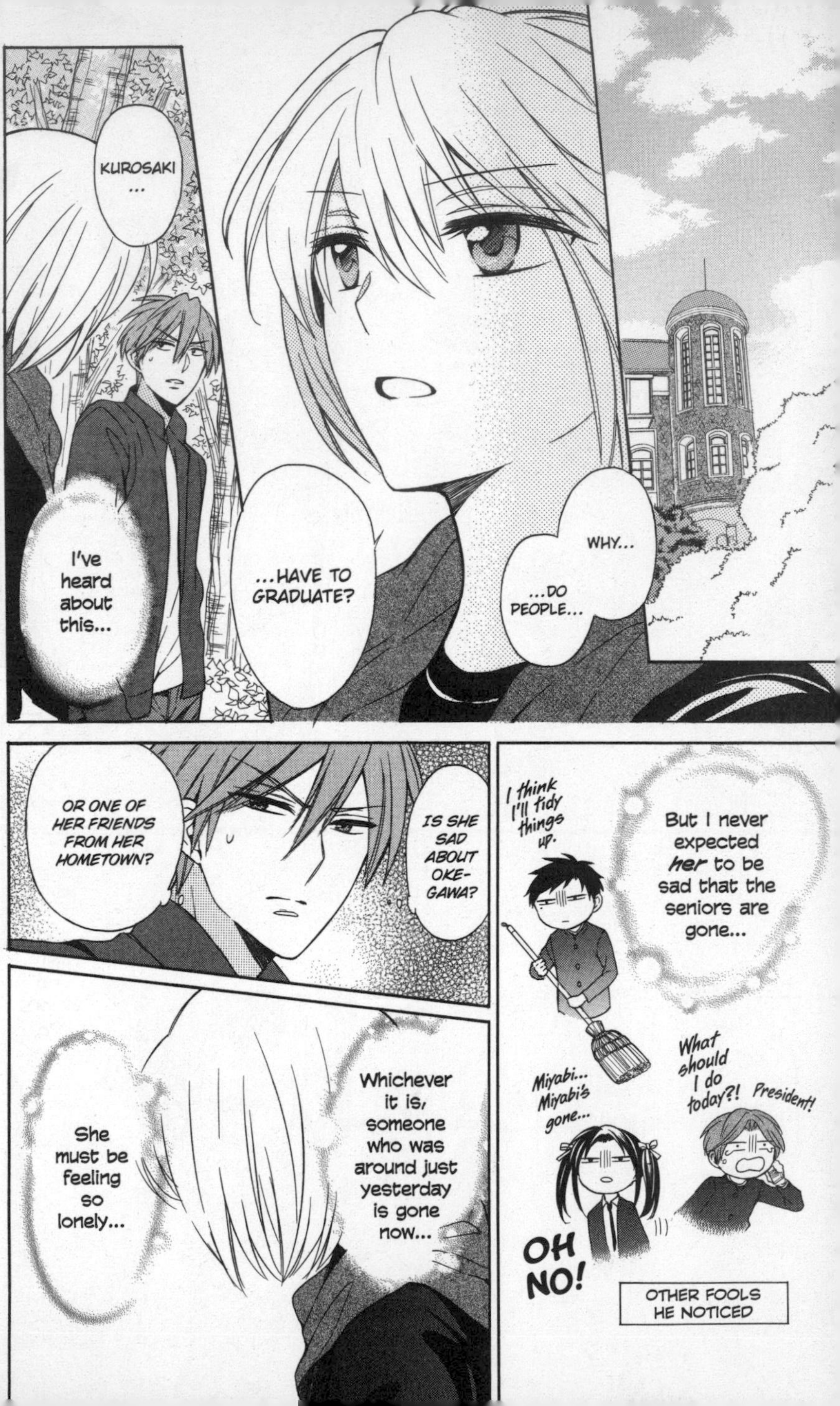
WHY...
...DO PEOPLE...
...HAVE TO GRADUATE?
KUROSAKI ...
I've heard about this...
But I never expected *her* to be sad that the seniors are gone...
I think I'll tidy things up.
What should I do today?!
President!
Miyabi... Miyabi's gone...
OH NO!
OTHER FOOLS HE NOTICED
IS SHE SAD ABOUT OKE-GAWA?
OR ONE OF HER FRIENDS FROM HER HOMETOWN?
Whichever it is, someone who was around just yesterday is gone now...
She must be feeling so lonely...

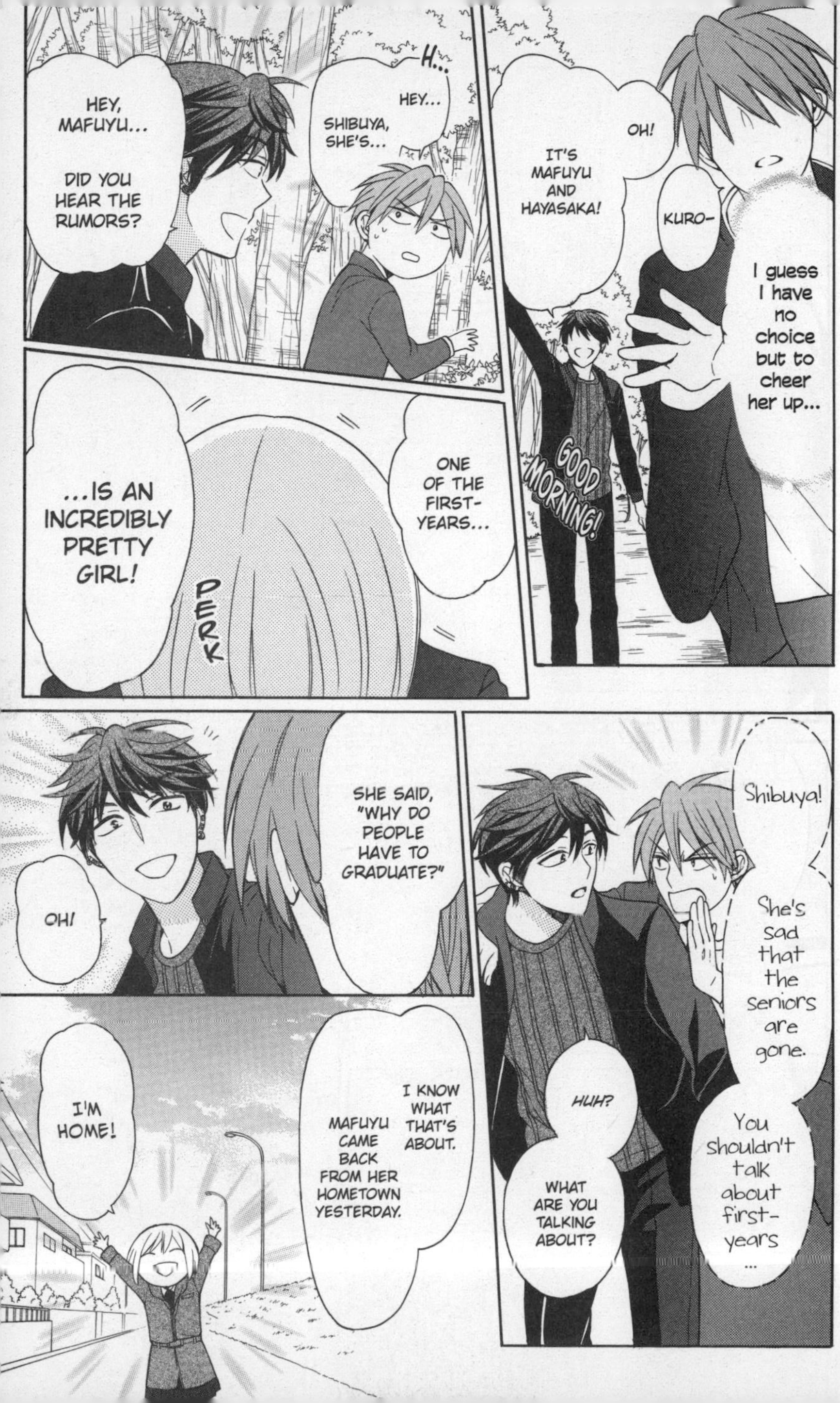
I guess I have no choice but to cheer her up...
OH!
IT'S MAFUYU AND HAYASAKA!
KURO-
GOOD MORNING!
H...
HEY... SHIBUYA, SHE'S...
HEY, MAFUYU... DID YOU HEAR THE RUMORS?
ONE OF THE FIRST-YEARS...
...IS AN INCREDIBLY PRETTY GIRL!
PERK
Shibuya!
She's sad that the seniors are gone.
You shouldn't talk about first-years ...
HUH?
WHAT ARE YOU TALKING ABOUT?
SHE SAID, "WHY DO PEOPLE HAVE TO GRADUATE?"
OH!
I KNOW WHAT THAT'S ABOUT.
MAFUYU CAME BACK FROM HER HOMETOWN YESTERDAY.
I'M HOME!

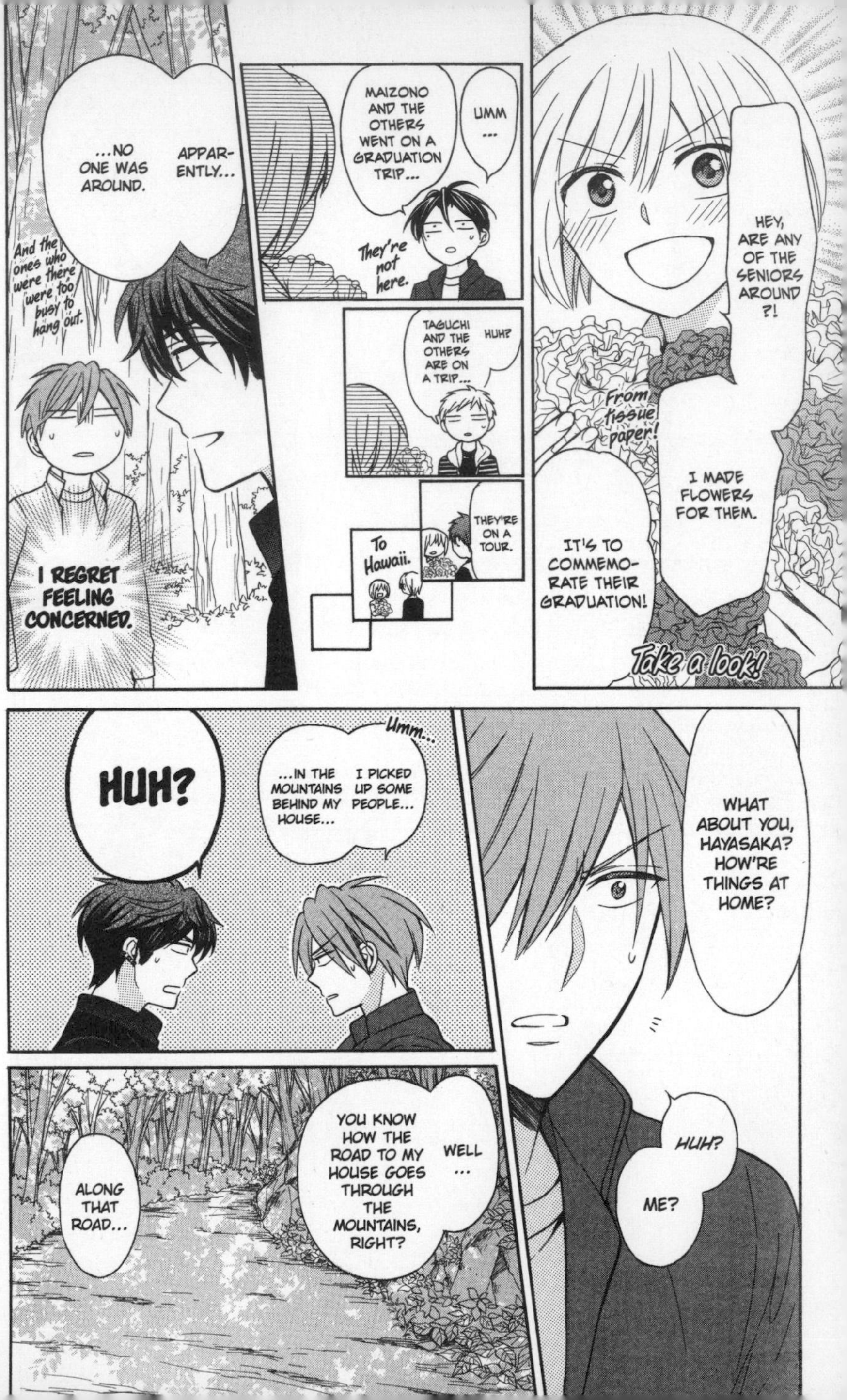
HEY, ARE ANY OF THE SENIORS AROUND?!
I MADE FLOWERS FOR THEM.
From tissue paper!
IT'S TO COMMEMORATE THEIR GRADUATION!
Take a look!
UMM ...
MAIZONO AND THE OTHERS WENT ON A GRADUATION TRIP...
They're not here.
HUH?
TAGUCHI AND THE OTHERS ARE ON A TRIP...
THEY'RE ON A TOUR.
To Hawaii.
APPARENTLY...
...NO ONE WAS AROUND.
And the ones who were there were too busy to hang out.
I REGRET FEELING CONCERNED.
WHAT ABOUT YOU, HAYASAKA? HOW'RE THINGS AT HOME?
HUH?
ME?
Umm...
I PICKED UP SOME PEOPLE...
...IN THE MOUNTAINS BEHIND MY HOUSE...
HUH?
WELL ...
YOU KNOW HOW THE ROAD TO MY HOUSE GOES THROUGH THE MOUNTAINS, RIGHT?
ALONG THAT ROAD...

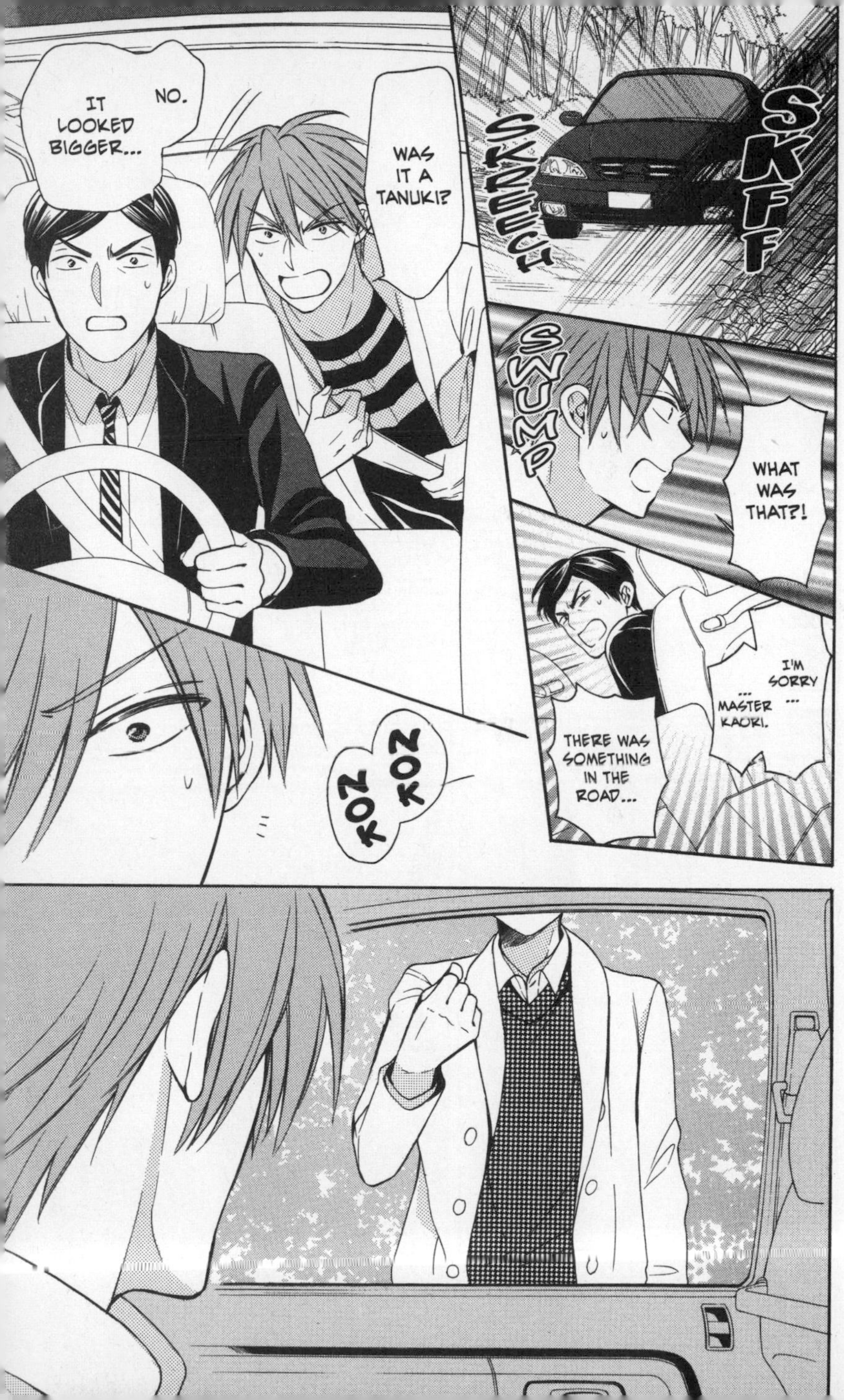
SKREECH
SKFF
SWUMP
WHAT WAS THAT?!
I'M SORRY... MASTER KAORI.
THERE WAS SOMETHING IN THE ROAD...
WAS IT A TANUKI?
NO.
IT LOOKED BIGGER...
KONK KONK

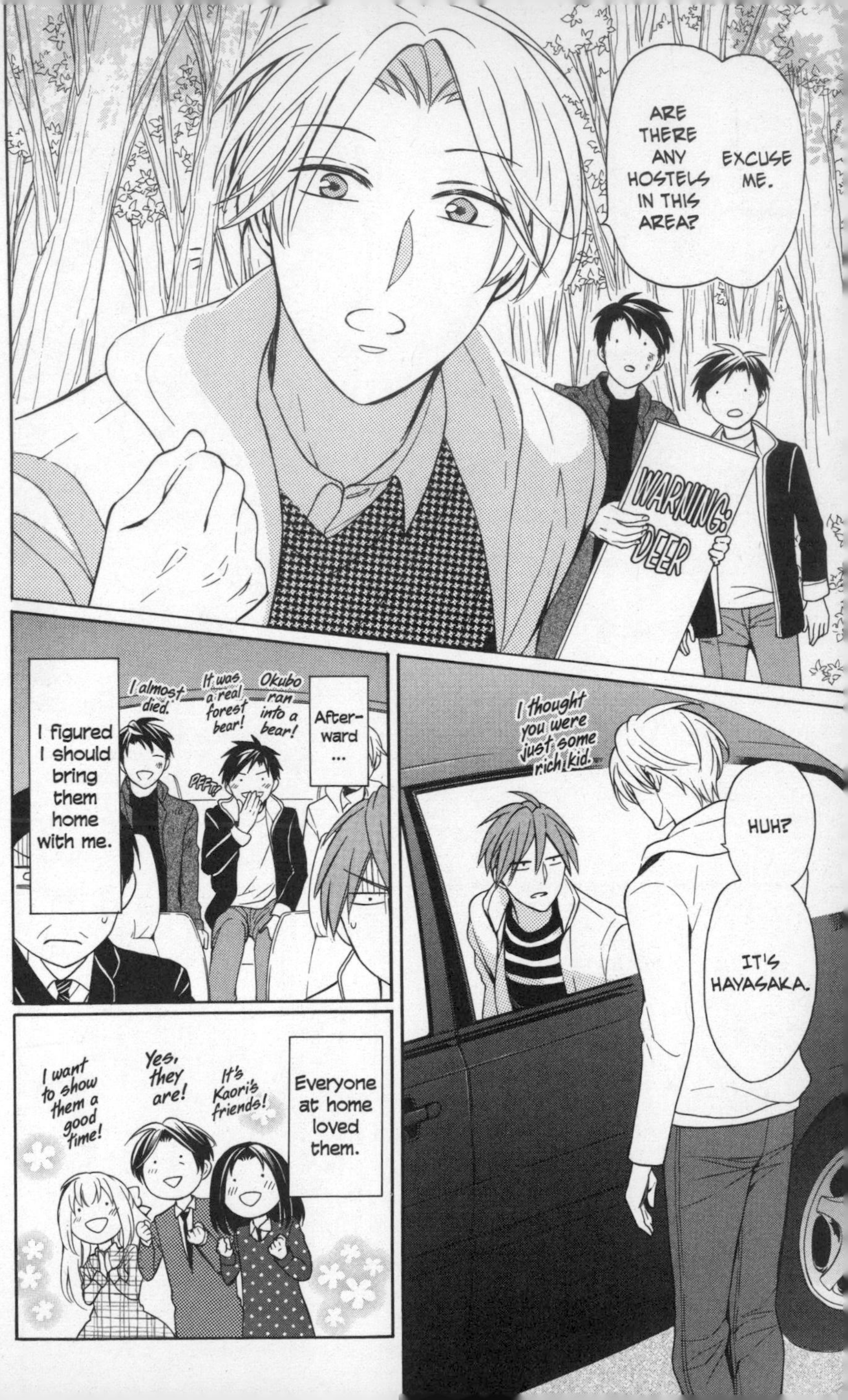
EXCUSE ME.
ARE THERE ANY HOSTELS IN THIS AREA?
WARNING: DEER
HUH?
IT'S HAYASAKA.
I thought you were just some rich kid.
Afterward...
Okubo ran into a bear!
It was a real forest bear!
I almost died.
PFFT!
I figured I should bring them home with me.
Everyone at home loved them.
It's Kaori's friends!
Yes, they are!
I want to show them a good time!

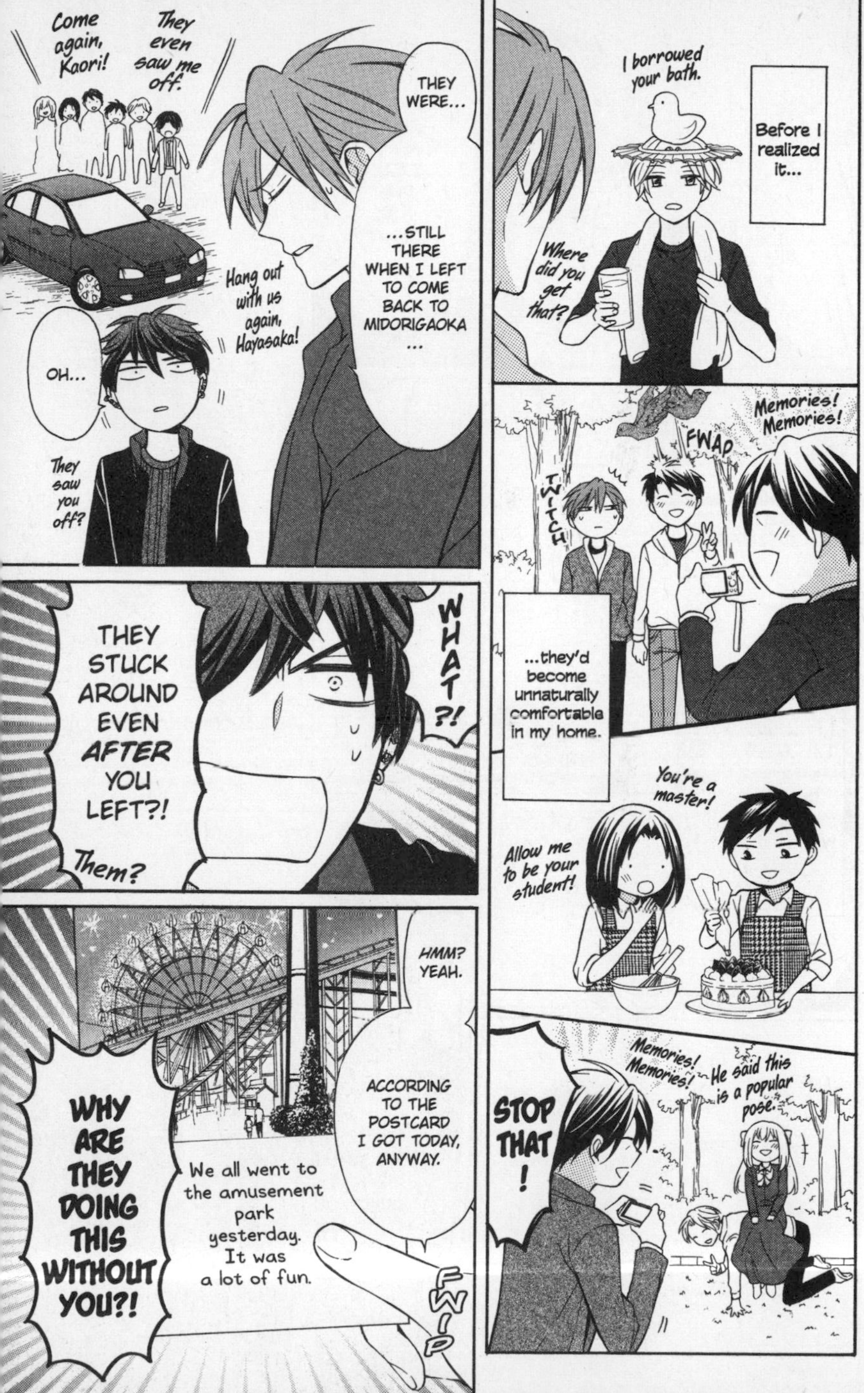
I borrowed your bath.
Before I realized it...
Where did you get that?
Memories! Memories!
FWAP
TWITCH
...they'd become unnaturally comfortable in my home.
You're a master!
Allow me to be your student!
Memories! Memories!
He said this is a popular pose.
STOP THAT!
THEY WERE...
...STILL THERE WHEN I LEFT TO COME BACK TO MIDORIGAOKA...
They even saw me off.
Come again, Kaori!
Hang out with us again, Hayasaka!
OH...
They saw you off?
WHAT?!
THEY STUCK AROUND EVEN AFTER YOU LEFT?!
Them?
HMM? YEAH.
ACCORDING TO THE POSTCARD I GOT TODAY, ANYWAY.
FWIP
We all went to the amusement park yesterday. It was a lot of fun.
WHY ARE THEY DOING THIS WITHOUT YOU?!

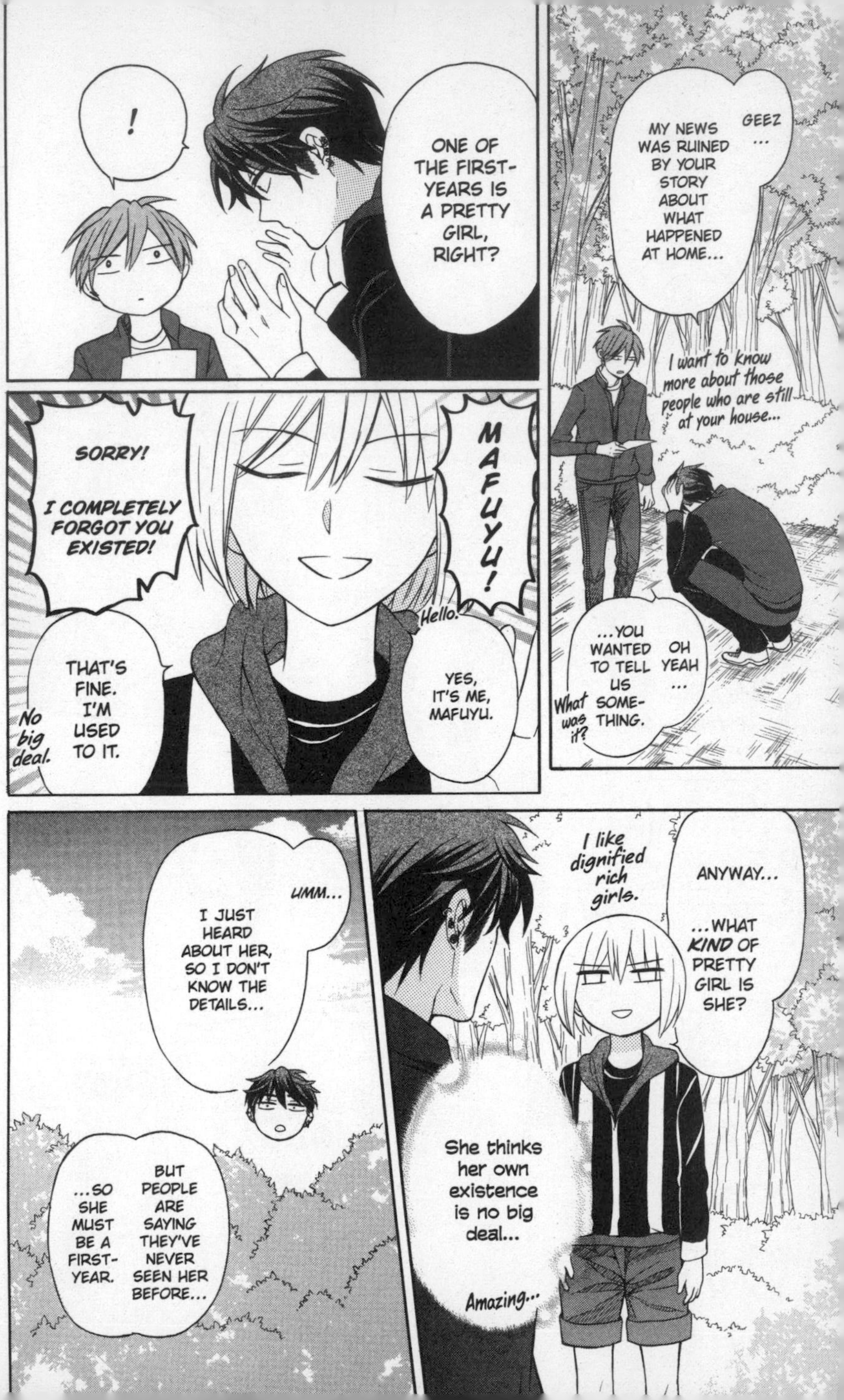
GEEZ...
MY NEWS WAS RUINED BY YOUR STORY ABOUT WHAT HAPPENED AT HOME...
I want to know more about those people who are still at your house...
OH YEAH...
...YOU WANTED TO TELL US SOMETHING.
What was it?
ONE OF THE FIRST-YEARS IS A PRETTY GIRL, RIGHT?
!
MAFUYU!
SORRY! I COMPLETELY FORGOT YOU EXISTED!
Hello.
YES, IT'S ME, MAFUYU.
THAT'S FINE. I'M USED TO IT.
No big deal.
ANYWAY... ...WHAT KIND OF PRETTY GIRL IS SHE?
I like dignified rich girls.
She thinks her own existence is no big deal...
Amazing...
UMM...
I JUST HEARD ABOUT HER, SO I DON'T KNOW THE DETAILS...
BUT PEOPLE ARE SAYING THEY'VE NEVER SEEN HER BEFORE...
...SO SHE MUST BE A FIRST-YEAR.

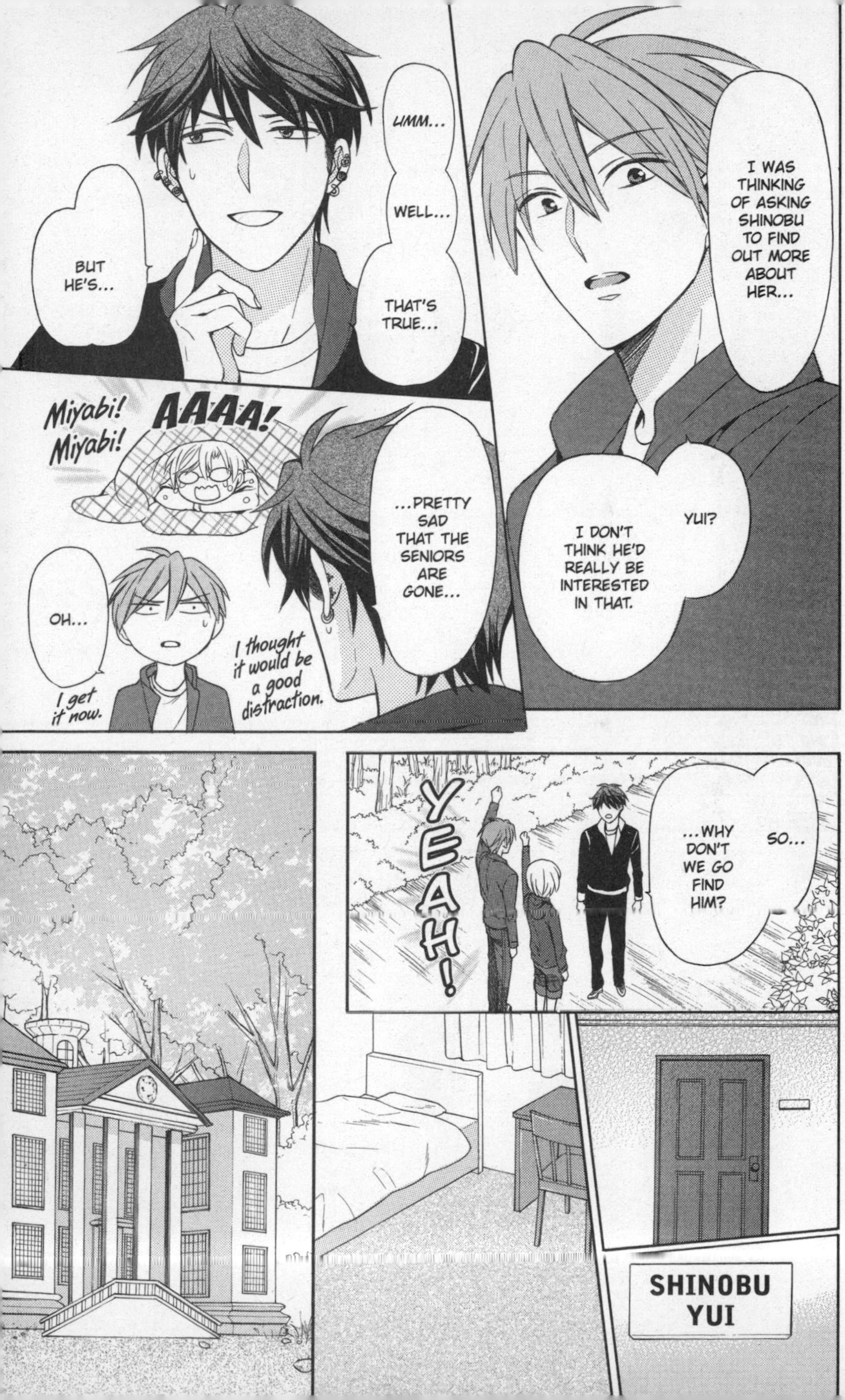
I WAS THINKING OF ASKING SHINOBU TO FIND OUT MORE ABOUT HER...
YUI?
I DON'T THINK HE'D REALLY BE INTERESTED IN THAT.
UMM...
WELL...
THAT'S TRUE...
BUT HE'S...
...PRETTY SAD THAT THE SENIORS ARE GONE...
AAAA!
Miyabi! Miyabi!
I thought it would be a good distraction.
OH...
I get it now.
SO...
...WHY DON'T WE GO FIND HIM?
YEAH!
SHINOBU YUI

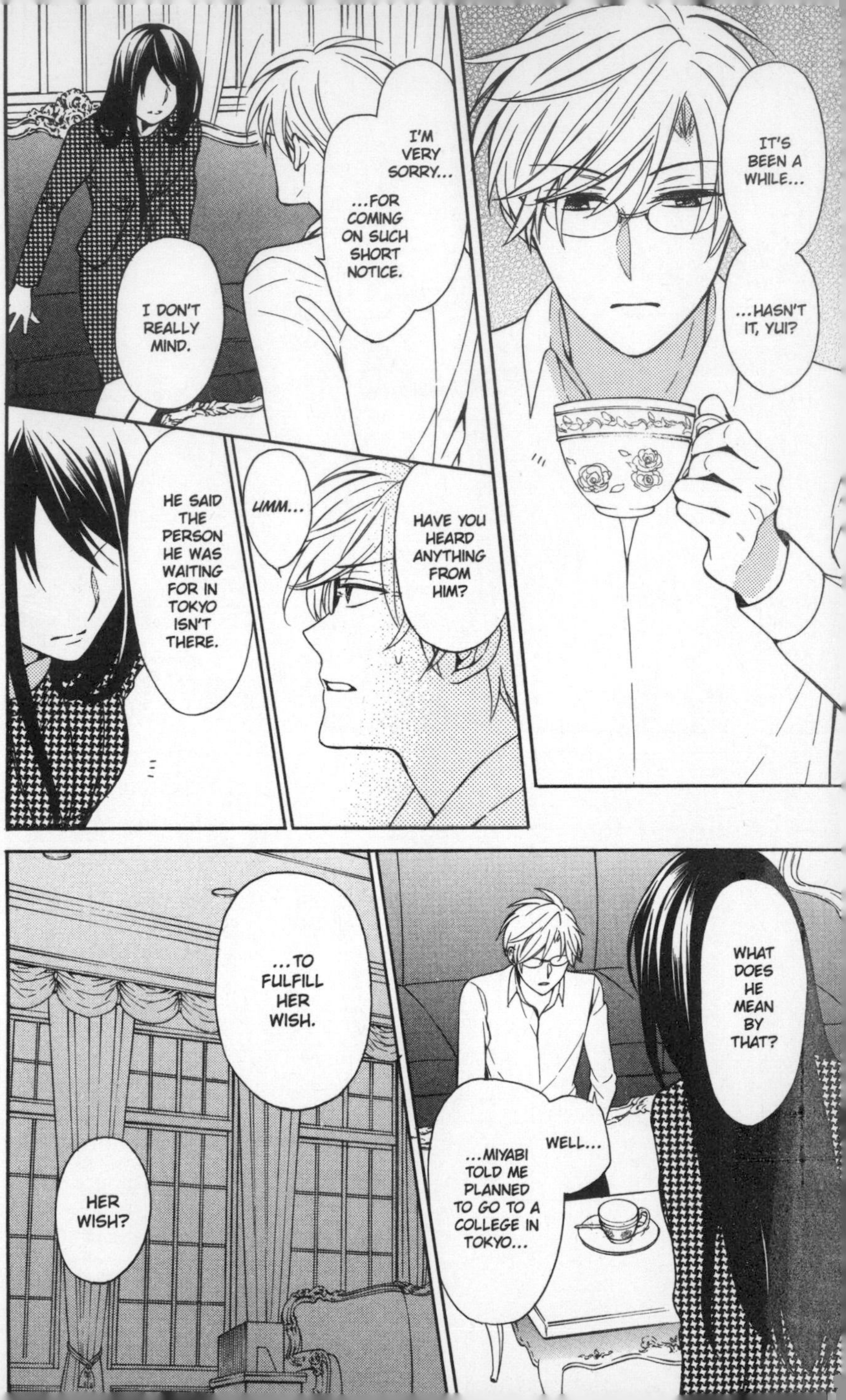
IT'S BEEN A WHILE...
...HASN'T IT, YUI?
I'M VERY SORRY...
...FOR COMING ON SUCH SHORT NOTICE.
I DON'T REALLY MIND.
HAVE YOU HEARD ANYTHING FROM HIM?
UMM...
HE SAID THE PERSON HE WAS WAITING FOR IN TOKYO ISN'T THERE.
WHAT DOES HE MEAN BY THAT?
WELL...
...MIYABI TOLD ME PLANNED TO GO TO A COLLEGE IN TOKYO...
...TO FULFILL HER WISH.
HER WISH?

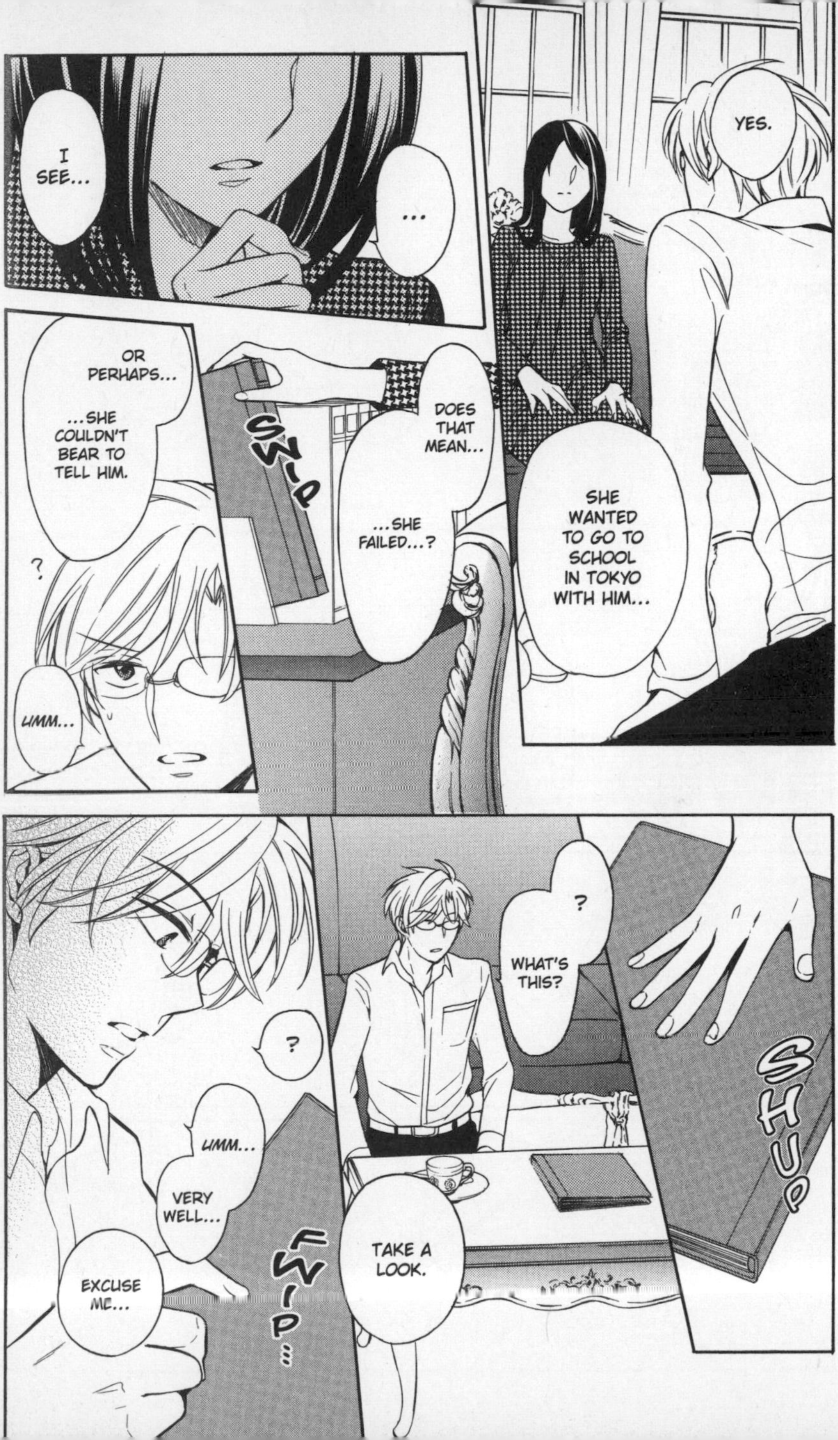
YES.
SHE WANTED TO GO TO SCHOOL IN TOKYO WITH HIM...
I SEE...
...
DOES THAT MEAN...
...SHE FAILED...?
OR PERHAPS...
...SHE COULDN'T BEAR TO TELL HIM.
SWIP
?
UMM...
SHUP
?
WHAT'S THIS?
TAKE A LOOK.
?
UMM...
VERY WELL...
FWIP..
EXCUSE ME...

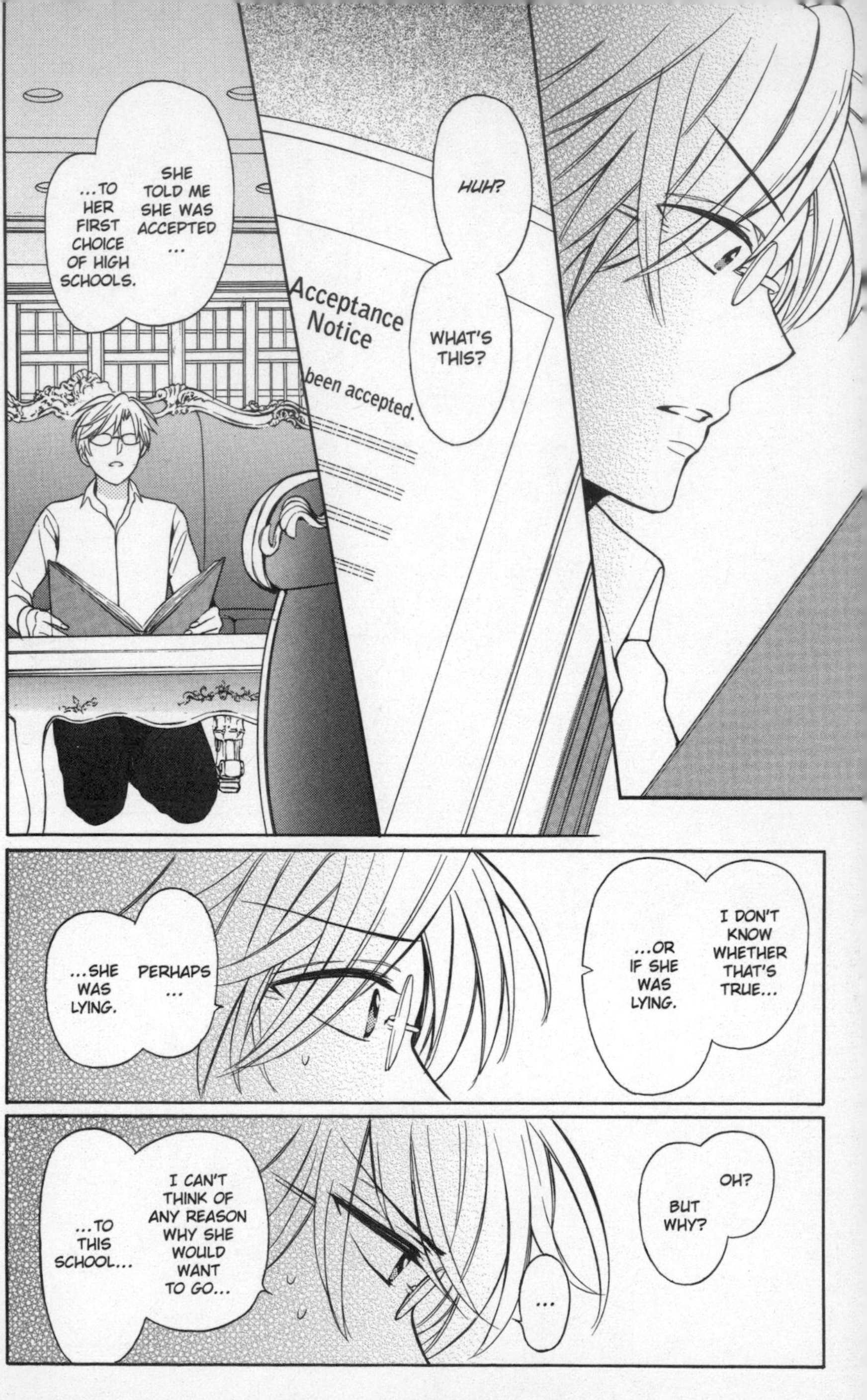
HUH?
WHAT'S THIS?
Acceptance Notice
been accepted.
SHE TOLD ME SHE WAS ACCEPTED...
...TO HER FIRST CHOICE OF HIGH SCHOOLS.
I DON'T KNOW WHETHER THAT'S TRUE...
...OR IF SHE WAS LYING.
PERHAPS...
...SHE WAS LYING.
OH?
BUT WHY?
...
I CAN'T THINK OF ANY REASON WHY SHE WOULD WANT TO GO...
...TO THIS SCHOOL...

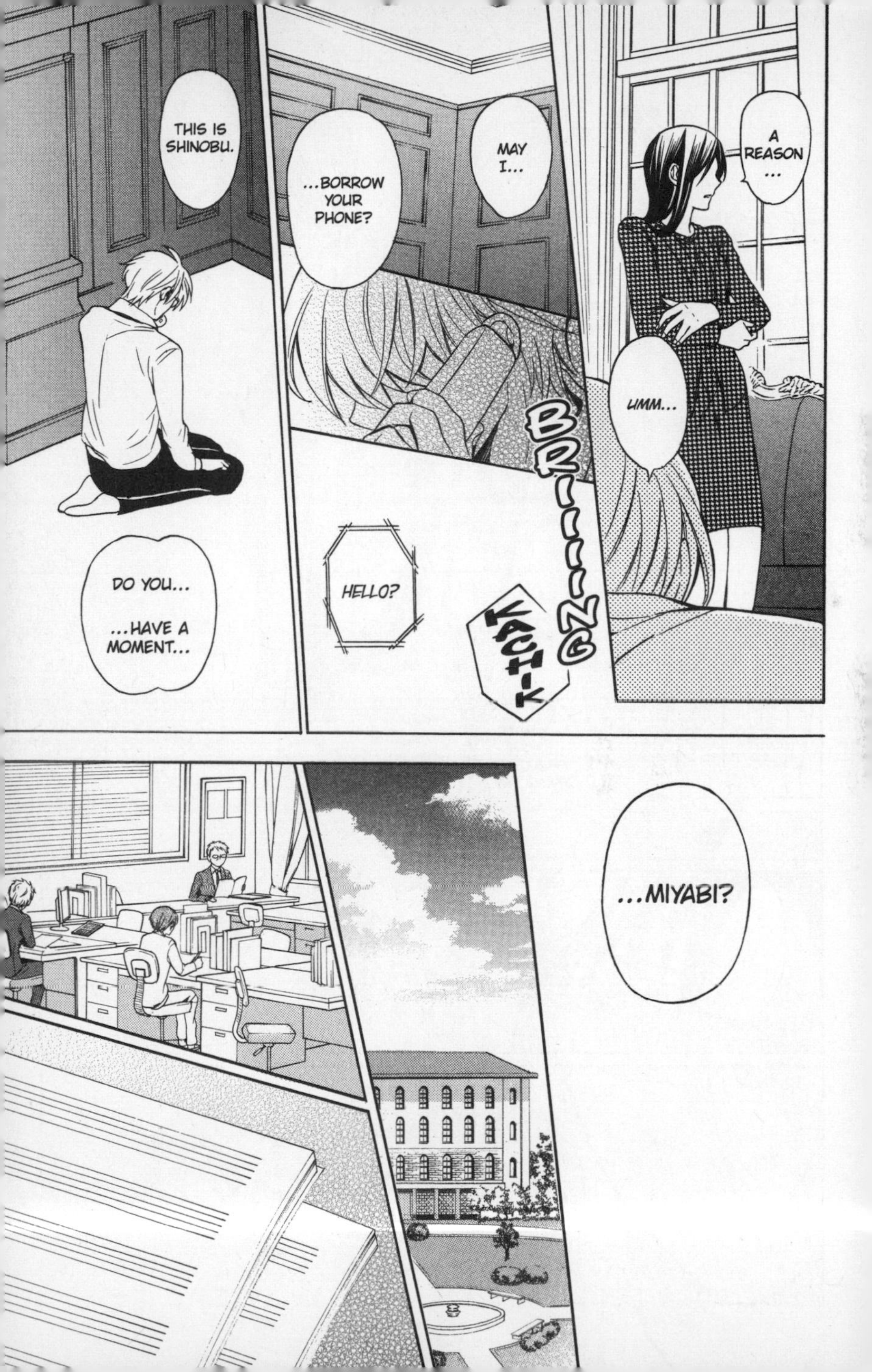
A REASON...
UMM...
BRIIIING
MAY I...
...BORROW YOUR PHONE?
HELLO?
KACHIK
THIS IS SHINOBU.
DO YOU... ...HAVE A MOMENT...
...MIYABI?

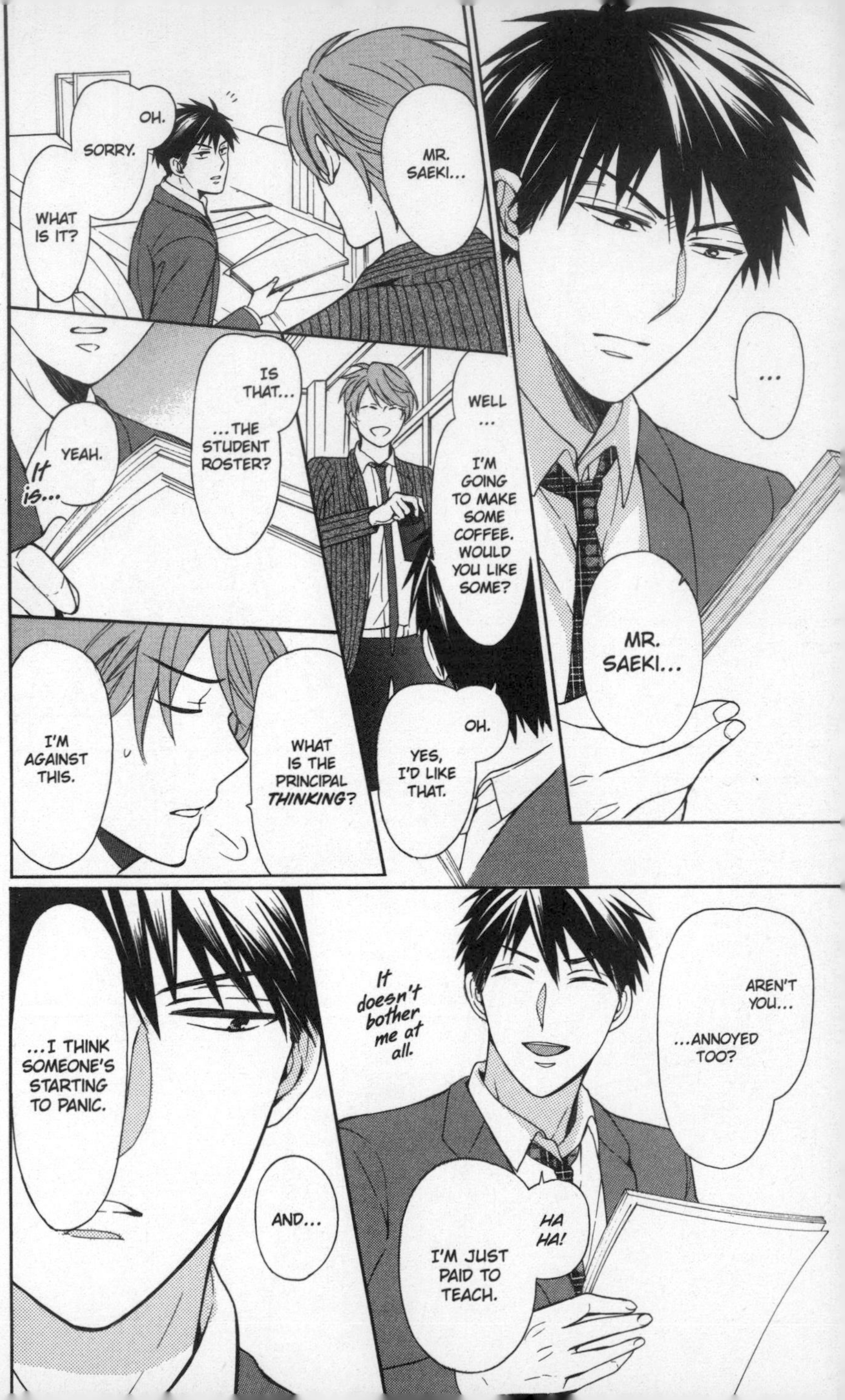
...
MR. SAEKI...
MR. SAEKI...
OH.
SORRY.
WHAT IS IT?
IS THAT...
...THE STUDENT ROSTER?
YEAH.
It is...
WELL...
I'M GOING TO MAKE SOME COFFEE. WOULD YOU LIKE SOME?
OH.
YES, I'D LIKE THAT.
WHAT IS THE PRINCIPAL *THINKING*?
I'M AGAINST THIS.
AREN'T YOU...
...ANNOYED TOO?
HA HA!
I'M JUST PAID TO TEACH.
It doesn't bother me at all.
AND...
...I THINK SOMEONE'S STARTING TO PANIC.

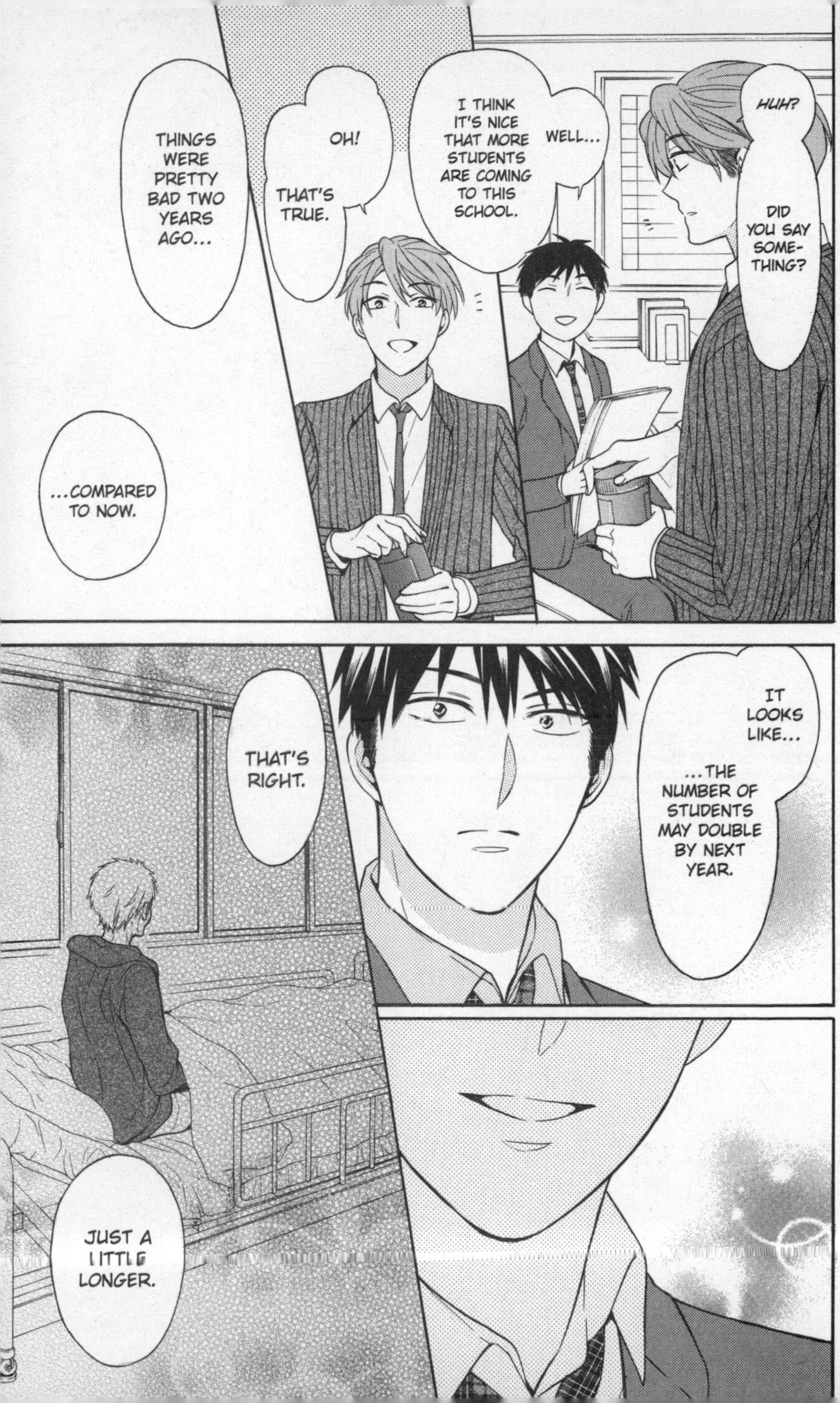
HUH?
DID YOU SAY SOMETHING?
WELL...
I THINK IT'S NICE THAT MORE STUDENTS ARE COMING TO THIS SCHOOL.
OH!
THAT'S TRUE.
THINGS WERE PRETTY BAD TWO YEARS AGO...
...COMPARED TO NOW.
IT LOOKS LIKE...
...THE NUMBER OF STUDENTS MAY DOUBLE BY NEXT YEAR.
THAT'S RIGHT.
JUST A LITTLE LONGER.

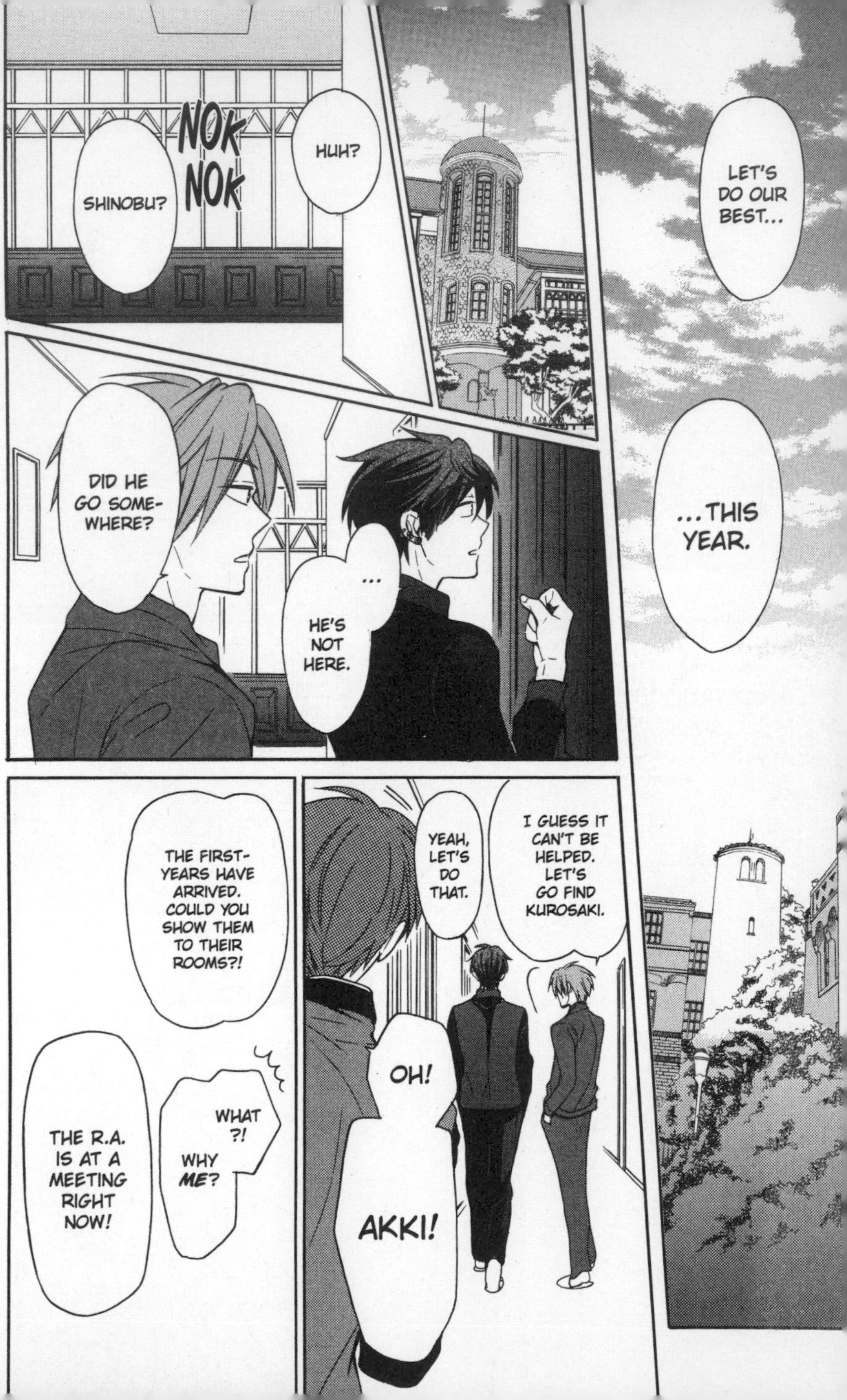
LET'S DO OUR BEST...
...THIS YEAR.
HUH?
NOK NOK
SHINOBU?
... HE'S NOT HERE.
DID HE GO SOME-WHERE?
I GUESS IT CAN'T BE HELPED. LET'S GO FIND KUROSAKI.
YEAH, LET'S DO THAT.
OH!
AKKI!
THE FIRST-YEARS HAVE ARRIVED. COULD YOU SHOW THEM TO THEIR ROOMS?!
WHAT?! WHY *ME*?
THE R.A. IS AT A MEETING RIGHT NOW!

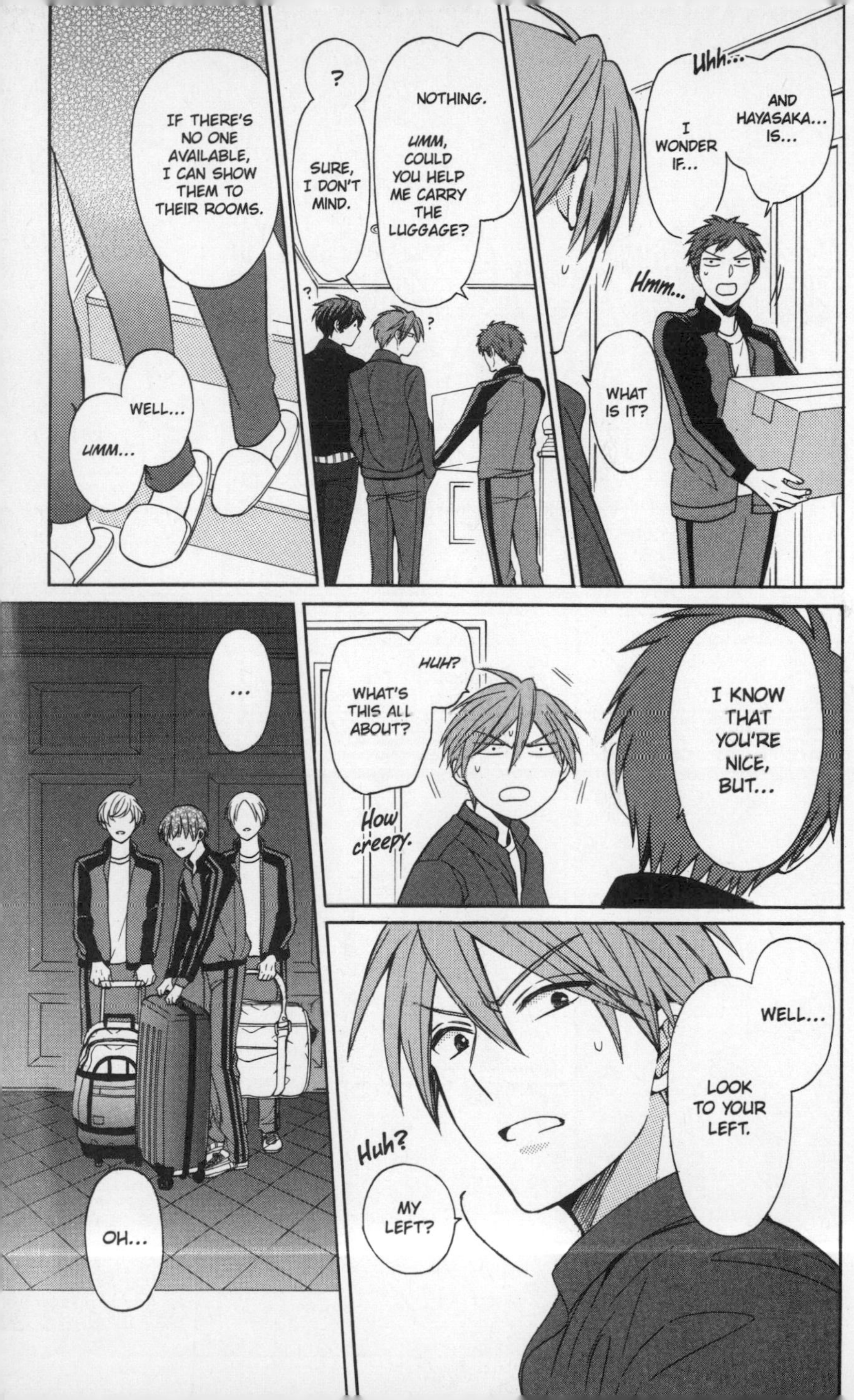
Uhh...
AND HAYASAKA... IS...
I WONDER IF...
Hmm...
WHAT IS IT?
NOTHING.
UMM, COULD YOU HELP ME CARRY THE LUGGAGE?
?
SURE, I DON'T MIND.
?
?
IF THERE'S NO ONE AVAILABLE, I CAN SHOW THEM TO THEIR ROOMS.
WELL...
UMM...
I KNOW THAT YOU'RE NICE, BUT...
HUH?
WHAT'S THIS ALL ABOUT?
How creepy.
WELL...
LOOK TO YOUR LEFT.
Huh?
MY LEFT?
...
OH...

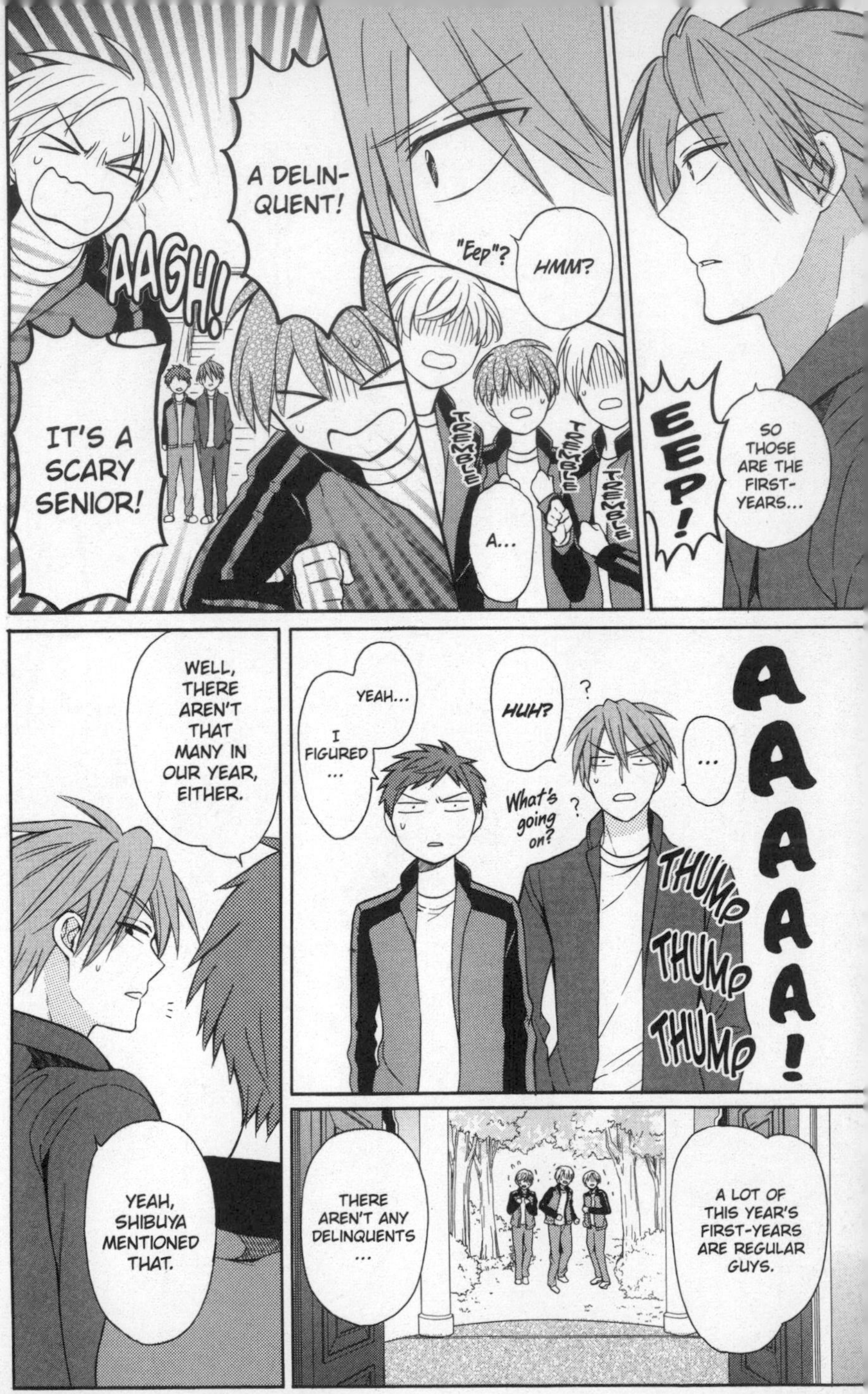
SO THOSE ARE THE FIRST-YEARS...
EEP!
HMM?
"Eep"?
TREMBLE
TREMBLE
TREMBLE
A...
A DELIN-QUENT!
AAGH!
IT'S A SCARY SENIOR!
AAAAAA!
THUMP THUMP THUMP
...
HUH?
What's going on?
YEAH...
I FIGURED...
A LOT OF THIS YEAR'S FIRST-YEARS ARE REGULAR GUYS.
THERE AREN'T ANY DELINQUENTS...
WELL, THERE AREN'T THAT MANY IN OUR YEAR, EITHER.
YEAH, SHIBUYA MENTIONED THAT.

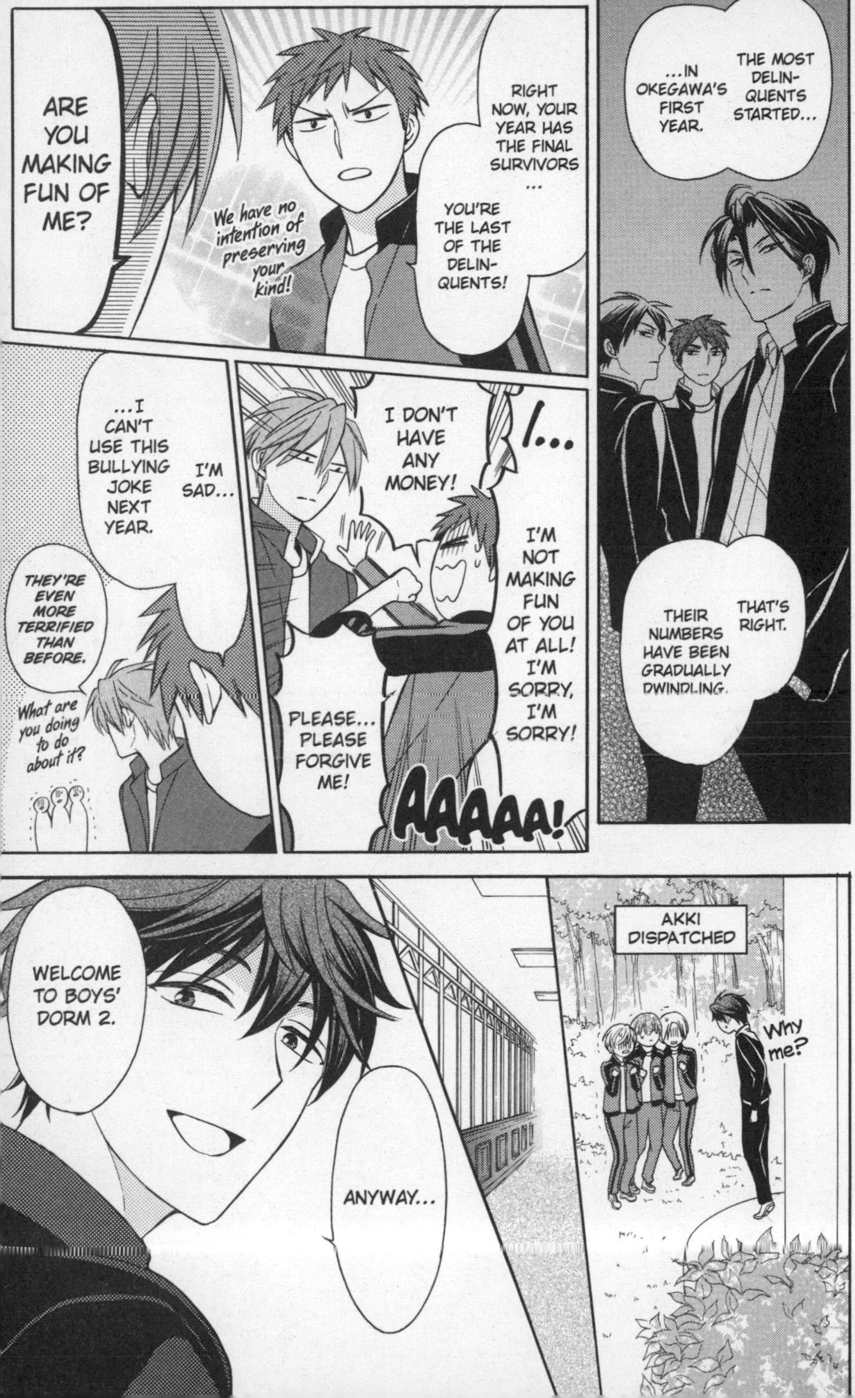
THE MOST DELIN-QUENTS STARTED...
...IN OKEGAWA'S FIRST YEAR.
THAT'S RIGHT.
THEIR NUMBERS HAVE BEEN GRADUALLY DWINDLING.
RIGHT NOW, YOUR YEAR HAS THE FINAL SURVIVORS ...
YOU'RE THE LAST OF THE DELIN-QUENTS!
We have no intention of preserving your kind!
ARE YOU MAKING FUN OF ME?
I...
I DON'T HAVE ANY MONEY!
I'M NOT MAKING FUN OF YOU AT ALL! I'M SORRY, I'M SORRY!
PLEASE... PLEASE FORGIVE ME!
AAAAA!
I'M SAD...
...I CAN'T USE THIS BULLYING JOKE NEXT YEAR.
THEY'RE EVEN MORE TERRIFIED THAN BEFORE.
What are you doing to do about it?
AKKI DISPATCHED
Why me?
WELCOME TO BOYS' DORM 2.
ANYWAY...

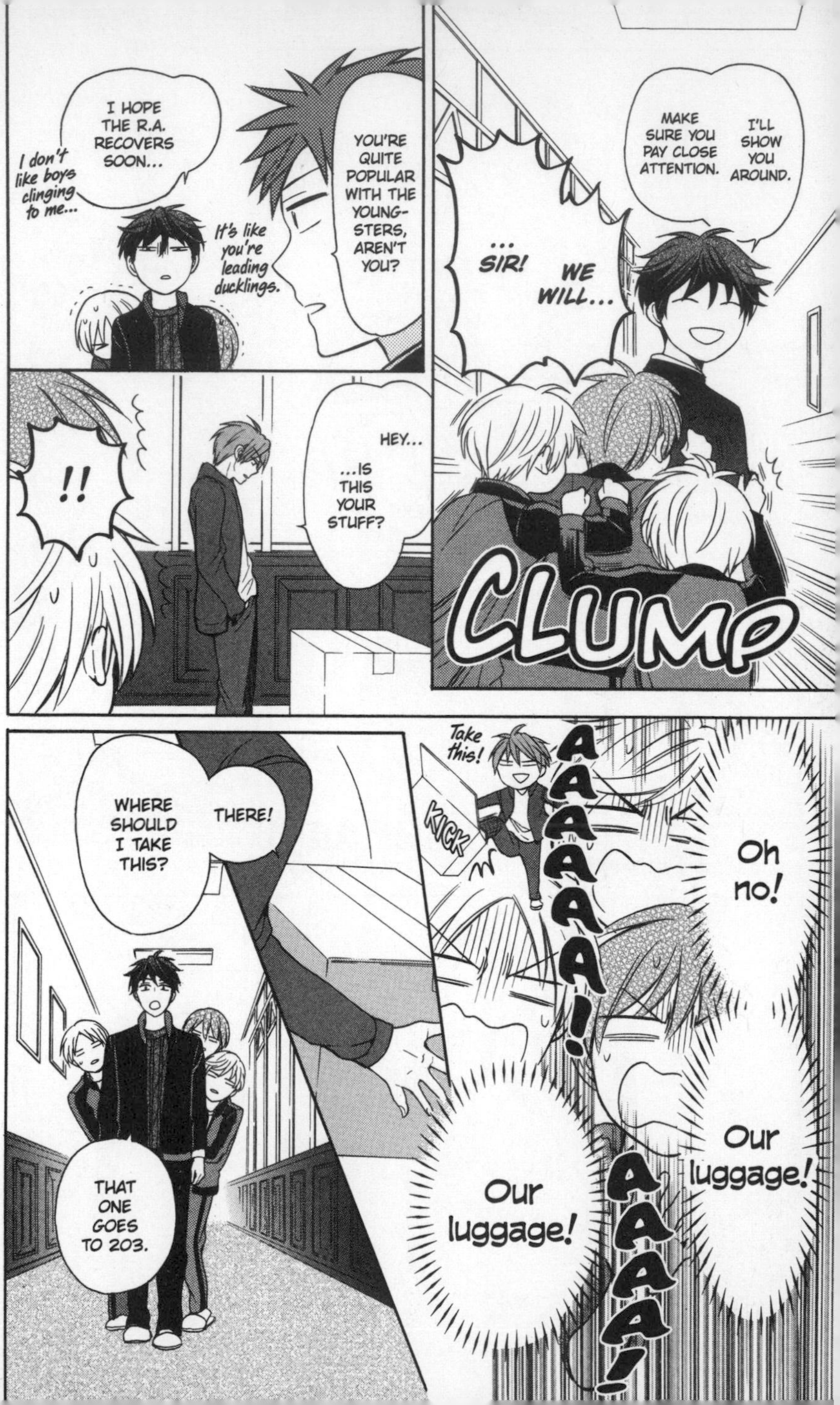
I'LL SHOW YOU AROUND.
MAKE SURE YOU PAY CLOSE ATTENTION.
WE WILL...
...SIR!
CLUMP
YOU'RE QUITE POPULAR WITH THE YOUNGSTERS, AREN'T YOU?
It's like you're leading ducklings.
I HOPE THE R.A. RECOVERS SOON...
I don't like boys clinging to me...
HEY...
...IS THIS YOUR STUFF?
!!
Take this!
KICK
AAAAAAA!
Oh no!
Our luggage!
Our luggage!
AAAAA!
THERE!
WHERE SHOULD I TAKE THIS?
THAT ONE GOES TO 203.

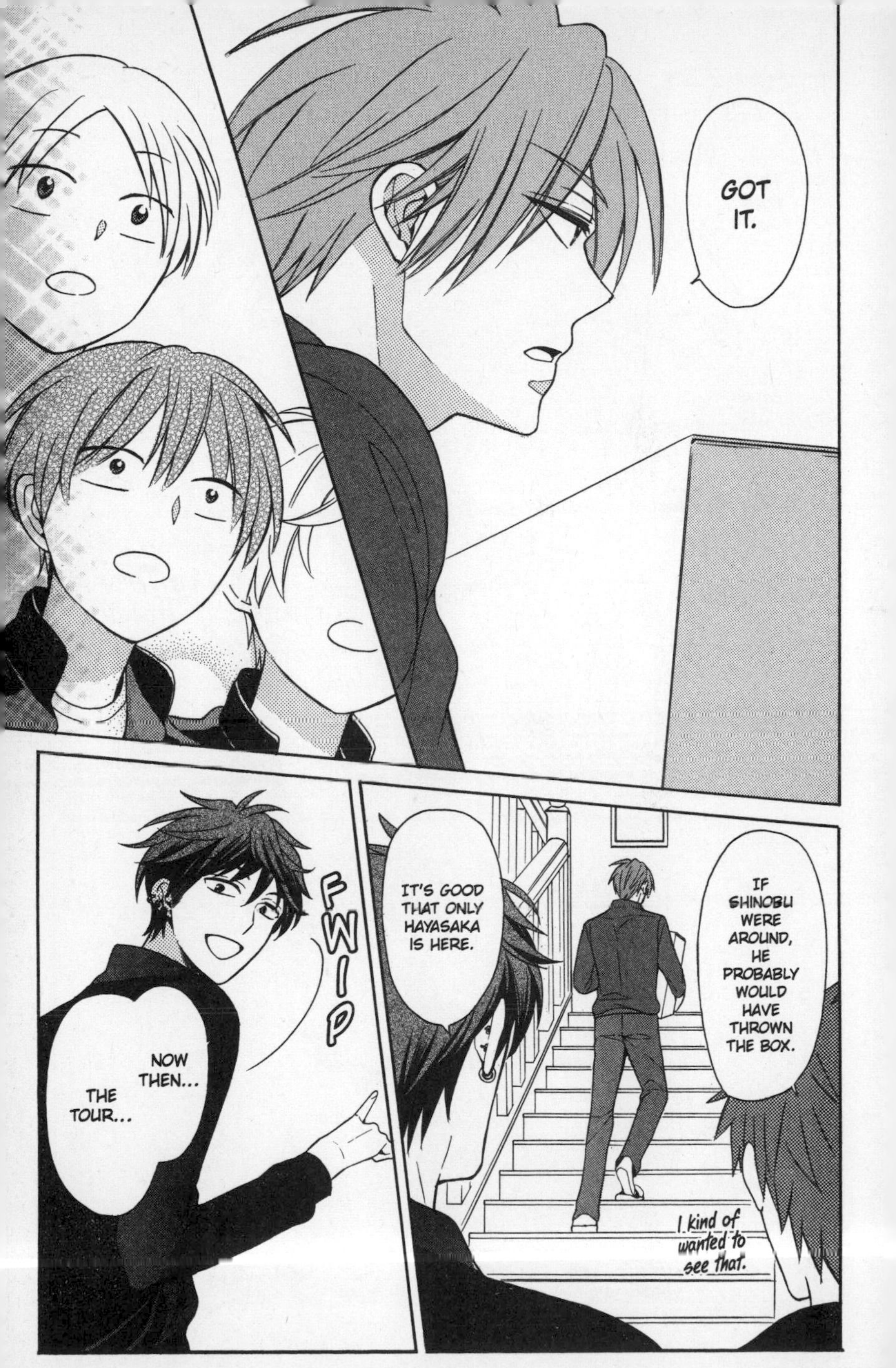
GOT IT.
IT'S GOOD THAT ONLY HAYASAKA IS HERE.
IF SHINOBU WERE AROUND, HE PROBABLY WOULD HAVE THROWN THE BOX.
I kind of wanted to see that.
FWIP
NOW THEN...
THE TOUR...

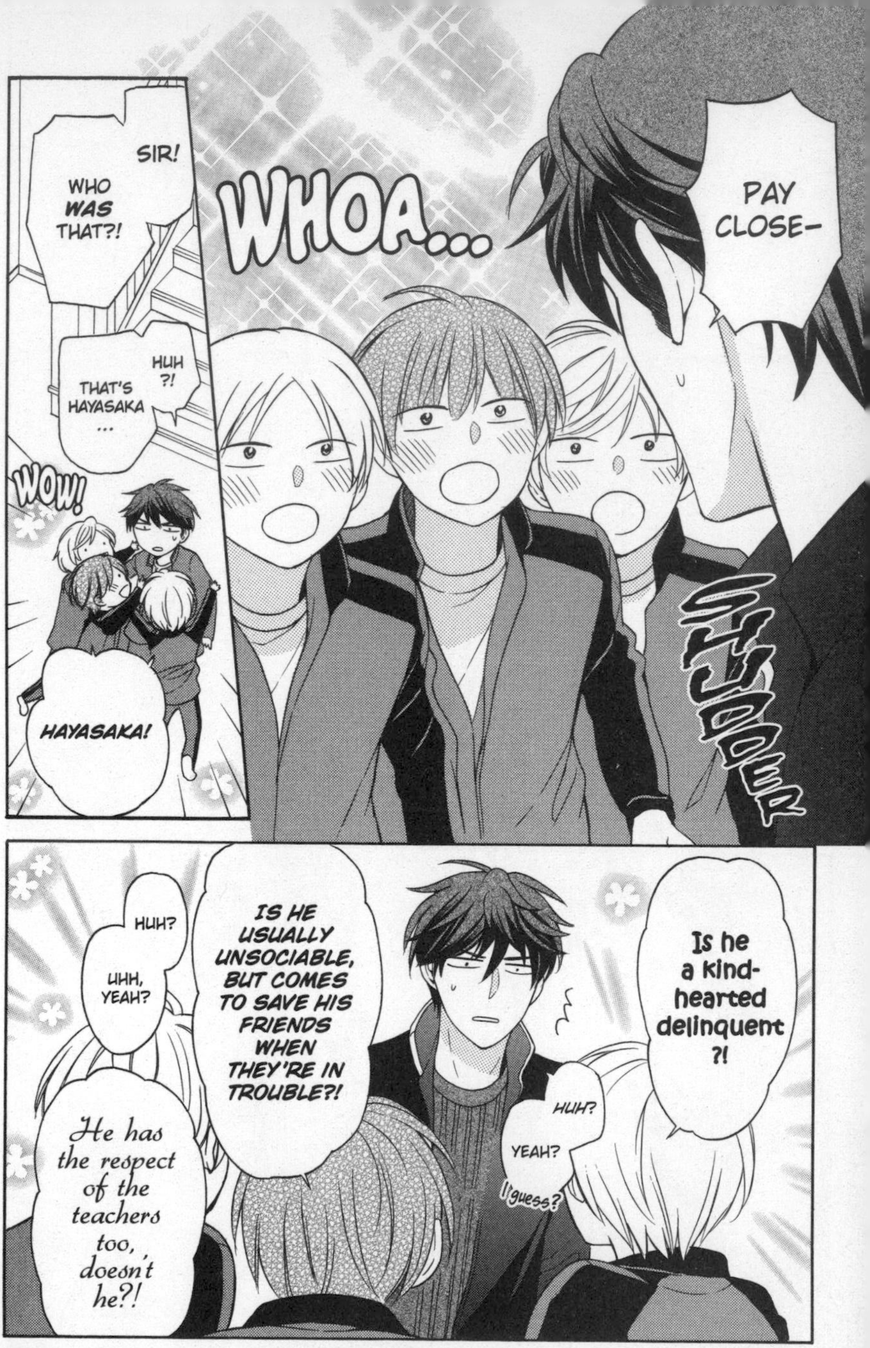
PAY CLOSE-
WHOA...
SHUDDER
SIR! WHO WAS THAT?!
HUH?! THAT'S HAYASAKA...
WOW!
HAYASAKA!
Is he a kind-hearted delinquent?!
HUH? YEAH? I guess?
IS HE USUALLY UNSOCIABLE, BUT COMES TO SAVE HIS FRIENDS WHEN THEY'RE IN TROUBLE?!
HUH? UHH, YEAH?
He has the respect of the teachers too, doesn't he?!

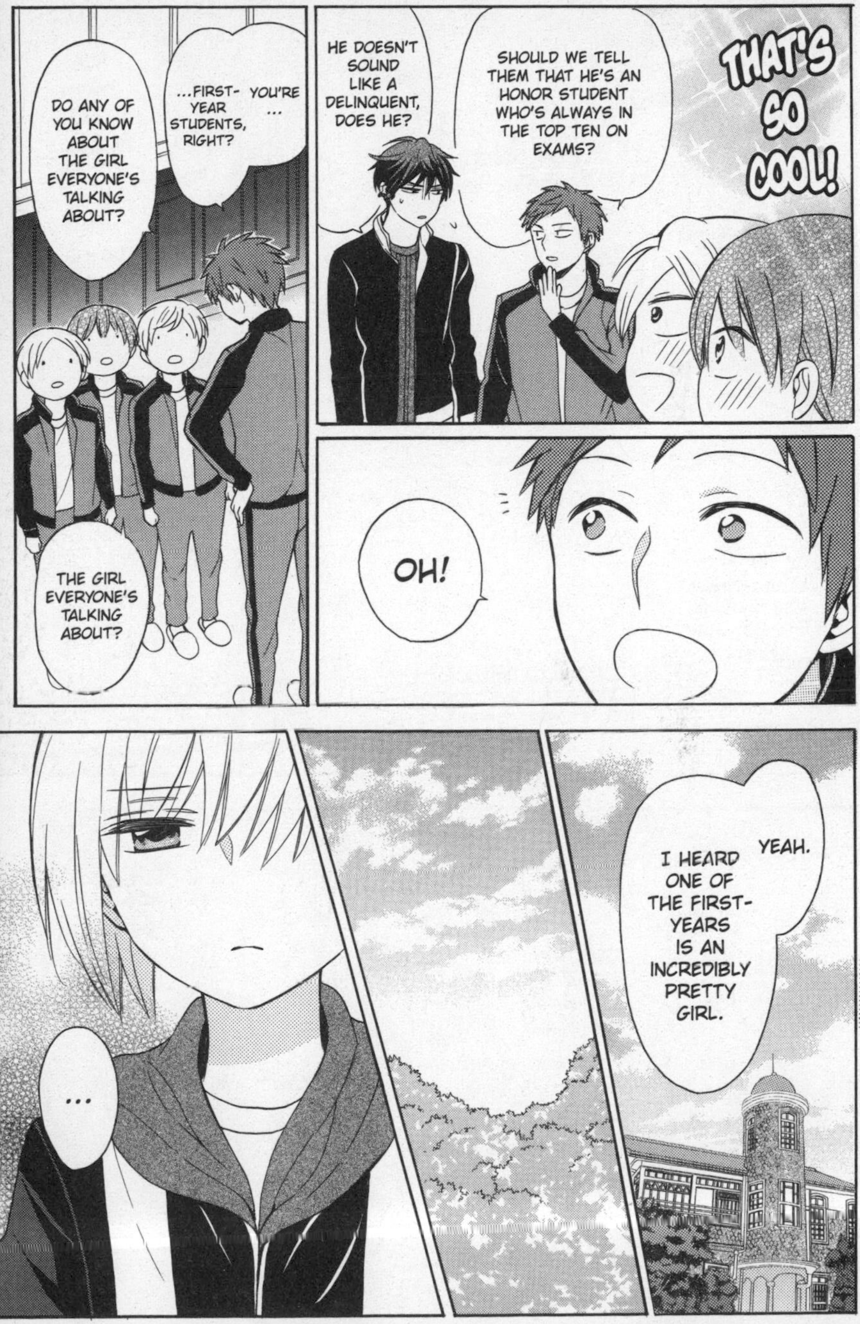
THAT'S SO COOL!
SHOULD WE TELL THEM THAT HE'S AN HONOR STUDENT WHO'S ALWAYS IN THE TOP TEN ON EXAMS?
HE DOESN'T SOUND LIKE A DELINQUENT, DOES HE?
OH!
YOU'RE ...
...FIRST-YEAR STUDENTS, RIGHT?
DO ANY OF YOU KNOW ABOUT THE GIRL EVERYONE'S TALKING ABOUT?
THE GIRL EVERYONE'S TALKING ABOUT?
YEAH.
I HEARD ONE OF THE FIRST-YEARS IS AN INCREDIBLY PRETTY GIRL.
...

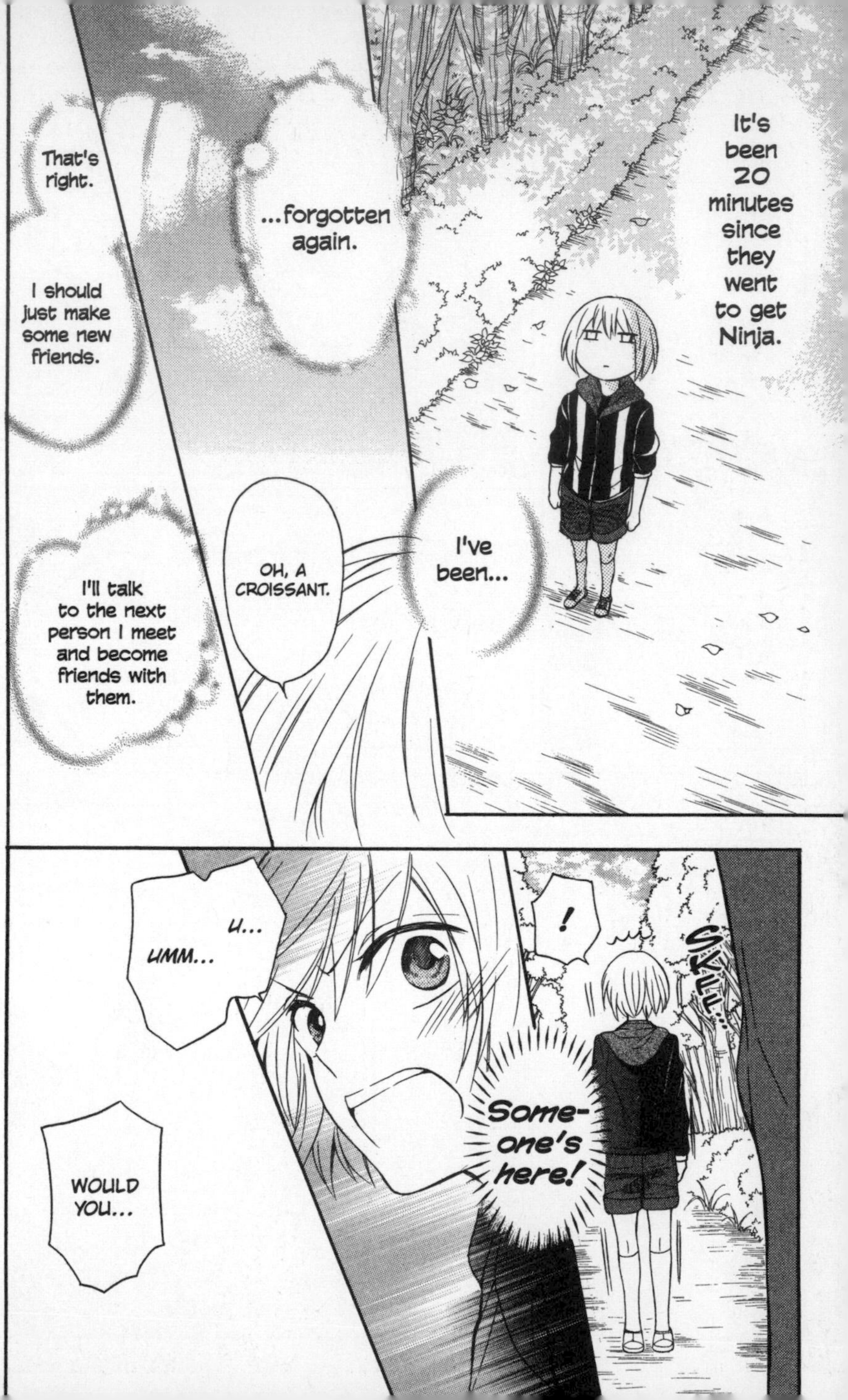

It's been 20 minutes since they went to get Ninja.
I've been...
...forgotten again.
That's right.
I should just make some new friends.
I'll talk to the next person I meet and become friends with them.
OH, A CROISSANT.
!
SKFF...
Some-one's here!
U...
UMM...
WOULD YOU...

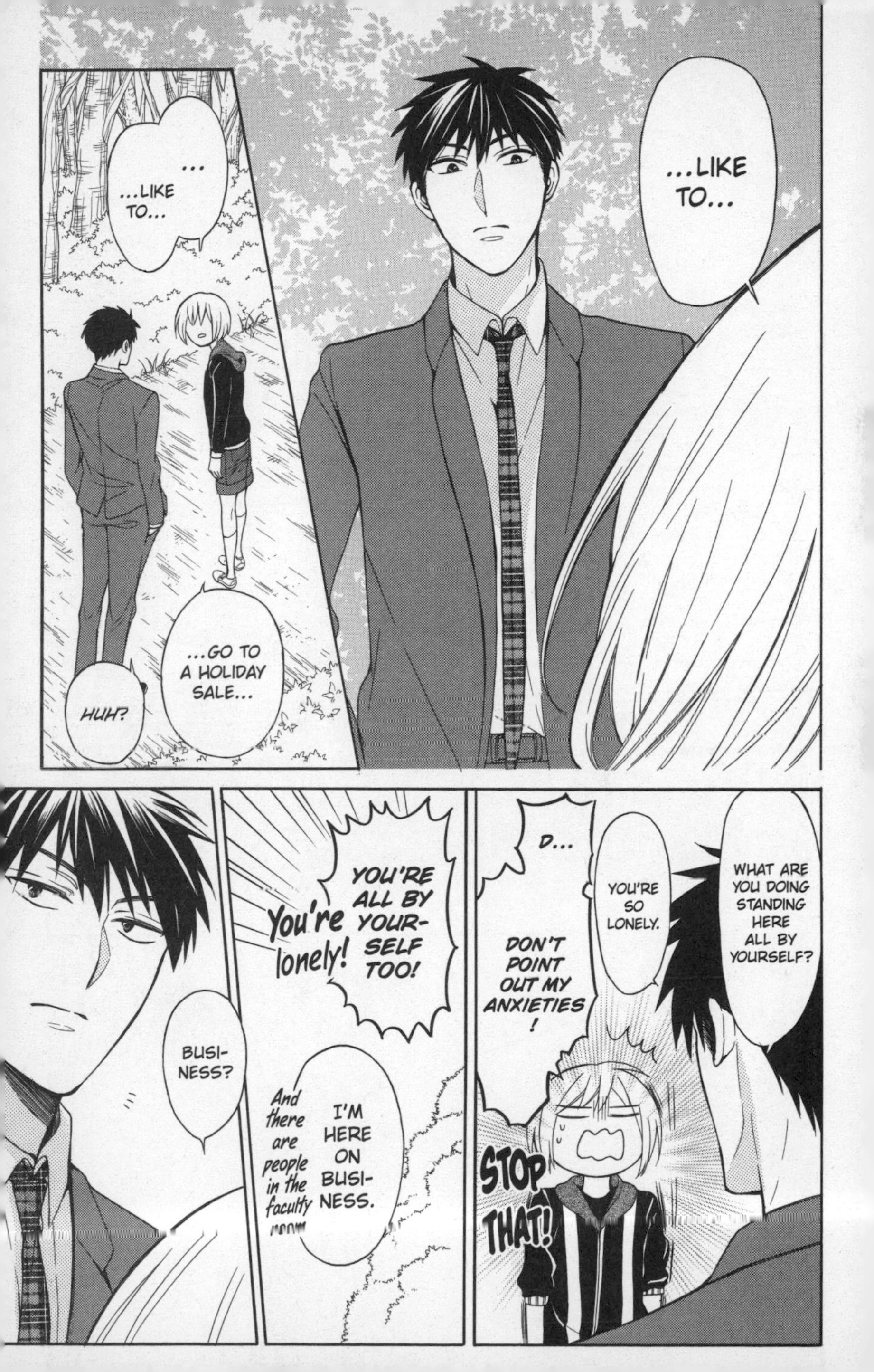
...LIKE TO...
...
...LIKE TO...
...GO TO A HOLIDAY SALE...
HUH?
WHAT ARE YOU DOING STANDING HERE ALL BY YOURSELF?
YOU'RE SO LONELY.
D...
DON'T POINT OUT MY ANXIETIES!
STOP THAT!
YOU'RE ALL BY YOURSELF TOO!
You're lonely!
I'M HERE ON BUSINESS.
And there are people in the faculty
BUSINESS?

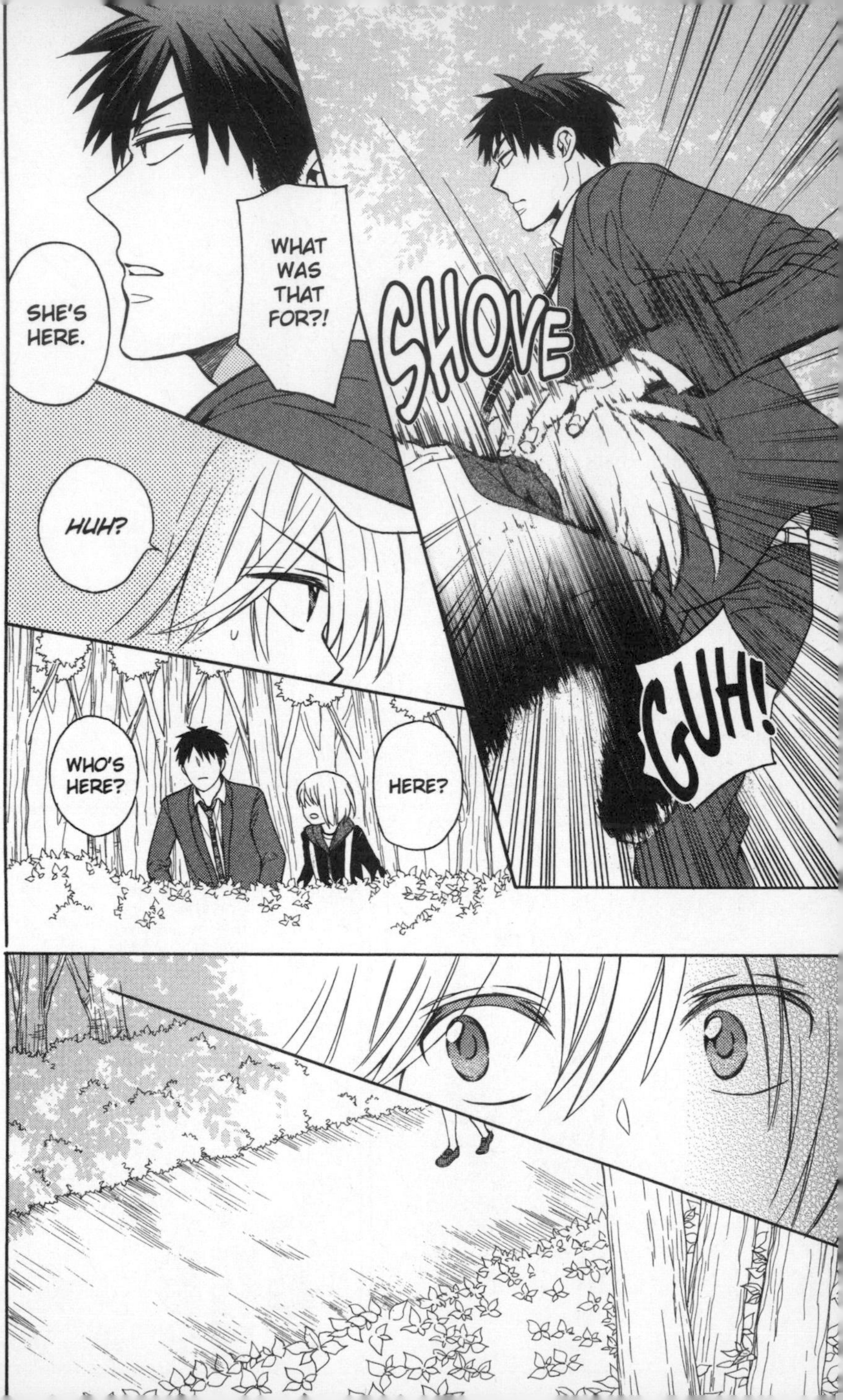
SHOVE
GUH!
WHAT WAS THAT FOR?!
SHE'S HERE.
HUH?
HERE?
WHO'S HERE?

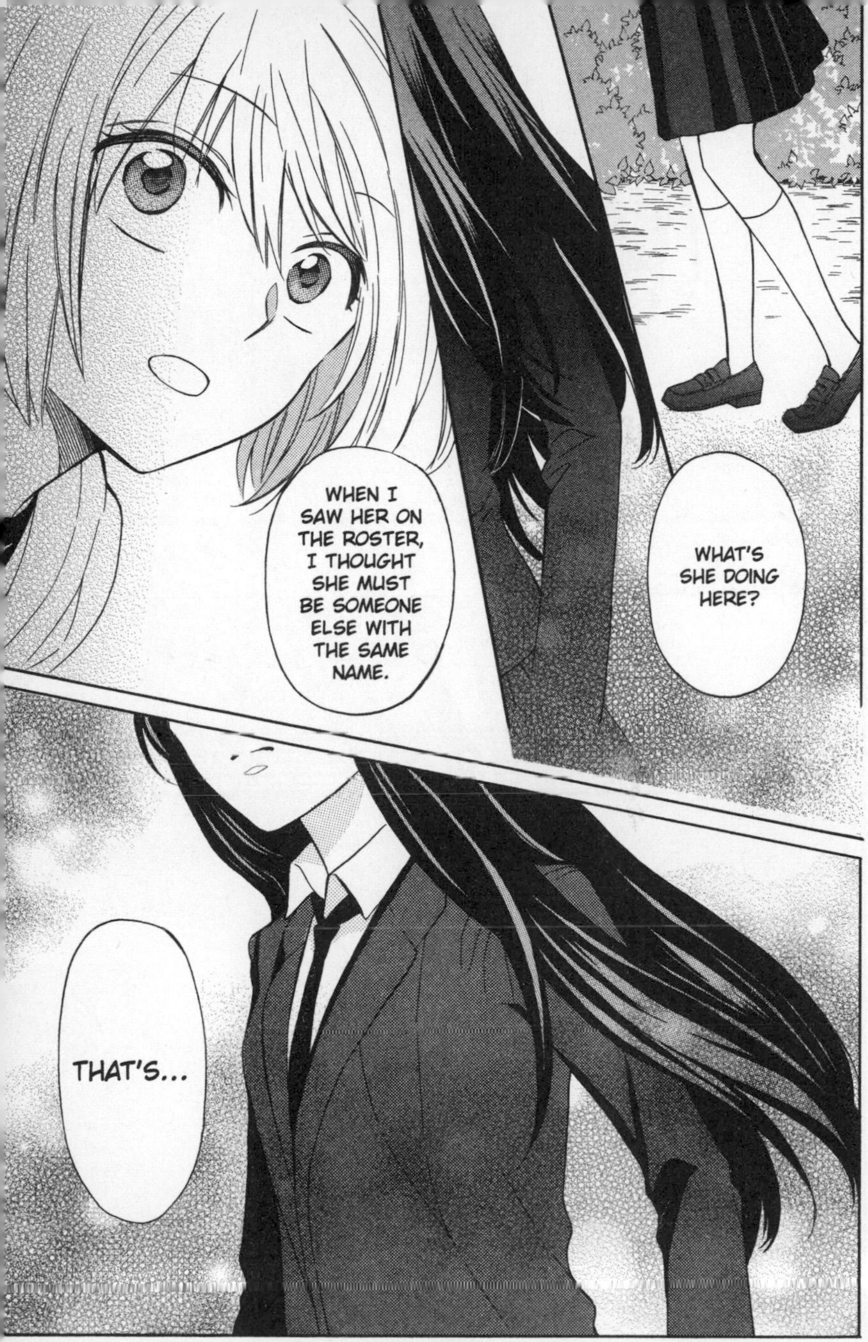
WHAT'S SHE DOING HERE?
WHEN I SAW HER ON THE ROSTER, I THOUGHT SHE MUST BE SOMEONE ELSE WITH THE SAME NAME.
THAT'S...

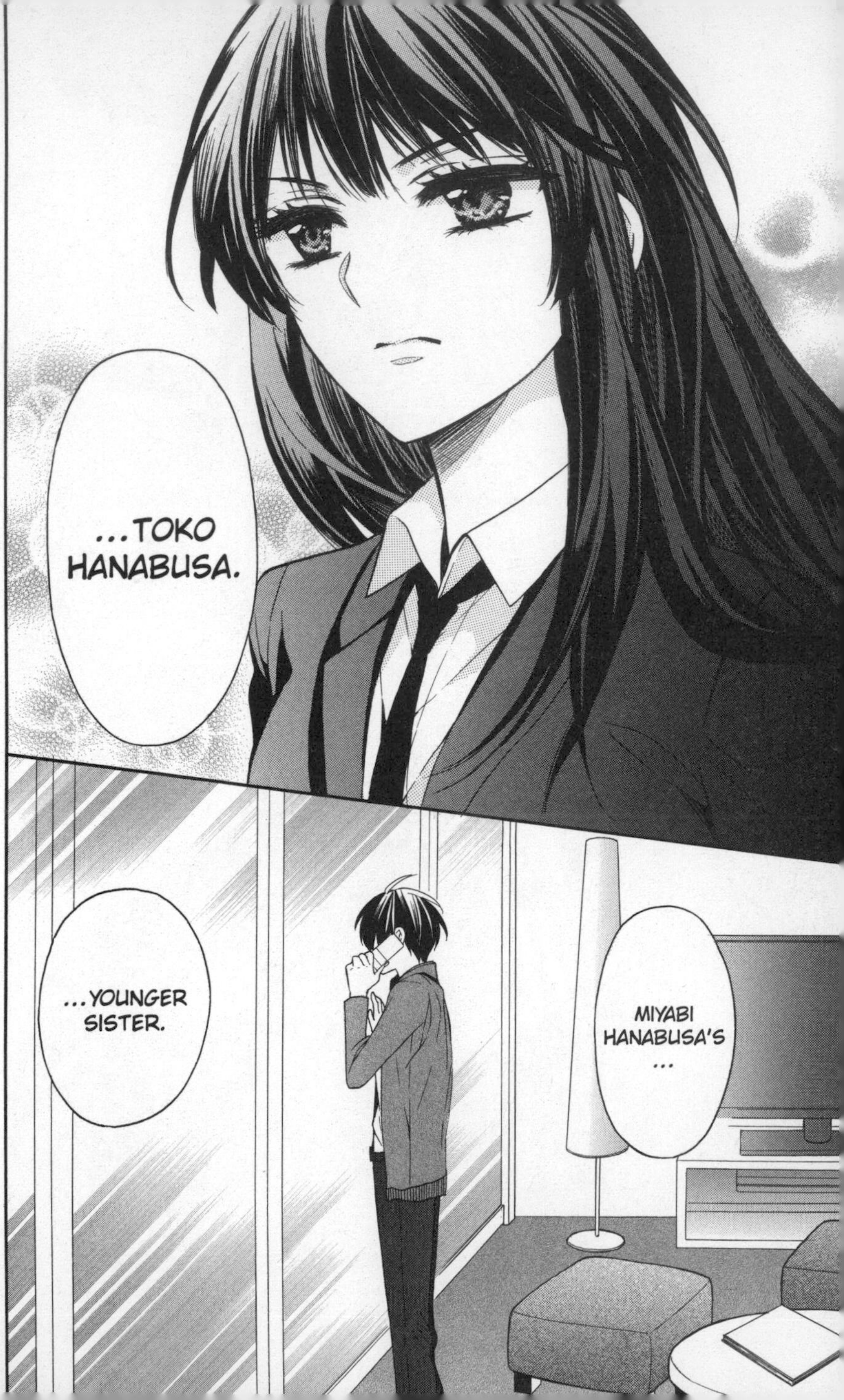
...TOKO HANABUSA.
MIYABI HANABUSA'S ...
...YOUNGER SISTER.

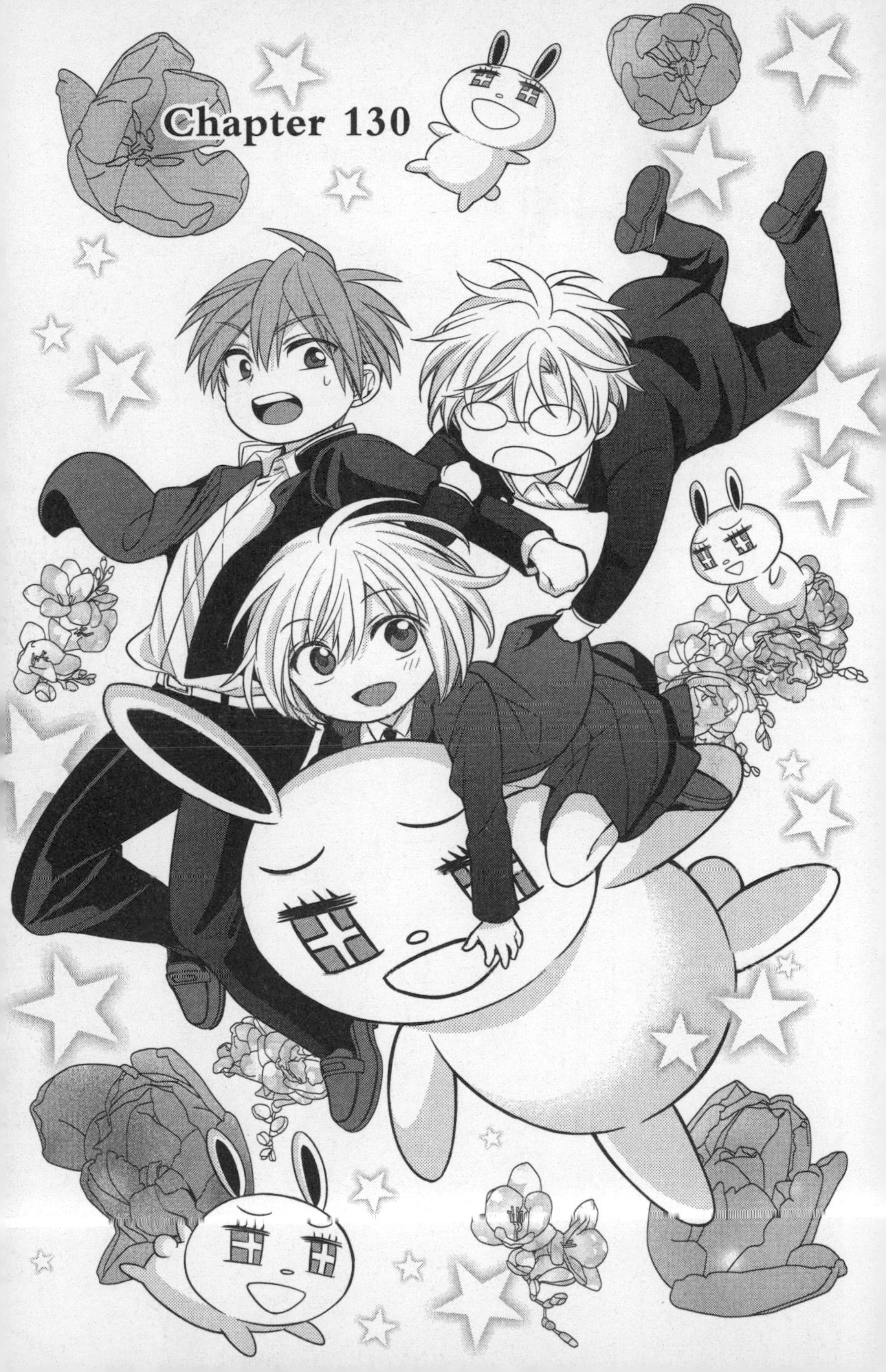
Chapter 130

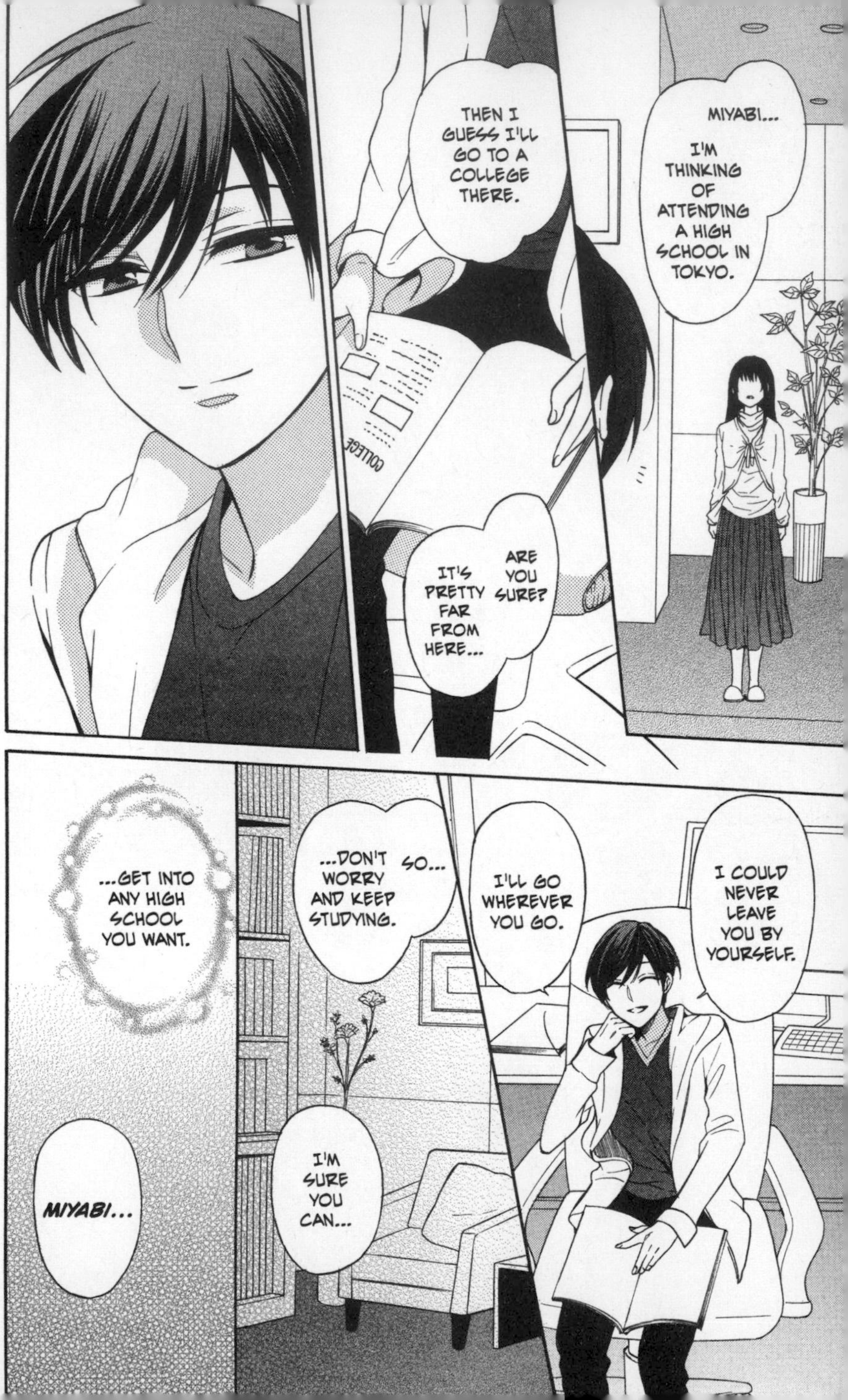
MIYABI...
I'M THINKING OF ATTENDING A HIGH SCHOOL IN TOKYO.
THEN I GUESS I'LL GO TO A COLLEGE THERE.
COLLEGE
ARE YOU SURE?
IT'S PRETTY FAR FROM HERE...
I COULD NEVER LEAVE YOU BY YOURSELF.
I'LL GO WHEREVER YOU GO.
SO...
...DON'T WORRY AND KEEP STUDYING.
I'M SURE YOU CAN...
...GET INTO ANY HIGH SCHOOL YOU WANT.
MIYABI...

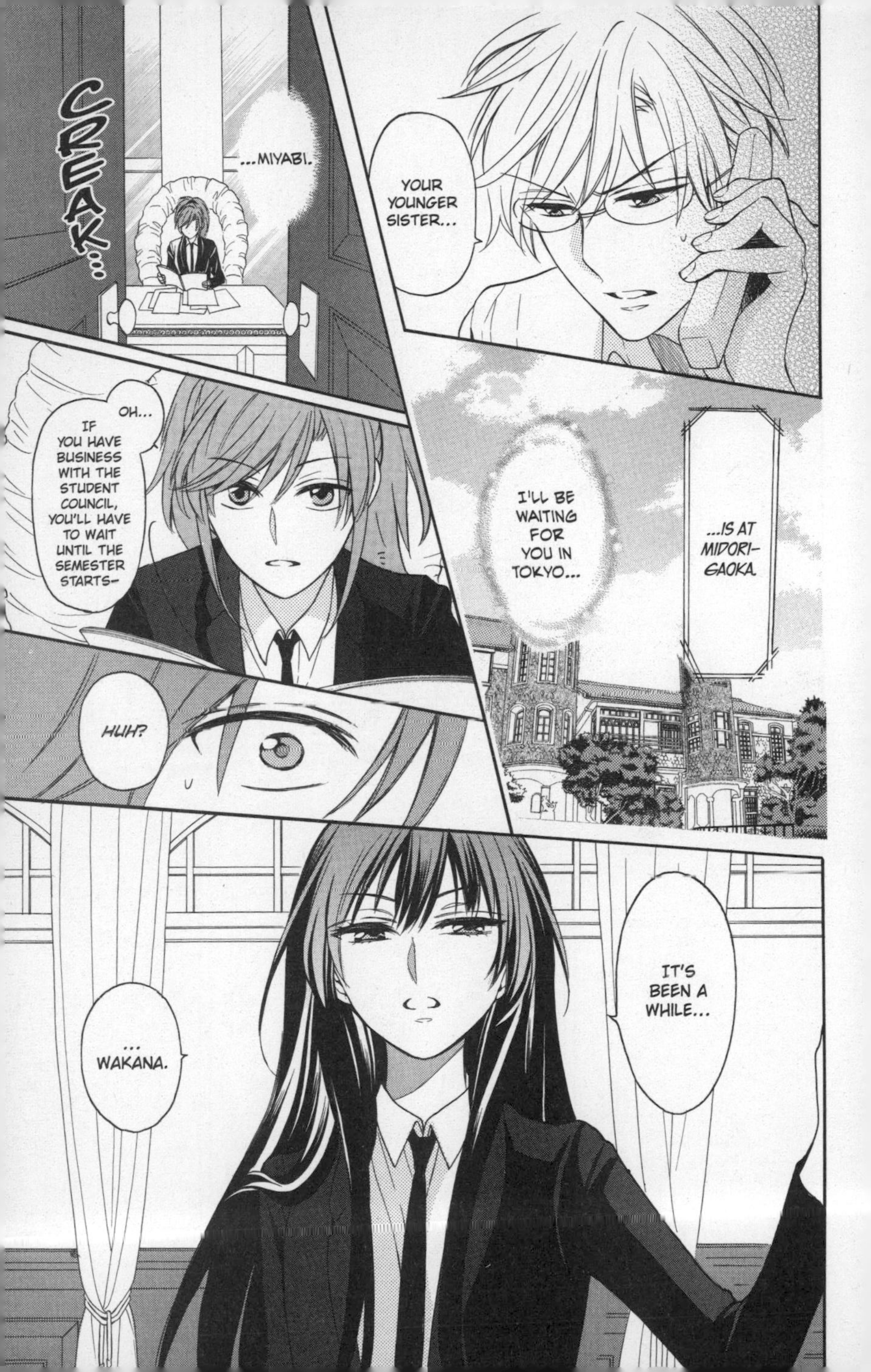
YOUR YOUNGER SISTER...
...IS AT MIDORI-GAOKA.
I'LL BE WAITING FOR YOU IN TOKYO...
...MIYABI.
CREAK...
OH... IF YOU HAVE BUSINESS WITH THE STUDENT COUNCIL, YOU'LL HAVE TO WAIT UNTIL THE SEMESTER STARTS-
HUH?
IT'S BEEN A WHILE...
... WAKANA.

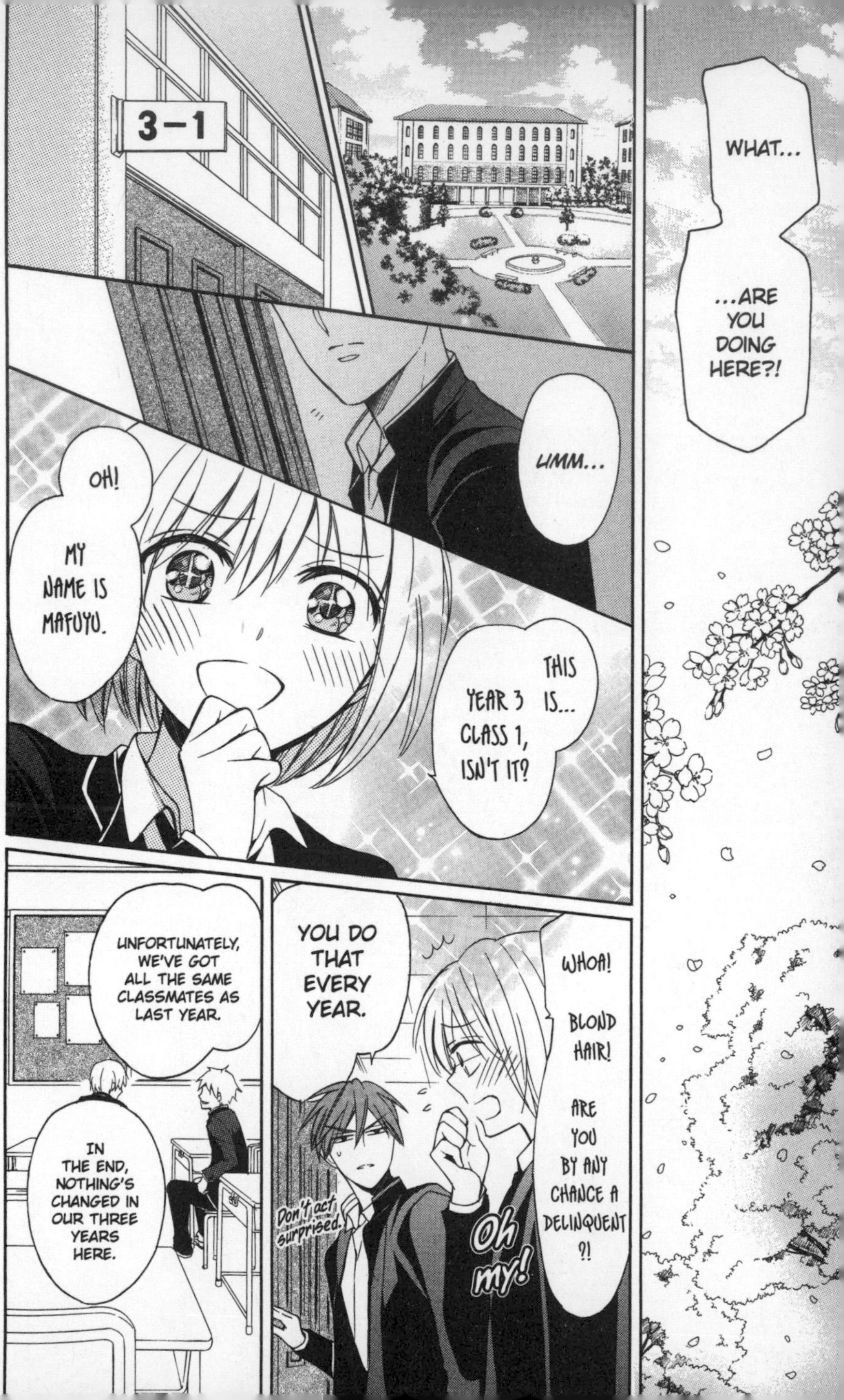

WHAT...
...ARE YOU DOING HERE?!
3-1
UMM...
OH!
MY NAME IS MAFUYU.
THIS IS... YEAR 3 CLASS 1, ISN'T IT?
WHOA!
BLOND HAIR!
ARE YOU BY ANY CHANCE A DELINQUENT?!
Oh my!
YOU DO THAT EVERY YEAR.
Don't act surprised.
UNFORTUNATELY, WE'VE GOT ALL THE SAME CLASSMATES AS LAST YEAR.
IN THE END, NOTHING'S CHANGED IN OUR THREE YEARS HERE.

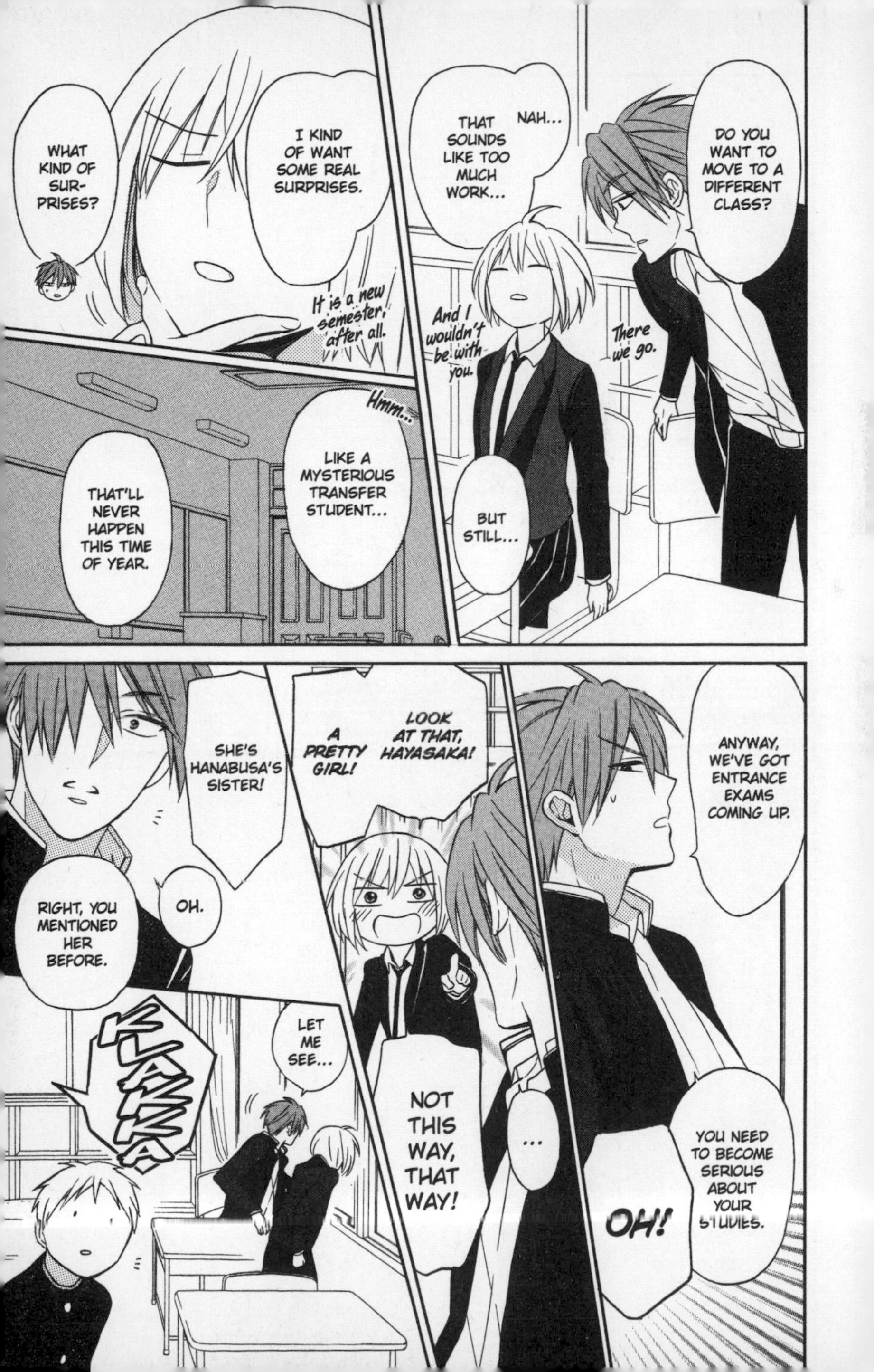
DO YOU WANT TO MOVE TO A DIFFERENT CLASS?
NAH...
THAT SOUNDS LIKE TOO MUCH WORK...
There we go.
And I wouldn't be with you.
BUT STILL...
I KIND OF WANT SOME REAL SURPRISES.
WHAT KIND OF SUR-PRISES?
It is a new semester, after all.
Hmm...
LIKE A MYSTERIOUS TRANSFER STUDENT...
THAT'LL NEVER HAPPEN THIS TIME OF YEAR.
ANYWAY, WE'VE GOT ENTRANCE EXAMS COMING UP.
YOU NEED TO BECOME SERIOUS ABOUT YOUR STUDIES.
OH!
...
LOOK AT THAT, HAYASAKA!
A PRETTY GIRL!
NOT THIS WAY, THAT WAY!
SHE'S HANABUSA'S SISTER!
OH.
RIGHT, YOU MENTIONED HER BEFORE.
LET ME SEE...

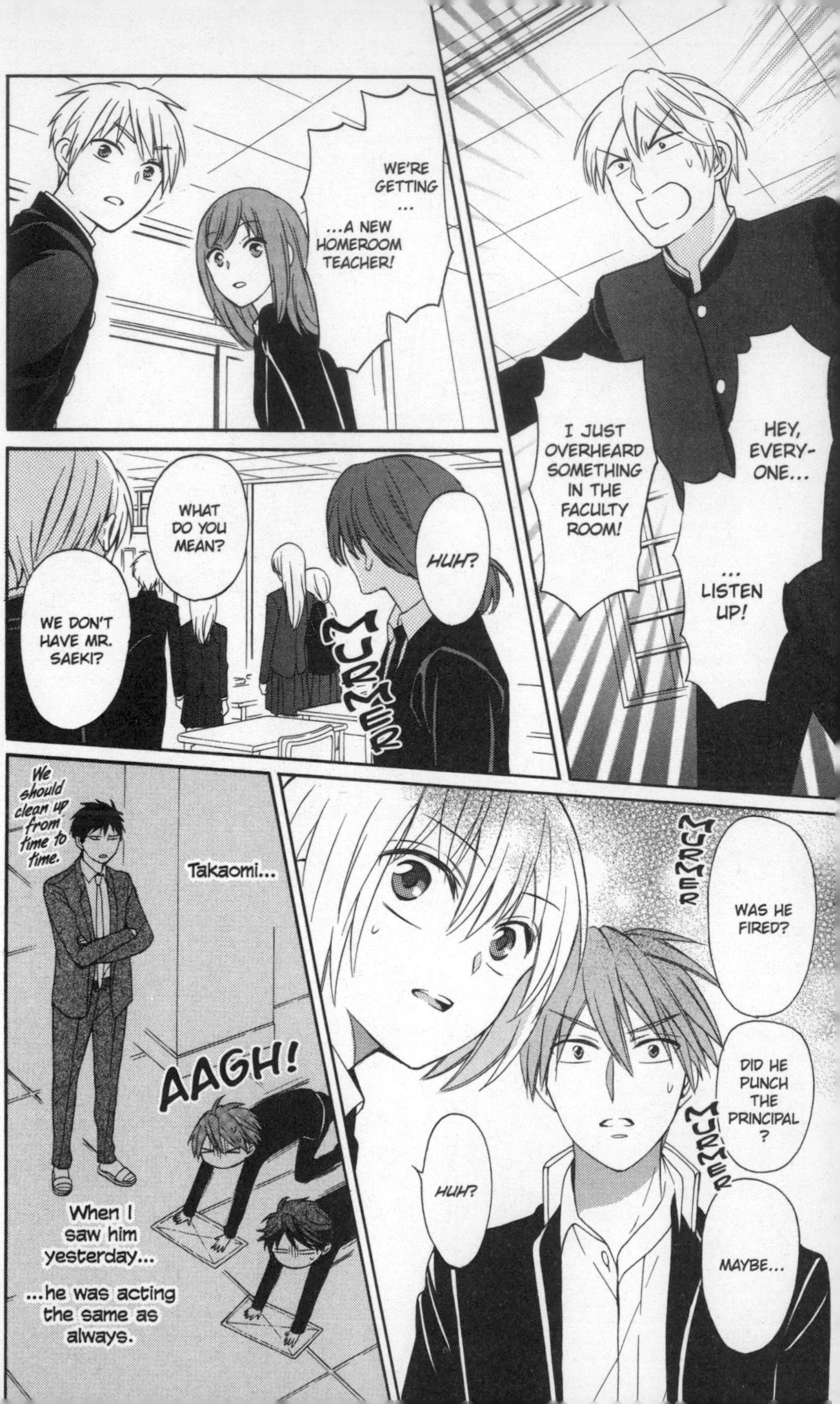
HEY, EVERY-ONE...
I JUST OVERHEARD SOMETHING IN THE FACULTY ROOM!
... LISTEN UP!
WE'RE GETTING ...
...A NEW HOMEROOM TEACHER!
HUH?
WHAT DO YOU MEAN?
WE DON'T HAVE MR. SAEKI?
MURMER
MURMER
WAS HE FIRED?
DID HE PUNCH THE PRINCIPAL?
MURMER
MAYBE...
HUH?
Takaomi...
When I saw him yesterday...
...he was acting the same as always.
AAGH!
We should clean up from time to time.

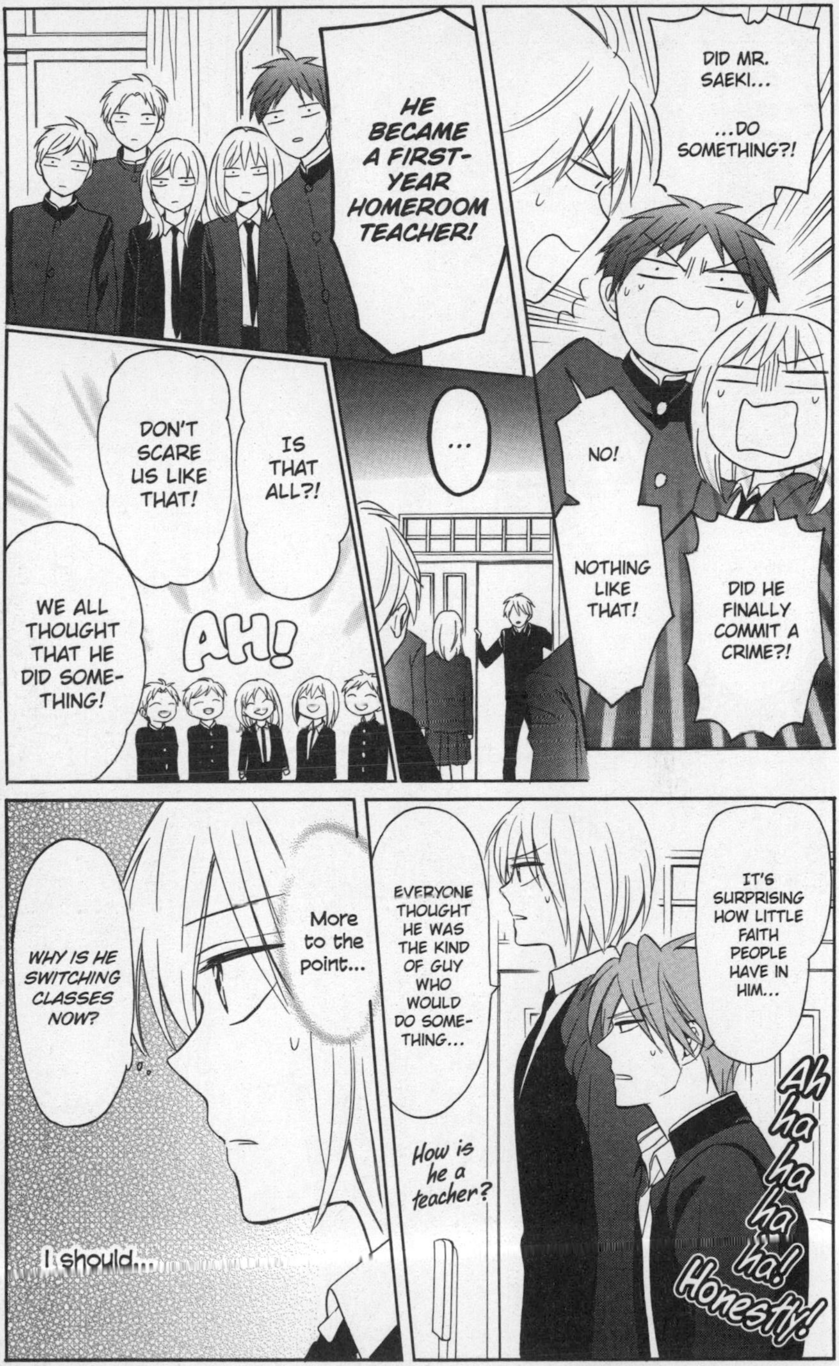
DID MR. SAEKI...
...DO SOMETHING?!
DID HE FINALLY COMMIT A CRIME?!
NO!
NOTHING LIKE THAT!
HE BECAME A FIRST-YEAR HOMEROOM TEACHER!
...
IS THAT ALL?!
DON'T SCARE US LIKE THAT!
AH!
WE ALL THOUGHT THAT HE DID SOME-THING!
IT'S SURPRISING HOW LITTLE FAITH PEOPLE HAVE IN HIM...
Ah ha ha ha ha! Honestly!
EVERYONE THOUGHT HE WAS THE KIND OF GUY WHO WOULD DO SOME-THING...
How is he a teacher?
More to the point...
WHY IS HE SWITCHING CLASSES NOW?
I should...

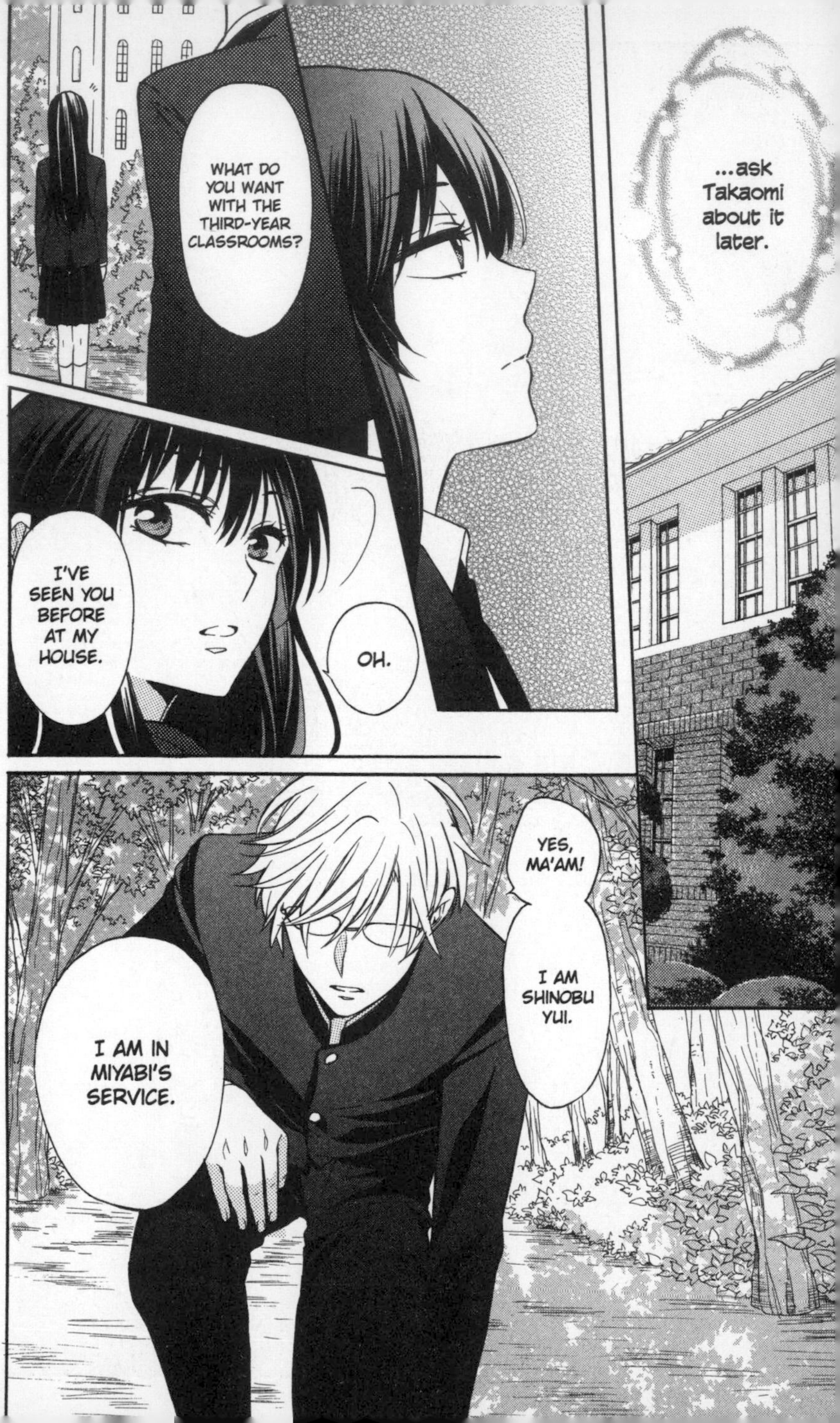
...ask Takaomi about it later.
WHAT DO YOU WANT WITH THE THIRD-YEAR CLASSROOMS?
OH.
I'VE SEEN YOU BEFORE AT MY HOUSE.
YES, MA'AM!
I AM SHINOBU YUI.
I AM IN MIYABI'S SERVICE.

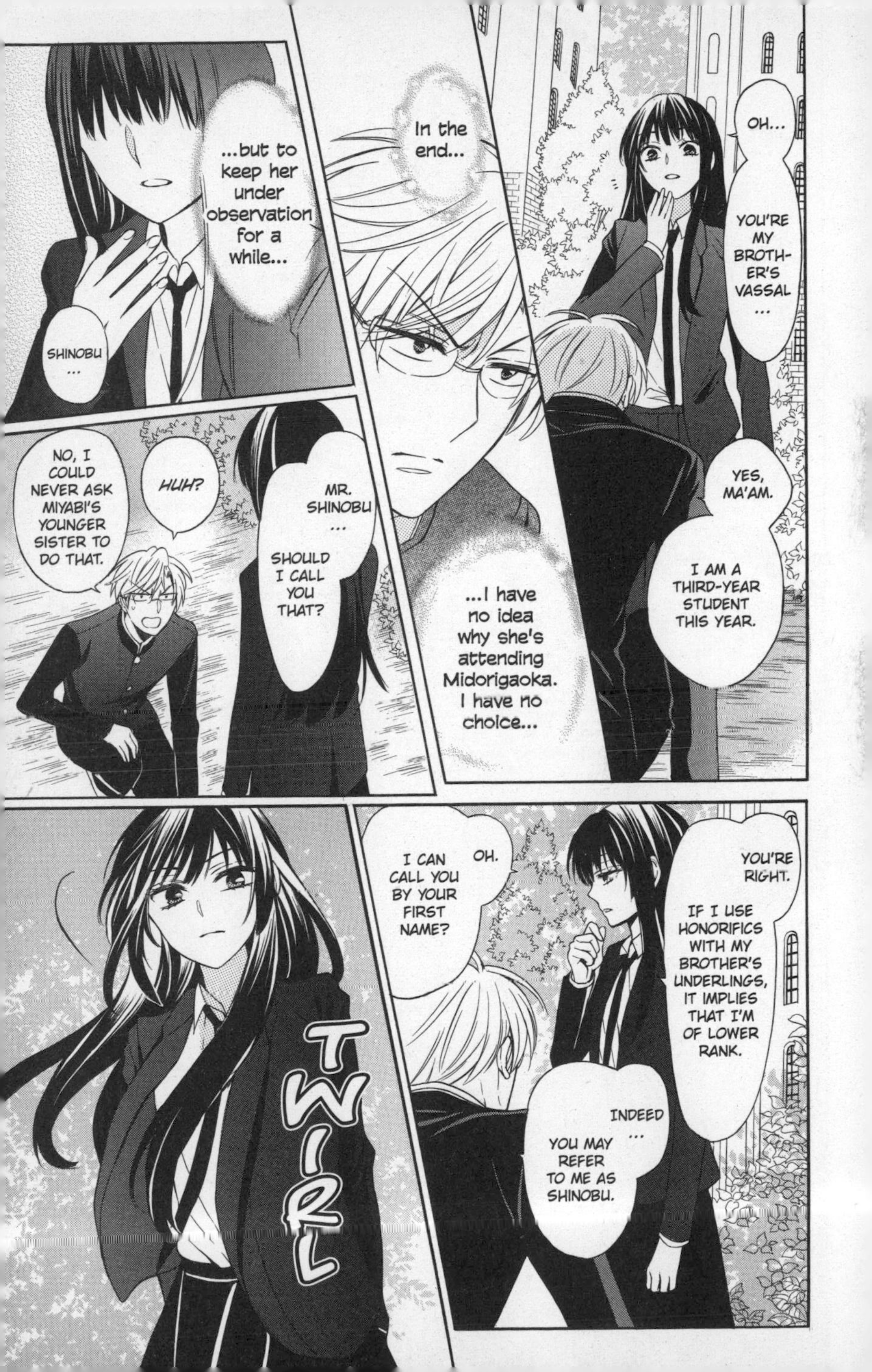
OH...
YOU'RE MY BROTHER'S VASSAL...
YES, MA'AM.
I AM A THIRD-YEAR STUDENT THIS YEAR.
In the end...
...I have no idea why she's attending Midorigaoka. I have no choice...
...but to keep her under observation for a while...
SHINOBU...
MR. SHINOBU...
SHOULD I CALL YOU THAT?
HUH?
NO, I COULD NEVER ASK MIYABI'S YOUNGER SISTER TO DO THAT.
YOU'RE RIGHT.
IF I USE HONORIFICS WITH MY BROTHER'S UNDERLINGS, IT IMPLIES THAT I'M OF LOWER RANK.
OH.
I CAN CALL YOU BY YOUR FIRST NAME?
INDEED...
YOU MAY REFER TO ME AS SHINOBU.
TWIRL

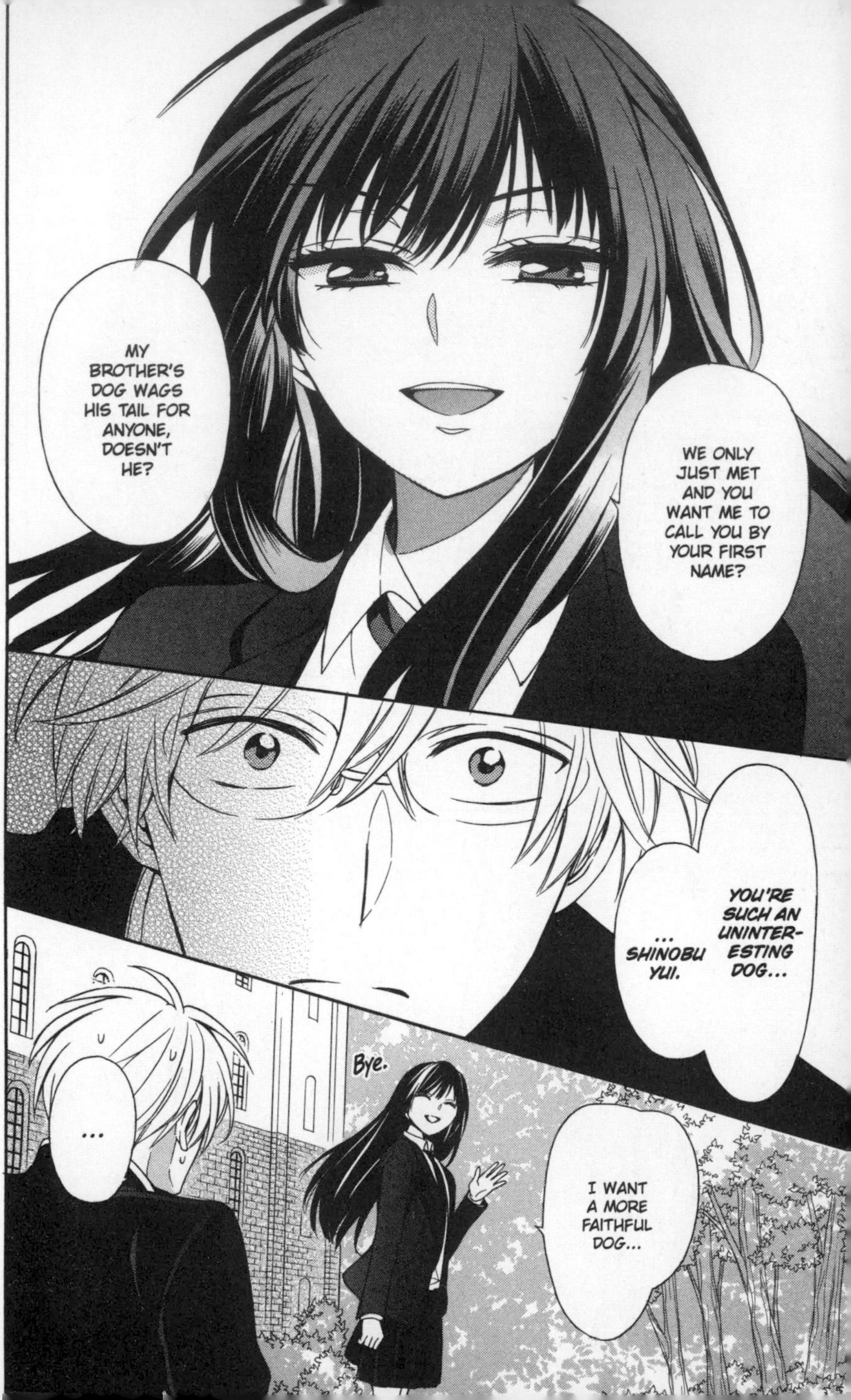
WE ONLY JUST MET AND YOU WANT ME TO CALL YOU BY YOUR FIRST NAME?
MY BROTHER'S DOG WAGS HIS TAIL FOR ANYONE, DOESN'T HE?
YOU'RE SUCH AN UNINTER-ESTING DOG...
...SHINOBU YUI.
I WANT A MORE FAITHFUL DOG...
Bye.
...

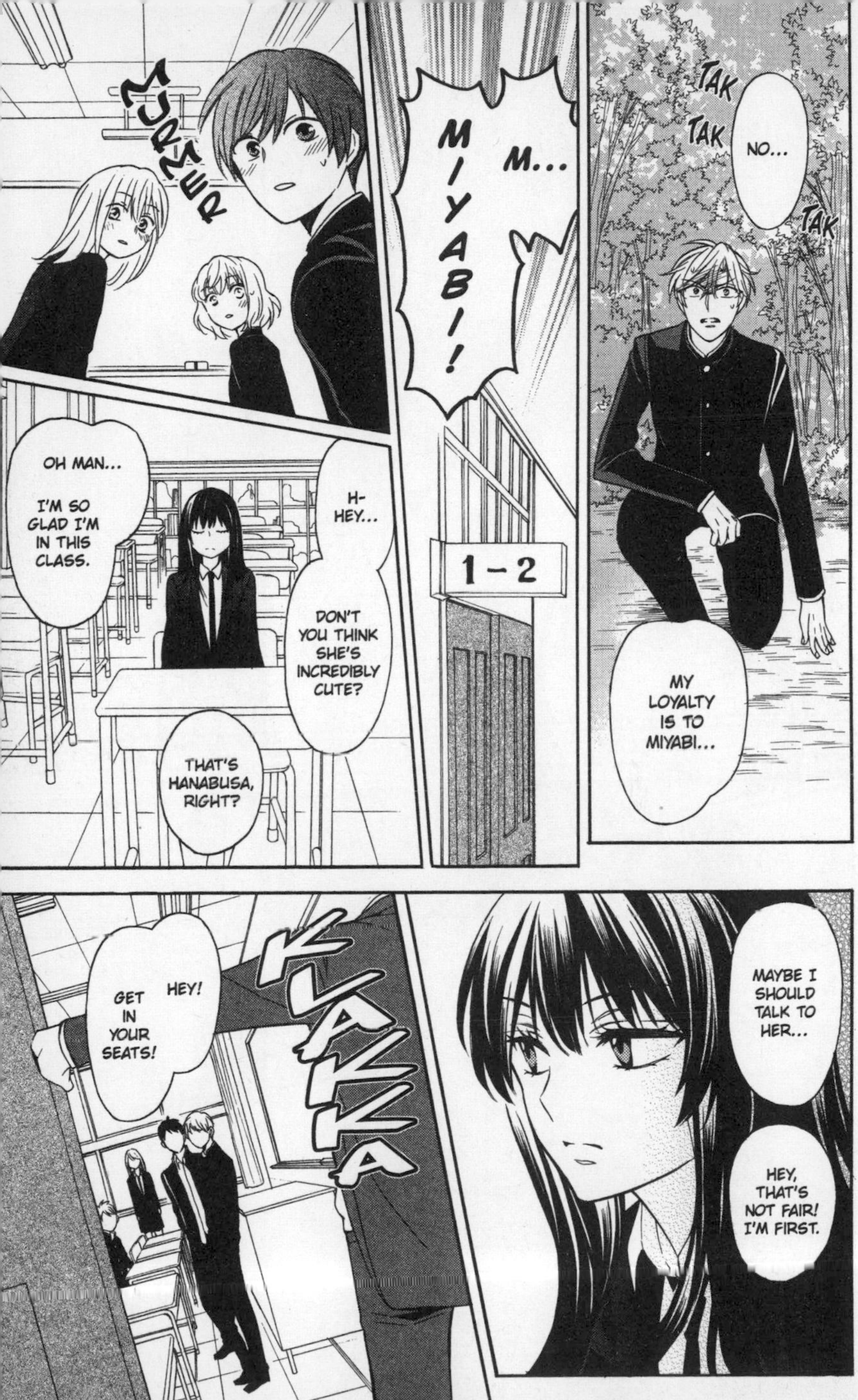
TAK
TAK
NO...
TAK
MY LOYALTY IS TO MIYABI...
M...
MIYABI!!
1-2
MURMER
H-HEY...
DON'T YOU THINK SHE'S INCREDIBLY CUTE?
OH MAN...
I'M SO GLAD I'M IN THIS CLASS.
THAT'S HANABUSA, RIGHT?
MAYBE I SHOULD TALK TO HER...
HEY, THAT'S NOT FAIR! I'M FIRST.
KLAKKA
HEY!
GET IN YOUR SEATS!

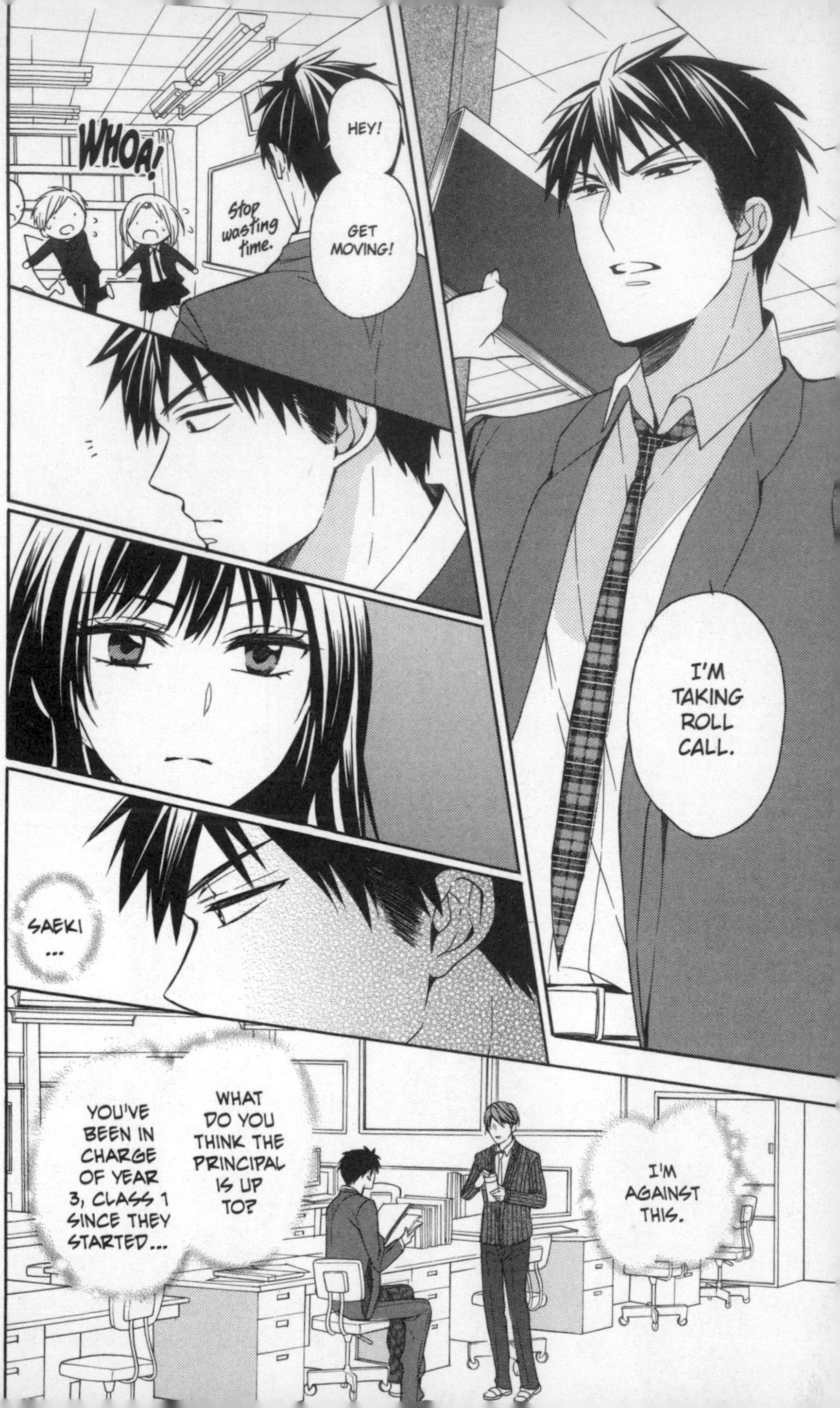
I'M TAKING ROLL CALL.
HEY!
GET MOVING!
Stop wasting time.
WHOA!
SAEKI ...
I'M AGAINST THIS.
WHAT DO YOU THINK THE PRINCIPAL IS UP TO?
YOU'VE BEEN IN CHARGE OF YEAR 3, CLASS 1 SINCE THEY STARTED...

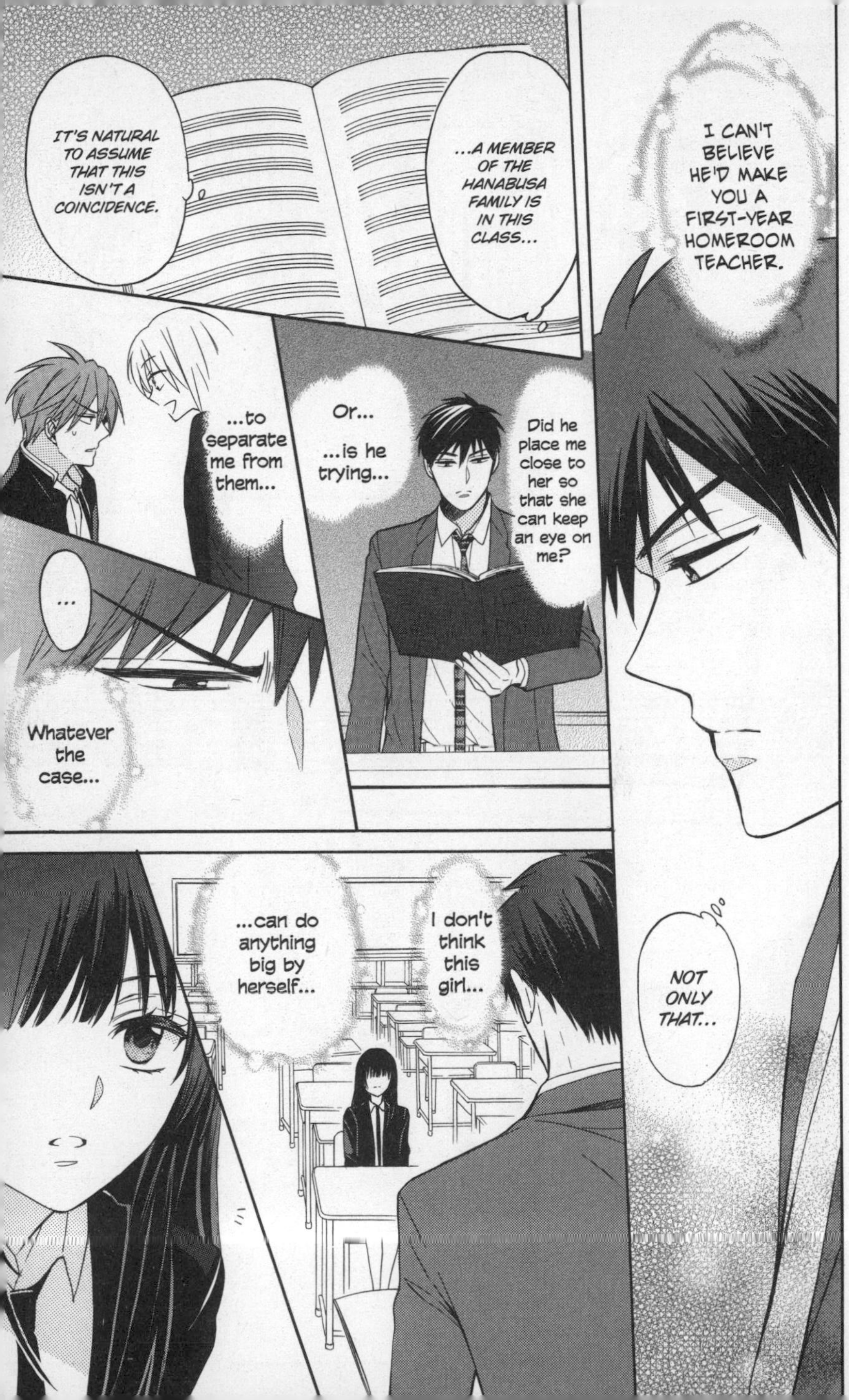
I CAN'T BELIEVE HE'D MAKE YOU A FIRST-YEAR HOMEROOM TEACHER.
NOT ONLY THAT...
...A MEMBER OF THE HANABUSA FAMILY IS IN THIS CLASS...
IT'S NATURAL TO ASSUME THAT THIS ISN'T A COINCIDENCE.
Did he place me close to her so that she can keep an eye on me?
Or...
...is he trying...
...to separate me from them...
...
Whatever the case...
I don't think this girl...
...can do anything big by herself...

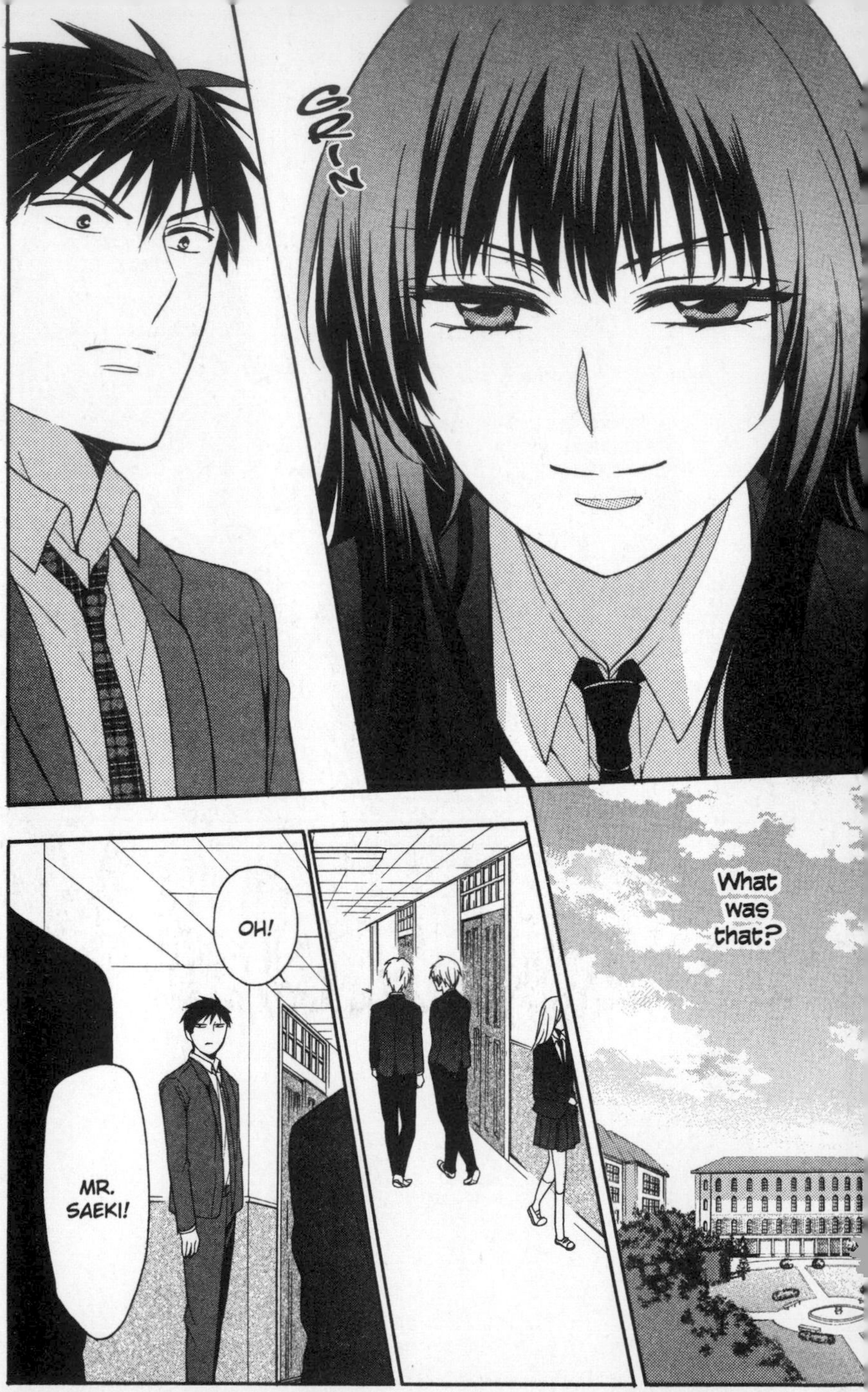
GRIN
What was that?
OH!
MR. SAEKI!

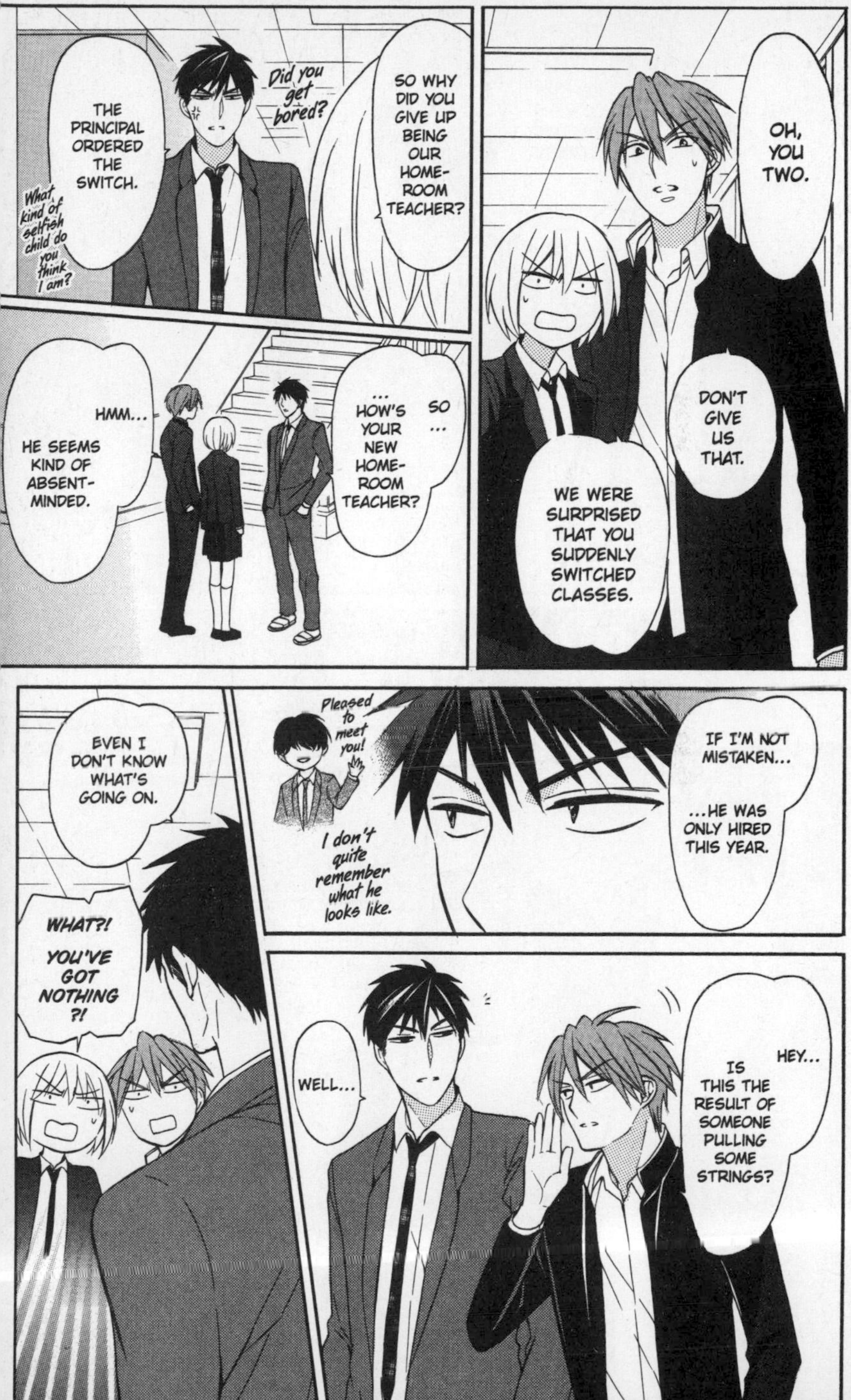
OH, YOU TWO.
DON'T GIVE US THAT.
WE WERE SURPRISED THAT YOU SUDDENLY SWITCHED CLASSES.
SO WHY DID YOU GIVE UP BEING OUR HOMEROOM TEACHER?
Did you get bored?
THE PRINCIPAL ORDERED THE SWITCH.
What kind of selfish child do you think I am?
SO...
...HOW'S YOUR NEW HOMEROOM TEACHER?
HMM...
HE SEEMS KIND OF ABSENT-MINDED.
IF I'M NOT MISTAKEN...
...HE WAS ONLY HIRED THIS YEAR.
Pleased to meet you!
I don't quite remember what he looks like.
HEY...
IS THIS THE RESULT OF SOMEONE PULLING SOME STRINGS?
WELL...
EVEN I DON'T KNOW WHAT'S GOING ON.
WHAT?!
YOU'VE GOT NOTHING?!

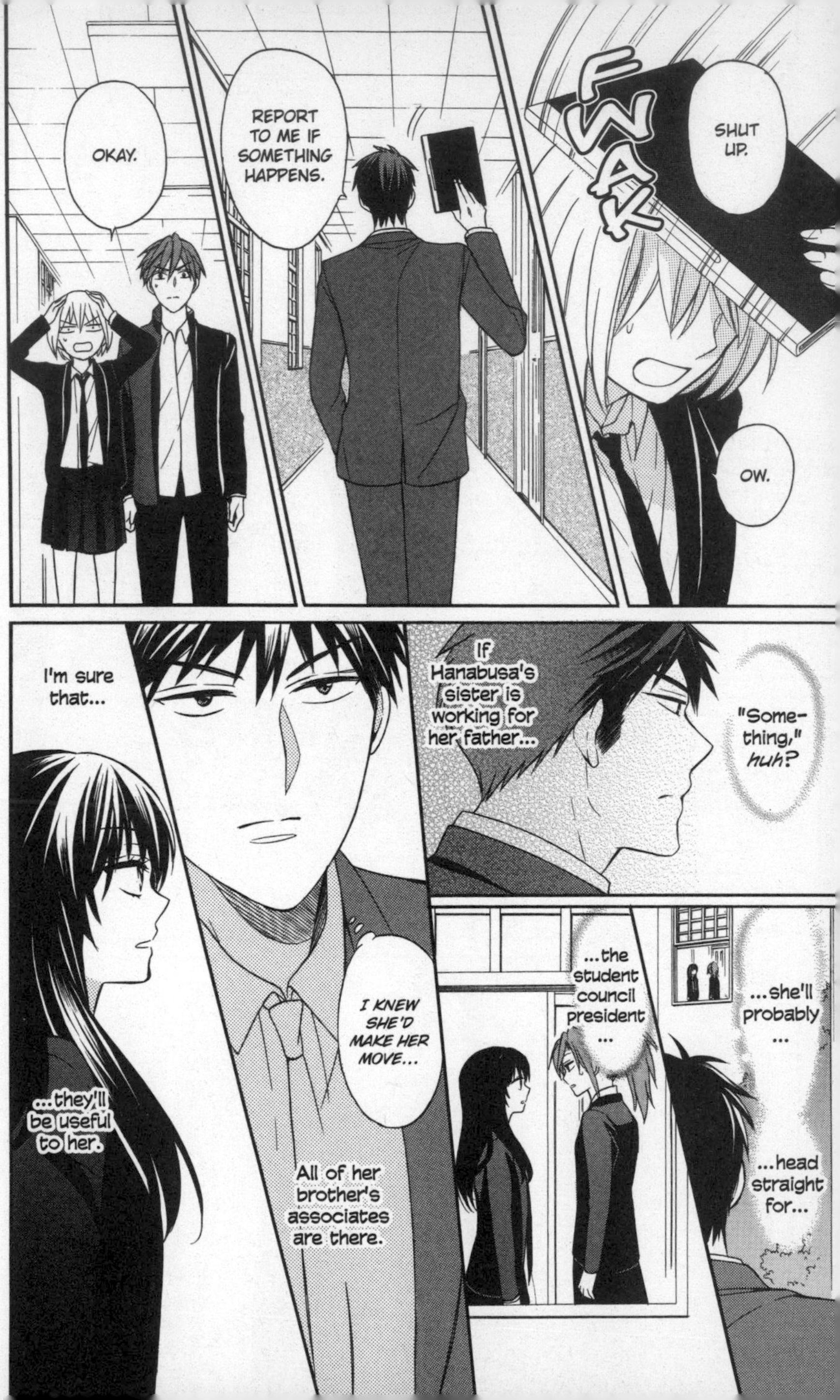
FWAK
SHUT UP.
OW.
REPORT TO ME IF SOMETHING HAPPENS.
OKAY.
"Something," huh?
If Hanabusa's sister is working for her father...
...she'll probably...
...head straight for...
...the student council president...
I KNEW SHE'D MAKE HER MOVE...
All of her brother's associates are there.
I'm sure that...
...they'll be useful to her.

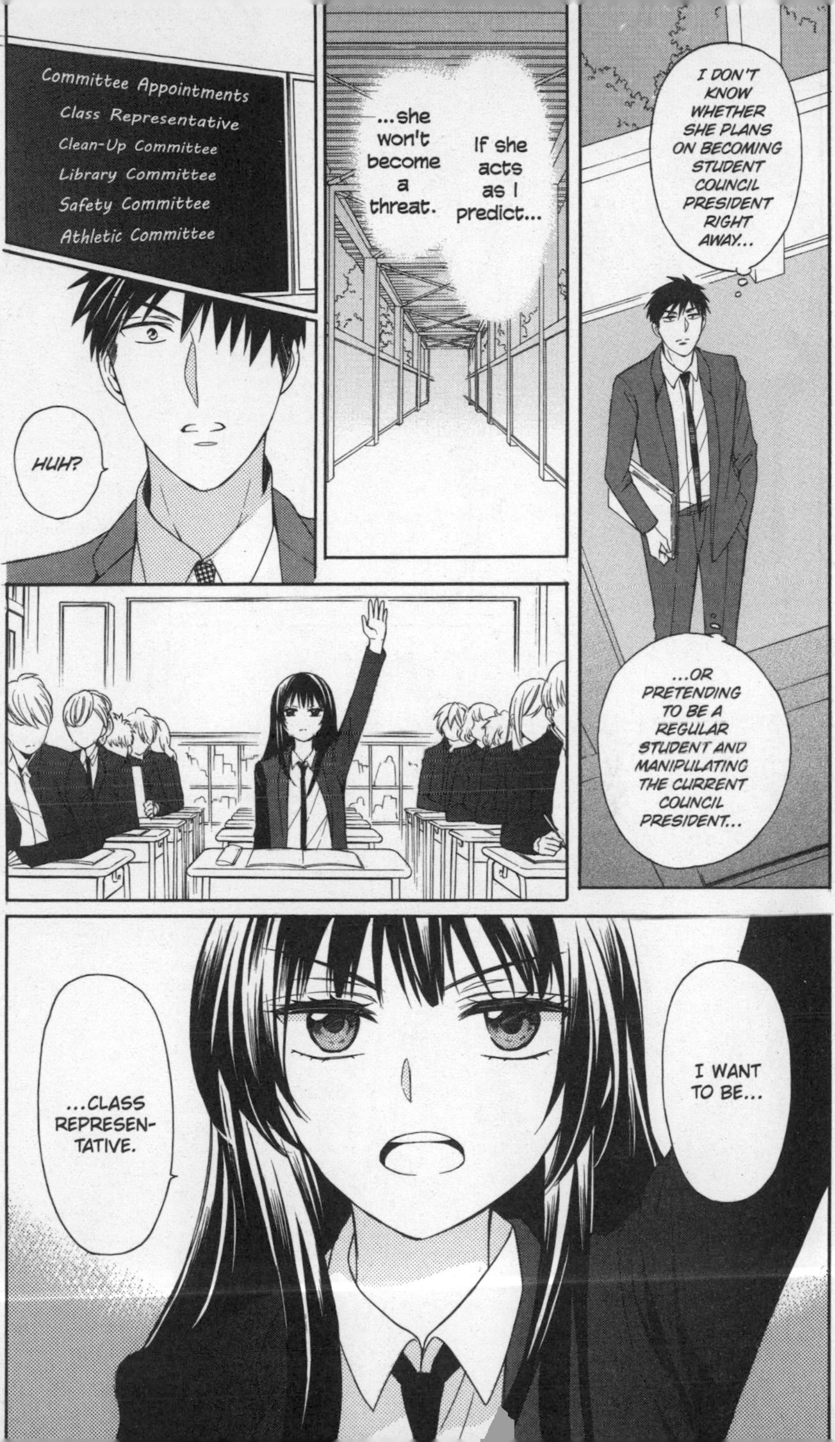
I DON'T KNOW WHETHER SHE PLANS ON BECOMING STUDENT COUNCIL PRESIDENT RIGHT AWAY...
...OR PRETENDING TO BE A REGULAR STUDENT AND MANIPULATING THE CURRENT COUNCIL PRESIDENT...
If she acts as I predict...
...she won't become a threat.
Committee Appointments
Class Representative
Clean-Up Committee
Library Committee
Safety Committee
Athletic Committee
HUH?
I WANT TO BE...
...CLASS REPRESEN-TATIVE.

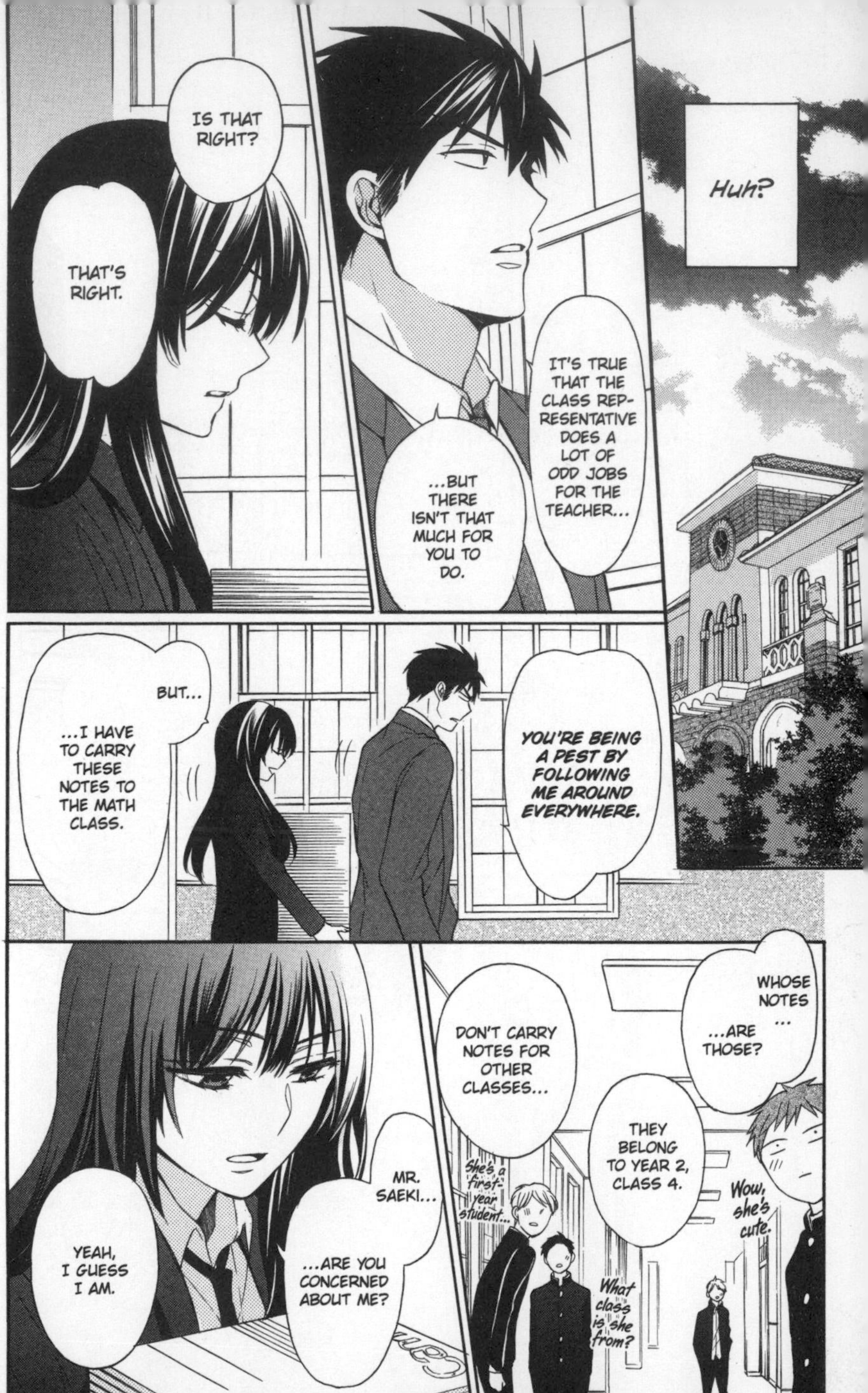
Huh?
IT'S TRUE THAT THE CLASS REP-RESENTATIVE DOES A LOT OF ODD JOBS FOR THE TEACHER...
...BUT THERE ISN'T THAT MUCH FOR YOU TO DO.
IS THAT RIGHT?
THAT'S RIGHT.
YOU'RE BEING A PEST BY FOLLOWING ME AROUND EVERYWHERE.
BUT...
...I HAVE TO CARRY THESE NOTES TO THE MATH CLASS.
WHOSE NOTES ...
...ARE THOSE?
THEY BELONG TO YEAR 2, CLASS 4.
DON'T CARRY NOTES FOR OTHER CLASSES...
Wow, she's cute.
What class is she from?
She's a first-year student...
MR. SAEKI...
...ARE YOU CONCERNED ABOUT ME?
YEAH, I GUESS I AM.

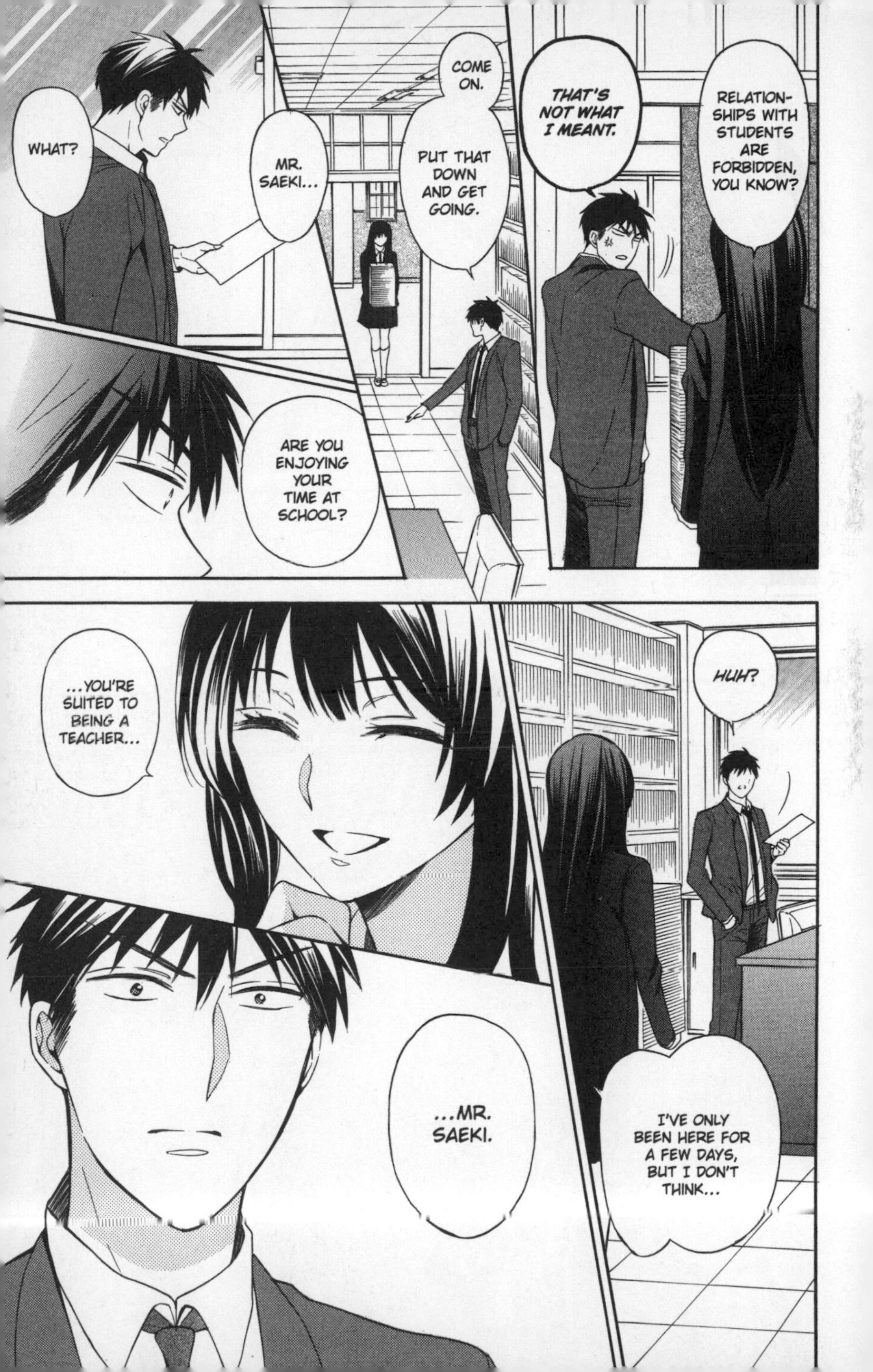
RELATION-SHIPS WITH STUDENTS ARE FORBIDDEN, YOU KNOW?
THAT'S NOT WHAT I MEANT.
COME ON.
PUT THAT DOWN AND GET GOING.
MR. SAEKI...
WHAT?
ARE YOU ENJOYING YOUR TIME AT SCHOOL?
HUH?
I'VE ONLY BEEN HERE FOR A FEW DAYS, BUT I DON'T THINK...
...YOU'RE SUITED TO BEING A TEACHER...
...MR. SAEKI.

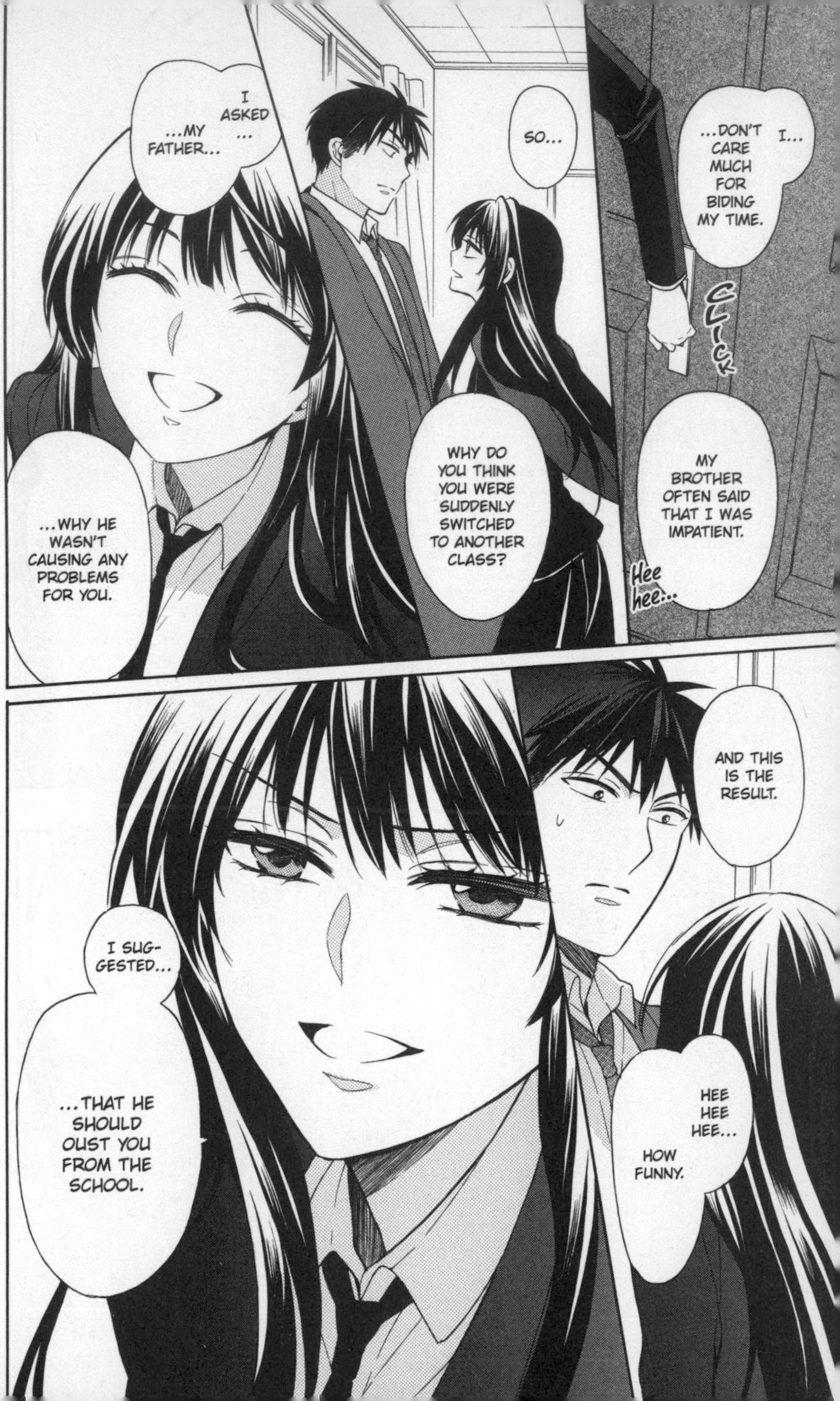
I... ...DON'T CARE MUCH FOR BIDING MY TIME.
CLICK
MY BROTHER OFTEN SAID THAT I WAS IMPATIENT.
Hee hee...
SO...
WHY DO YOU THINK YOU WERE SUDDENLY SWITCHED TO ANOTHER CLASS?
I ASKED... ...MY FATHER...
...WHY HE WASN'T CAUSING ANY PROBLEMS FOR YOU.
AND THIS IS THE RESULT.
I SUG-GESTED...
...THAT HE SHOULD OUST YOU FROM THE SCHOOL.
HEE HEE HEE... HOW FUNNY.

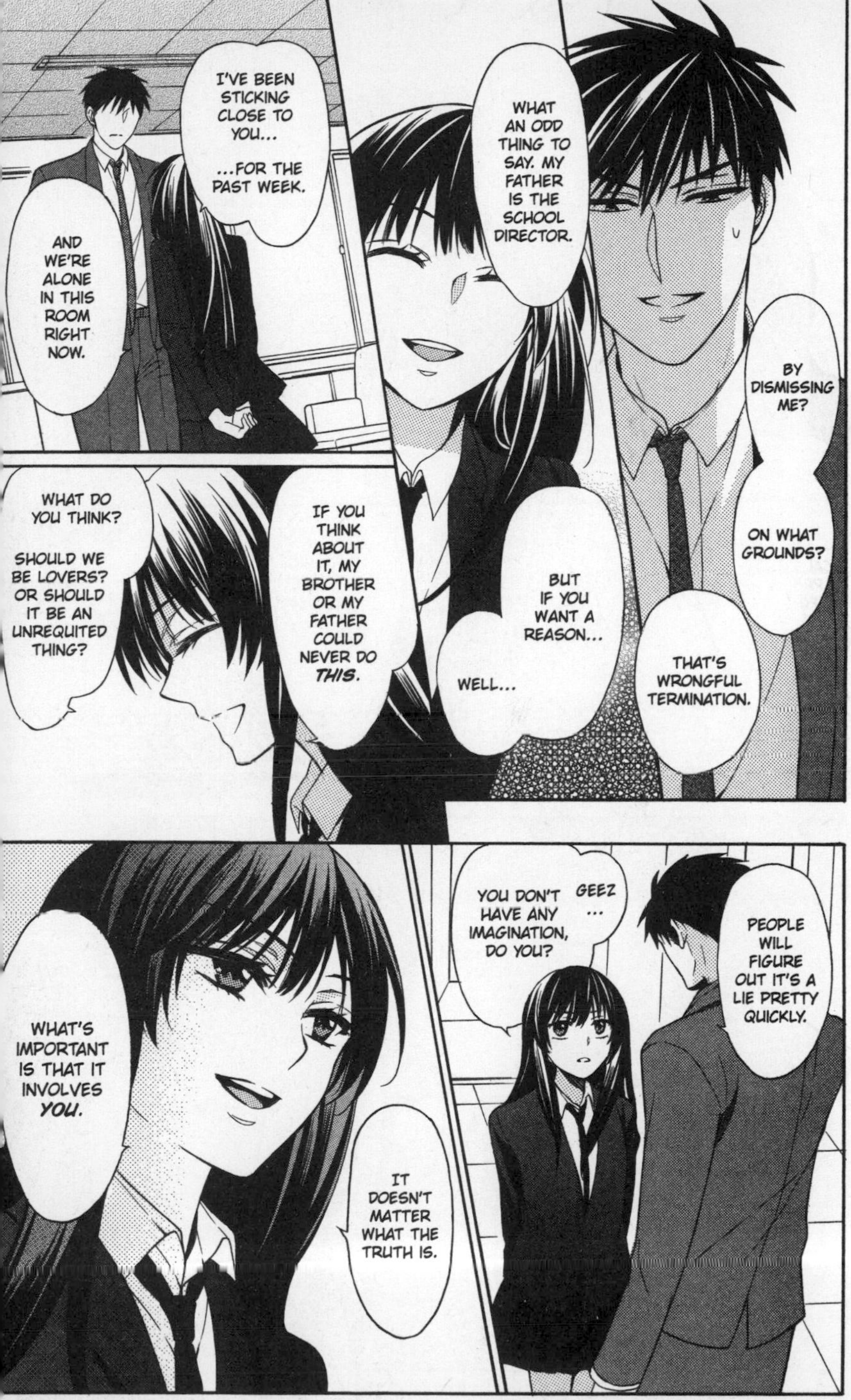
BY DISMISSING ME?
ON WHAT GROUNDS?
THAT'S WRONGFUL TERMINATION.
WHAT AN ODD THING TO SAY. MY FATHER IS THE SCHOOL DIRECTOR.
BUT IF YOU WANT A REASON...
WELL...
I'VE BEEN STICKING CLOSE TO YOU...
...FOR THE PAST WEEK.
AND WE'RE ALONE IN THIS ROOM RIGHT NOW.
IF YOU THINK ABOUT IT, MY BROTHER OR MY FATHER COULD NEVER DO *THIS*.
WHAT DO YOU THINK?
SHOULD WE BE LOVERS? OR SHOULD IT BE AN UNREQUITED THING?
PEOPLE WILL FIGURE OUT IT'S A LIE PRETTY QUICKLY.
GEEZ...
YOU DON'T HAVE ANY IMAGINATION, DO YOU?
IT DOESN'T MATTER WHAT THE TRUTH IS.
WHAT'S IMPORTANT IS THAT IT INVOLVES *YOU*.

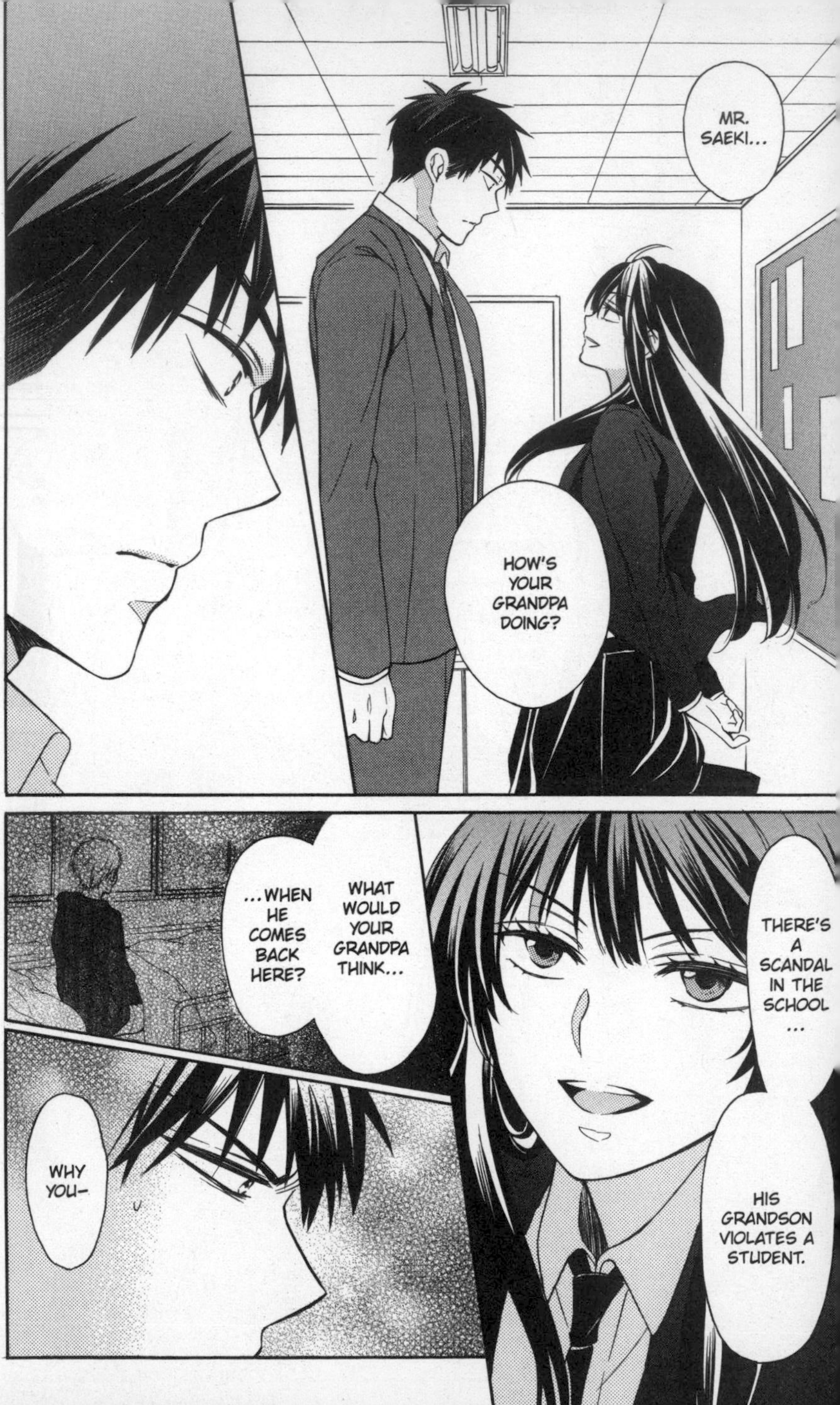
MR. SAEKI...
HOW'S YOUR GRANDPA DOING?
THERE'S A SCANDAL IN THE SCHOOL ...
HIS GRANDSON VIOLATES A STUDENT.
WHAT WOULD YOUR GRANDPA THINK...
...WHEN HE COMES BACK HERE?
WHY YOU-

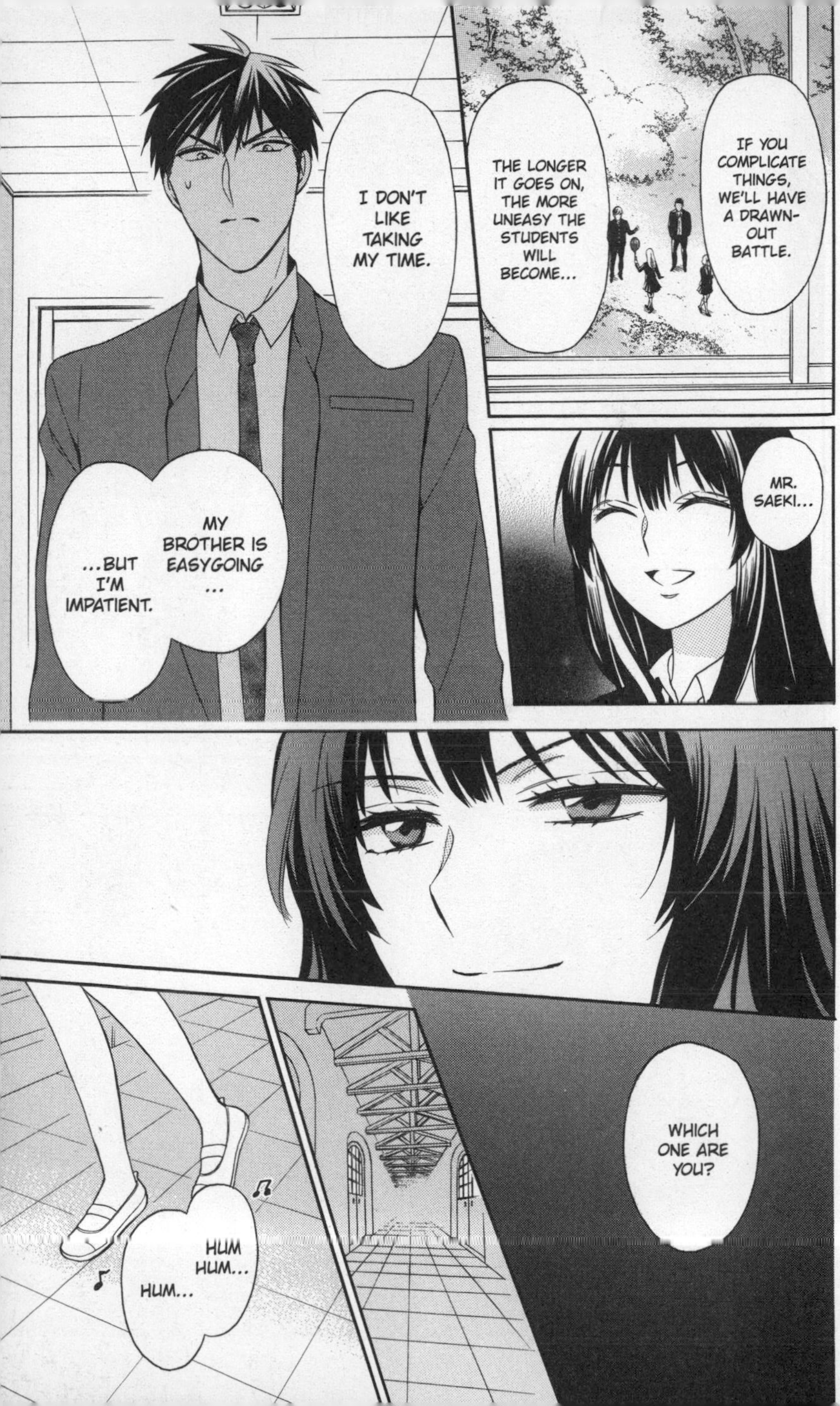
IF YOU COMPLICATE THINGS, WE'LL HAVE A DRAWN-OUT BATTLE.
THE LONGER IT GOES ON, THE MORE UNEASY THE STUDENTS WILL BECOME...
MR. SAEKI...
I DON'T LIKE TAKING MY TIME.
MY BROTHER IS EASYGOING...
...BUT I'M IMPATIENT.
WHICH ONE ARE YOU?
HUM HUM... HUM...

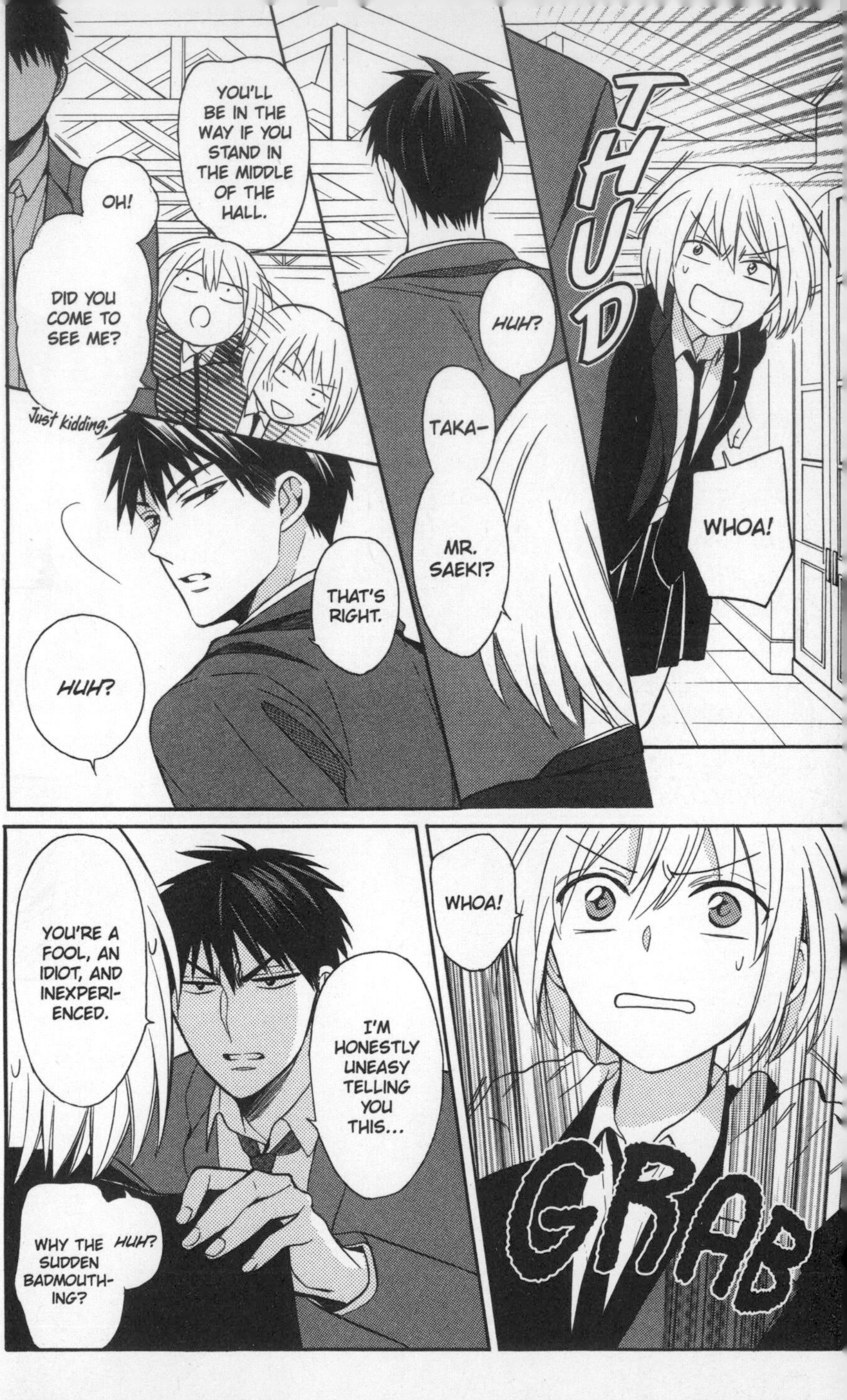

THUD
WHOA!
HUH?
TAKA-
MR. SAEKI?
YOU'LL BE IN THE WAY IF YOU STAND IN THE MIDDLE OF THE HALL.
OH!
DID YOU COME TO SEE ME?
Just kidding.
THAT'S RIGHT.
HUH?
WHOA!
GRAB
I'M HONESTLY UNEASY TELLING YOU THIS...
YOU'RE A FOOL, AN IDIOT, AND INEXPERIENCED.
HUH?
WHY THE SUDDEN BADMOUTHING?

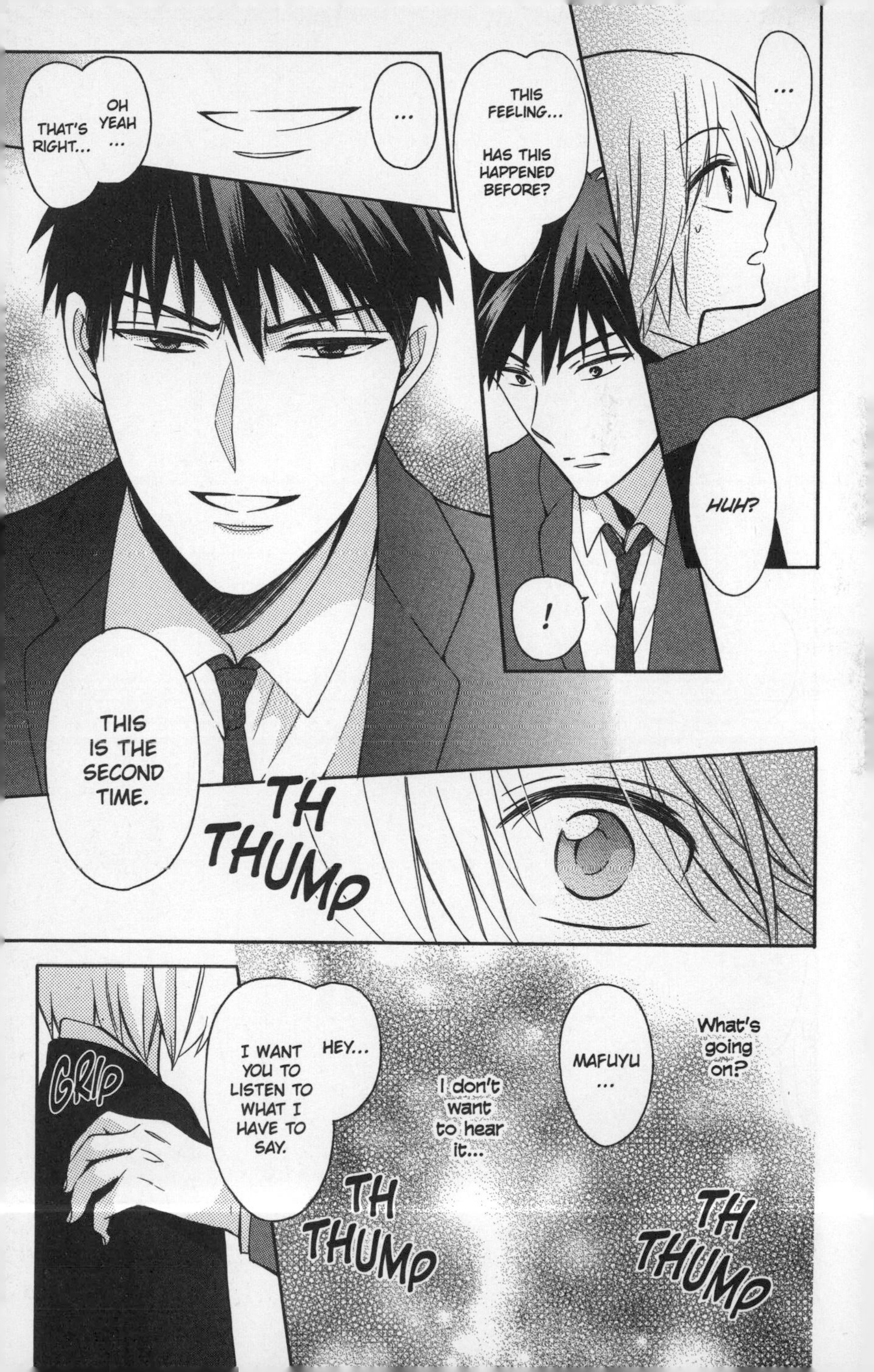
...
THIS FEELING... HAS THIS HAPPENED BEFORE?
HUH?
!
...
OH YEAH... THAT'S RIGHT...
THIS IS THE SECOND TIME.
TH THUMP
What's going on?
MAFUYU...
I don't want to hear it...
TH THUMP
HEY... I WANT YOU TO LISTEN TO WHAT I HAVE TO SAY.
GRIP
TH THUMP

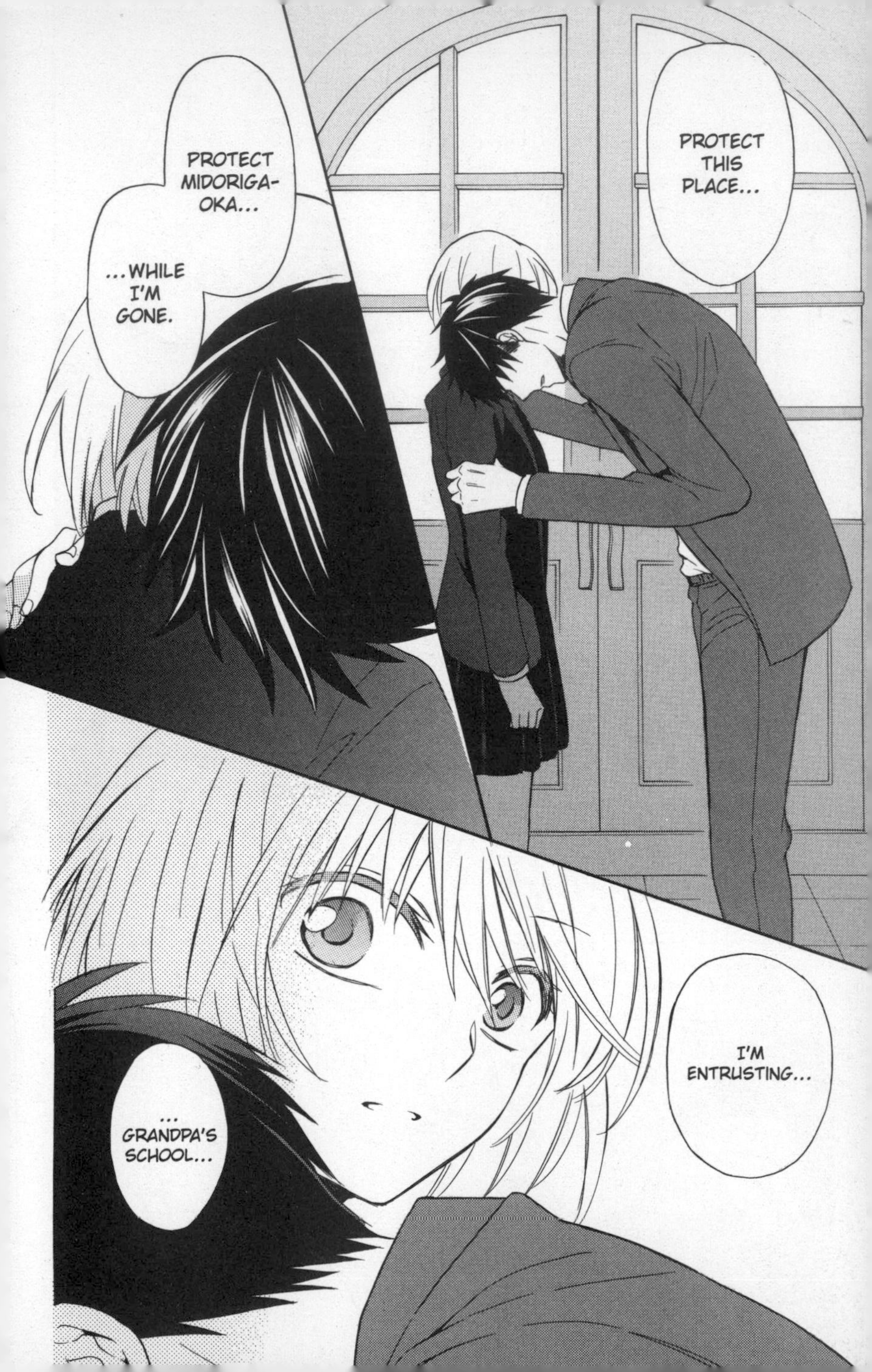
PROTECT THIS PLACE...
PROTECT MIDORIGA-OKA...
...WHILE I'M GONE.
I'M ENTRUSTING...
...GRANDPA'S SCHOOL...

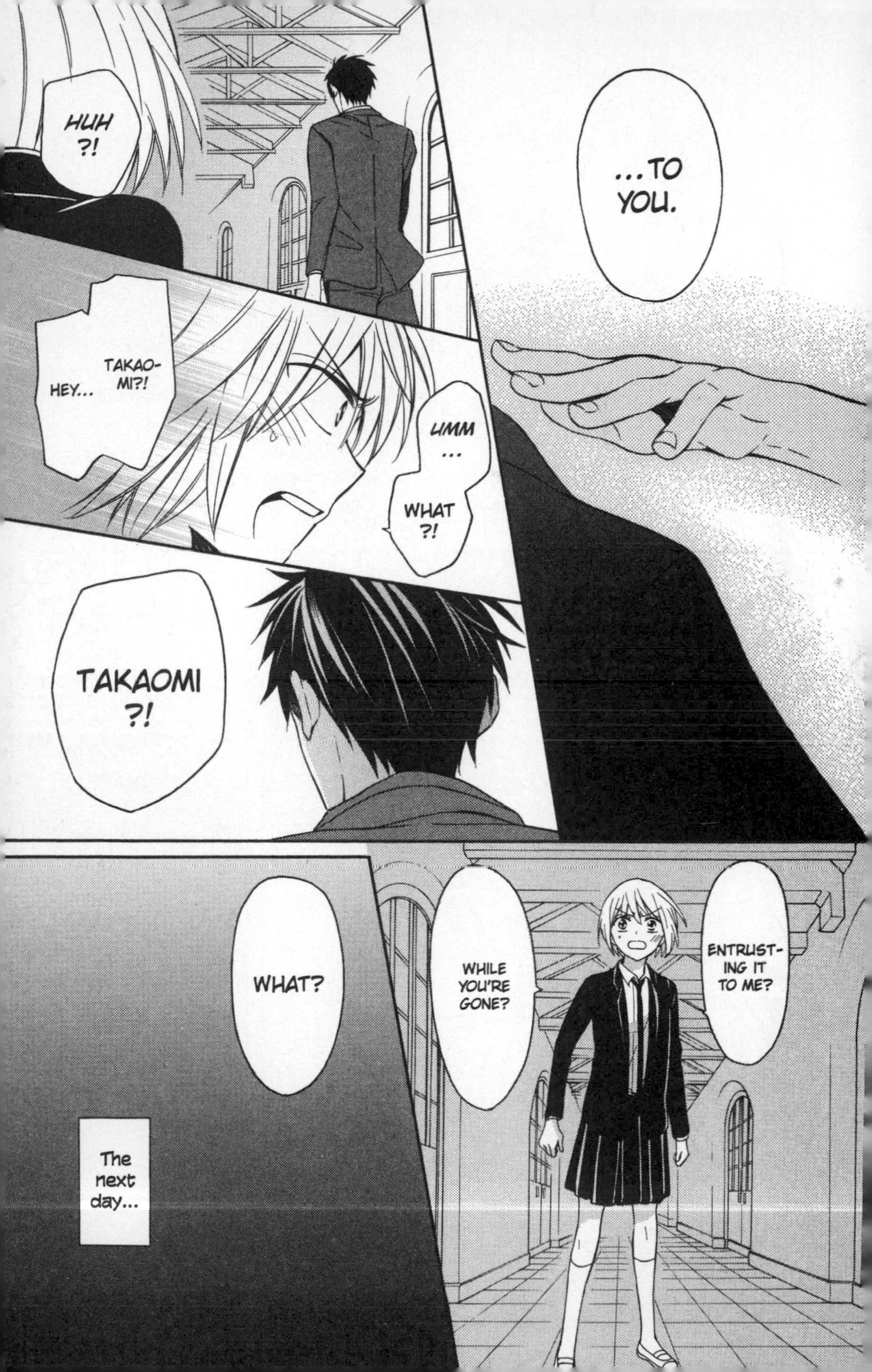
...TO YOU.
HUH ?!
UMM ... WHAT ?!
HEY... TAKAO-MI?!
TAKAOMI ?!
ENTRUST-ING IT TO ME?
WHILE YOU'RE GONE?
WHAT?
The next day...

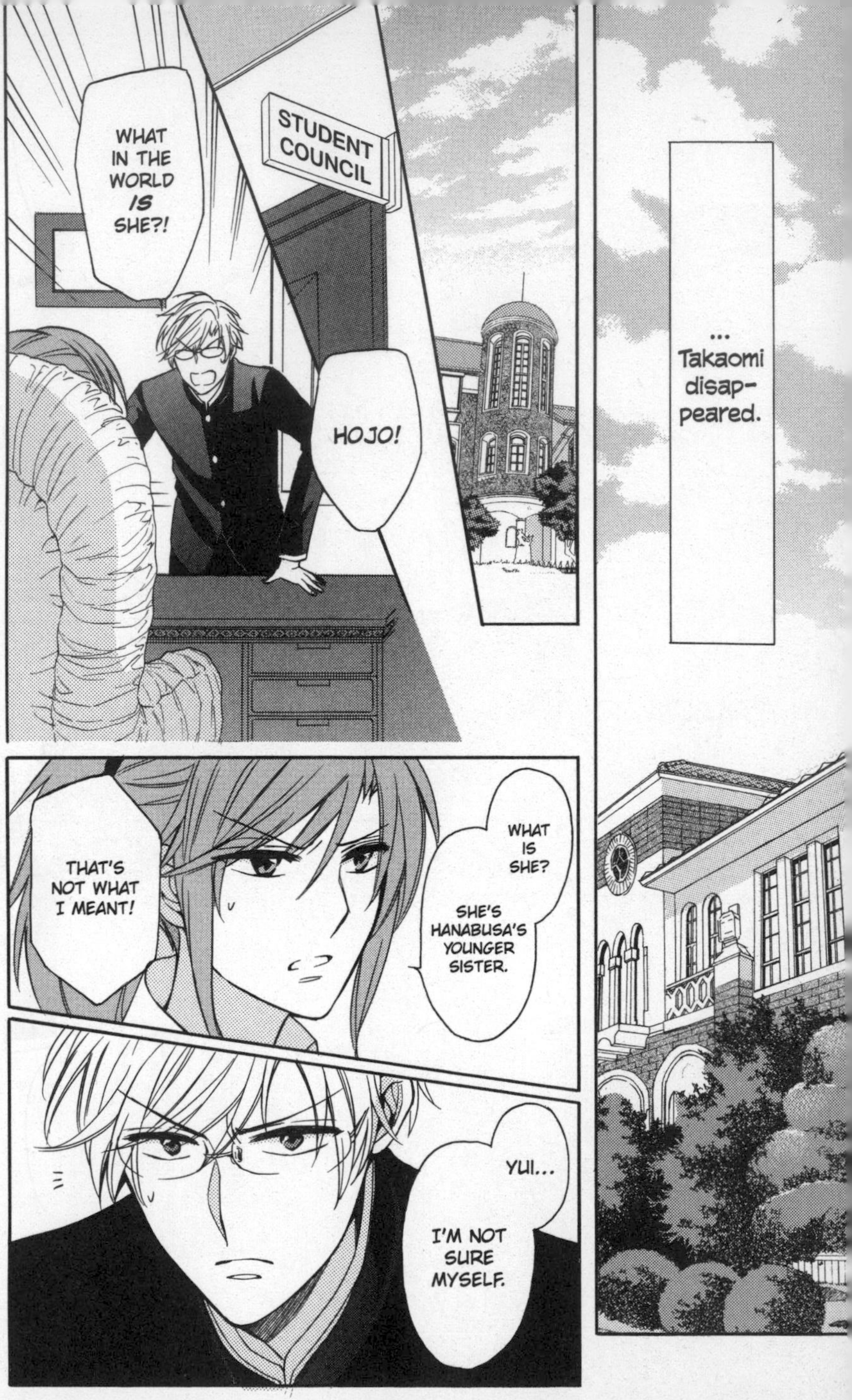
...Takaomi disappeared.
HOJO!
WHAT IN THE WORLD *IS* SHE?!
WHAT IS SHE?
SHE'S HANABUSA'S YOUNGER SISTER.
THAT'S NOT WHAT I MEANT!
YUI...
I'M NOT SURE MYSELF.

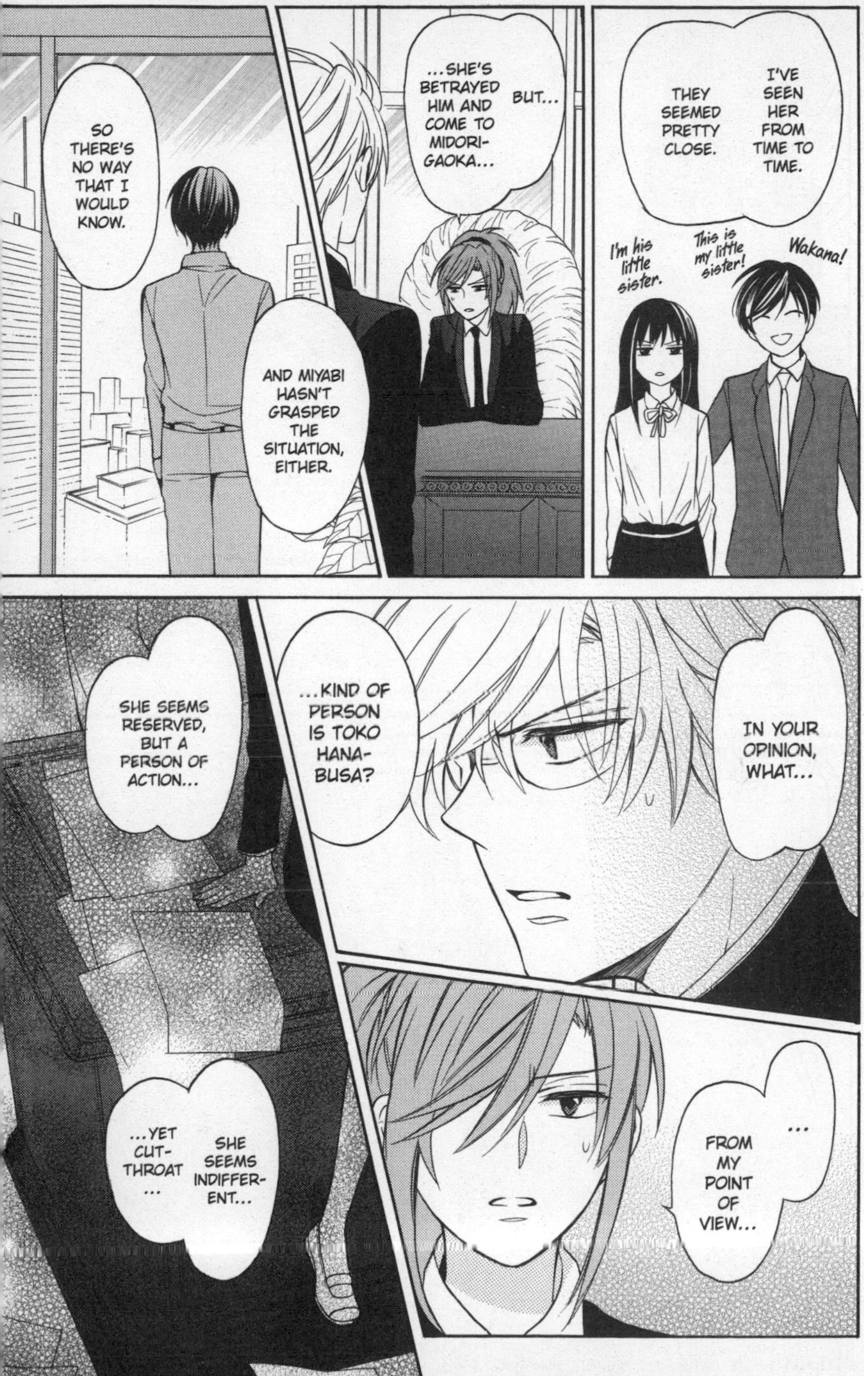
I'VE SEEN HER FROM TIME TO TIME.
THEY SEEMED PRETTY CLOSE.
Wakana!
This is my little sister!
I'm his little sister.
BUT...
...SHE'S BETRAYED HIM AND COME TO MIDORI-GAOKA...
AND MIYABI HASN'T GRASPED THE SITUATION, EITHER.
SO THERE'S NO WAY THAT I WOULD KNOW.
IN YOUR OPINION, WHAT...
...KIND OF PERSON IS TOKO HANA-BUSA?
...
FROM MY POINT OF VIEW...
SHE SEEMS RESERVED, BUT A PERSON OF ACTION...
SHE SEEMS INDIFFER-ENT...
...YET CUT-THROAT...

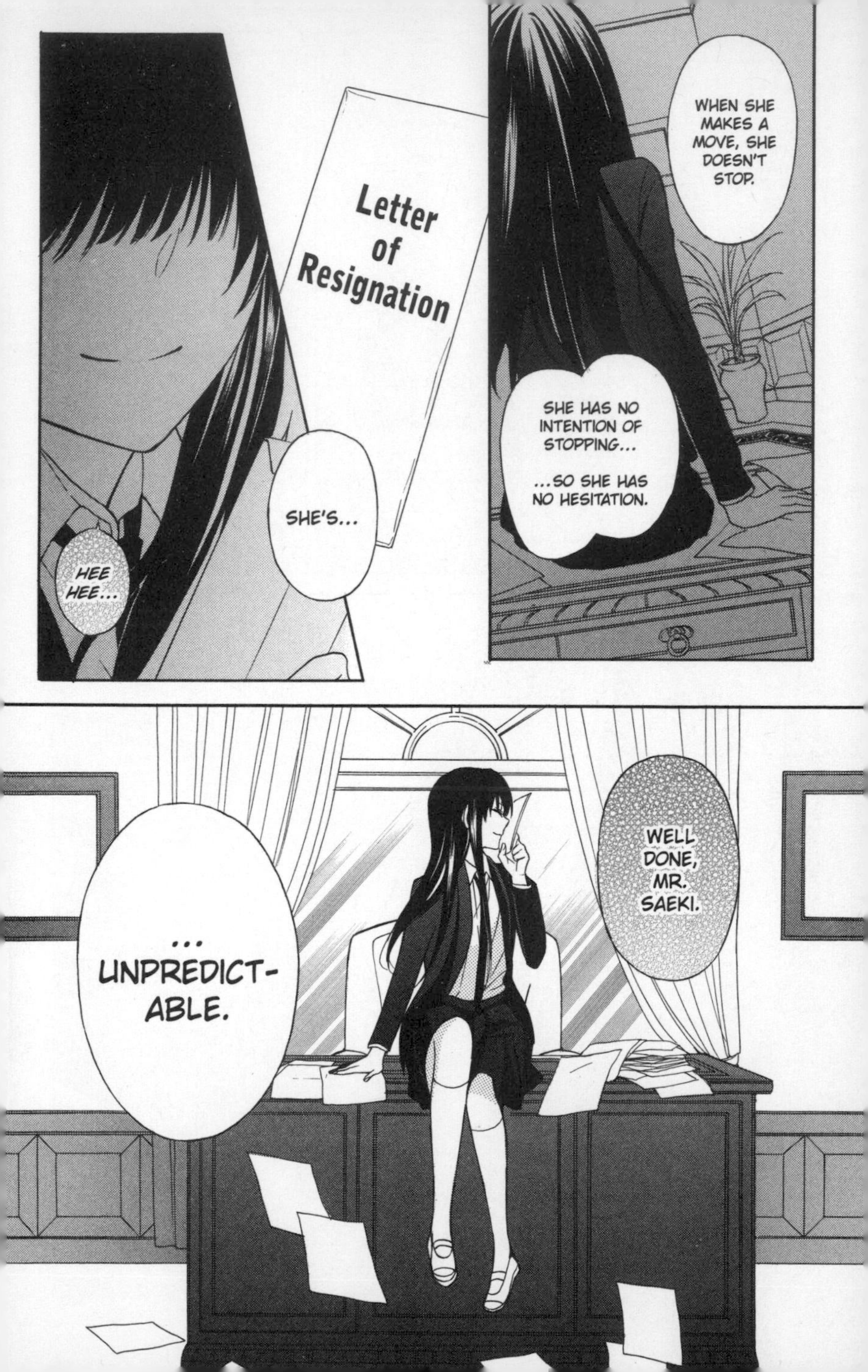
WHEN SHE MAKES A MOVE, SHE DOESN'T STOP.
SHE HAS NO INTENTION OF STOPPING...
...SO SHE HAS NO HESITATION.
Letter of Resignation
SHE'S...
HEE HEE...
WELL DONE, MR. SAEKI.
...UNPREDICTABLE.

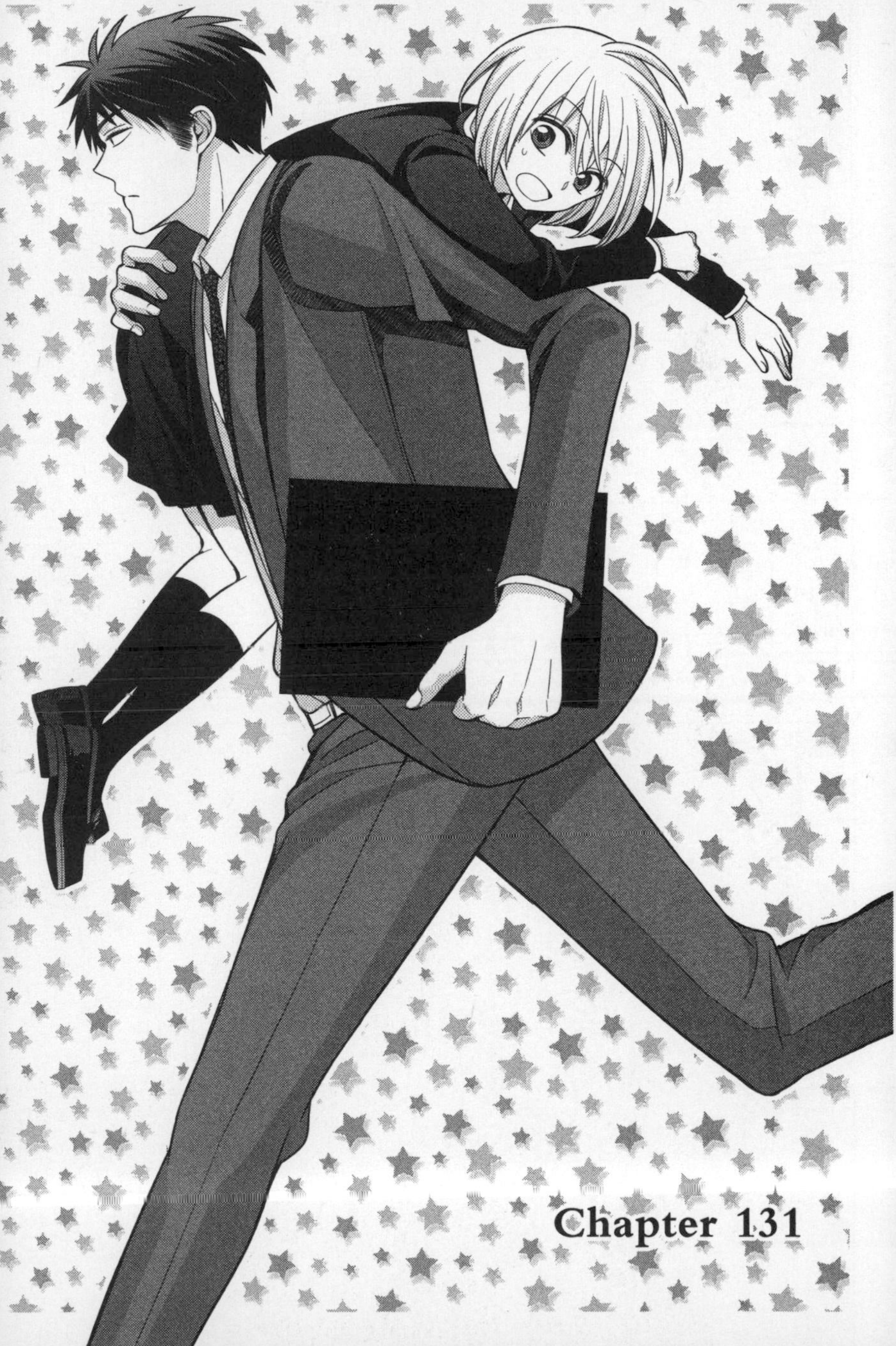

Chapter 131

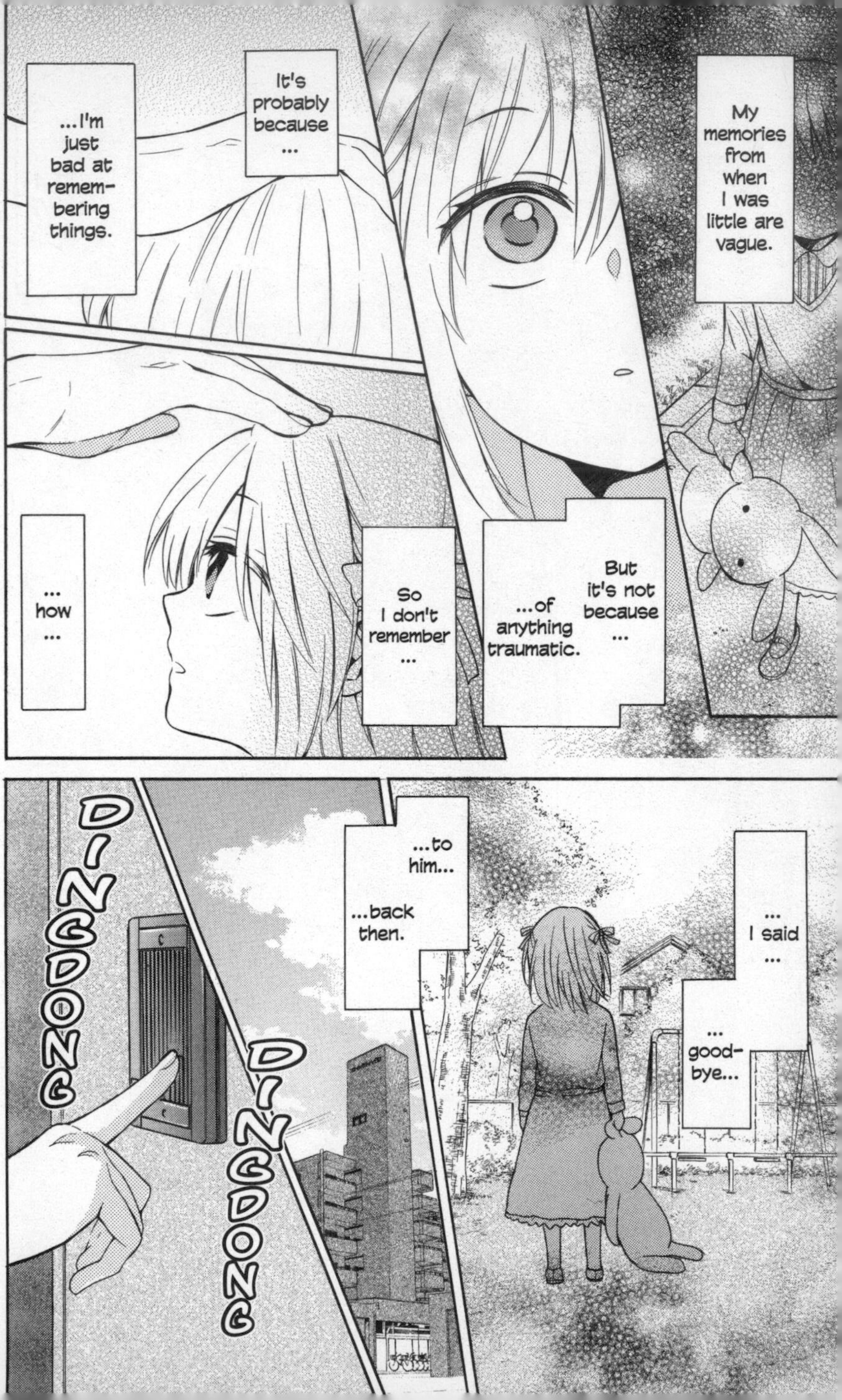
My memories from when I was little are vague.
It's probably because ...
...I'm just bad at remem-bering things.
But it's not because ...
...of anything traumatic.
So I don't remember ...
... how ...
... I said ...
... good-bye...
...to him...
...back then.
DINGDONG
DINGDONG

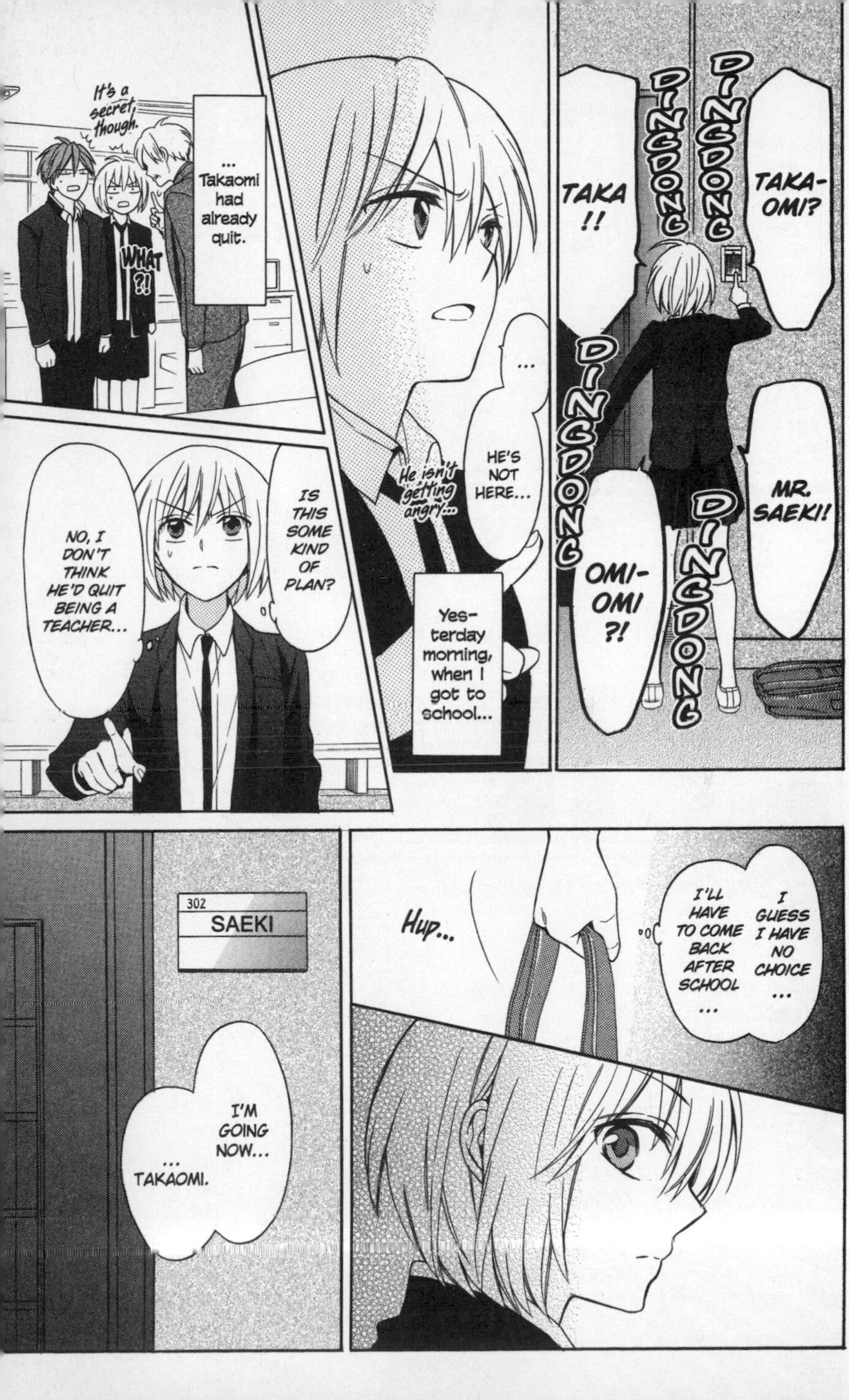
TAKA-OMI?
DINGDONG
DINGDONG
TAKA!!
DINGDONG
DINGDONG
MR. SAEKI!
OMI-OMI?!
...
HE'S NOT HERE...
He isn't getting angry...
Yesterday morning, when I got to school...
...Takaomi had already quit.
WHAT?!
It's a secret, though.
IS THIS SOME KIND OF PLAN?
NO, I DON'T THINK HE'D QUIT BEING A TEACHER...
I GUESS I HAVE NO CHOICE...
I'LL HAVE TO COME BACK AFTER SCHOOL...
Hup...
302
SAEKI
I'M GOING NOW...
...TAKAOMI.

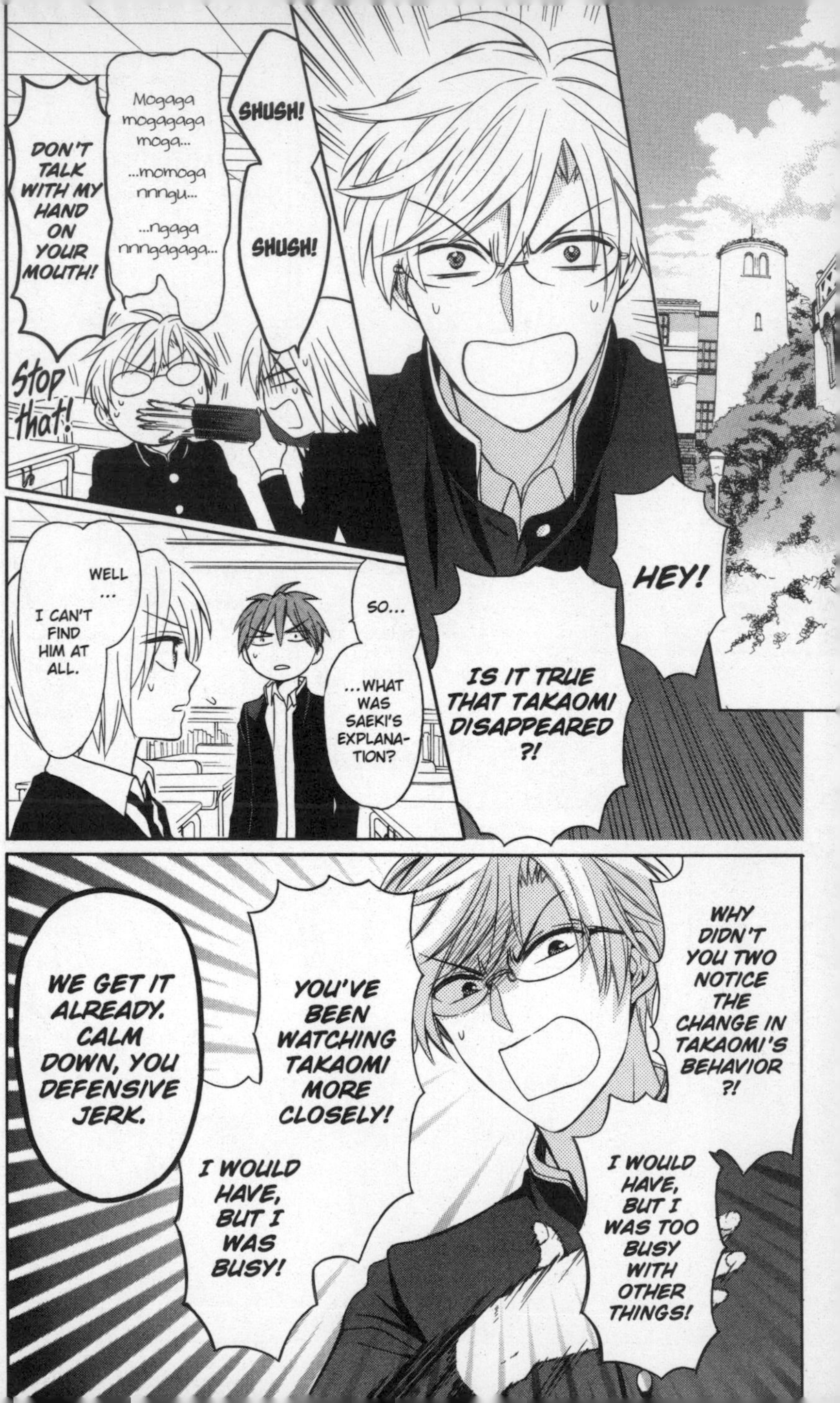
HEY!
IS IT TRUE THAT TAKAOMI DISAPPEARED ?!
SHUSH!
SHUSH!
Mogaga mogagaga moga... ...momoga nnngu... ...ngaga nnngagaga...
DON'T TALK WITH MY HAND ON YOUR MOUTH!
Stop that!
SO... ...WHAT WAS SAEKI'S EXPLANATION?
WELL... I CAN'T FIND HIM AT ALL.
WHY DIDN'T YOU TWO NOTICE THE CHANGE IN TAKAOMI'S BEHAVIOR ?!
I WOULD HAVE, BUT I WAS TOO BUSY WITH OTHER THINGS!
YOU'VE BEEN WATCHING TAKAOMI MORE CLOSELY!
I WOULD HAVE, BUT I WAS BUSY!
WE GET IT ALREADY. CALM DOWN, YOU DEFENSIVE JERK.

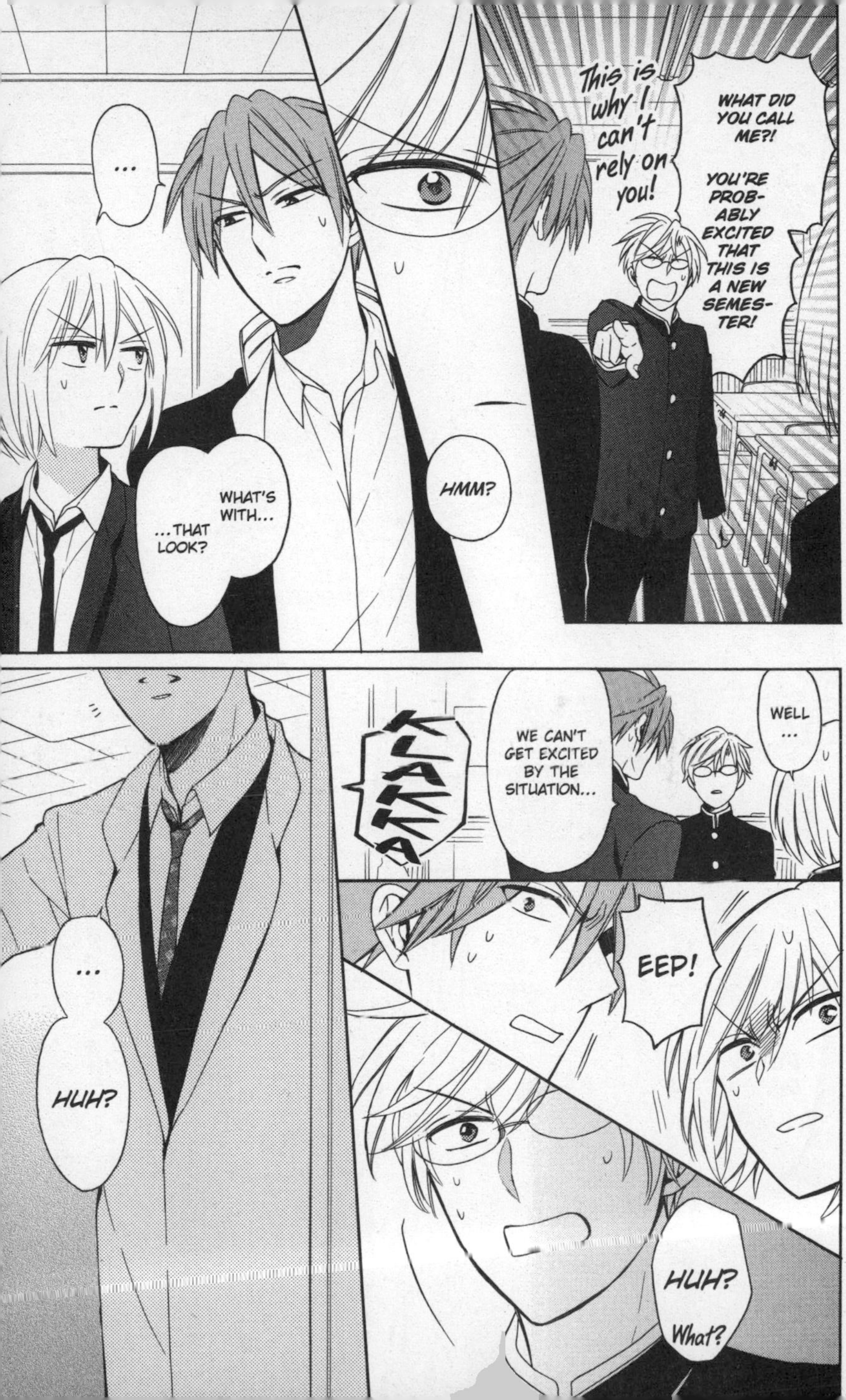
WHAT DID YOU CALL ME?!
YOU'RE PROB-ABLY EXCITED THAT THIS IS A NEW SEMES-TER!
This is why I can't rely on you!
HMM?
...
WHAT'S WITH... ...THAT LOOK?
WELL...
WE CAN'T GET EXCITED BY THE SITUATION...
KLAKKA
EEP!
HUH?
What?
...
HUH?

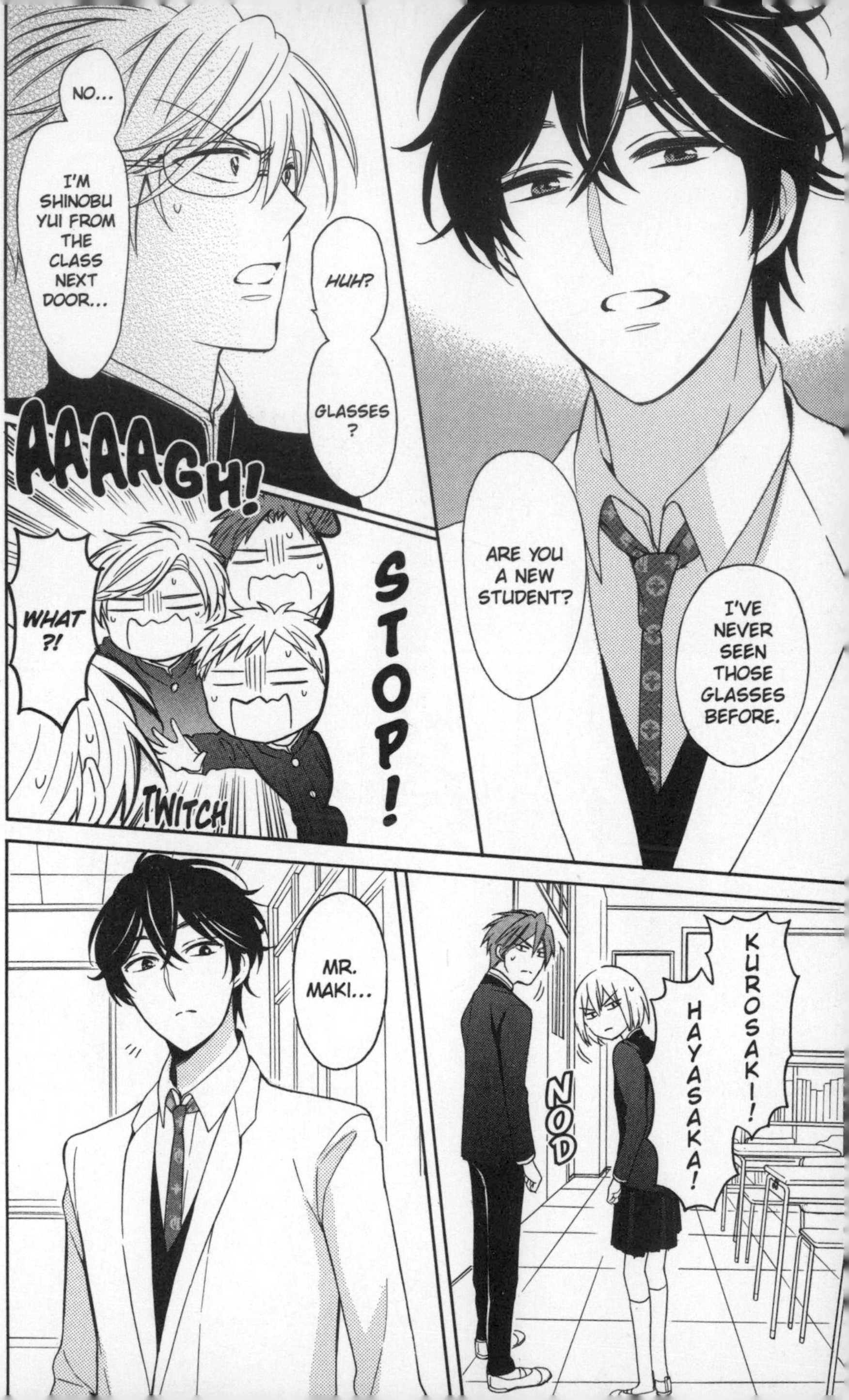
I'VE NEVER SEEN THOSE GLASSES BEFORE.
ARE YOU A NEW STUDENT?
HUH?
GLASSES ?
NO...
I'M SHINOBU YUI FROM THE CLASS NEXT DOOR...
STOP!
AAAAGH!
WHAT ?!
TWITCH
KUROSAKI!
HAYASAKA!
NOD
MR. MAKI...

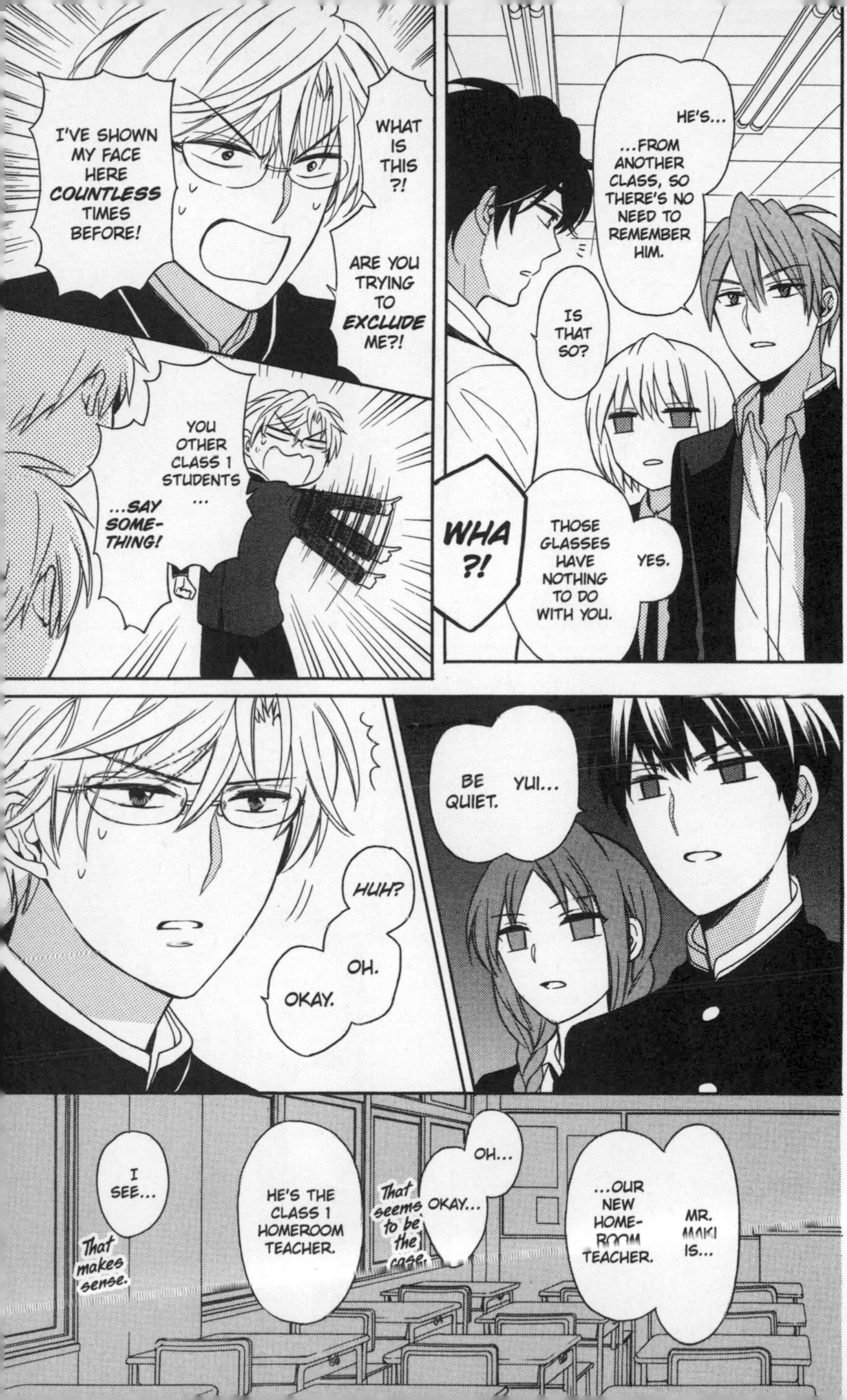
HE'S...
...FROM ANOTHER CLASS, SO THERE'S NO NEED TO REMEMBER HIM.
IS THAT SO?
YES.
THOSE GLASSES HAVE NOTHING TO DO WITH YOU.
WHA ?!
WHAT IS THIS ?!
I'VE SHOWN MY FACE HERE COUNTLESS TIMES BEFORE!
ARE YOU TRYING TO EXCLUDE ME?!
YOU OTHER CLASS 1 STUDENTS ...
...SAY SOME-THING!
YUI...
BE QUIET.
HUH?
OH.
OKAY.
MR. MAKI IS...
...OUR NEW HOME-ROOM TEACHER.
OH...
OKAY...
That seems to be the case.
HE'S THE CLASS 1 HOMEROOM TEACHER.
I SEE...
That makes sense.

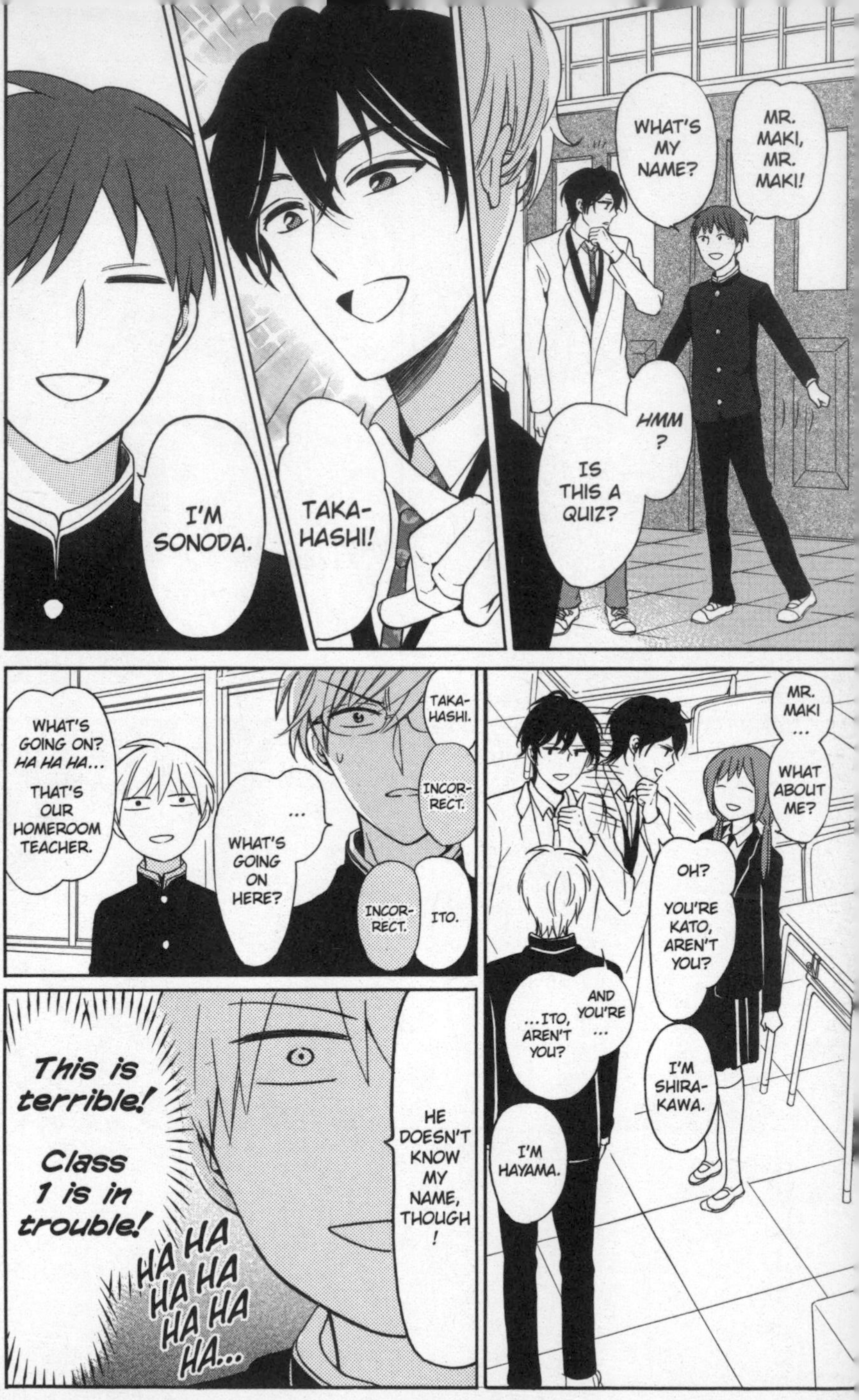
MR. MAKI, MR. MAKI!
WHAT'S MY NAME?
HMM?
IS THIS A QUIZ?
TAKA-HASHI!
I'M SONODA.
MR. MAKI... WHAT ABOUT ME?
OH? YOU'RE KATO, AREN'T YOU?
I'M SHIRA-KAWA.
AND YOU'RE...
...ITO, AREN'T YOU?
I'M HAYAMA.
TAKA-HASHI.
INCOR-RECT.
...
ITO.
INCOR-RECT.
WHAT'S GOING ON HERE?
WHAT'S GOING ON? HA HA HA...
THAT'S OUR HOMEROOM TEACHER.
HE DOESN'T KNOW MY NAME, THOUGH!
This is terrible!
Class 1 is in trouble!
HA HA HA HA HA HA HA...

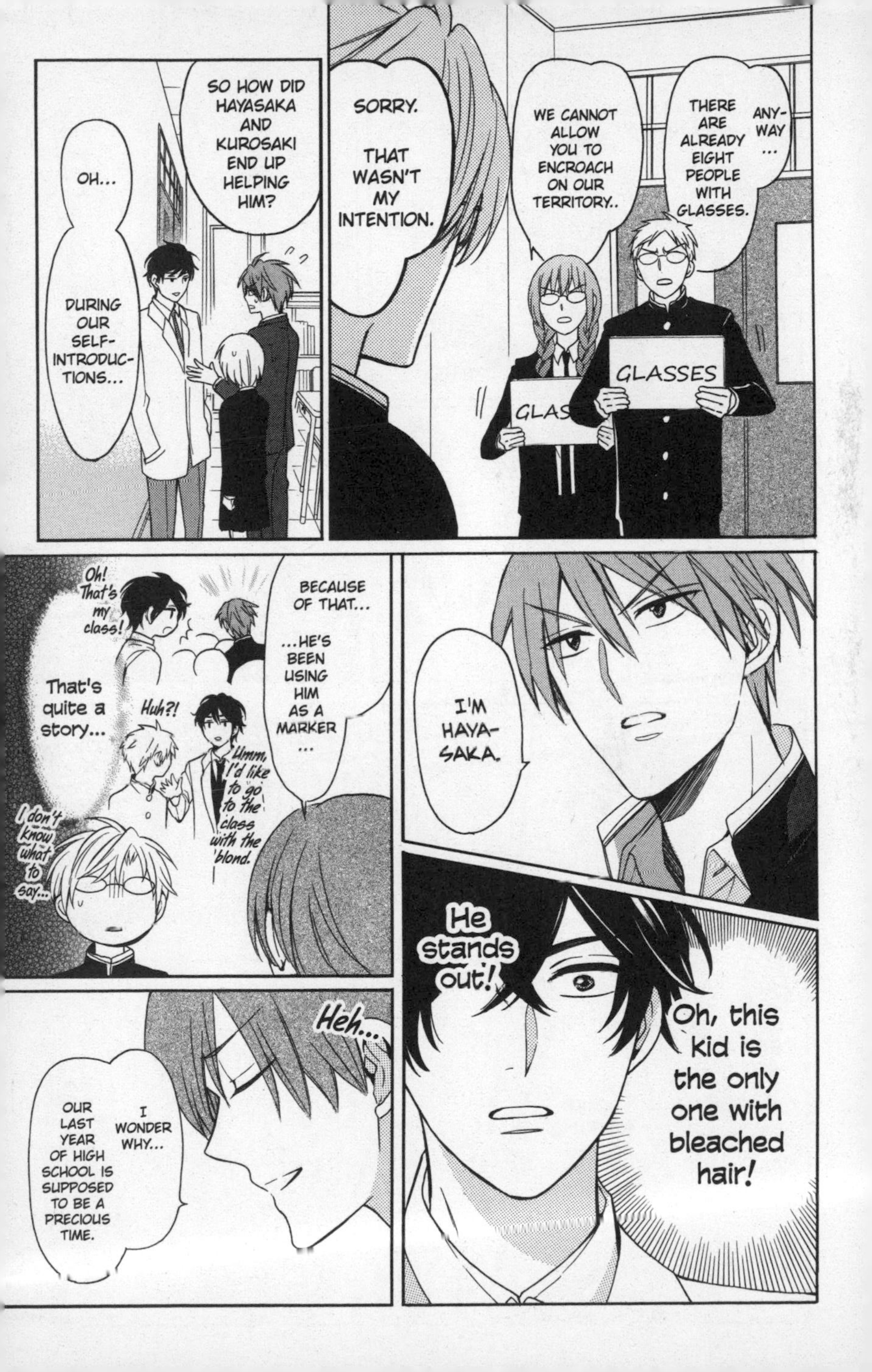

ANYWAY...
THERE ARE ALREADY EIGHT PEOPLE WITH GLASSES.
WE CANNOT ALLOW YOU TO ENCROACH ON OUR TERRITORY..
GLASSES
GLAS
SORRY.
THAT WASN'T MY INTENTION.
SO HOW DID HAYASAKA AND KUROSAKI END UP HELPING HIM?
OH...
DURING OUR SELF-INTRODUCTIONS...
I'M HAYA-SAKA.
He stands out!
Oh, this kid is the only one with bleached hair!
BECAUSE OF THAT...
...HE'S BEEN USING HIM AS A MARKER...
Oh! That's my class!
Huh?!
Umm, I'd like to go to the class with the blond.
That's quite a story...
I don't know what to say...
Heh...
I WONDER WHY...
OUR LAST YEAR OF HIGH SCHOOL IS SUPPOSED TO BE A PRECIOUS TIME.

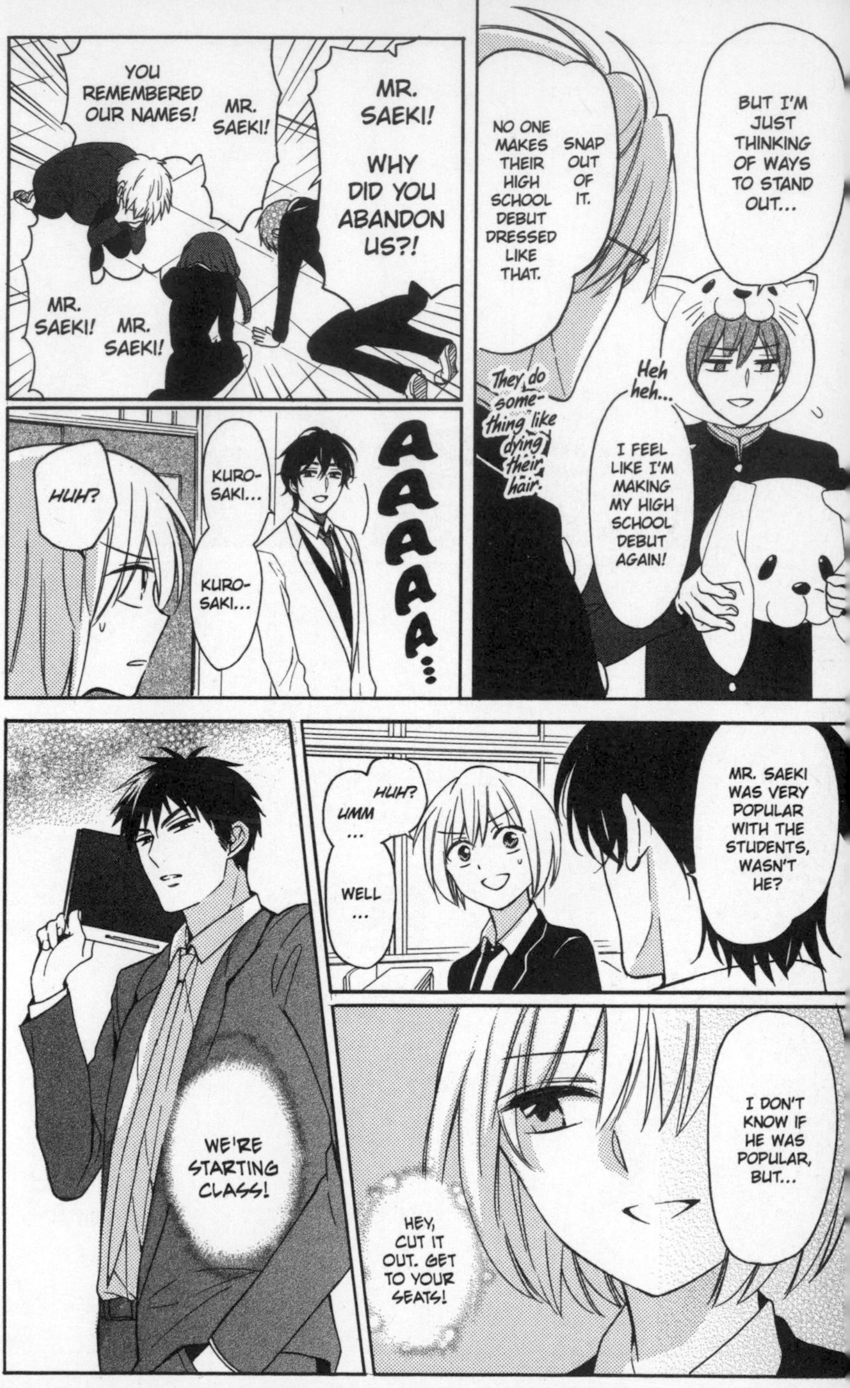
BUT I'M JUST THINKING OF WAYS TO STAND OUT...
SNAP OUT OF IT.
NO ONE MAKES THEIR HIGH SCHOOL DEBUT DRESSED LIKE THAT.
Heh heh...
I FEEL LIKE I'M MAKING MY HIGH SCHOOL DEBUT AGAIN!
They do something like dying their hair.
MR. SAEKI! WHY DID YOU ABANDON US?!
MR. SAEKI!
YOU REMEMBERED OUR NAMES!
MR. SAEKI!
MR. SAEKI!
AAAAAA..
KURO-SAKI...
KURO-SAKI...
HUH?
MR. SAEKI WAS VERY POPULAR WITH THE STUDENTS, WASN'T HE?
HUH? UMM...
WELL...
I DON'T KNOW IF HE WAS POPULAR, BUT...
HEY, CUT IT OUT. GET TO YOUR SEATS!
WE'RE STARTING CLASS!

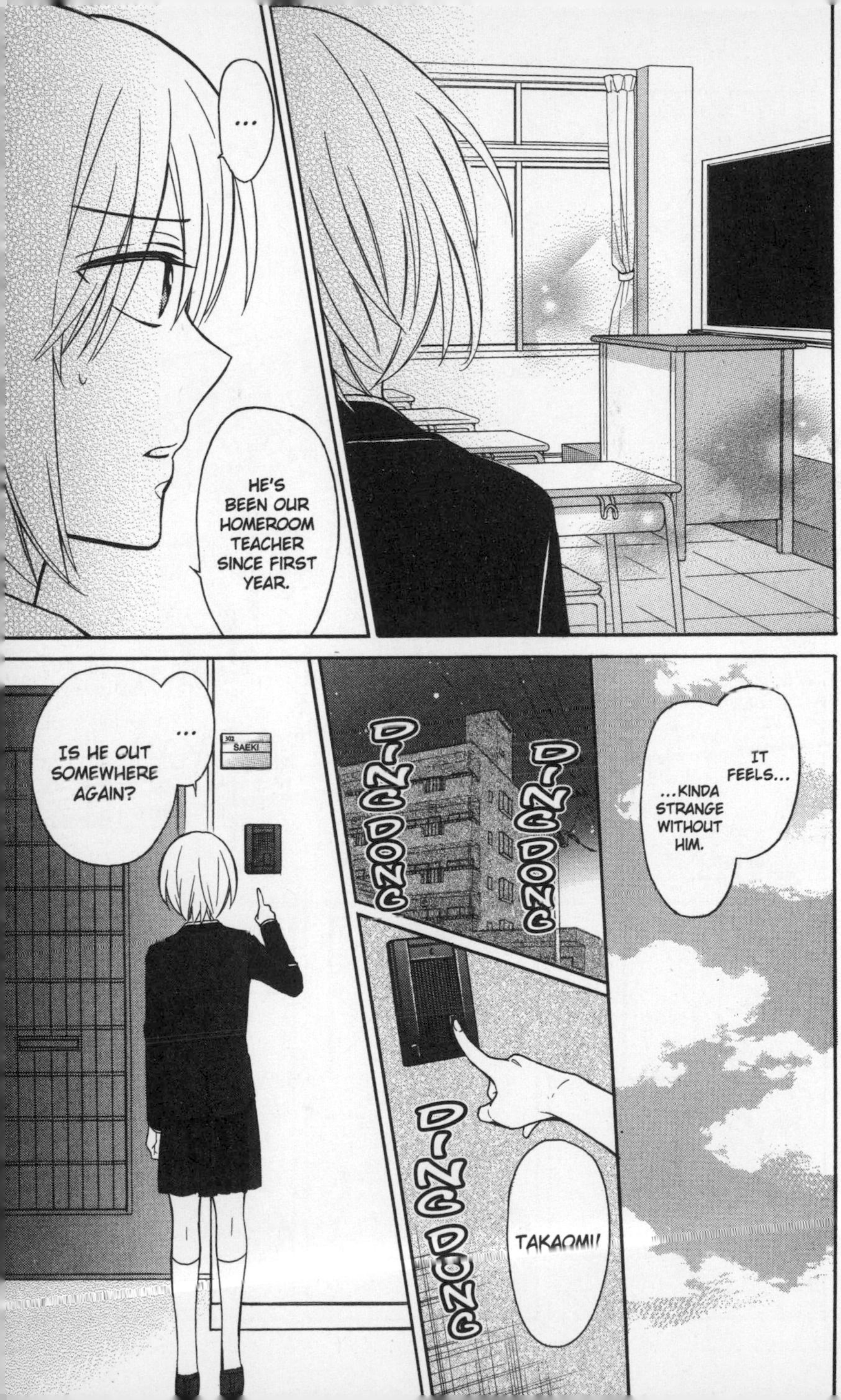
...
HE'S BEEN OUR HOMEROOM TEACHER SINCE FIRST YEAR.
IT FEELS... ...KINDA STRANGE WITHOUT HIM.
DING DONG
DING DONG
DING DONG
TAKAOMI!!
302 SAEKI
... IS HE OUT SOMEWHERE AGAIN?

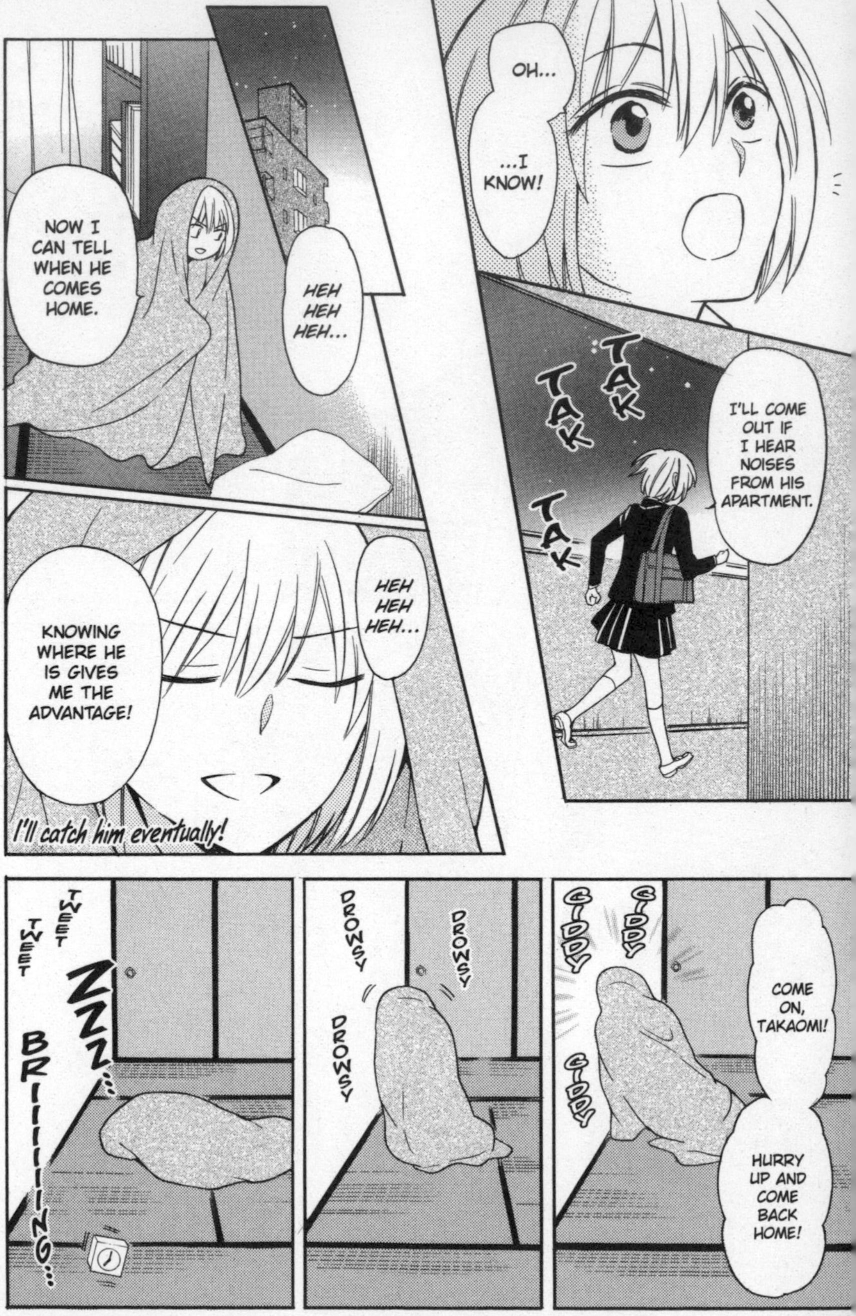
OH...
...I KNOW!
TAK TAK TAK
I'LL COME OUT IF I HEAR NOISES FROM HIS APARTMENT.
NOW I CAN TELL WHEN HE COMES HOME.
HEH HEH HEH...
HEH HEH HEH...
KNOWING WHERE HE IS GIVES ME THE ADVANTAGE!
I'll catch him eventually!
GIDDY GIDDY
COME ON, TAKAOMI!
HURRY UP AND COME BACK HOME!
GIDDY
DROWSY
DROWSY
DROWSY
TWEET
TWEET
ZZZ...
BRIIIIIING...

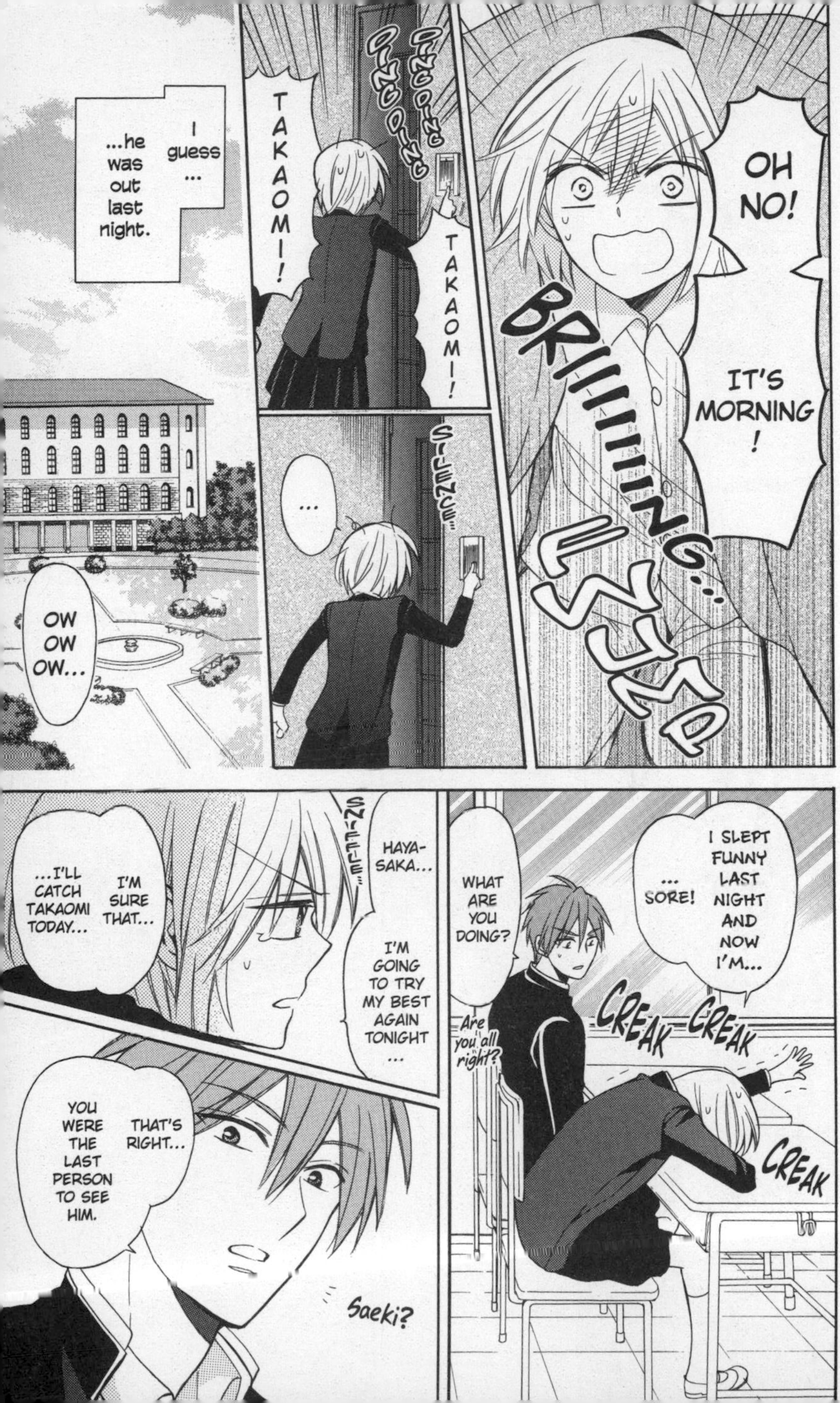
OH NO!
BRIIIIIING...
IT'S MORNING!
DING DONG DING DONG
TAKAOMI!
TAKAOMI!
SILENCE...
...
I guess... ...he was out last night.
OW OW OW...
I SLEPT FUNNY LAST NIGHT AND NOW I'M... ...SORE!
CREAK CREAK
CREAK
WHAT ARE YOU DOING?
Are you all right?
HAYA-SAKA...
SNIFFLE...
I'M GOING TO TRY MY BEST AGAIN TONIGHT...
I'M SURE THAT... ...I'LL CATCH TAKAOMI TODAY...
THAT'S RIGHT... YOU WERE THE LAST PERSON TO SEE HIM.
Saeki?

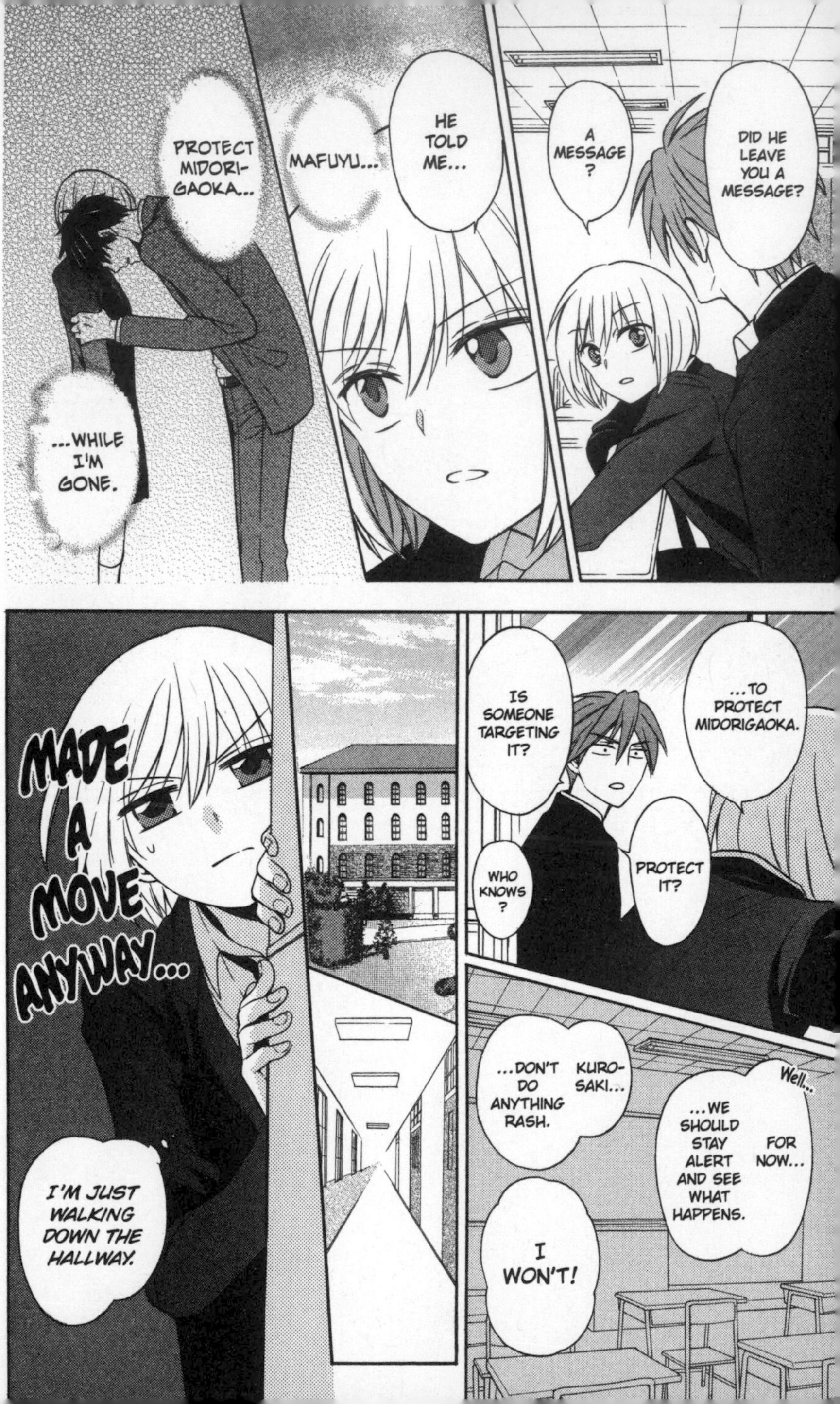
DID HE LEAVE YOU A MESSAGE?
A MESSAGE?
HE TOLD ME...
MAFUYU...
PROTECT MIDORI-GAOKA...
...WHILE I'M GONE.
...TO PROTECT MIDORIGAOKA.
IS SOMEONE TARGETING IT?
PROTECT IT?
WHO KNOWS?
Well...
FOR NOW...
...WE SHOULD STAY ALERT AND SEE WHAT HAPPENS.
KURO-SAKI...
...DON'T DO ANYTHING RASH.
I WON'T!
MADE A MOVE ANYWAY...
I'M JUST WALKING DOWN THE HALLWAY.

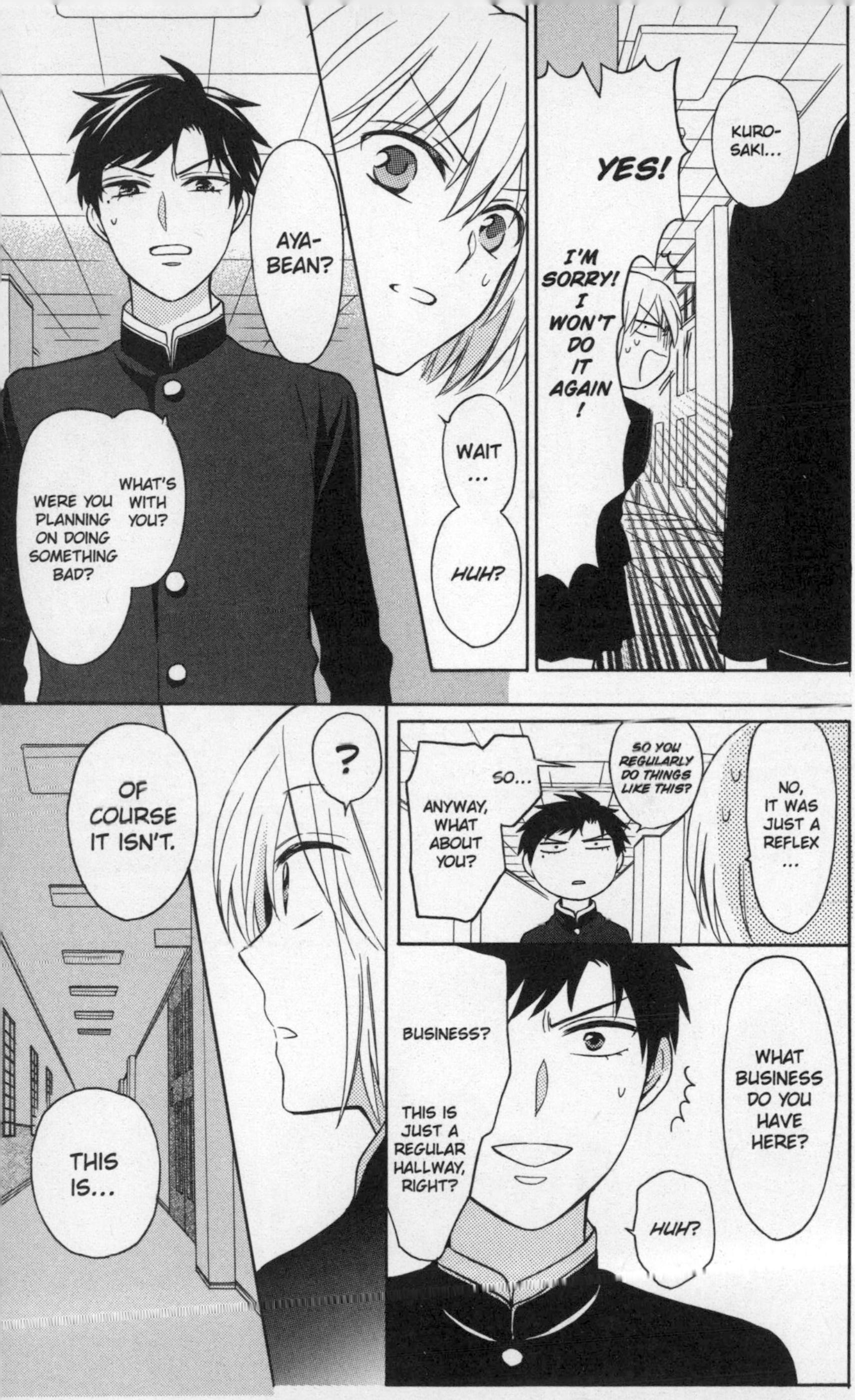
KURO-SAKI...
YES!
I'M SORRY! I WON'T DO IT AGAIN!
AYA-BEAN?
WAIT...
HUH?
WHAT'S WITH YOU?
WERE YOU PLANNING ON DOING SOMETHING BAD?
SO YOU REGULARLY DO THINGS LIKE THIS?
NO, IT WAS JUST A REFLEX...
SO... ANYWAY, WHAT ABOUT YOU?
WHAT BUSINESS DO YOU HAVE HERE?
HUH?
BUSINESS?
THIS IS JUST A REGULAR HALLWAY, RIGHT?
?
OF COURSE IT ISN'T.
THIS IS...

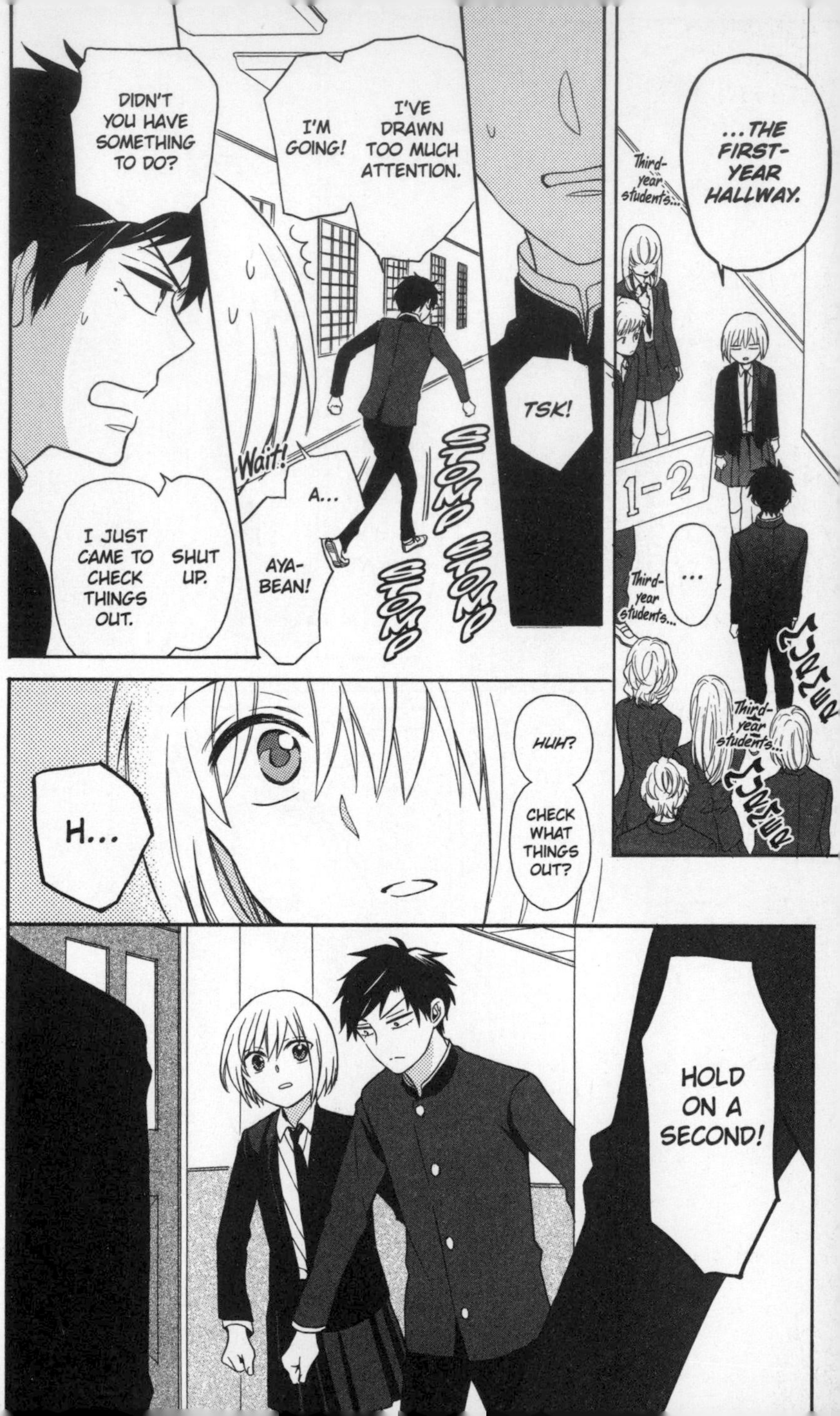
...THE FIRST-YEAR HALLWAY.
Third-year students...
...
Third-year students...
Third-year students...
1-2
TSK!
I'VE DRAWN TOO MUCH ATTENTION.
I'M GOING!
Wait!
A...
AYA-BEAN!
STOMP STOMP STOMP
DIDN'T YOU HAVE SOMETHING TO DO?
SHUT UP.
I JUST CAME TO CHECK THINGS OUT.
HUH?
CHECK WHAT THINGS OUT?
H...
HOLD ON A SECOND!

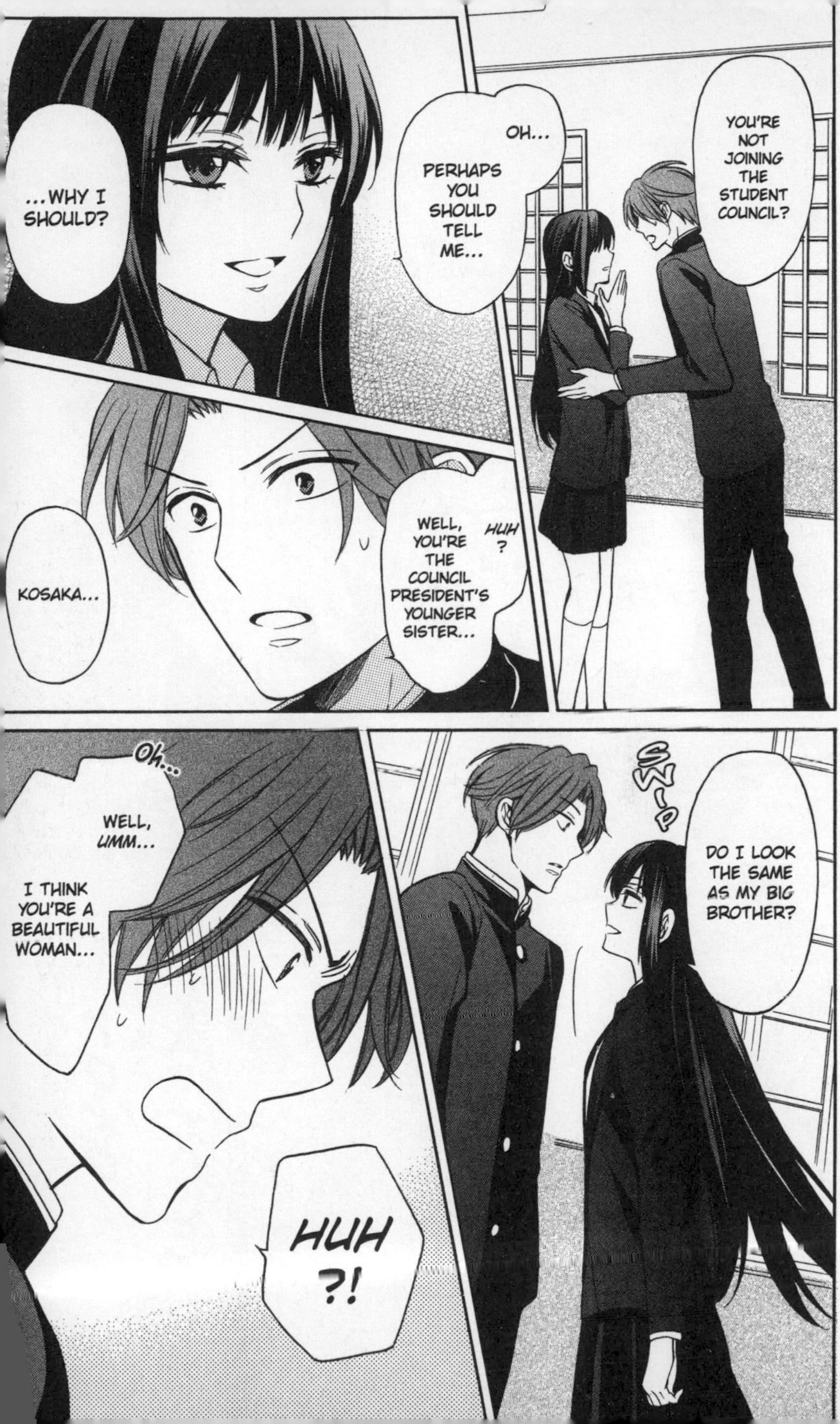
YOU'RE NOT JOINING THE STUDENT COUNCIL?
OH... PERHAPS YOU SHOULD TELL ME...
...WHY I SHOULD?
HUH?
WELL, YOU'RE THE COUNCIL PRESIDENT'S YOUNGER SISTER...
KOSAKA...
SWIP
DO I LOOK THE SAME AS MY BIG BROTHER?
Oh...
WELL, UMM...
I THINK YOU'RE A BEAUTIFUL WOMAN...
HUH ?!

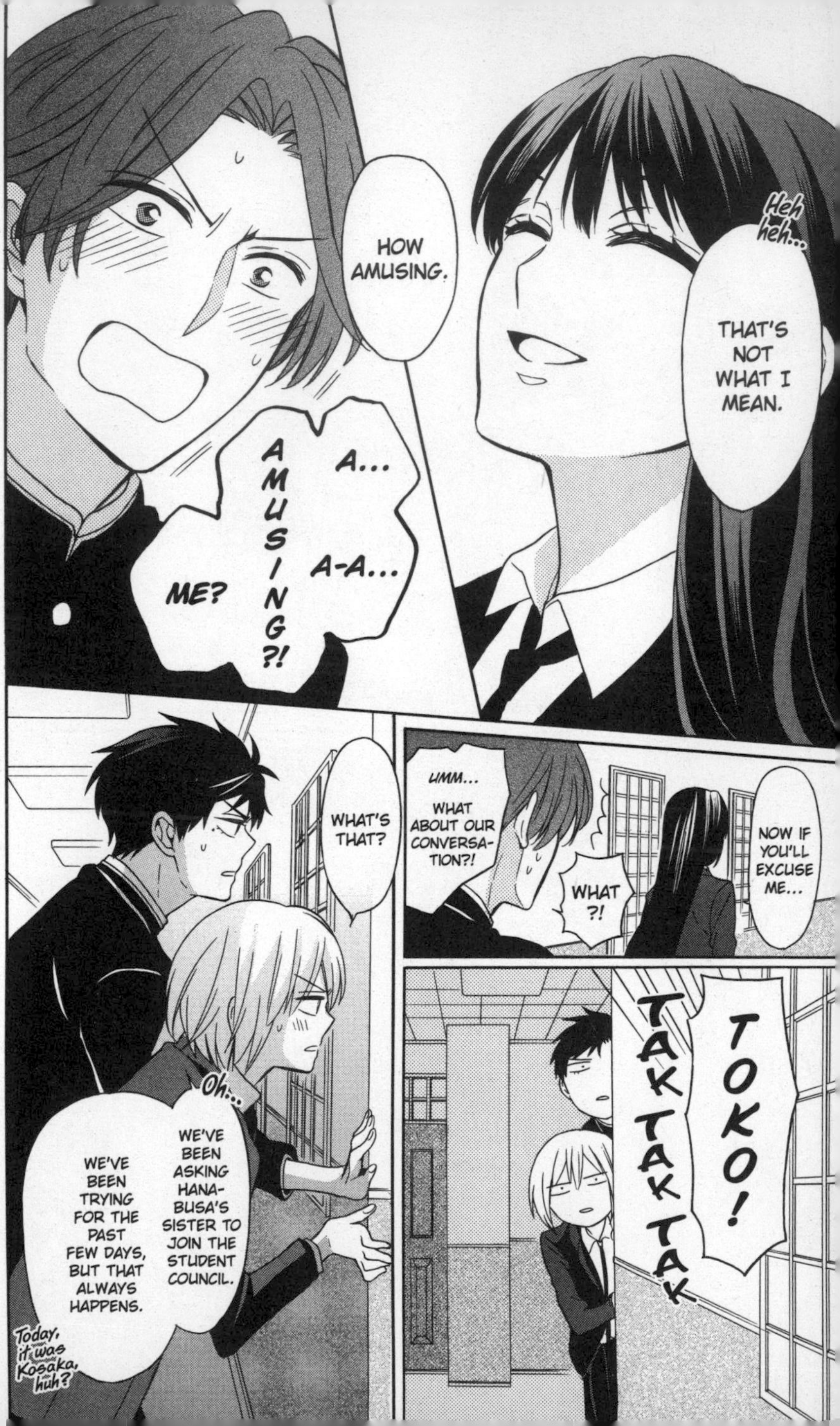
Heh heh...
THAT'S NOT WHAT I MEAN.
HOW AMUSING.
A...
A-A...
AMUSING ?!
ME?
NOW IF YOU'LL EXCUSE ME...
WHAT ?!
UMM... WHAT ABOUT OUR CONVERSA-TION?!
TOKO!
TAK TAK TAK TAK
WHAT'S THAT?
Oh...
WE'VE BEEN ASKING HANA-BUSA'S SISTER TO JOIN THE STUDENT COUNCIL.
WE'VE BEEN TRYING FOR THE PAST FEW DAYS, BUT THAT ALWAYS HAPPENS.
Today, it was Kosaka, huh?

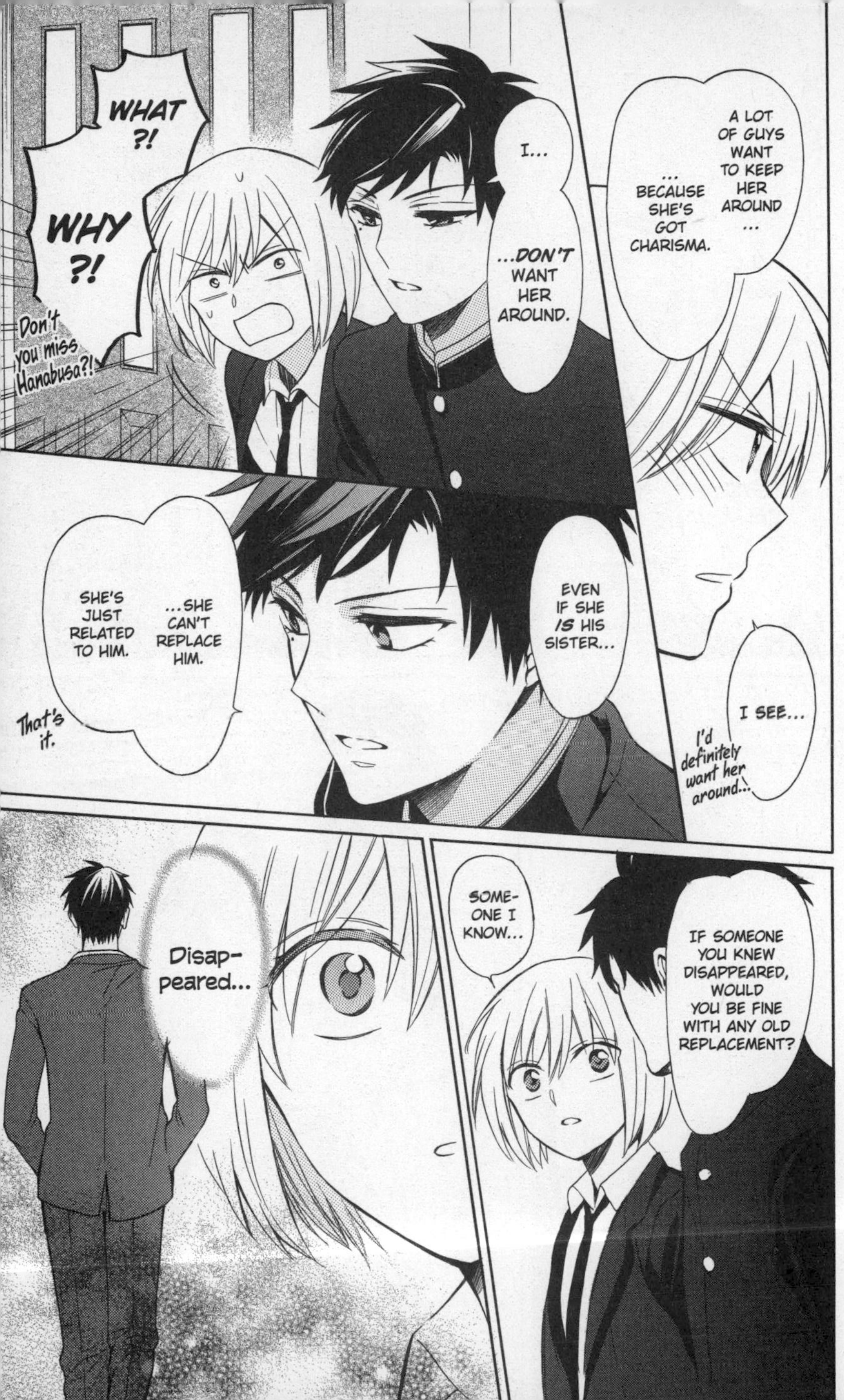
A LOT OF GUYS WANT TO KEEP HER AROUND ...
... BECAUSE SHE'S GOT CHARISMA.
I...
...*DON'T* WANT HER AROUND.
WHAT ?!
WHY ?!
Don't you miss Hanabusa?!
I SEE...
I'd definitely want her around...
EVEN IF SHE *IS* HIS SISTER...
...SHE CAN'T REPLACE HIM.
SHE'S JUST RELATED TO HIM.
That's it.
IF SOMEONE YOU KNEW DISAPPEARED, WOULD YOU BE FINE WITH ANY OLD REPLACEMENT?
SOME-ONE I KNOW...
Disap-peared...

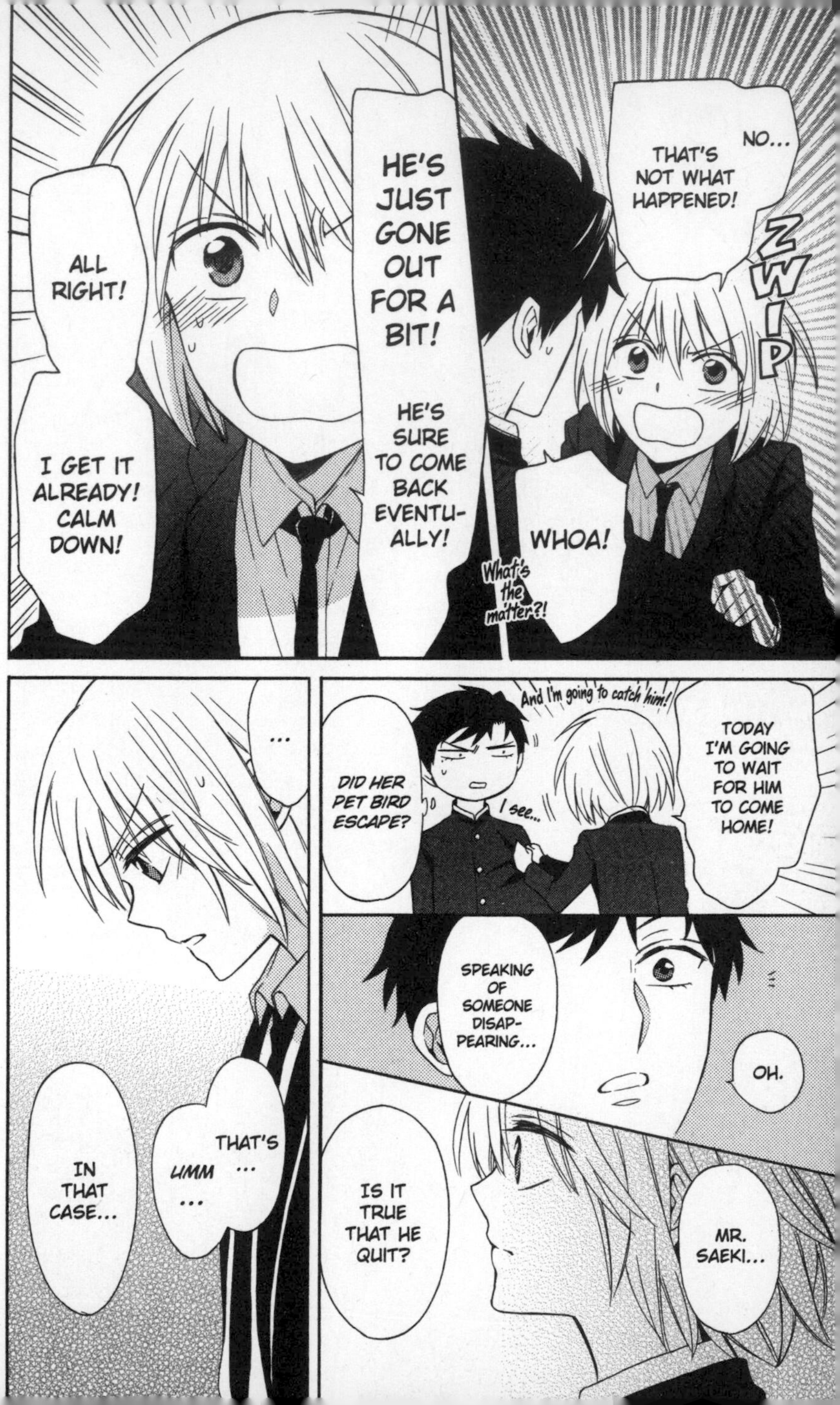
NO...
THAT'S NOT WHAT HAPPENED!
ZWIP
WHOA!
What's the matter?!
HE'S JUST GONE OUT FOR A BIT!
HE'S SURE TO COME BACK EVENTUALLY!
ALL RIGHT!
I GET IT ALREADY! CALM DOWN!
TODAY I'M GOING TO WAIT FOR HIM TO COME HOME!
And I'm going to catch him!
I see...
DID HER PET BIRD ESCAPE?
SPEAKING OF SOMEONE DISAP-PEARING...
OH.
MR. SAEKI...
IS IT TRUE THAT HE QUIT?
...
THAT'S...
UMM...
IN THAT CASE...

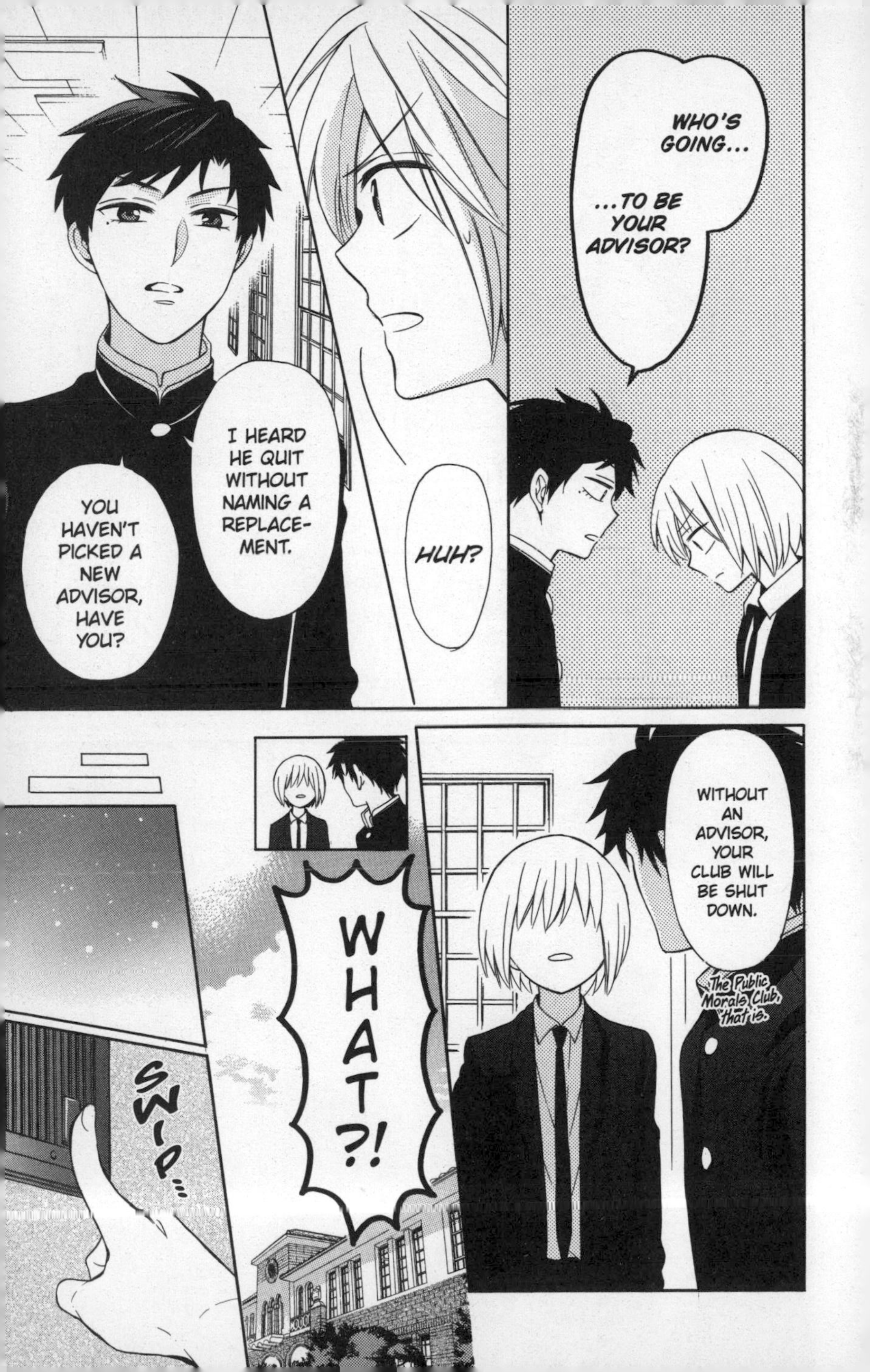
WHO'S GOING...
...TO BE YOUR ADVISOR?
HUH?
I HEARD HE QUIT WITHOUT NAMING A REPLACEMENT.
YOU HAVEN'T PICKED A NEW ADVISOR, HAVE YOU?
WITHOUT AN ADVISOR, YOUR CLUB WILL BE SHUT DOWN.
The Public Morals Club, that is.
WHAT?!
SWIP...

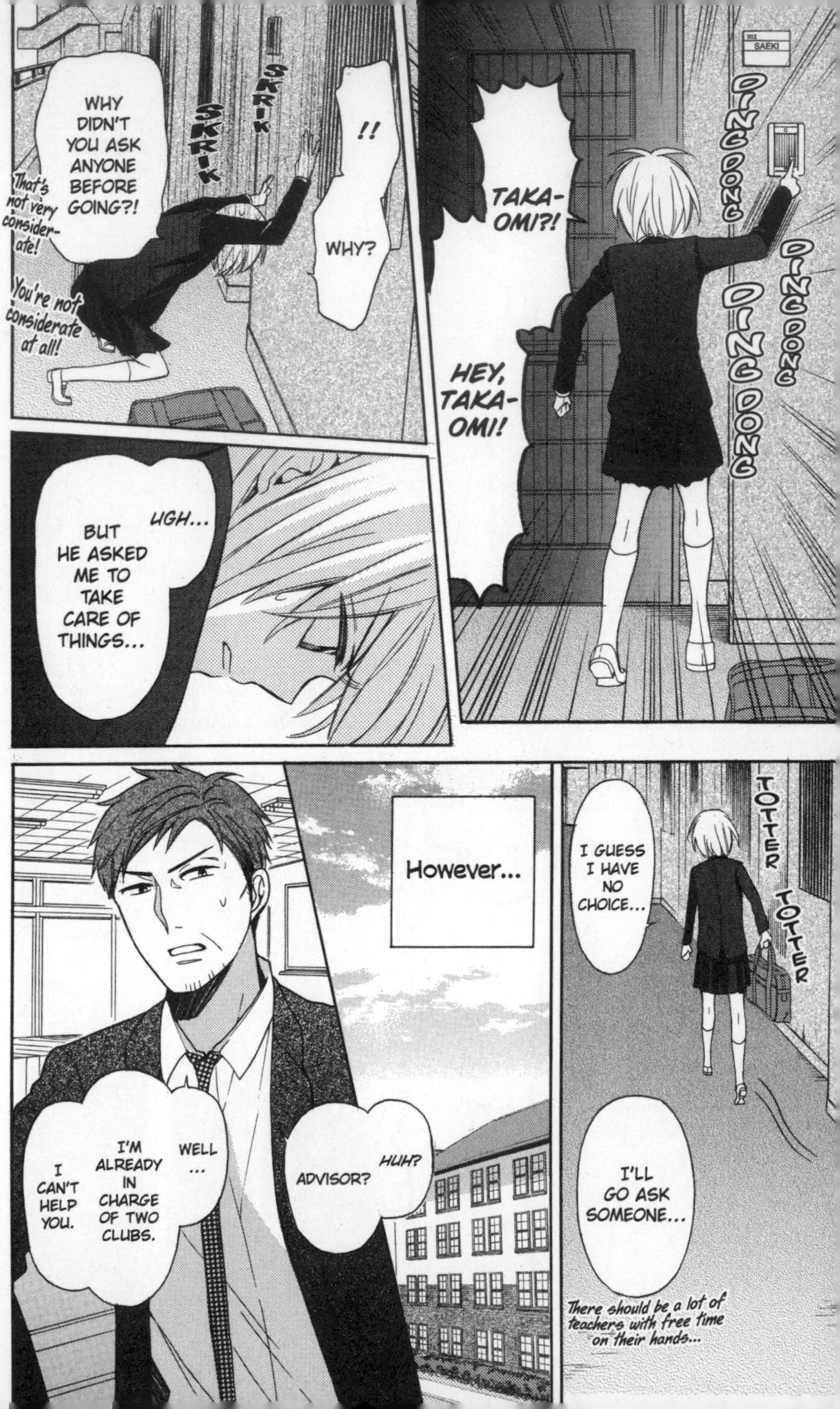
SAEKI
DING DONG DING DONG DING DONG
TAKA-OMI?!
HEY, TAKA-OMI!
!!
WHY?
SKRIK SKRIK
WHY DIDN'T YOU ASK ANYONE BEFORE GOING?!
That's not very considerate!
You're not considerate at all!
UGH...
BUT HE ASKED ME TO TAKE CARE OF THINGS...
TOTTER TOTTER
I GUESS I HAVE NO CHOICE...
I'LL GO ASK SOMEONE...
There should be a lot of teachers with free time on their hands...
However...
HUH?
ADVISOR?
WELL...
I'M ALREADY IN CHARGE OF TWO CLUBS.
I CAN'T HELP YOU.

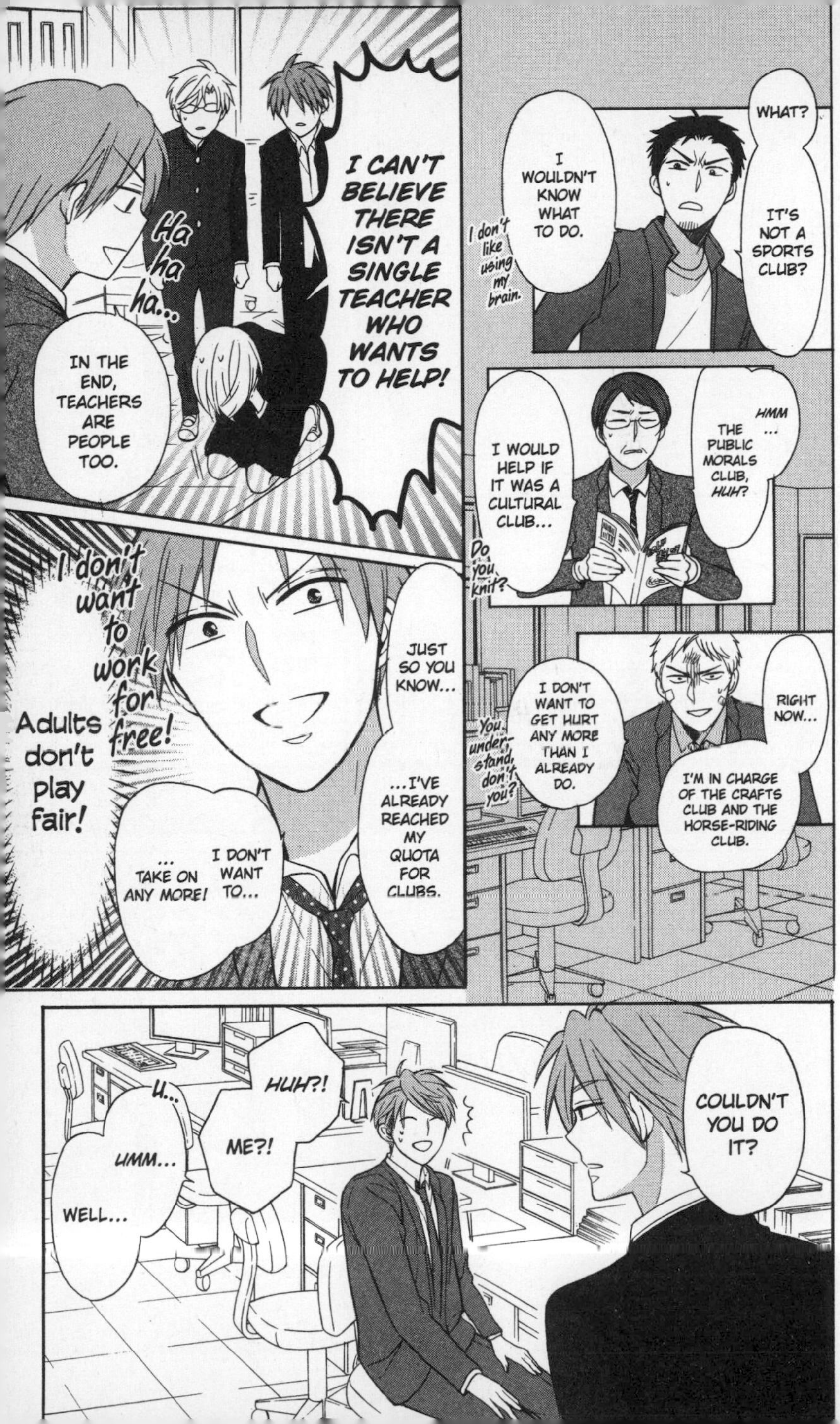
WHAT?
IT'S NOT A SPORTS CLUB?
I WOULDN'T KNOW WHAT TO DO.
I don't like using my brain.
HMM... THE PUBLIC MORALS CLUB, HUH?
I WOULD HELP IF IT WAS A CULTURAL CLUB...
Do you knit?
RIGHT NOW...
I'M IN CHARGE OF THE CRAFTS CLUB AND THE HORSE-RIDING CLUB.
I DON'T WANT TO GET HURT ANY MORE THAN I ALREADY DO.
You understand, don't you?
I CAN'T BELIEVE THERE ISN'T A SINGLE TEACHER WHO WANTS TO HELP!
Ha ha ha...
IN THE END, TEACHERS ARE PEOPLE TOO.
JUST SO YOU KNOW...
...I'VE ALREADY REACHED MY QUOTA FOR CLUBS.
I DON'T WANT TO...
... TAKE ON ANY MORE!
I don't want to work for free!
Adults don't play fair!
COULDN'T YOU DO IT?
HUH?!
ME?!
U...
UMM...
WELL...

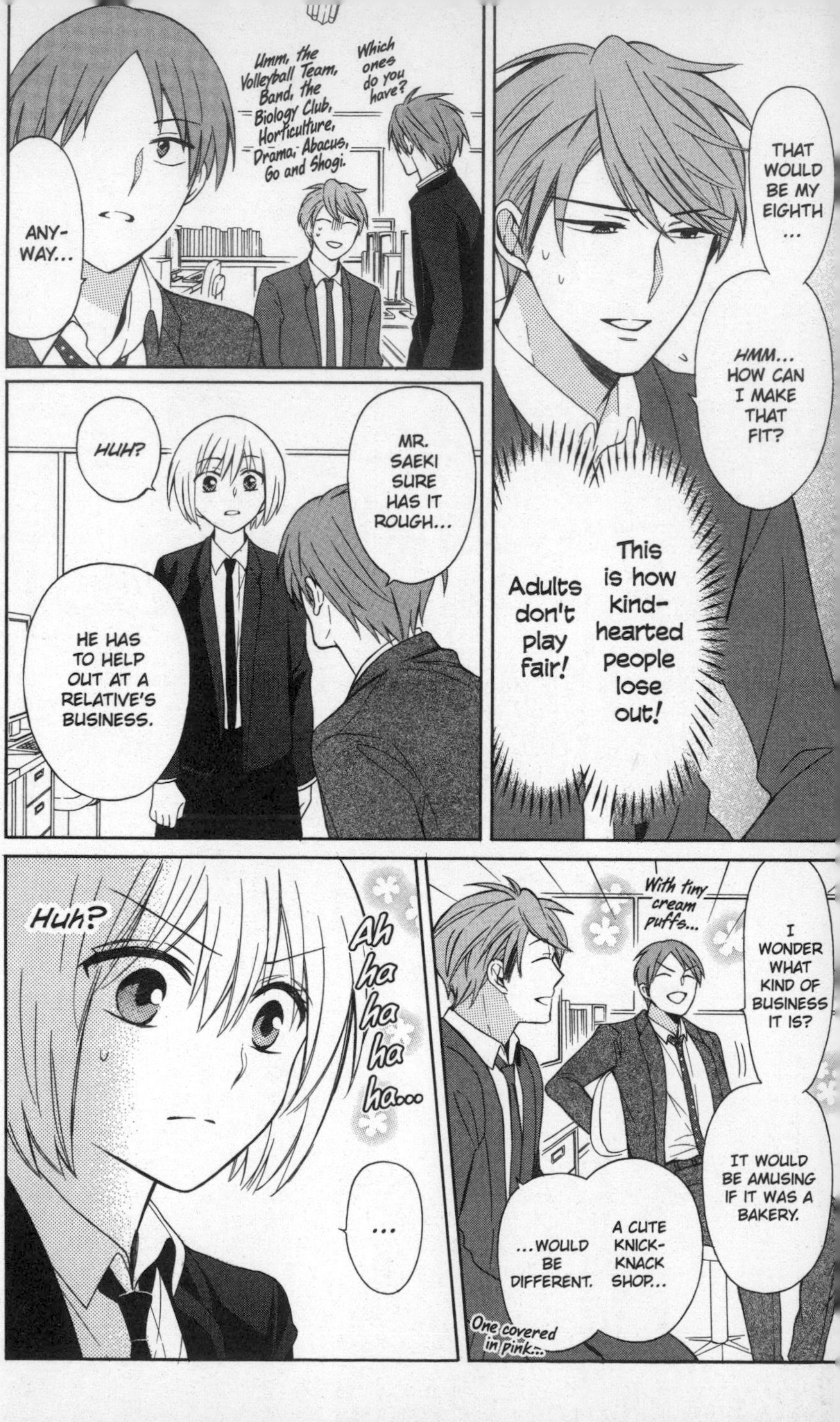
THAT WOULD BE MY EIGHTH...
HMM... HOW CAN I MAKE THAT FIT?
This is how kind-hearted people lose out!
Adults don't play fair!
Which ones do you have?
Umm, the Volleyball Team, Band, the Biology Club, Horticulture, Drama, Abacus, Go and Shogi.
ANY-WAY...
MR. SAEKI SURE HAS IT ROUGH...
HUH?
HE HAS TO HELP OUT AT A RELATIVE'S BUSINESS.
I WONDER WHAT KIND OF BUSINESS IT IS?
With tiny cream puffs...
IT WOULD BE AMUSING IF IT WAS A BAKERY.
A CUTE KNICK-KNACK SHOP...
...WOULD BE DIFFERENT.
One covered in pink...
Ah ha ha ha ha...
Huh?
...

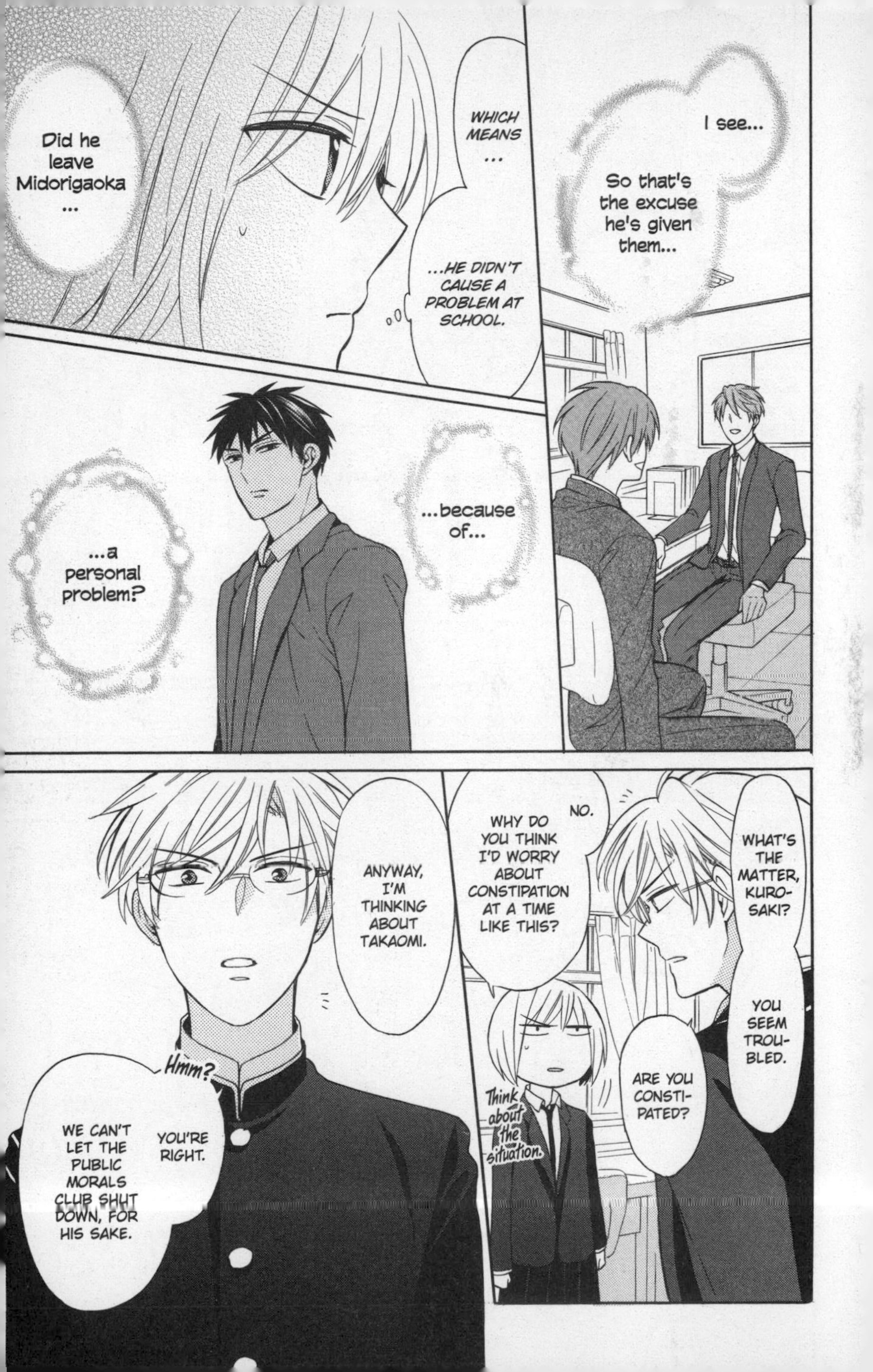
I see...
So that's the excuse he's given them...
WHICH MEANS ...
...HE DIDN'T CAUSE A PROBLEM AT SCHOOL.
Did he leave Midorigaoka ...
...because of...
...a personal problem?
WHAT'S THE MATTER, KURO-SAKI?
YOU SEEM TROU-BLED.
ARE YOU CONSTI-PATED?
NO.
WHY DO YOU THINK I'D WORRY ABOUT CONSTIPATION AT A TIME LIKE THIS?
Think about the situation.
ANYWAY, I'M THINKING ABOUT TAKAOMI.
Hmm?
YOU'RE RIGHT.
WE CAN'T LET THE PUBLIC MORALS CLUB SHUT DOWN, FOR HIS SAKE.

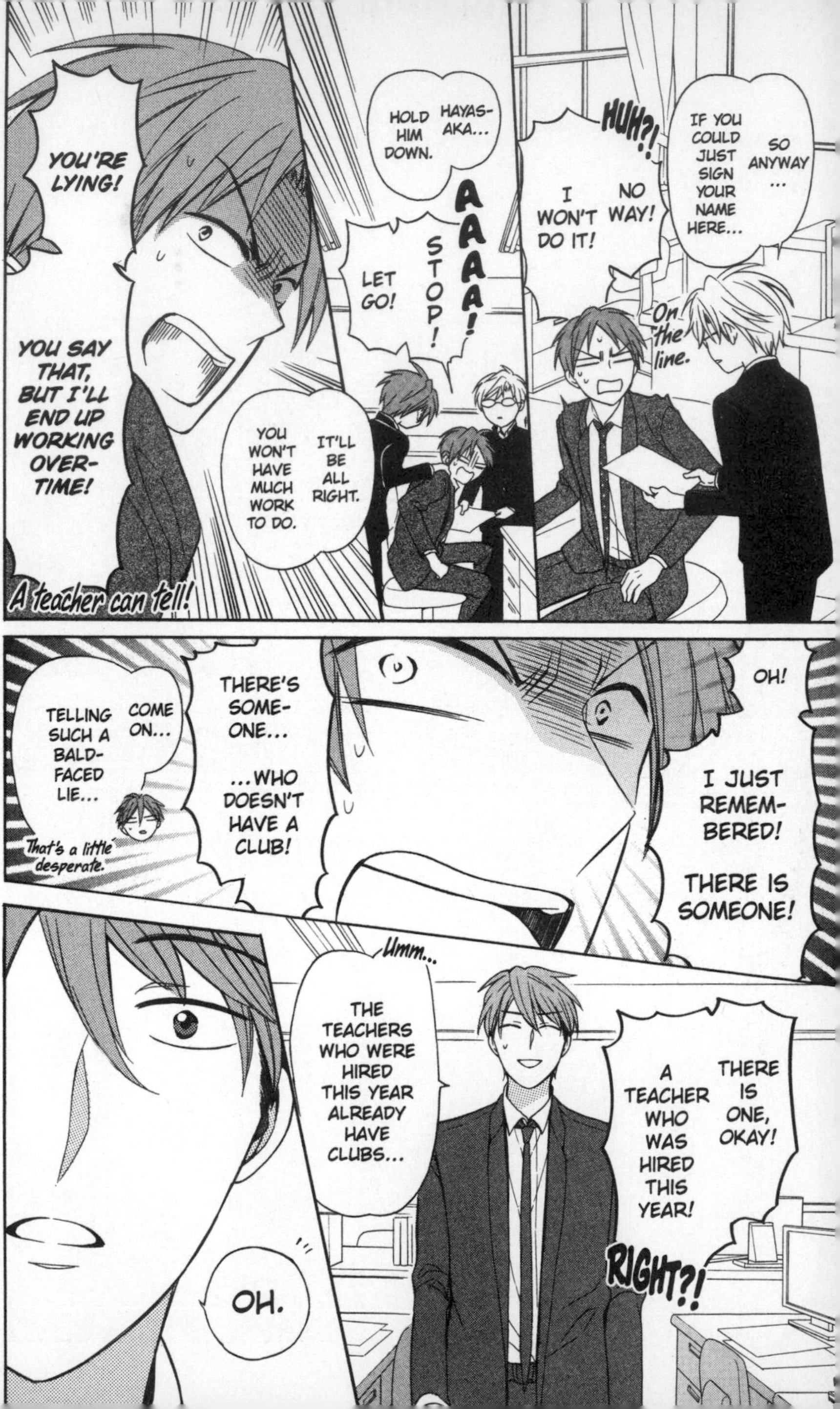
SO ANYWAY...
IF YOU COULD JUST SIGN YOUR NAME HERE...
On the line.
HUH?!
NO WAY!
I WON'T DO IT!
HAYAS-AKA... HOLD HIM DOWN.
AAAA!
STOP!
LET GO!
IT'LL BE ALL RIGHT.
YOU WON'T HAVE MUCH WORK TO DO.
YOU'RE LYING!
YOU SAY THAT, BUT I'LL END UP WORKING OVER-TIME!
A teacher can tell!
OH!
I JUST REMEM-BERED!
THERE IS SOMEONE!
THERE'S SOME-ONE...
...WHO DOESN'T HAVE A CLUB!
COME ON...
TELLING SUCH A BALD-FACED LIE...
That's a little desperate.
THERE IS ONE, OKAY!
A TEACHER WHO WAS HIRED THIS YEAR!
RIGHT?!
Umm...
THE TEACHERS WHO WERE HIRED THIS YEAR ALREADY HAVE CLUBS...
OH.

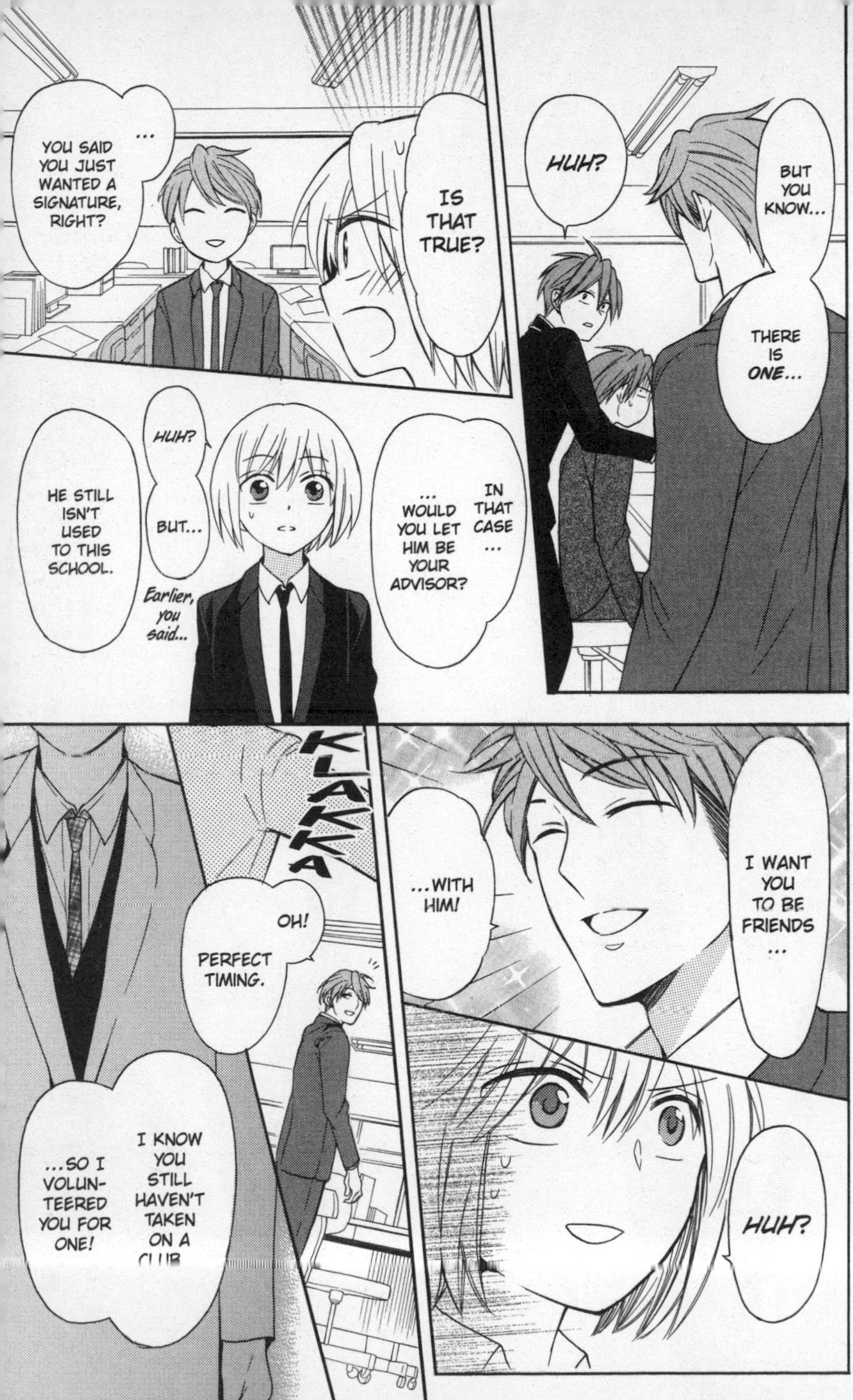
BUT YOU KNOW...
THERE IS ONE...
HUH?
IS THAT TRUE?
... YOU SAID YOU JUST WANTED A SIGNATURE, RIGHT?
IN THAT CASE ...
... WOULD YOU LET HIM BE YOUR ADVISOR?
HUH?
BUT...
Earlier, you said...
HE STILL ISN'T USED TO THIS SCHOOL.
I WANT YOU TO BE FRIENDS ...
...WITH HIM!
HUH?
KLAKKA
OH!
PERFECT TIMING.
I KNOW YOU STILL HAVEN'T TAKEN ON A CLUB
...SO I VOLUNTEERED YOU FOR ONE!

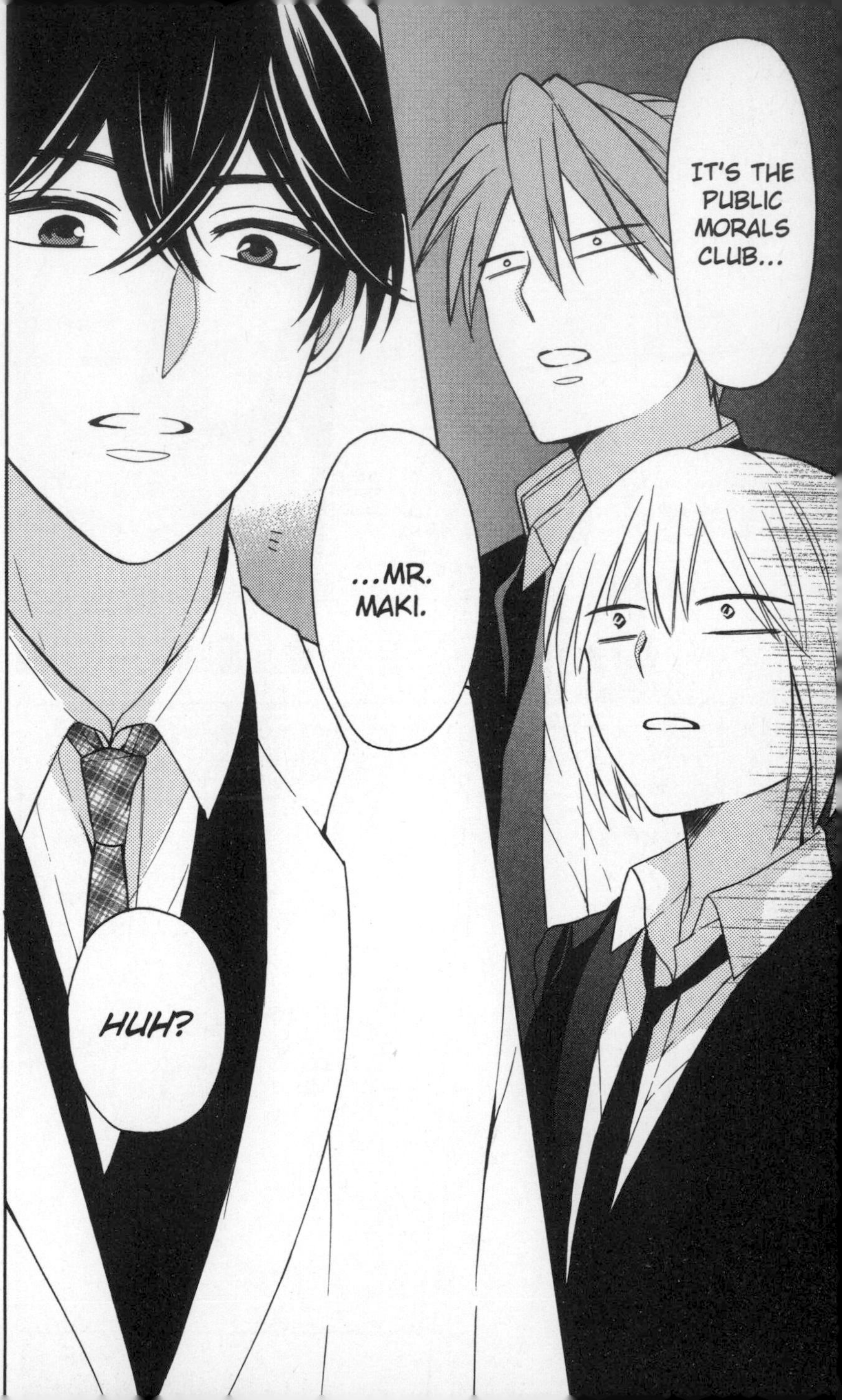
IT'S THE PUBLIC MORALS CLUB...
...MR. MAKI.
HUH?

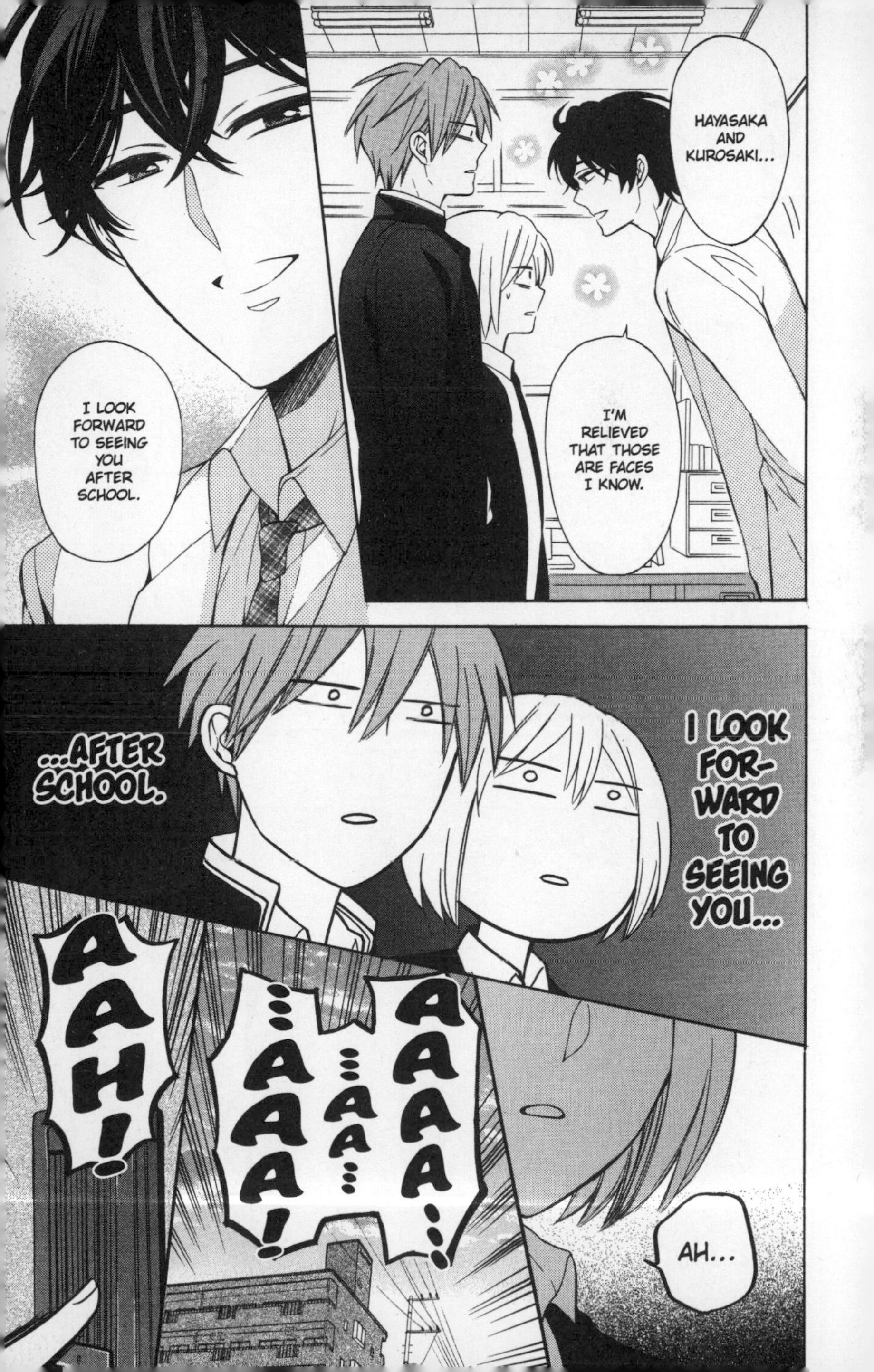
HAYASAKA AND KUROSAKI...
I'M RELIEVED THAT THOSE ARE FACES I KNOW.
I LOOK FORWARD TO SEEING YOU AFTER SCHOOL.
I LOOK FOR-WARD TO SEEING YOU...
...AFTER SCHOOL.
AH...
AAAA...
...AAA...!
AAH!

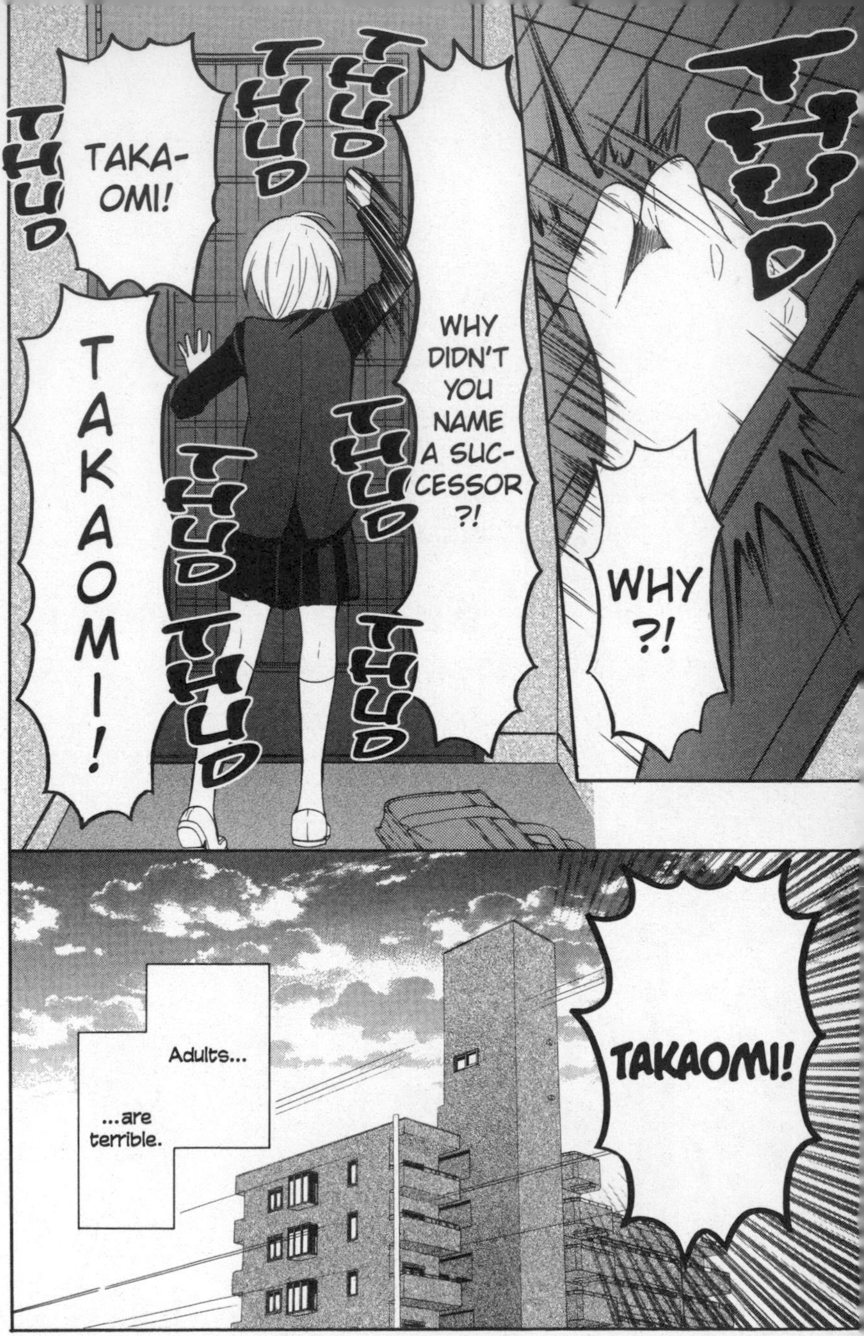
THUD
WHY ?!
THUD THUD
TAKA-OMI!
THUD
WHY DIDN'T YOU NAME A SUC-CESSOR ?!
THUD THUD THUD THUD
TAKAOMI!
TAKAOMI!
Adults...
...are terrible.

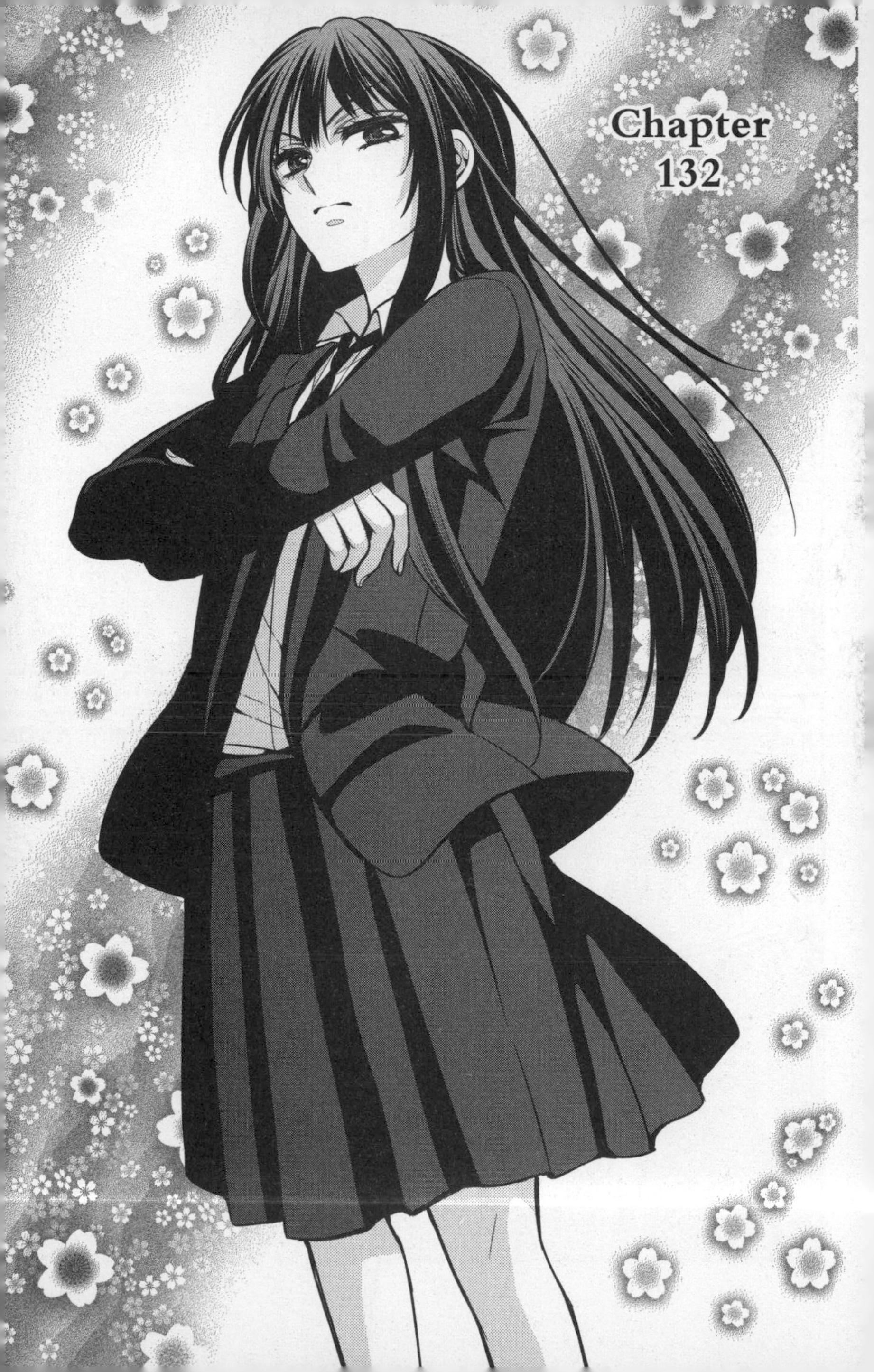
Chapter
132

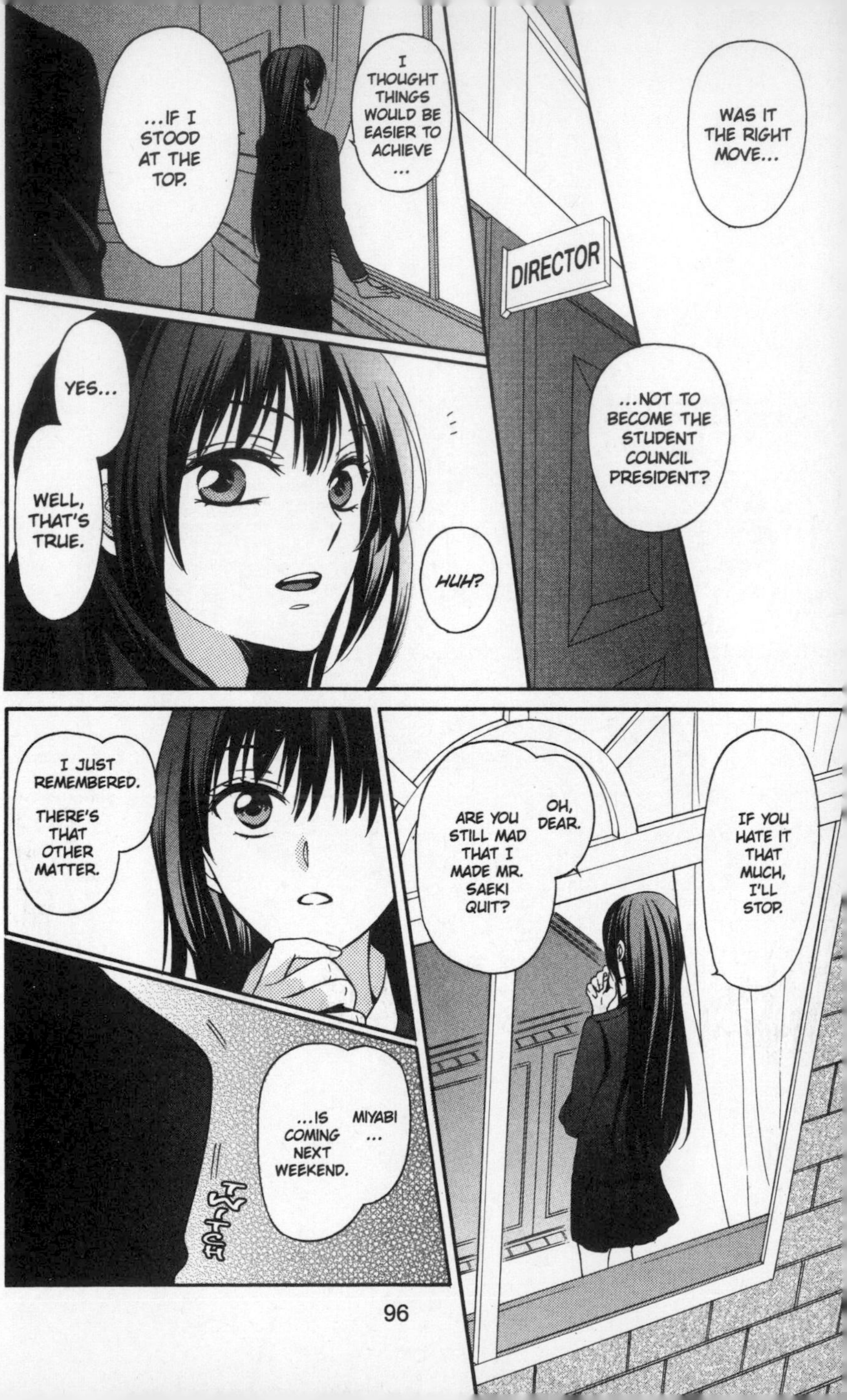
WAS IT THE RIGHT MOVE...
...NOT TO BECOME THE STUDENT COUNCIL PRESIDENT?
HUH?
YES...
WELL, THAT'S TRUE.
I THOUGHT THINGS WOULD BE EASIER TO ACHIEVE ...
...IF I STOOD AT THE TOP.
DIRECTOR
IF YOU HATE IT THAT MUCH, I'LL STOP.
OH, DEAR.
ARE YOU STILL MAD THAT I MADE MR. SAEKI QUIT?
I JUST REMEMBERED.
THERE'S THAT OTHER MATTER.
MIYABI ...
...IS COMING NEXT WEEKEND.

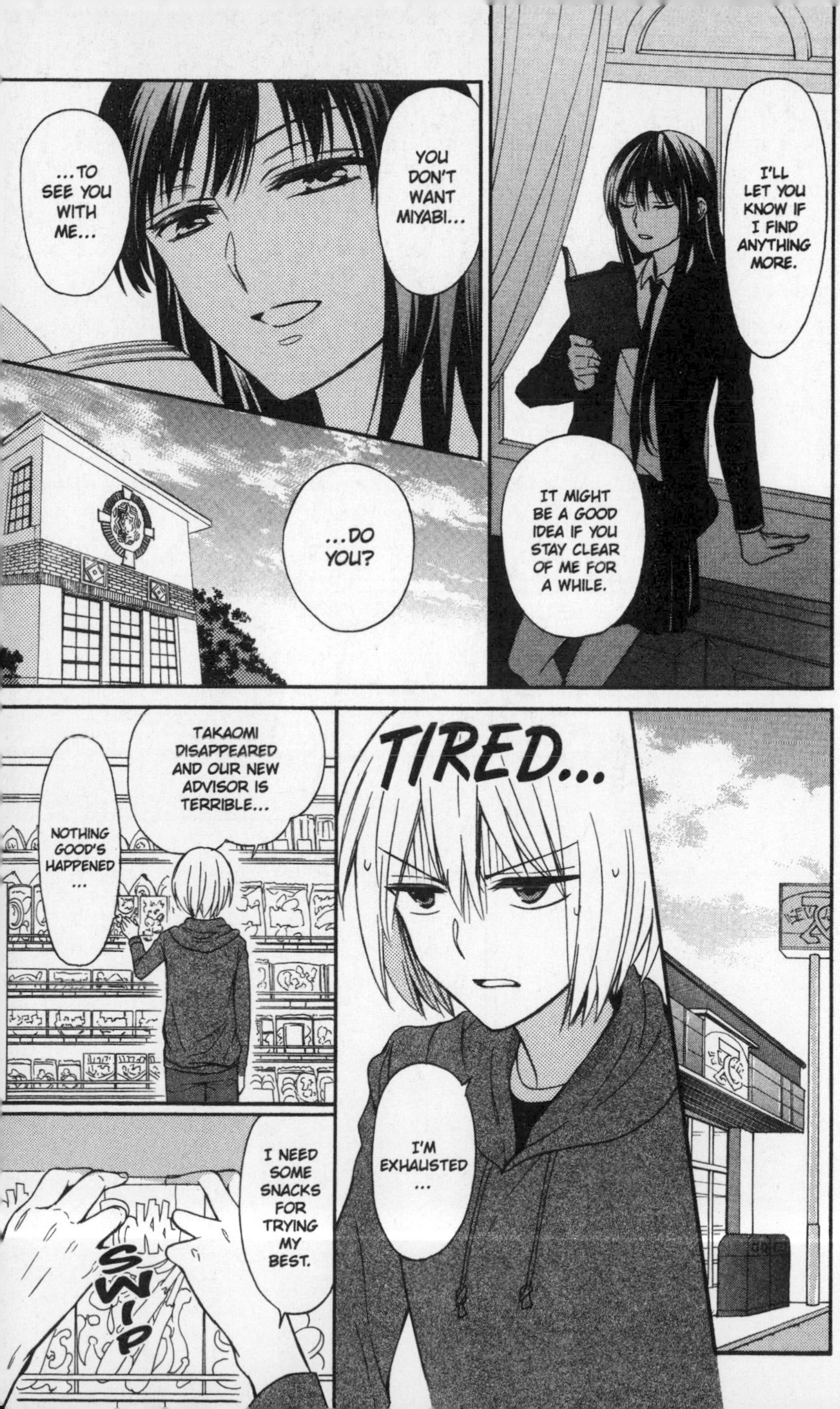
I'LL LET YOU KNOW IF I FIND ANYTHING MORE.
IT MIGHT BE A GOOD IDEA IF YOU STAY CLEAR OF ME FOR A WHILE.
YOU DON'T WANT MIYABI...
...TO SEE YOU WITH ME...
...DO YOU?
TIRED...
I'M EXHAUSTED...
TAKAOMI DISAPPEARED AND OUR NEW ADVISOR IS TERRIBLE...
NOTHING GOOD'S HAPPENED...
I NEED SOME SNACKS FOR TRYING MY BEST.
SWIP

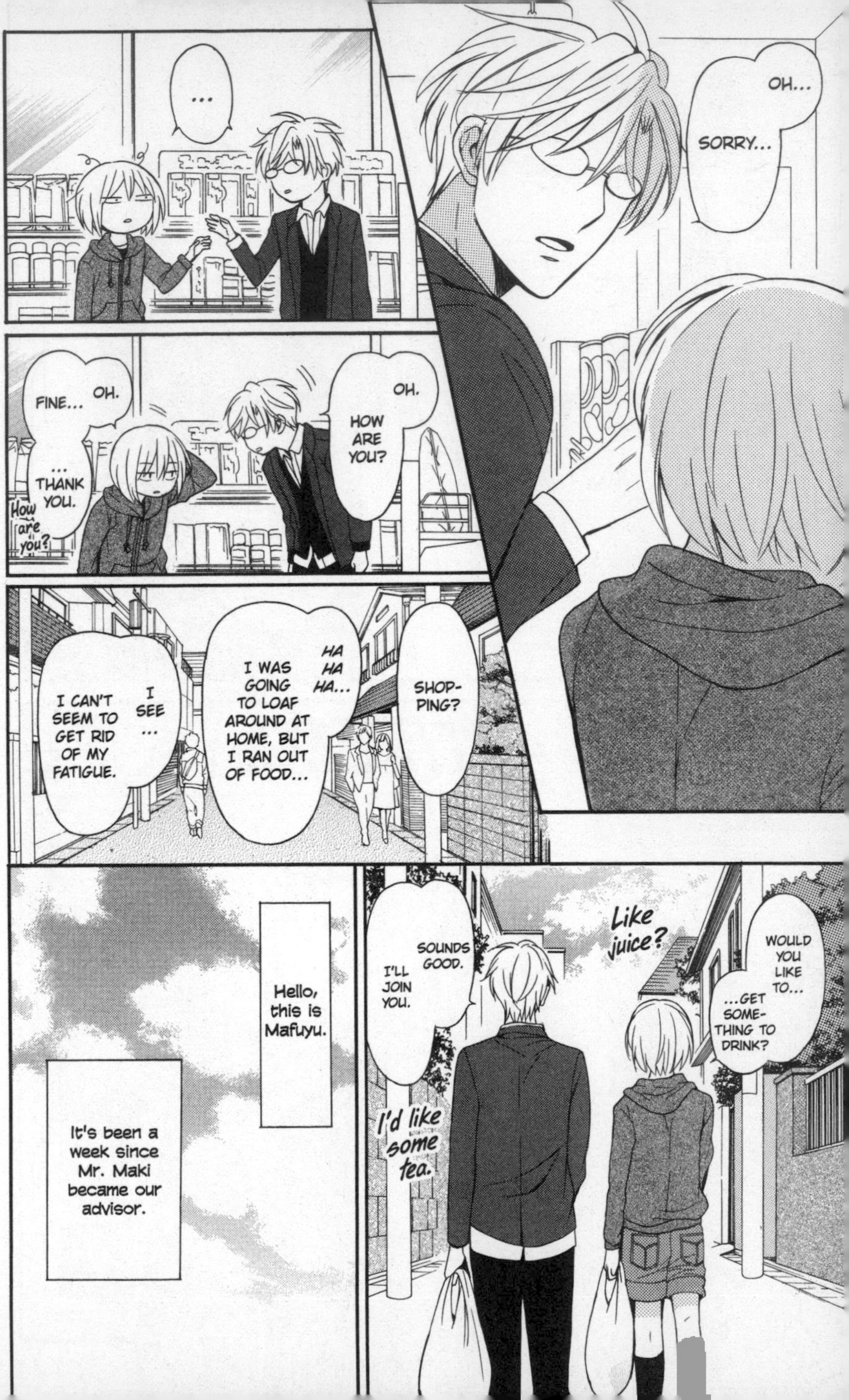
OH... SORRY...
...
OH. HOW ARE YOU?
OH. FINE... ...THANK YOU.
How are you?
SHOP-PING?
HA HA HA...
I WAS GOING TO LOAF AROUND AT HOME, BUT I RAN OUT OF FOOD...
I SEE...
I CAN'T SEEM TO GET RID OF MY FATIGUE.
WOULD YOU LIKE TO... ...GET SOME-THING TO DRINK?
Like juice?
SOUNDS GOOD. I'LL JOIN YOU.
I'd like some tea.
Hello, this is Mafuyu.
It's been a week since Mr. Maki became our advisor.

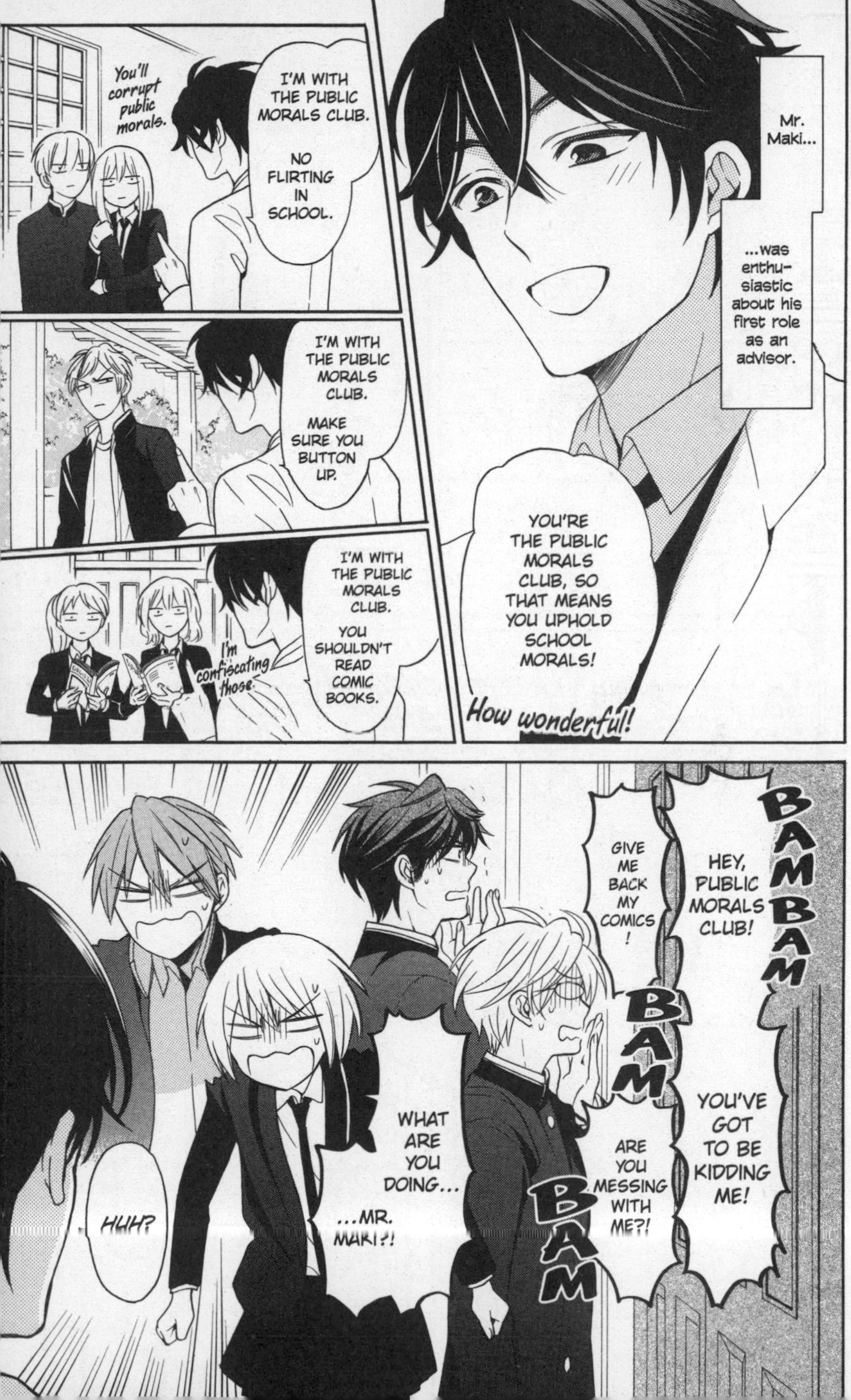
Mr. Maki...
...was enthusiastic about his first role as an advisor.
YOU'RE THE PUBLIC MORALS CLUB, SO THAT MEANS YOU UPHOLD SCHOOL MORALS!
How wonderful!
I'M WITH THE PUBLIC MORALS CLUB.
NO FLIRTING IN SCHOOL.
You'll corrupt public morals.
I'M WITH THE PUBLIC MORALS CLUB.
MAKE SURE YOU BUTTON UP.
I'M WITH THE PUBLIC MORALS CLUB.
YOU SHOULDN'T READ COMIC BOOKS.
I'm confiscating those.
BAM BAM
HEY, PUBLIC MORALS CLUB!
GIVE ME BACK MY COMICS!
BAM BAM
YOU'VE GOT TO BE KIDDING ME!
ARE YOU MESSING WITH ME?!
BAM BAM
WHAT ARE YOU DOING...
...MR. MAKI?!
HUH?

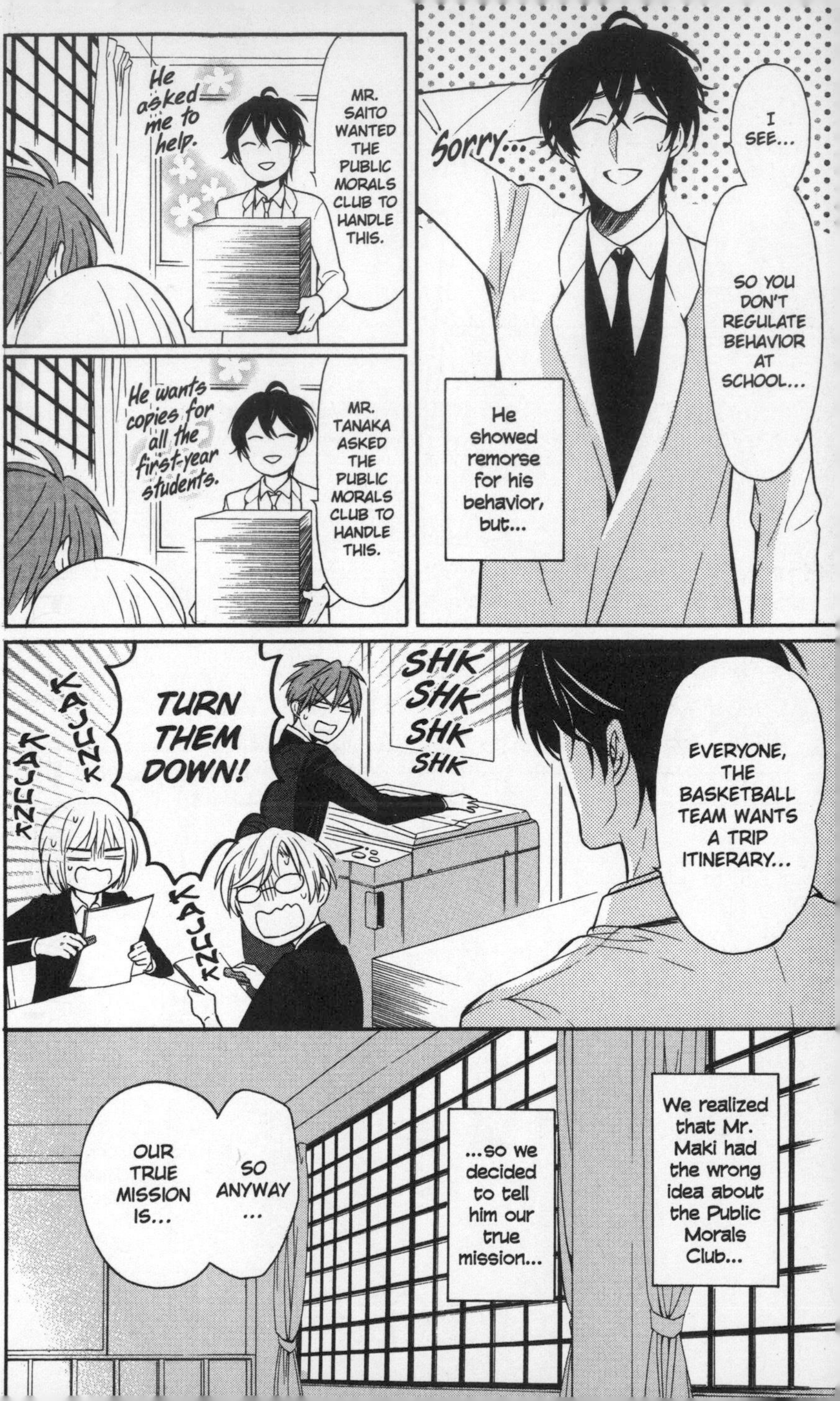
I SEE...
Sorry...
SO YOU DON'T REGULATE BEHAVIOR AT SCHOOL...
He showed remorse for his behavior, but...
MR. SAITO WANTED THE PUBLIC MORALS CLUB TO HANDLE THIS.
He asked me to help.
MR. TANAKA ASKED THE PUBLIC MORALS CLUB TO HANDLE THIS.
He wants copies for all the first-year students.
EVERYONE, THE BASKETBALL TEAM WANTS A TRIP ITINERARY...
SHK SHK SHK SHK
TURN THEM DOWN!
KAJUNK
KAJUNK
KAJUNK
We realized that Mr. Maki had the wrong idea about the Public Morals Club...
...so we decided to tell him our true mission...
SO ANYWAY...
OUR TRUE MISSION IS...

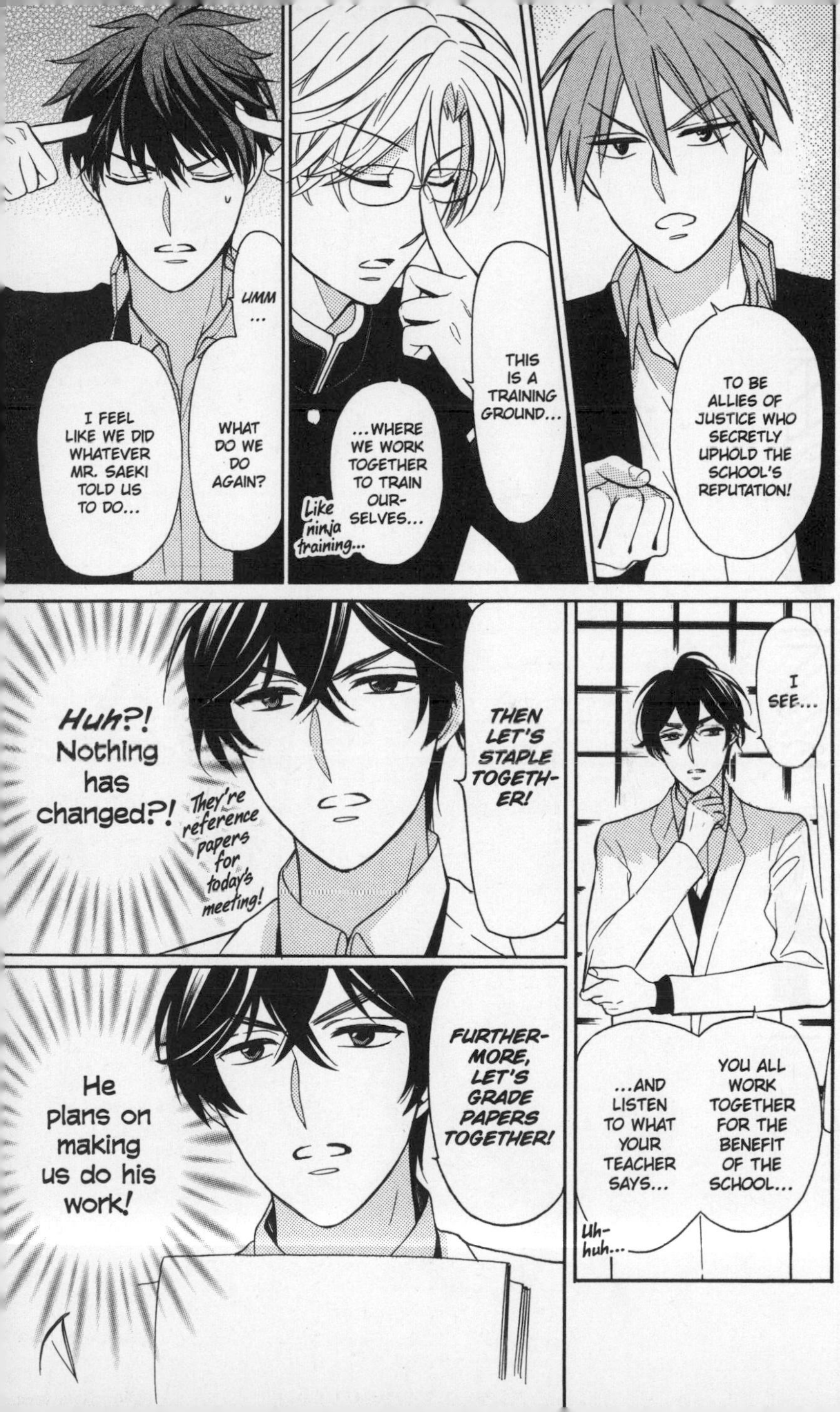
TO BE ALLIES OF JUSTICE WHO SECRETLY UPHOLD THE SCHOOL'S REPUTATION!
THIS IS A TRAINING GROUND...
...WHERE WE WORK TOGETHER TO TRAIN OUR-SELVES...
Like ninja training...
UMM...
WHAT DO WE DO AGAIN?
I FEEL LIKE WE DID WHATEVER MR. SAEKI TOLD US TO DO...
I SEE...
YOU ALL WORK TOGETHER FOR THE BENEFIT OF THE SCHOOL...
...AND LISTEN TO WHAT YOUR TEACHER SAYS...
Uh-huh...
THEN LET'S STAPLE TOGETHER!
They're reference papers for today's meeting!
Huh?! Nothing has changed?!
FURTHER-MORE, LET'S GRADE PAPERS TOGETHER!
He plans on making us do his work!

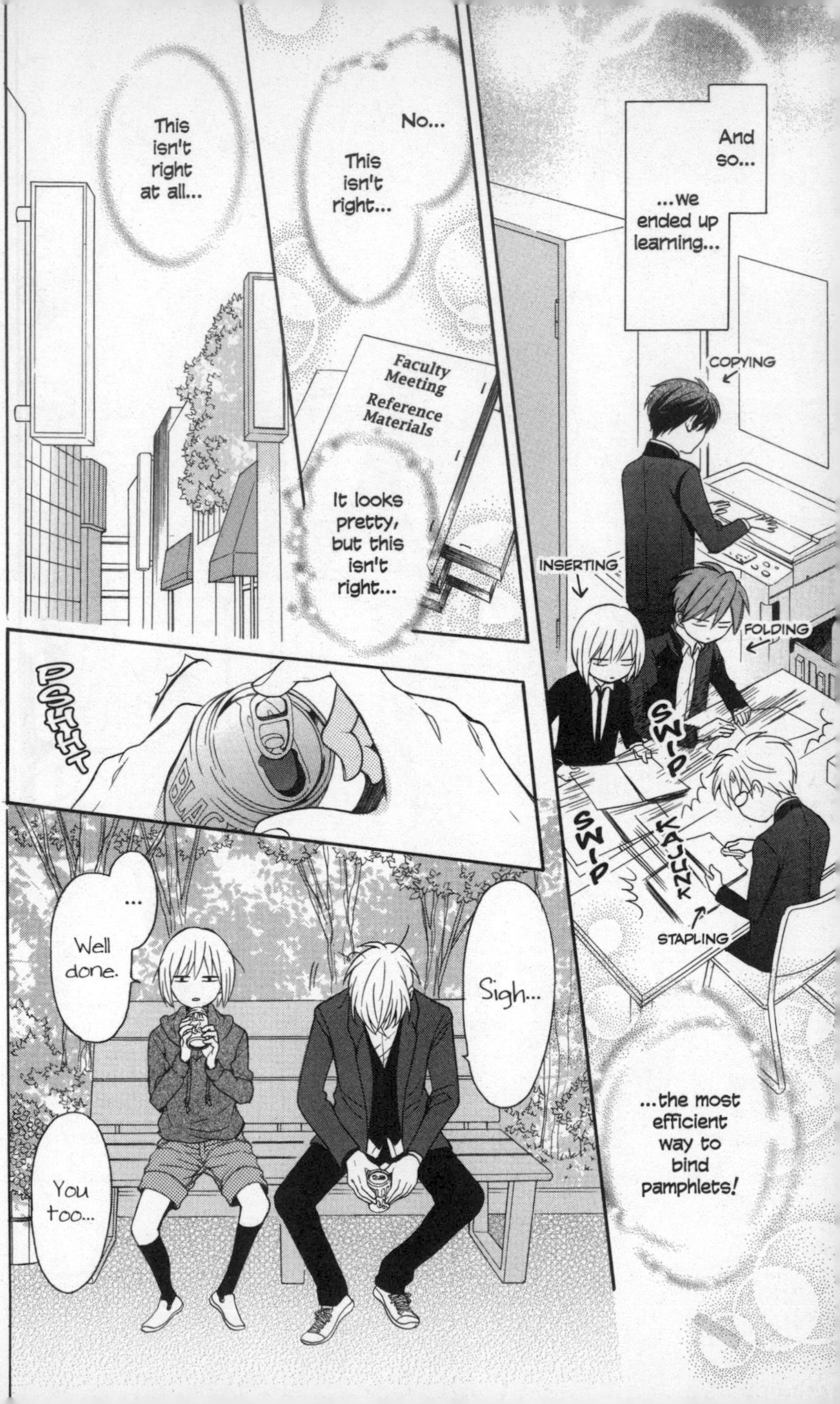
And so...
...we ended up learning...
COPYING
FOLDING
INSERTING
SWIP
SWIP
KAJUNK
STAPLING
...the most efficient way to bind pamphlets!
No...
This isn't right...
Faculty Meeting
Reference Materials
It looks pretty, but this isn't right...
This isn't right at all...
PSHHT
Sigh...
...
Well done.
You too...

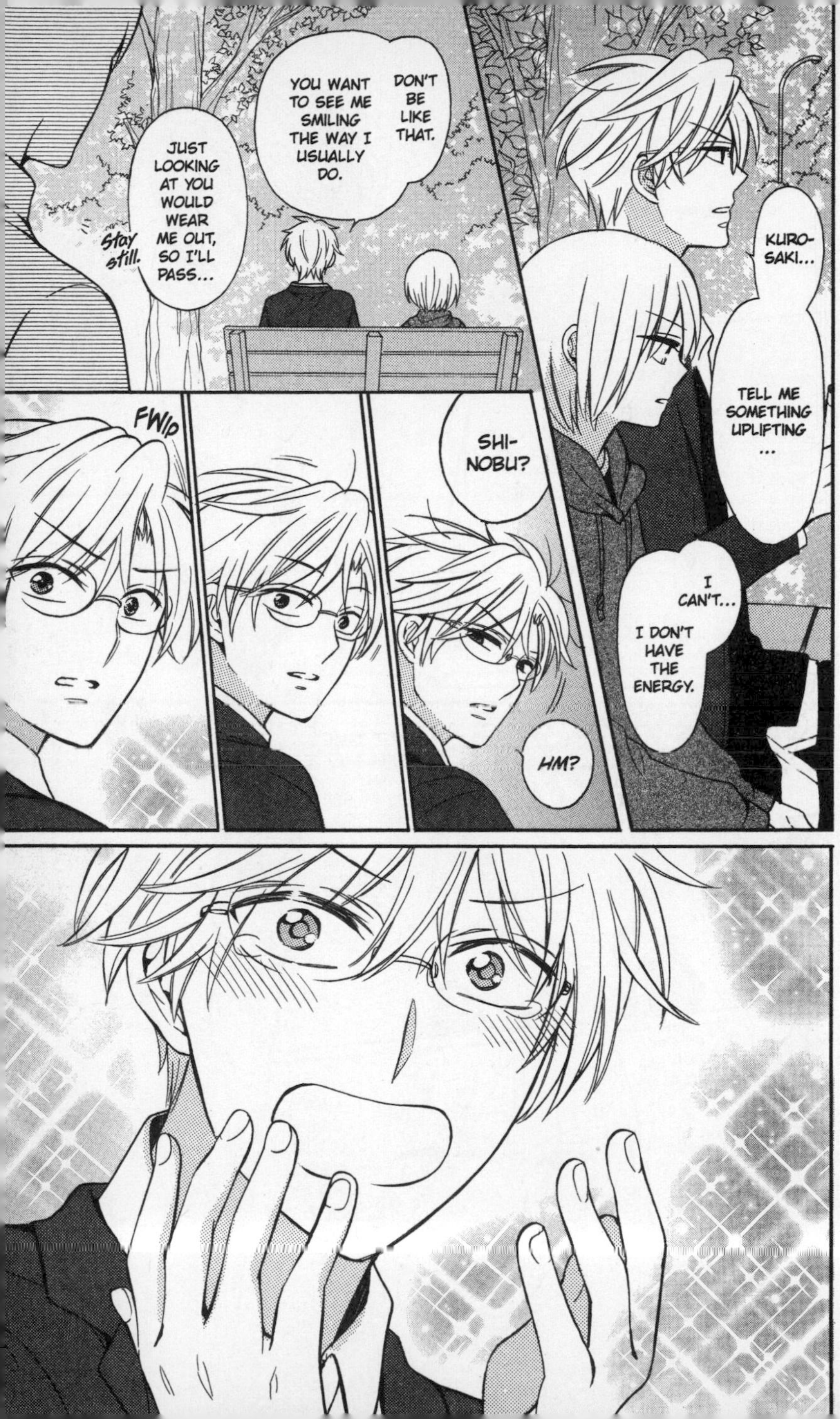
KURO-SAKI...
TELL ME SOMETHING UPLIFTING...
I CAN'T... I DON'T HAVE THE ENERGY.
DON'T BE LIKE THAT.
YOU WANT TO SEE ME SMILING THE WAY I USUALLY DO.
JUST LOOKING AT YOU WOULD WEAR ME OUT, SO I'LL PASS...
Stay still.
SHI-NOBU?
HM?
FWIP

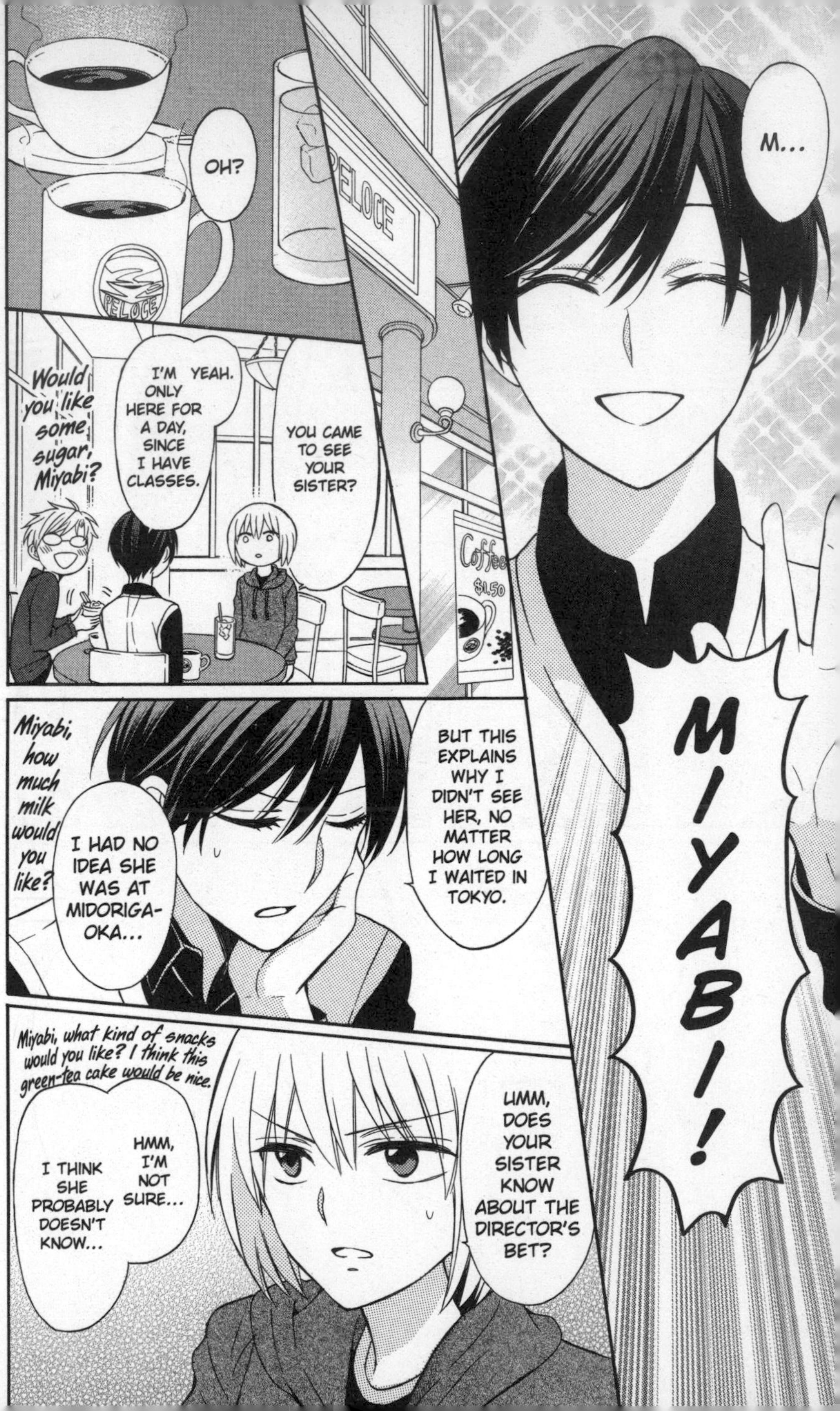
M...
MIYABI!!
OH?
PELOCE
PELOCE
YOU CAME TO SEE YOUR SISTER?
YEAH. I'M ONLY HERE FOR A DAY, SINCE I HAVE CLASSES.
Would you like some sugar, Miyabi?
Coffee $1.50
BUT THIS EXPLAINS WHY I DIDN'T SEE HER, NO MATTER HOW LONG I WAITED IN TOKYO.
I HAD NO IDEA SHE WAS AT MIDORIGA-OKA...
Miyabi, how much milk would you like?
UMM, DOES YOUR SISTER KNOW ABOUT THE DIRECTOR'S BET?
HMM, I'M NOT SURE...
I THINK SHE PROBABLY DOESN'T KNOW...
Miyabi, what kind of snacks would you like? I think this green-tea cake would be nice.

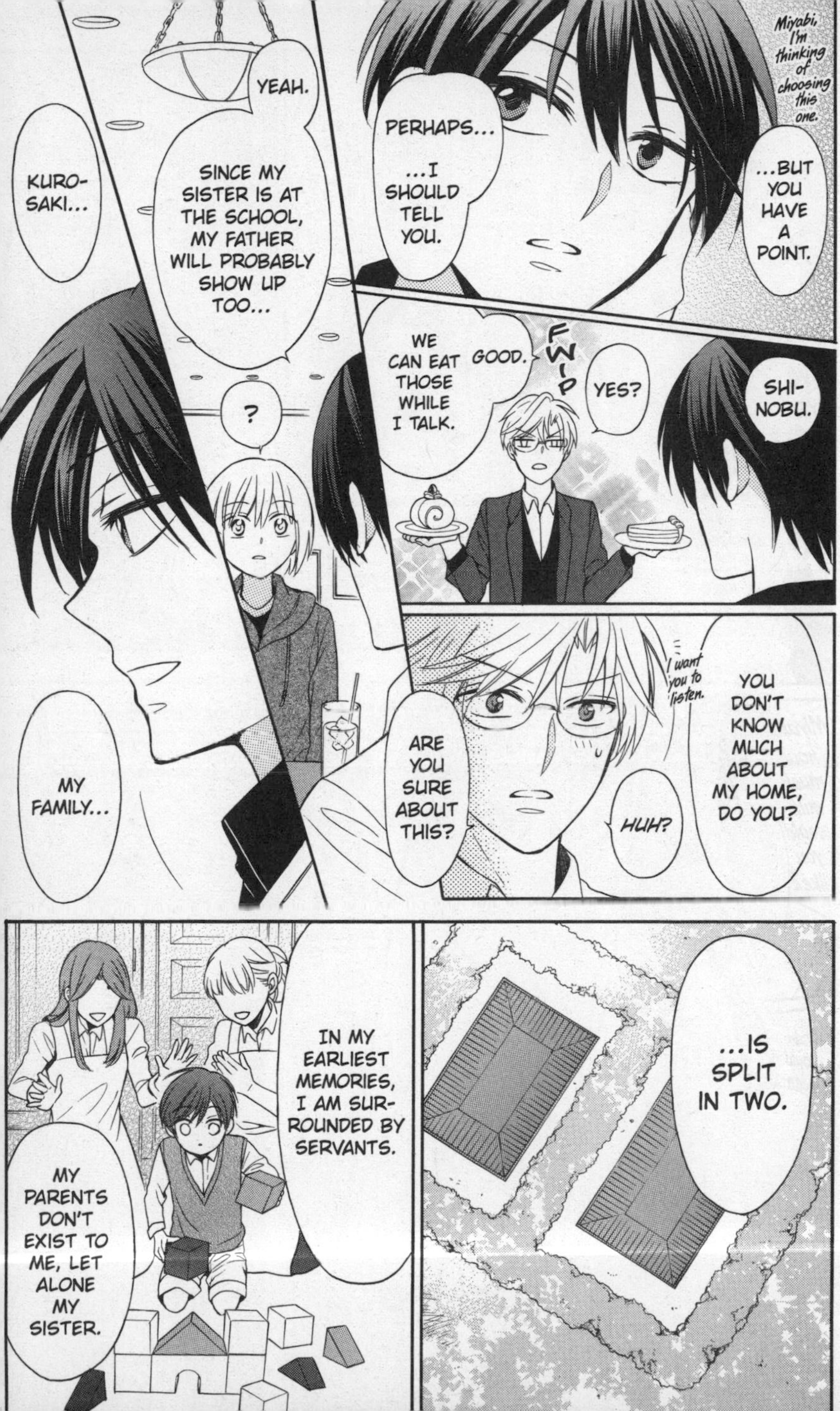
Miyabi, I'm thinking of choosing this one.
...BUT YOU HAVE A POINT.
PERHAPS...
...I SHOULD TELL YOU.
SHI-NOBU.
YES?
FWIP
GOOD.
WE CAN EAT THOSE WHILE I TALK.
YOU DON'T KNOW MUCH ABOUT MY HOME, DO YOU?
I want you to listen.
HUH?
ARE YOU SURE ABOUT THIS?
YEAH.
SINCE MY SISTER IS AT THE SCHOOL, MY FATHER WILL PROBABLY SHOW UP TOO...
KURO-SAKI...
?
MY FAMILY...
...IS SPLIT IN TWO.
IN MY EARLIEST MEMORIES, I AM SUR-ROUNDED BY SERVANTS.
MY PARENTS DON'T EXIST TO ME, LET ALONE MY SISTER.

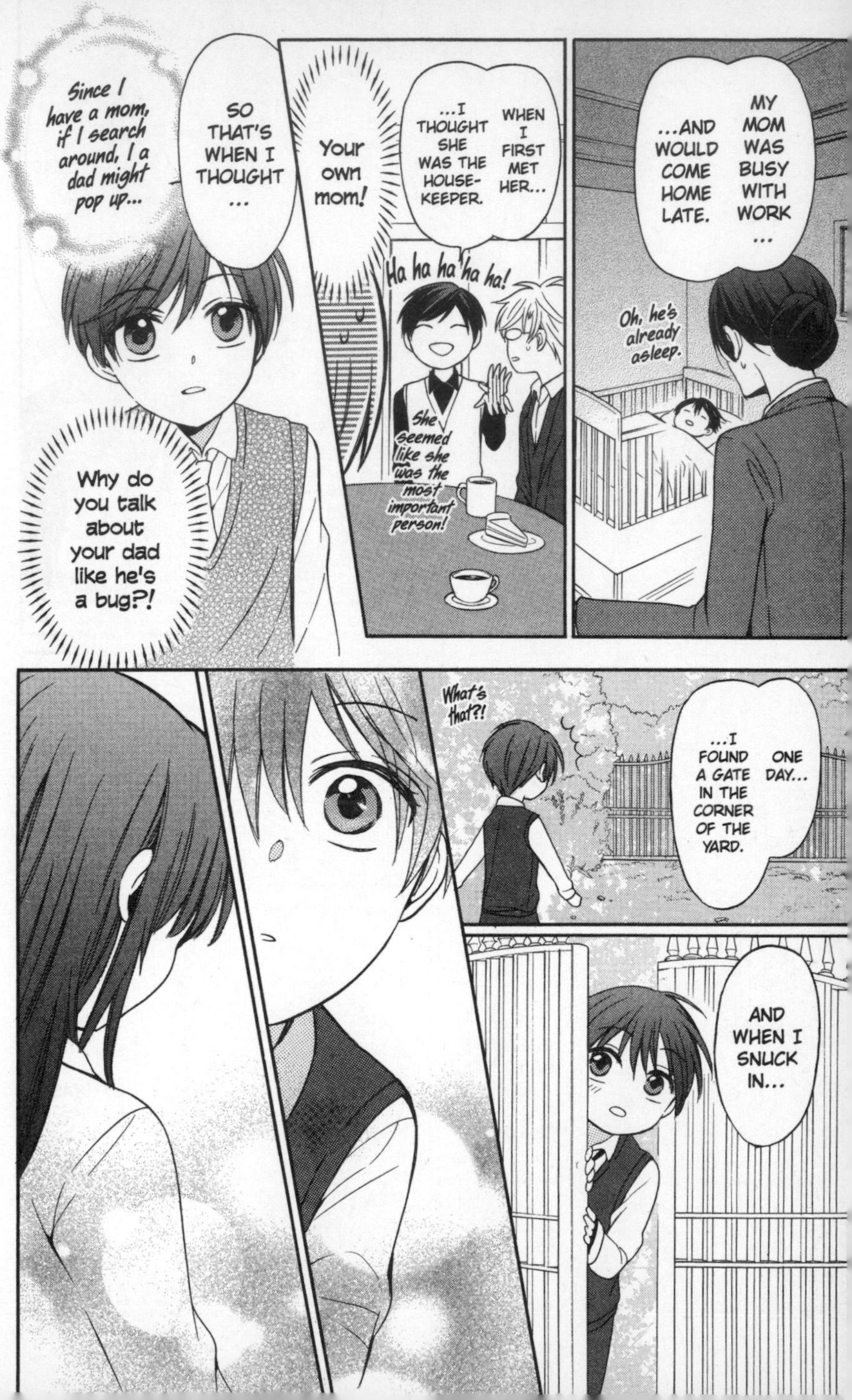
MY MOM WAS BUSY WITH WORK...
...AND WOULD COME HOME LATE.
Oh, he's already asleep.
WHEN I FIRST MET HER...
...I THOUGHT SHE WAS THE HOUSE-KEEPER.
Your own mom!
Ha ha ha ha ha!
She seemed like she was the most important person!
SO THAT'S WHEN I THOUGHT...
Since I have a mom, if I search around, I a dad might pop up...
Why do you talk about your dad like he's a bug?!
ONE DAY...
...I FOUND A GATE IN THE CORNER OF THE YARD.
What's that?!
AND WHEN I SNUCK IN...

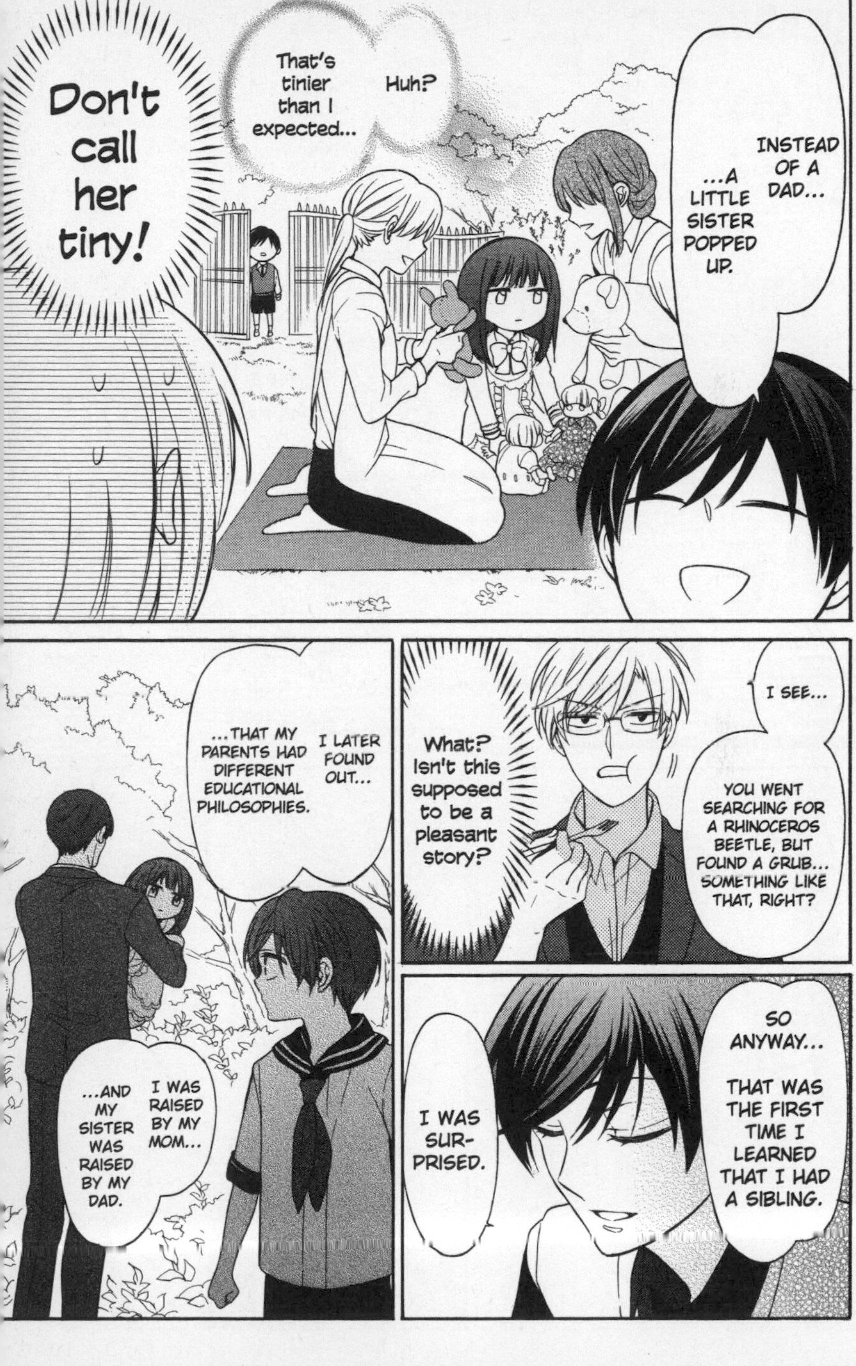
INSTEAD OF A DAD...
...A LITTLE SISTER POPPED UP.
Huh?
That's tinier than I expected...
Don't call her tiny!
I SEE...
YOU WENT SEARCHING FOR A RHINOCEROS BEETLE, BUT FOUND A GRUB... SOMETHING LIKE THAT, RIGHT?
What? Isn't this supposed to be a pleasant story?
SO ANYWAY...
THAT WAS THE FIRST TIME I LEARNED THAT I HAD A SIBLING.
I WAS SUR-PRISED.
I LATER FOUND OUT...
...THAT MY PARENTS HAD DIFFERENT EDUCATIONAL PHILOSOPHIES.
I WAS RAISED BY MY MOM...
...AND MY SISTER WAS RAISED BY MY DAD.

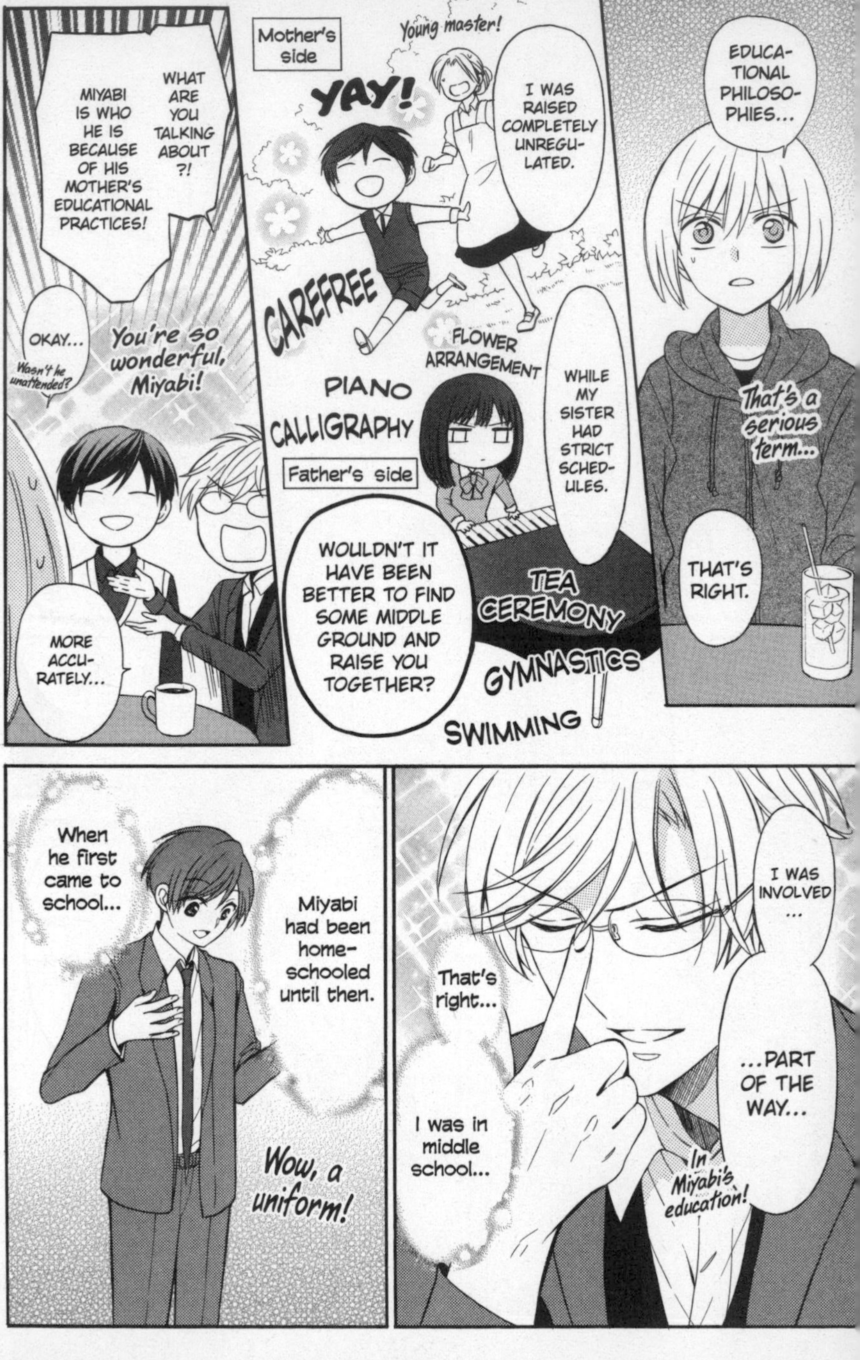
EDUCATIONAL PHILOSOPHIES...
That's a serious term...
THAT'S RIGHT.
I WAS RAISED COMPLETELY UNREGULATED.
Mother's side
Young master!
YAY!
CAREFREE
WHILE MY SISTER HAD STRICT SCHEDULES.
FLOWER ARRANGEMENT
PIANO
CALLIGRAPHY
Father's side
TEA CEREMONY
GYMNASTICS
SWIMMING
WOULDN'T IT HAVE BEEN BETTER TO FIND SOME MIDDLE GROUND AND RAISE YOU TOGETHER?
WHAT ARE YOU TALKING ABOUT?!
MIYABI IS WHO HE IS BECAUSE OF HIS MOTHER'S EDUCATIONAL PRACTICES!
You're so wonderful, Miyabi!
OKAY...
Wasn't he unattended?
MORE ACCURATELY...
I WAS INVOLVED...
...PART OF THE WAY...
In Miyabi's education!
That's right...
I was in middle school...
Miyabi had been home-schooled until then.
When he first came to school...
Wow, a uniform!

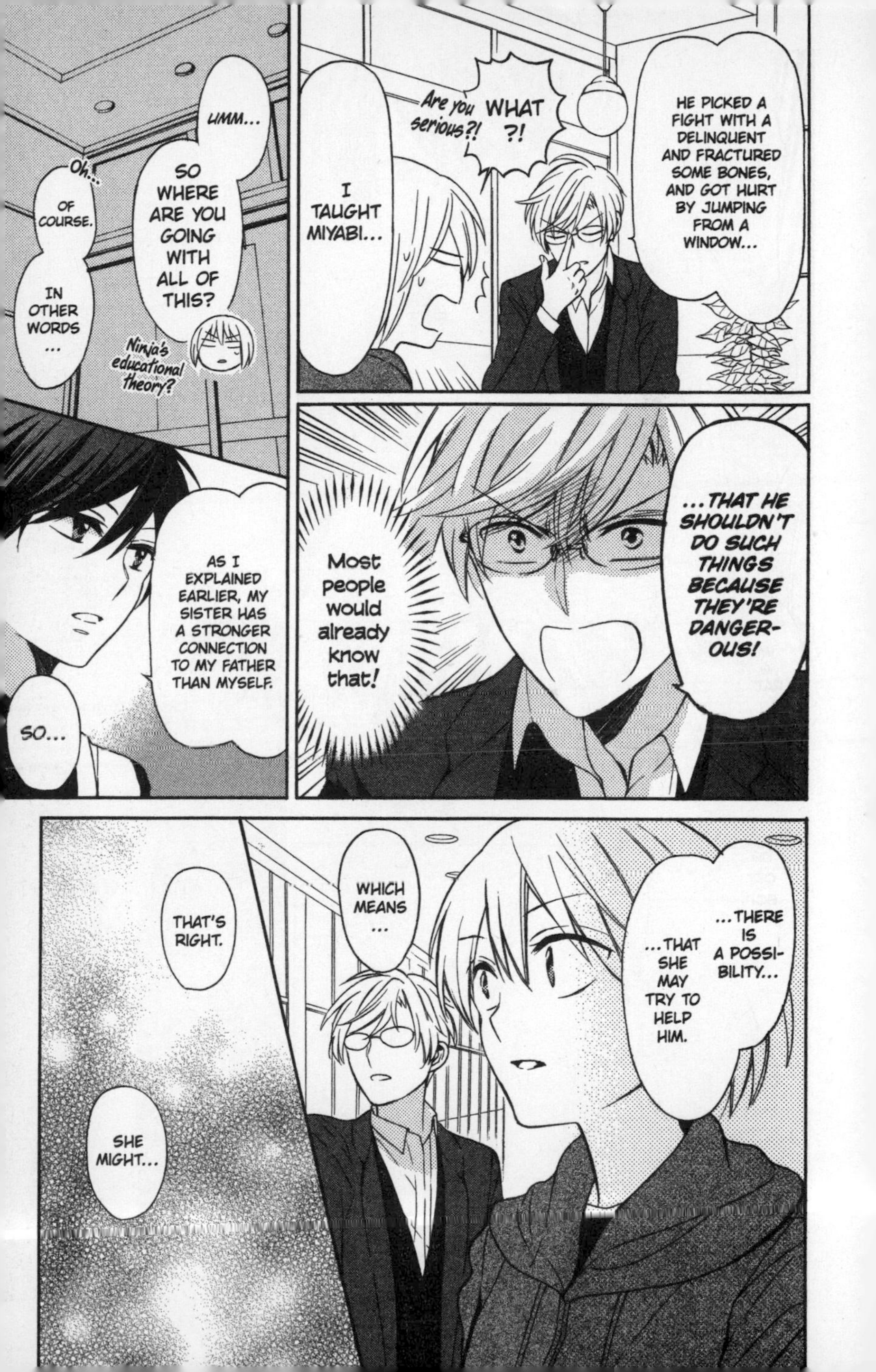
HE PICKED A FIGHT WITH A DELINQUENT AND FRACTURED SOME BONES, AND GOT HURT BY JUMPING FROM A WINDOW...
WHAT ?!
Are you serious?!
I TAUGHT MIYABI...
UMM...
SO WHERE ARE YOU GOING WITH ALL OF THIS?
Ninja's educational theory?
Oh...
OF COURSE.
IN OTHER WORDS ...
...THAT HE SHOULDN'T DO SUCH THINGS BECAUSE THEY'RE DANGER-OUS!
Most people would already know that!
AS I EXPLAINED EARLIER, MY SISTER HAS A STRONGER CONNECTION TO MY FATHER THAN MYSELF.
SO...
...THERE IS A POSSI-BILITY...
...THAT SHE MAY TRY TO HELP HIM.
WHICH MEANS ...
THAT'S RIGHT.
SHE MIGHT...

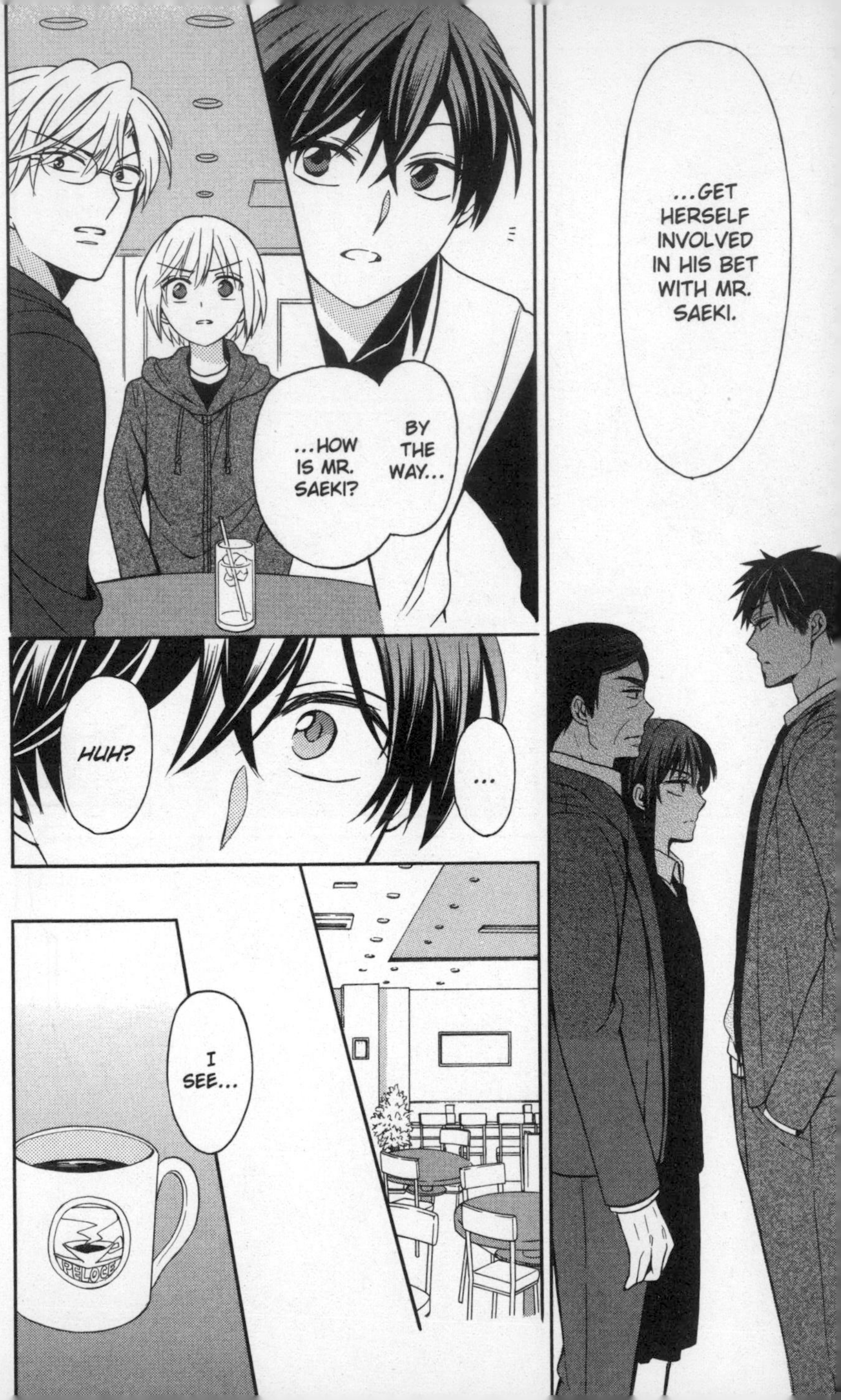
...GET HERSELF INVOLVED IN HIS BET WITH MR. SAEKI.
BY THE WAY...
...HOW IS MR. SAEKI?
...
HUH?
I SEE...

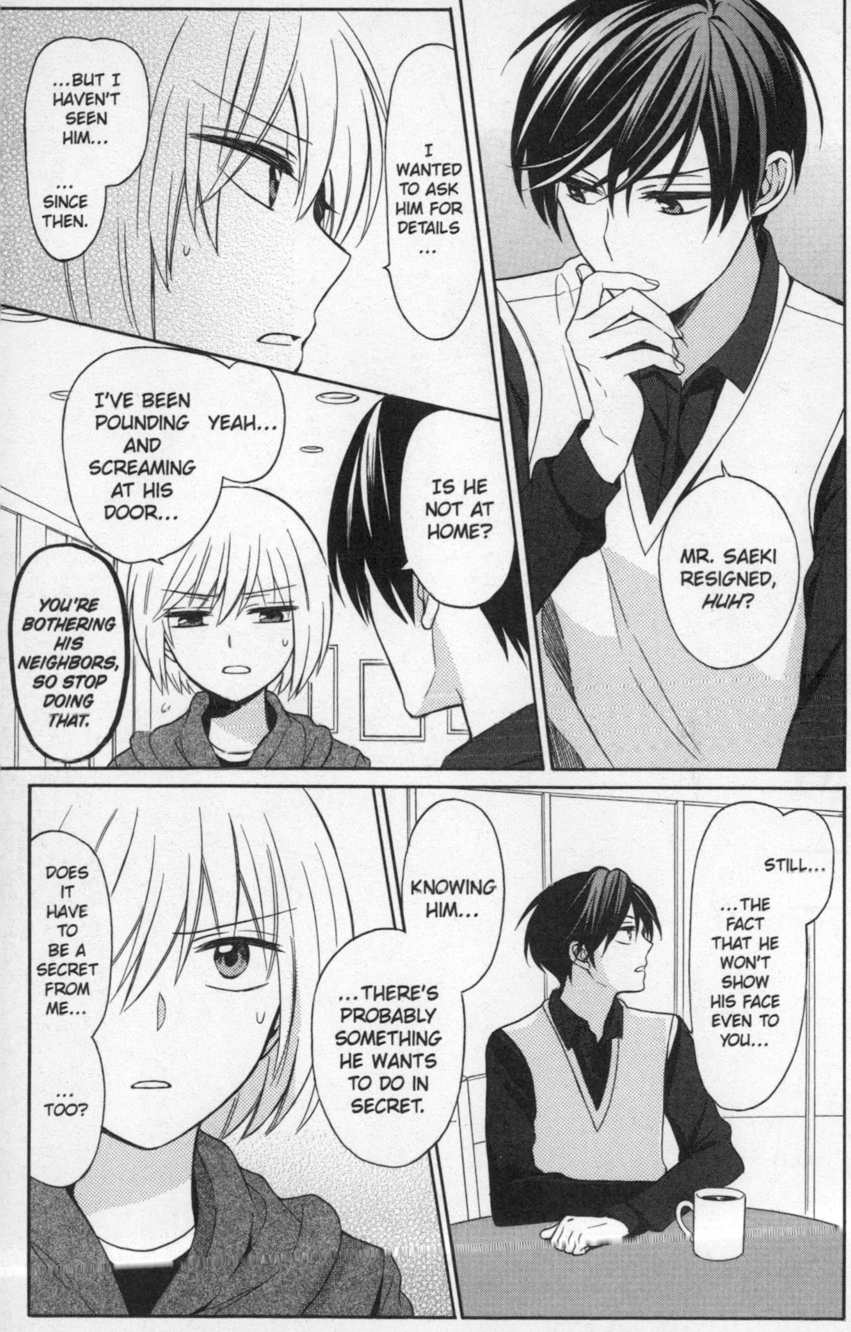
MR. SAEKI RESIGNED, HUH?
I WANTED TO ASK HIM FOR DETAILS ...
...BUT I HAVEN'T SEEN HIM...
... SINCE THEN.
IS HE NOT AT HOME?
YEAH... I'VE BEEN POUNDING AND SCREAMING AT HIS DOOR...
YOU'RE BOTHERING HIS NEIGHBORS, SO STOP DOING THAT.
STILL...
...THE FACT THAT HE WON'T SHOW HIS FACE EVEN TO YOU...
KNOWING HIM...
...THERE'S PROBABLY SOMETHING HE WANTS TO DO IN SECRET.
DOES IT HAVE TO BE A SECRET FROM ME...
... TOO?

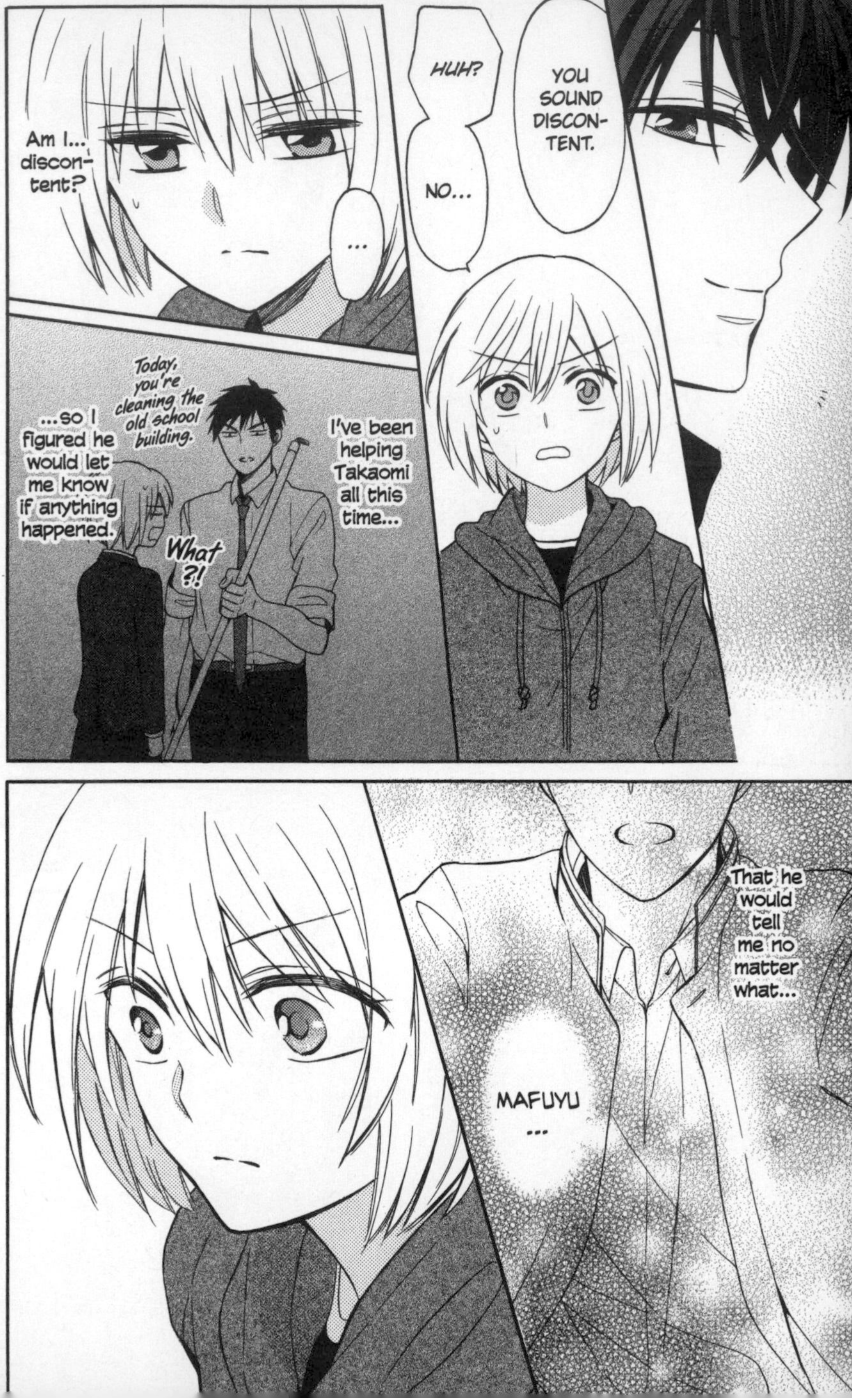
YOU SOUND DISCONTENT.
HUH?
NO...
...
Am I... discontent?
I've been helping Takaomi all this time...
Today, you're cleaning the old school building.
What?!
...so I figured he would let me know if anything happened.
That he would tell me no matter what...
MAFUYU...

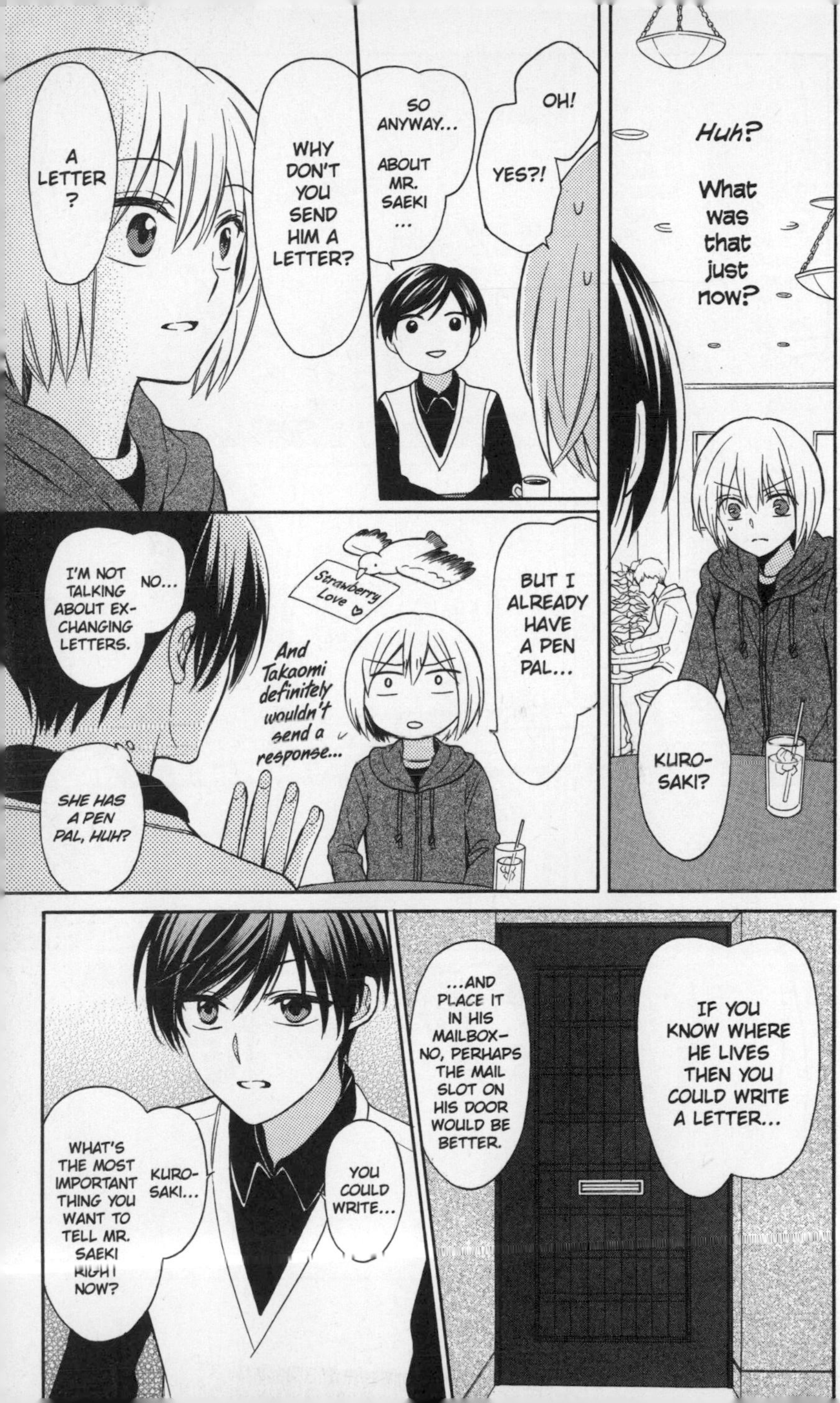
Huh?
What was that just now?
KURO-SAKI?
OH! YES?!
SO ANYWAY... ABOUT MR. SAEKI...
WHY DON'T YOU SEND HIM A LETTER?
A LETTER?
BUT I ALREADY HAVE A PEN PAL...
Strawberry Love
And Takaomi definitely wouldn't send a response...
NO...
I'M NOT TALKING ABOUT EX-CHANGING LETTERS.
SHE HAS A PEN PAL, HUH?
IF YOU KNOW WHERE HE LIVES THEN YOU COULD WRITE A LETTER...
...AND PLACE IT IN HIS MAILBOX—NO, PERHAPS THE MAIL SLOT ON HIS DOOR WOULD BE BETTER.
YOU COULD WRITE...
KURO-SAKI...
WHAT'S THE MOST IMPORTANT THING YOU WANT TO TELL MR. SAEKI RIGHT NOW?

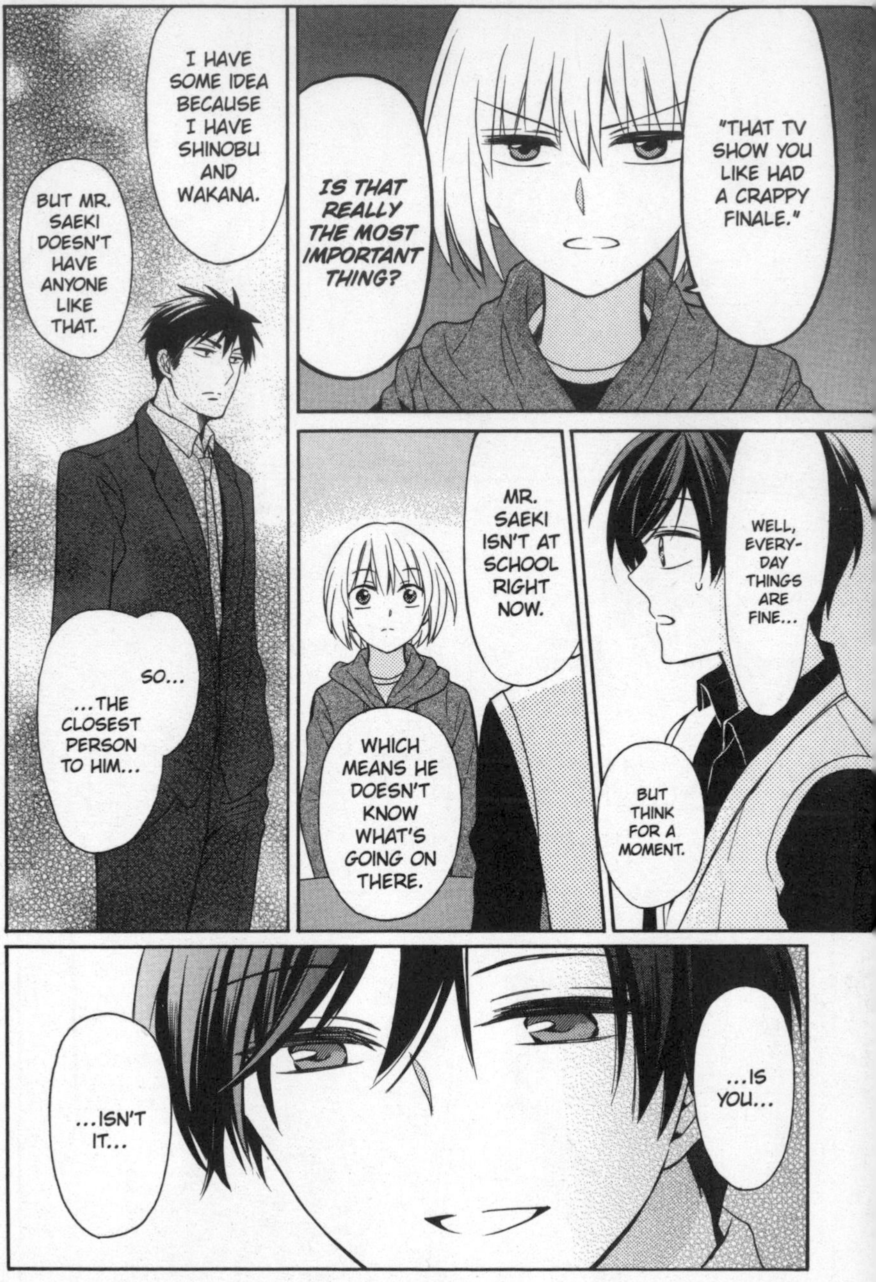
"THAT TV SHOW YOU LIKE HAD A CRAPPY FINALE."
IS THAT REALLY THE MOST IMPORTANT THING?
WELL, EVERY-DAY THINGS ARE FINE...
BUT THINK FOR A MOMENT.
MR. SAEKI ISN'T AT SCHOOL RIGHT NOW.
WHICH MEANS HE DOESN'T KNOW WHAT'S GOING ON THERE.
I HAVE SOME IDEA BECAUSE I HAVE SHINOBU AND WAKANA.
BUT MR. SAEKI DOESN'T HAVE ANYONE LIKE THAT.
SO...
...THE CLOSEST PERSON TO HIM...
...IS YOU...
...ISN'T IT...

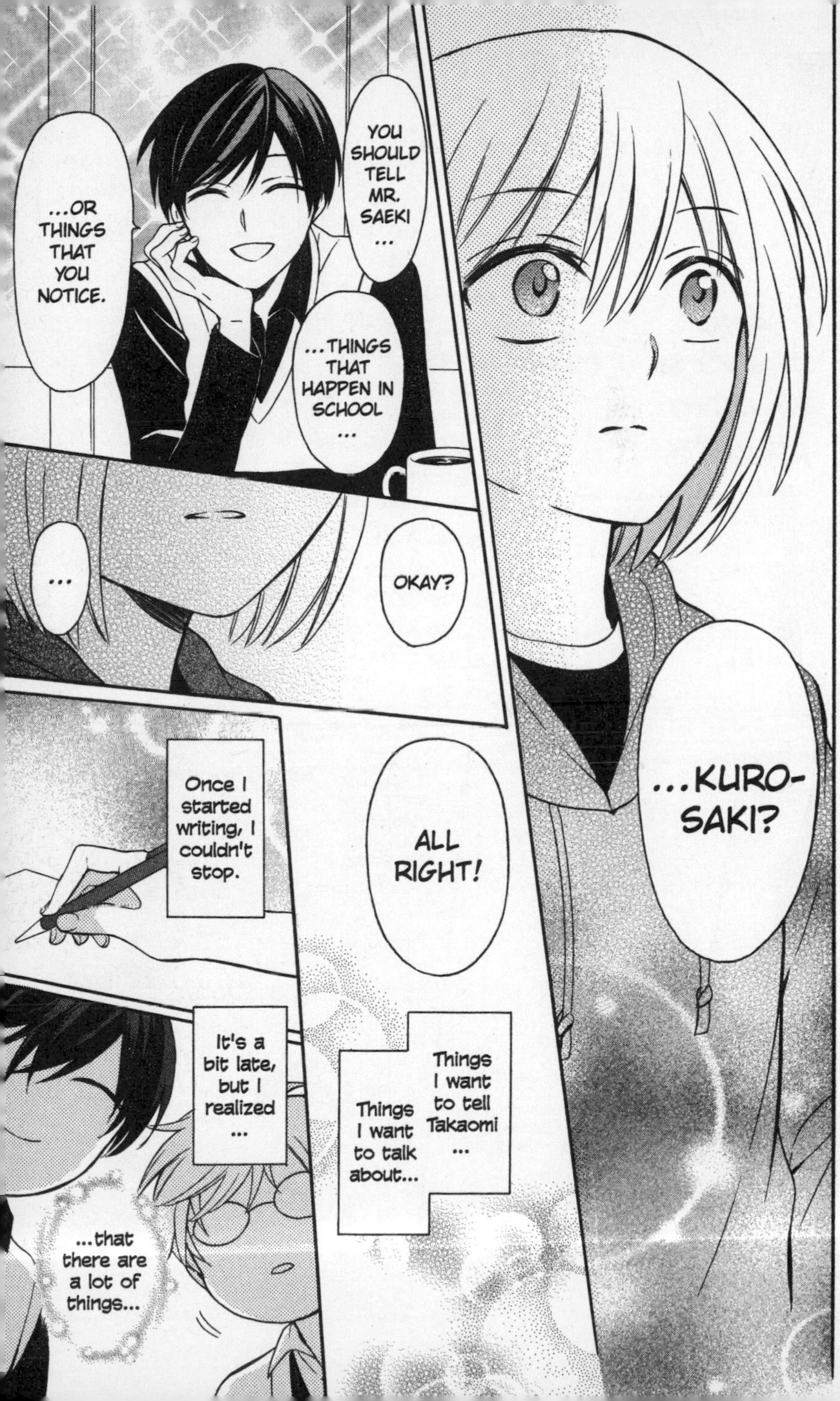
...KURO-SAKI?
ALL RIGHT!
Things I want to tell Takaomi...
Things I want to talk about...
YOU SHOULD TELL MR. SAEKI...
...THINGS THAT HAPPEN IN SCHOOL...
...OR THINGS THAT YOU NOTICE.
OKAY?
...
Once I started writing, I couldn't stop.
It's a bit late, but I realized...
...that there are a lot of things...

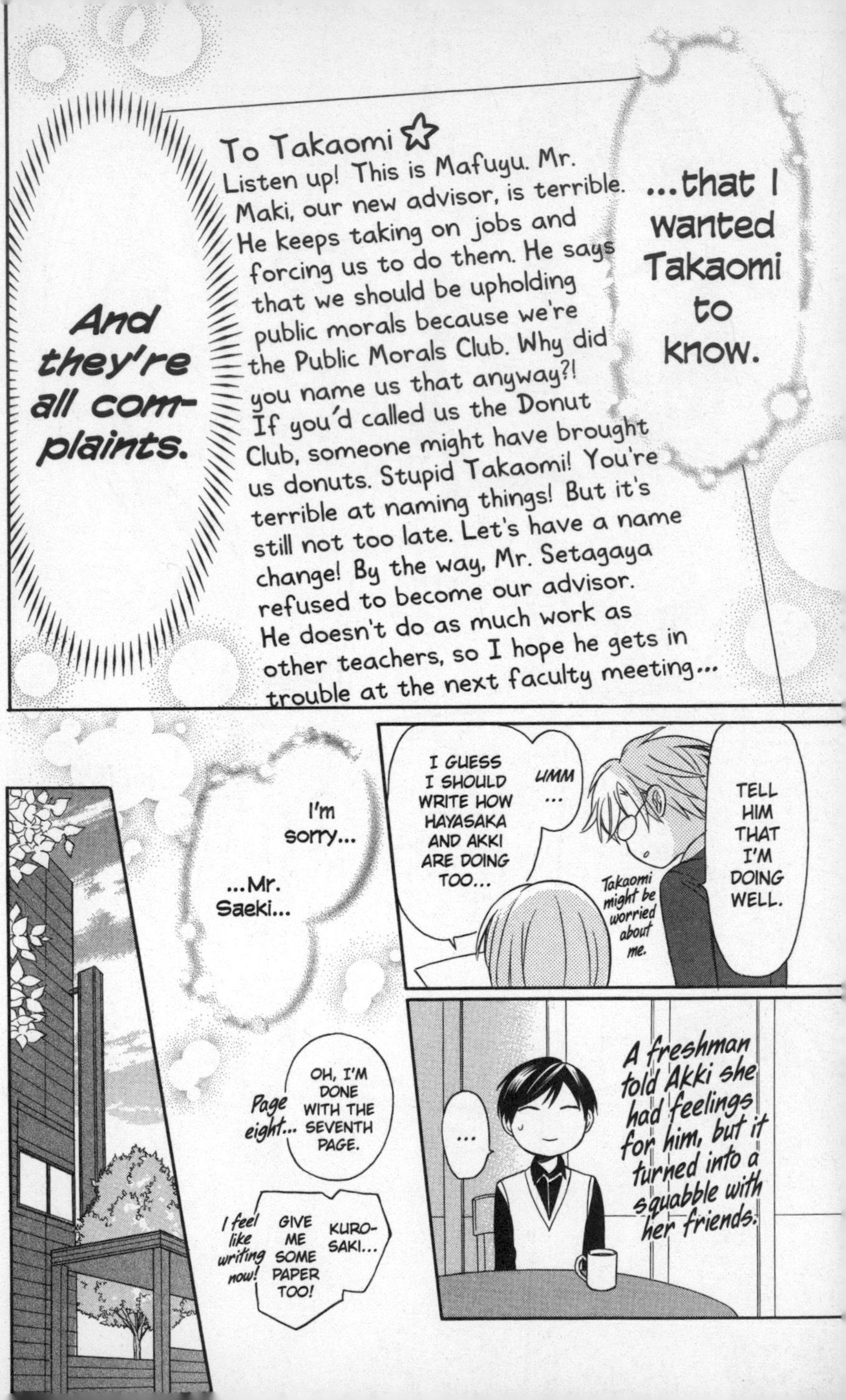
...that I wanted Takaomi to know.
To Takaomi ☆
Listen up! This is Mafuyu. Mr. Maki, our new advisor, is terrible. He keeps taking on jobs and forcing us to do them. He says that we should be upholding public morals because we're the Public Morals Club. Why did you name us that anyway?! If you'd called us the Donut Club, someone might have brought us donuts. Stupid Takaomi! You're terrible at naming things! But it's still not too late. Let's have a name change! By the way, Mr. Setagaya refused to become our advisor. He doesn't do as much work as other teachers, so I hope he gets in trouble at the next faculty meeting...
And they're all com-plaints.
TELL HIM THAT I'M DOING WELL.
Takaomi might be worried about me.
UMM...
I GUESS I SHOULD WRITE HOW HAYASAKA AND AKKI ARE DOING TOO...
A freshman told Akki she had feelings for him, but it turned into a squabble with her friends.
...
I'm sorry...
...Mr. Saeki...
OH, I'M DONE WITH THE SEVENTH PAGE.
Page eight...
KURO-SAKI...
GIVE ME SOME PAPER TOO!
I feel like writing now!

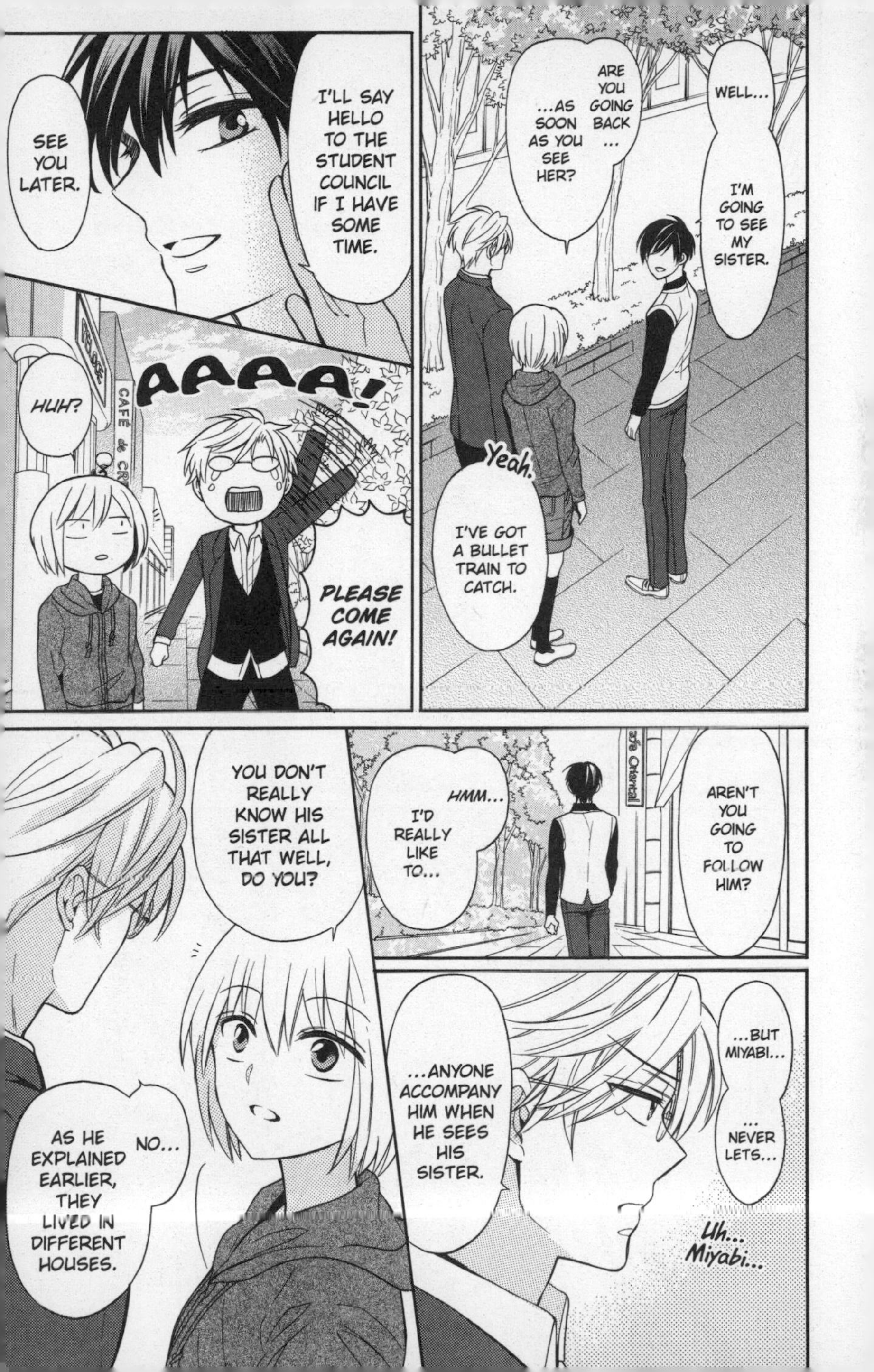
WELL...
I'M GOING TO SEE MY SISTER.
ARE YOU GOING BACK...
...AS SOON AS YOU SEE HER?
Yeah.
I'VE GOT A BULLET TRAIN TO CATCH.
I'LL SAY HELLO TO THE STUDENT COUNCIL IF I HAVE SOME TIME.
SEE YOU LATER.
AAAA!
PLEASE COME AGAIN!
HUH?
AREN'T YOU GOING TO FOLLOW HIM?
HMM...
I'D REALLY LIKE TO...
...BUT MIYABI...
...NEVER LETS...
...ANYONE ACCOMPANY HIM WHEN HE SEES HIS SISTER.
Uh... Miyabi...
YOU DON'T REALLY KNOW HIS SISTER ALL THAT WELL, DO YOU?
NO...
AS HE EXPLAINED EARLIER, THEY LIVED IN DIFFERENT HOUSES.

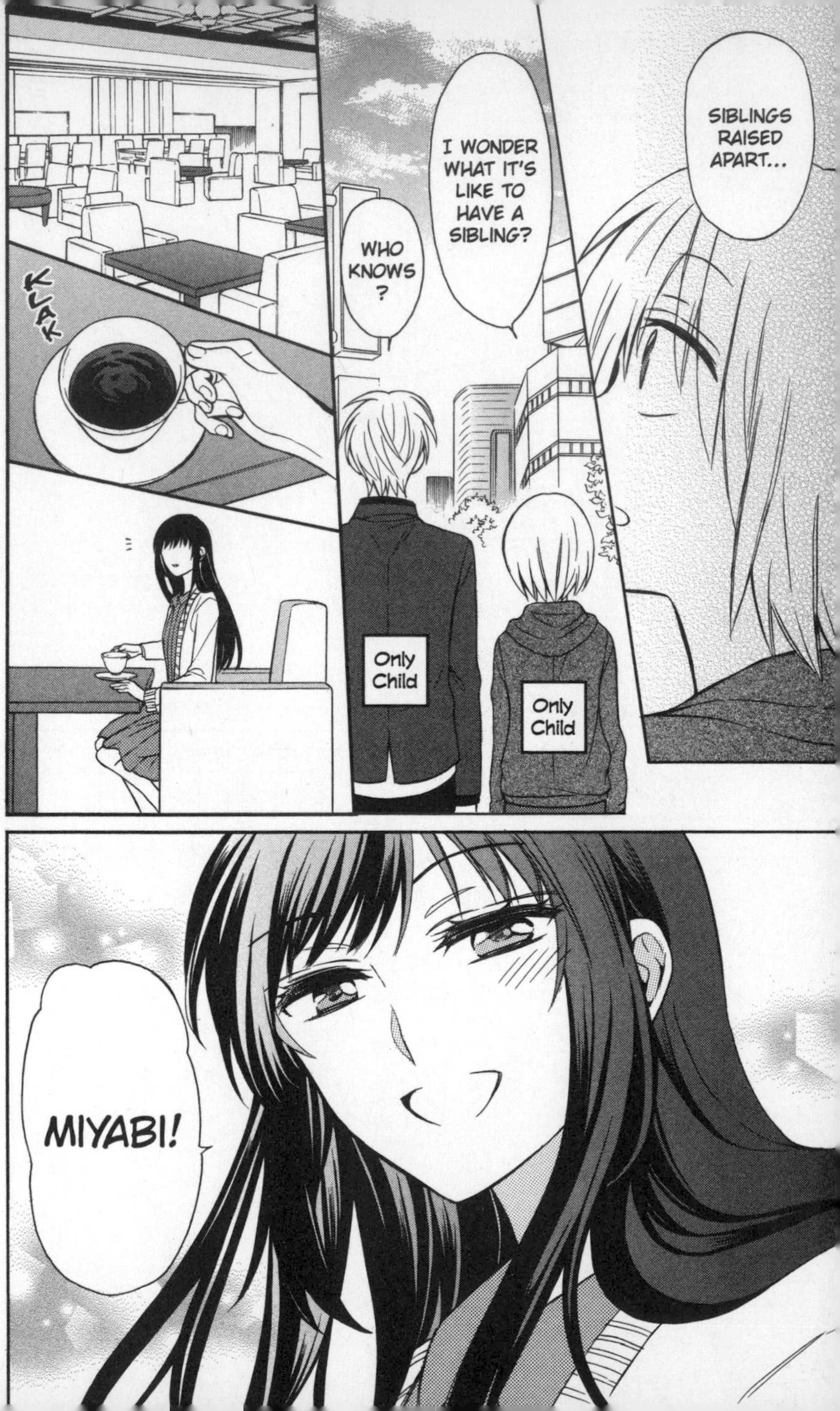
SIBLINGS RAISED APART...
I WONDER WHAT IT'S LIKE TO HAVE A SIBLING?
WHO KNOWS?
Only Child
Only Child
KLAK
MIYABI!

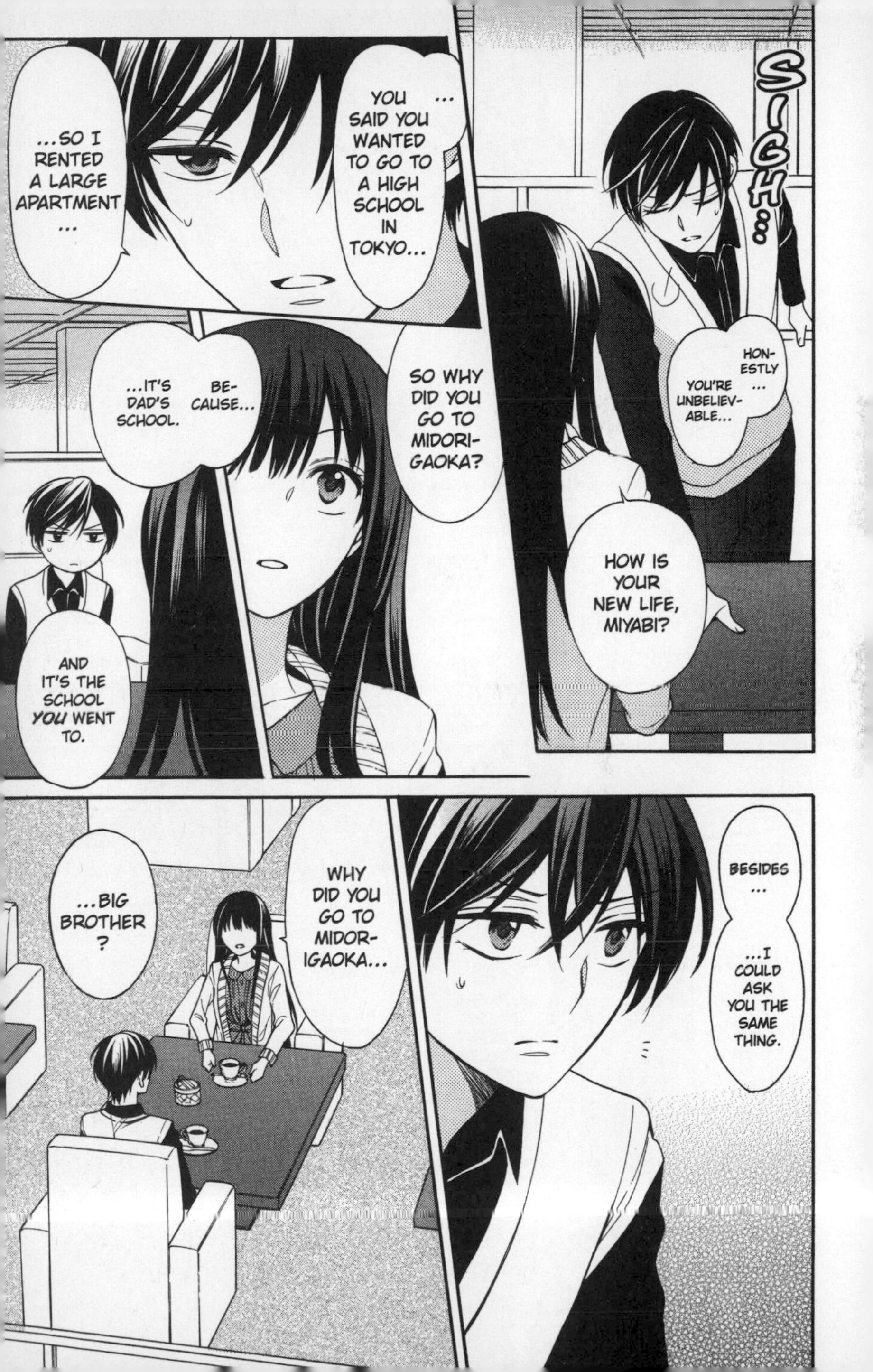
SIGH...
HONESTLY... YOU'RE UNBELIEVABLE...
HOW IS YOUR NEW LIFE, MIYABI?
YOU... SAID YOU WANTED TO GO TO A HIGH SCHOOL IN TOKYO...
...SO I RENTED A LARGE APARTMENT...
SO WHY DID YOU GO TO MIDORIGAOKA?
BECAUSE... ...IT'S DAD'S SCHOOL.
AND IT'S THE SCHOOL *YOU* WENT TO.
BESIDES...
...I COULD ASK YOU THE SAME THING.
WHY DID YOU GO TO MIDORIGAOKA...
...BIG BROTHER?

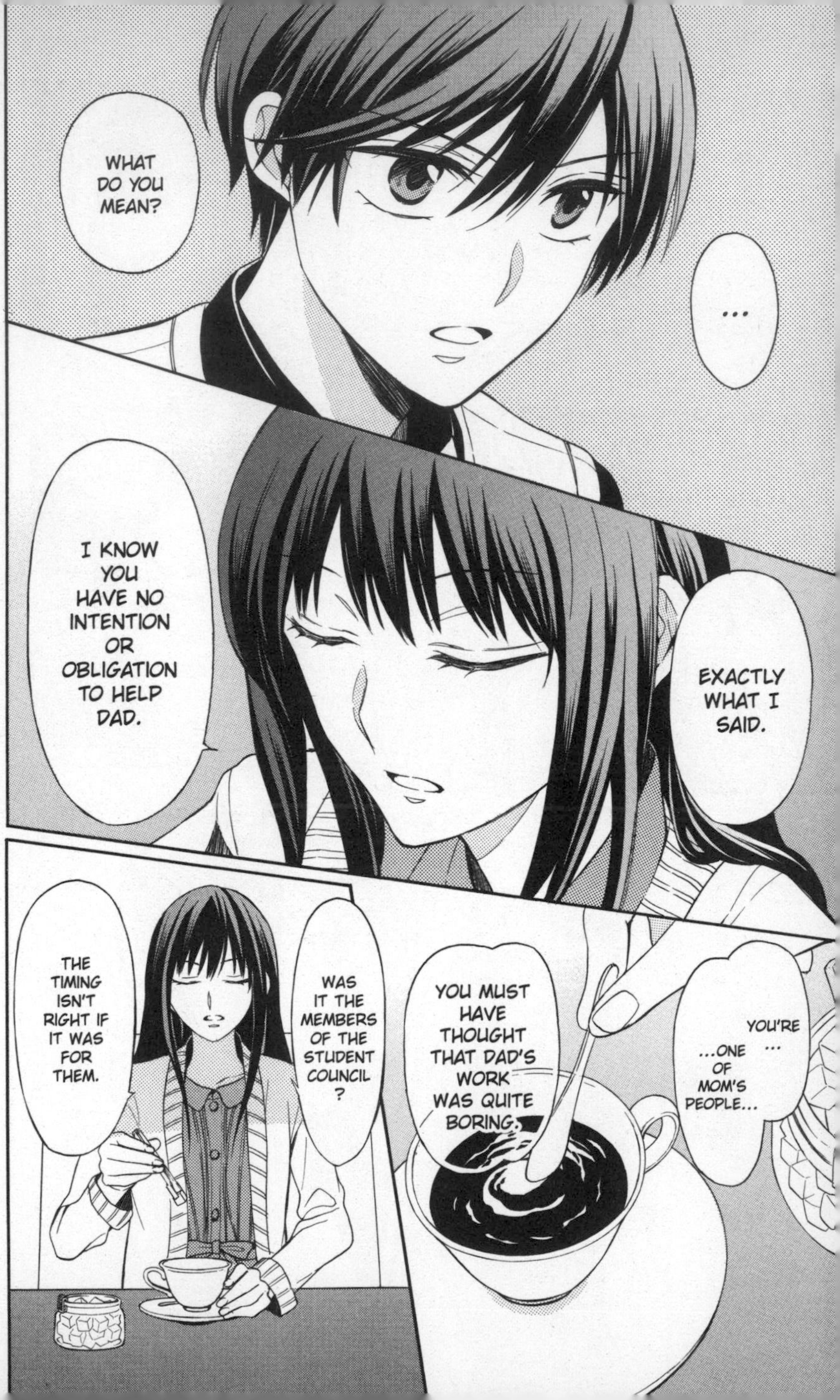
...
WHAT DO YOU MEAN?
EXACTLY WHAT I SAID.
I KNOW YOU HAVE NO INTENTION OR OBLIGATION TO HELP DAD.
YOU'RE ...
...ONE OF MOM'S PEOPLE...
YOU MUST HAVE THOUGHT THAT DAD'S WORK WAS QUITE BORING.
WAS IT THE MEMBERS OF THE STUDENT COUNCIL?
THE TIMING ISN'T RIGHT IF IT WAS FOR THEM.

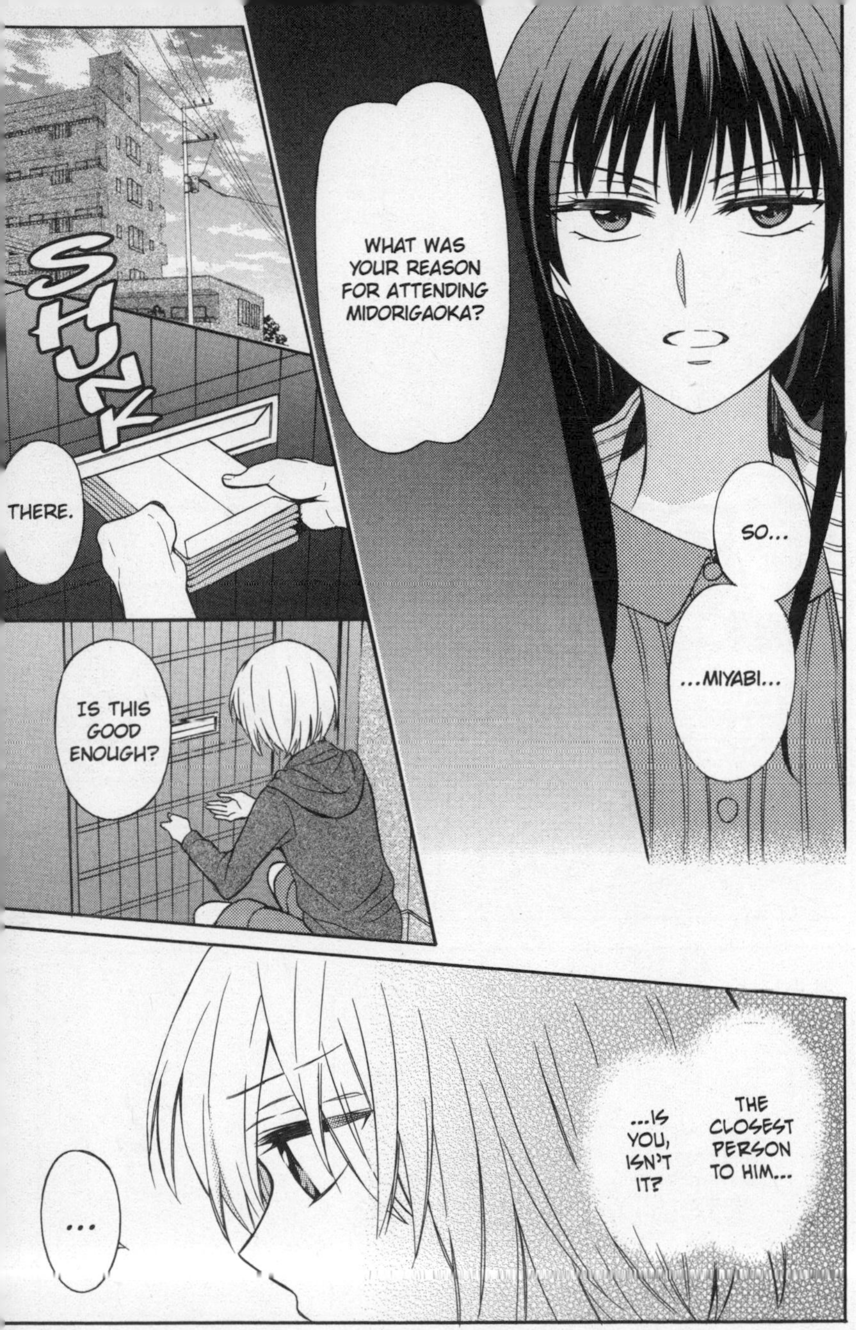
SO...
...MIYABI...
WHAT WAS YOUR REASON FOR ATTENDING MIDORIGAOKA?
SHUNK
THERE.
IS THIS GOOD ENOUGH?
THE CLOSEST PERSON TO HIM...
...IS YOU, ISN'T IT?
...

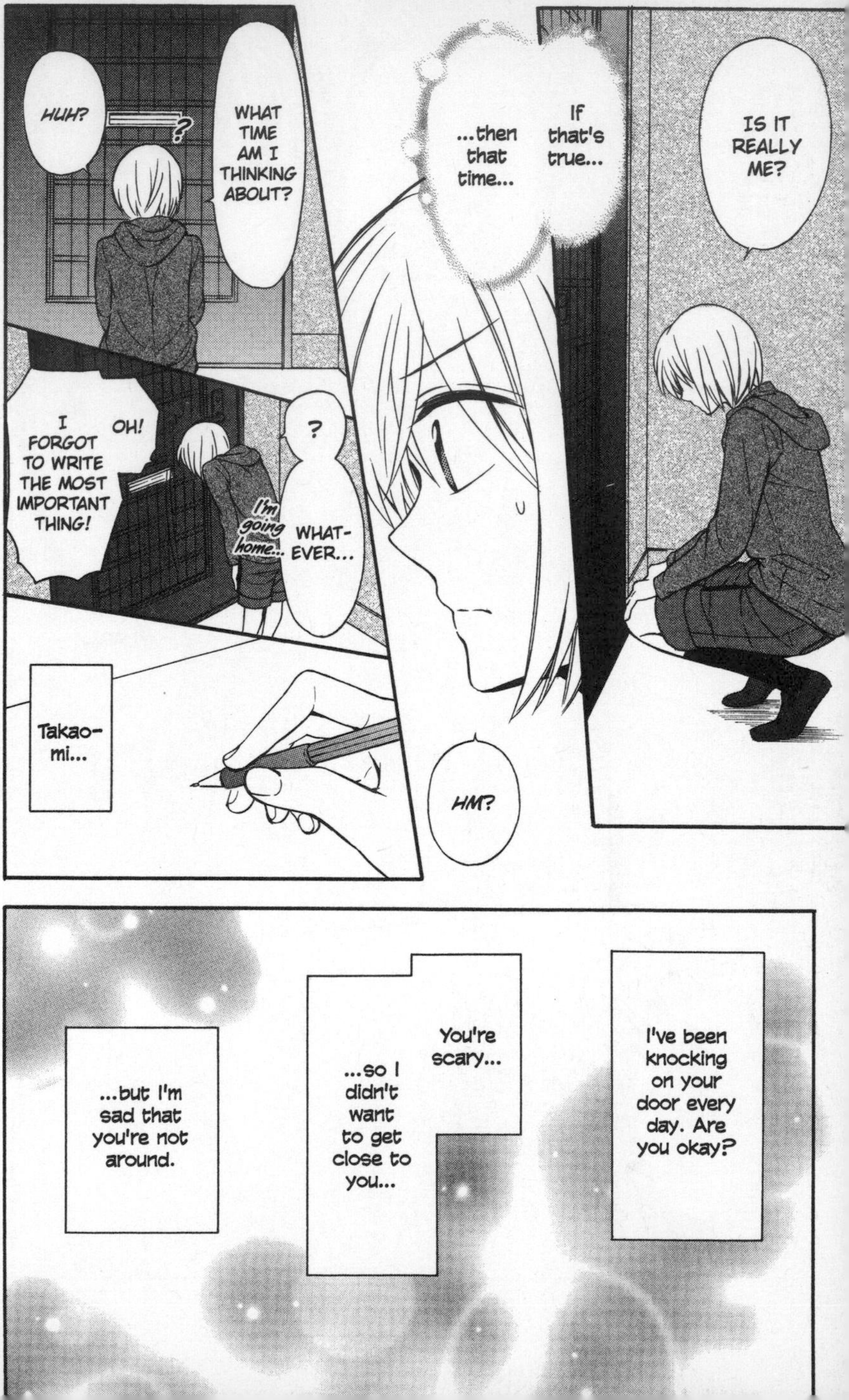
IS IT REALLY ME?
If that's true...
...then that time...
HM?
WHAT TIME AM I THINKING ABOUT?
HUH?
?
OH!
I FORGOT TO WRITE THE MOST IMPORTANT THING!
WHAT-EVER...
I'm going home...
Takao-mi...
I've been knocking on your door every day. Are you okay?
You're scary...
...so I didn't want to get close to you...
...but I'm sad that you're not around.

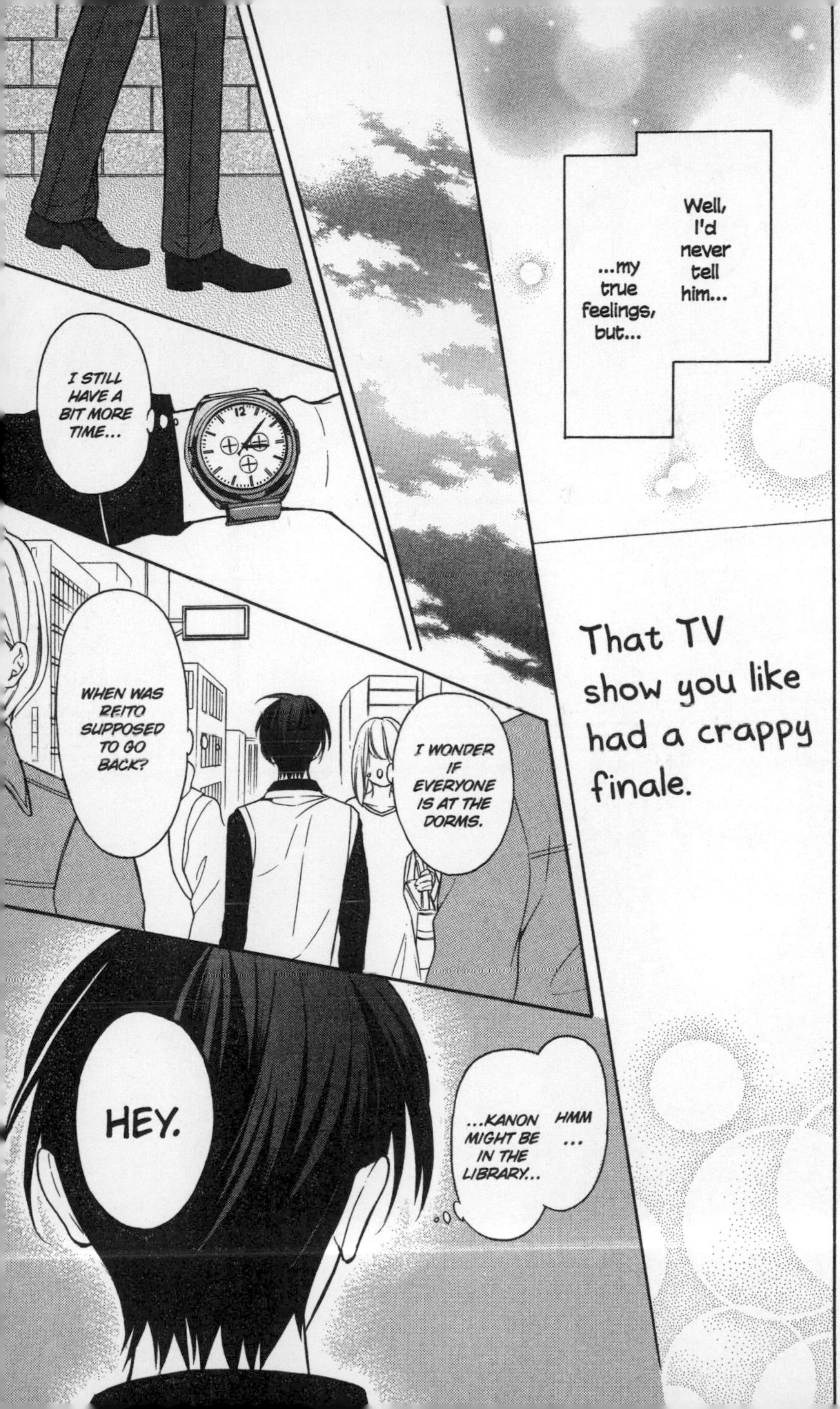
Well, I'd never tell him...
...my true feelings, but...
That TV show you like had a crappy finale.
I STILL HAVE A BIT MORE TIME...
I WONDER IF EVERYONE IS AT THE DORMS.
WHEN WAS REITO SUPPOSED TO GO BACK?
HMM ...
...KANON MIGHT BE IN THE LIBRARY...
HEY.

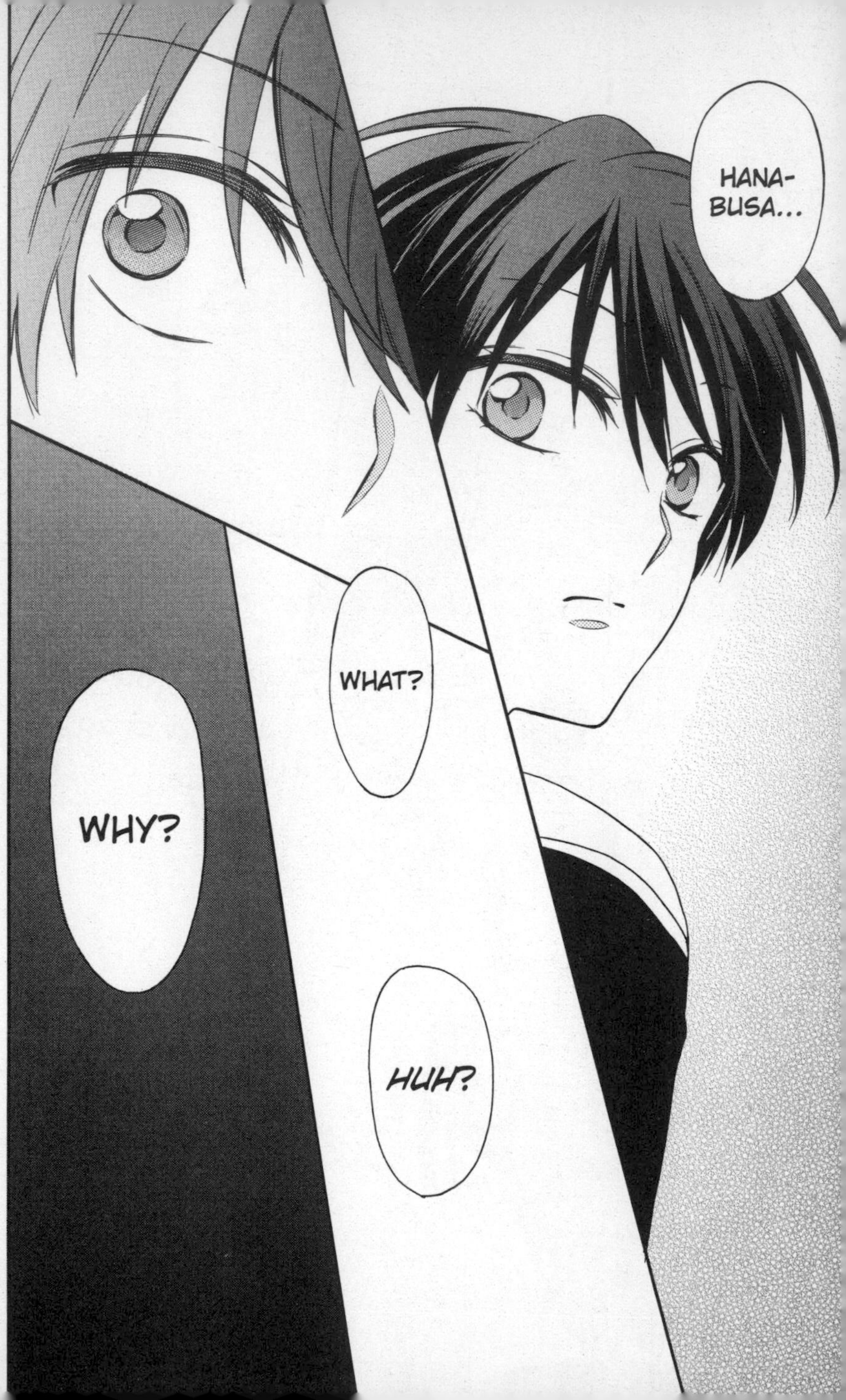
HANA-BUSA...
WHAT?
HUH?
WHY?

Chapter 133

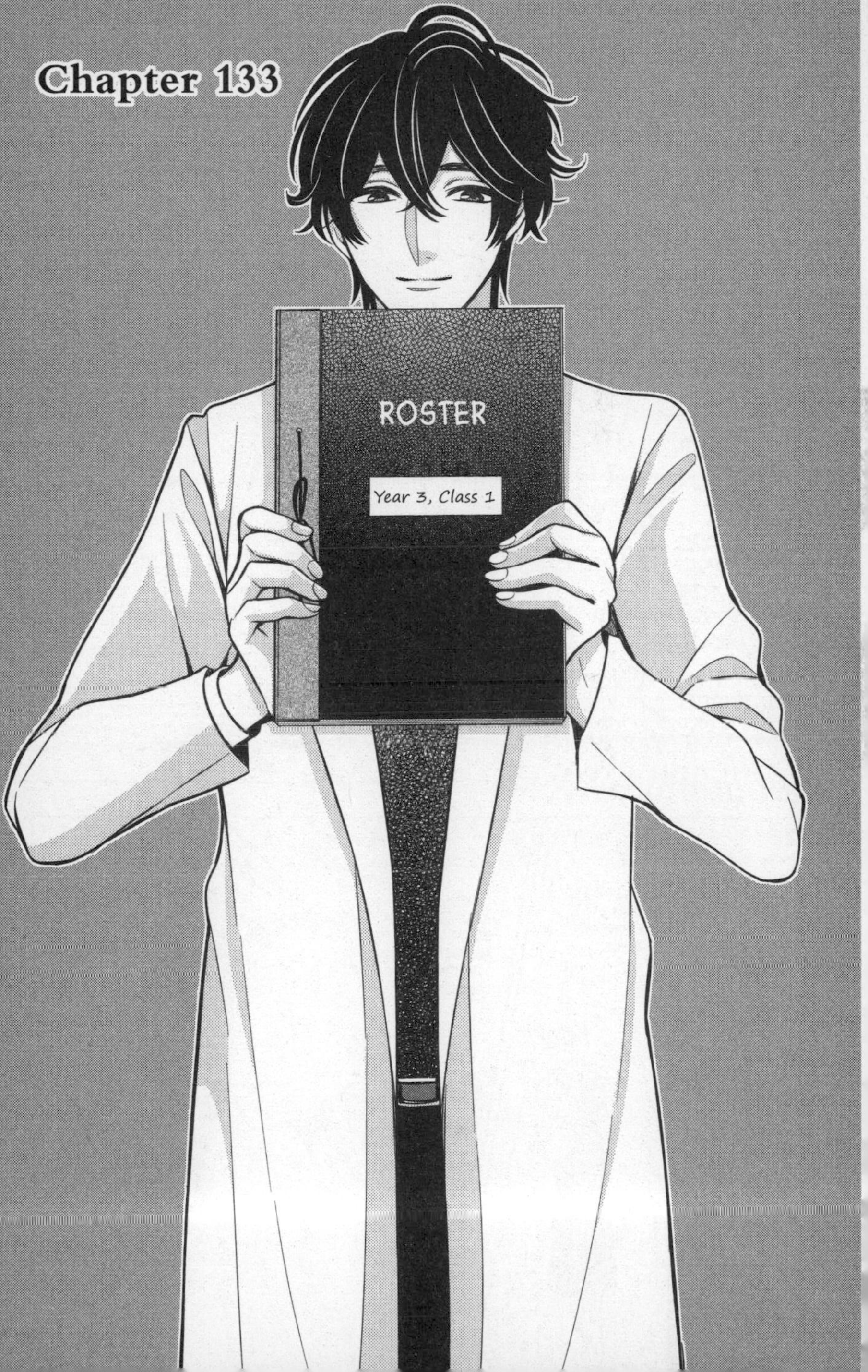
ROSTER
Year 3, Class 1

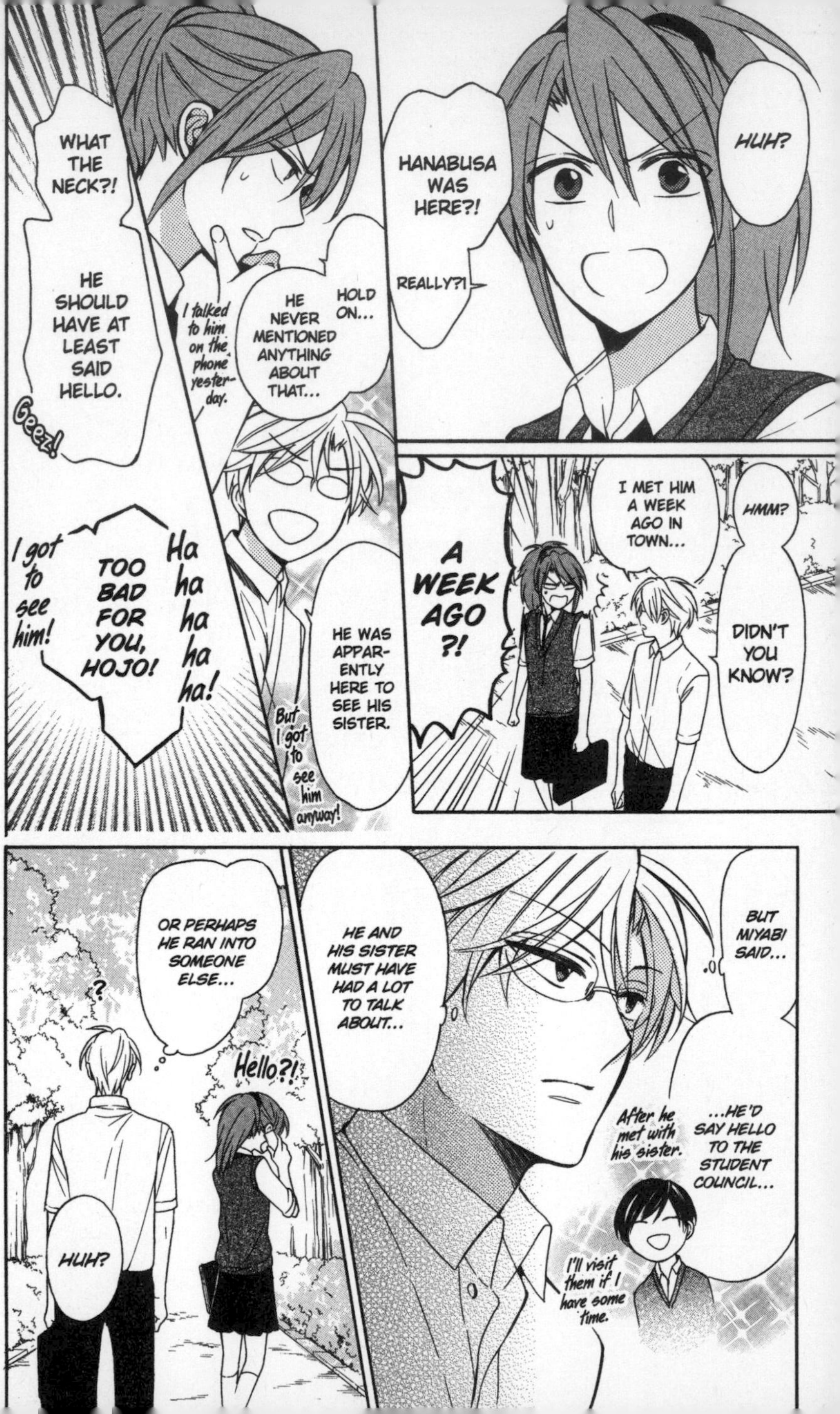
HUH?
HANABUSA WAS HERE?!
REALLY?!
HMM?
DIDN'T YOU KNOW?
I MET HIM A WEEK AGO IN TOWN...
A WEEK AGO?!
HE WAS APPARENTLY HERE TO SEE HIS SISTER.
But I got to see him anyway!
HOLD ON...
HE NEVER MENTIONED ANYTHING ABOUT THAT...
I talked to him on the phone yesterday.
WHAT THE NECK?!
HE SHOULD HAVE AT LEAST SAID HELLO.
Geez!
TOO BAD FOR YOU, HOJO!
Ha ha ha ha ha ha!
I got to see him!
BUT MIYABI SAID...
...HE'D SAY HELLO TO THE STUDENT COUNCIL...
After he met with his sister.
I'll visit them if I have some time.
HE AND HIS SISTER MUST HAVE HAD A LOT TO TALK ABOUT...
OR PERHAPS HE RAN INTO SOMEONE ELSE...
?
Hello?!
HUH?

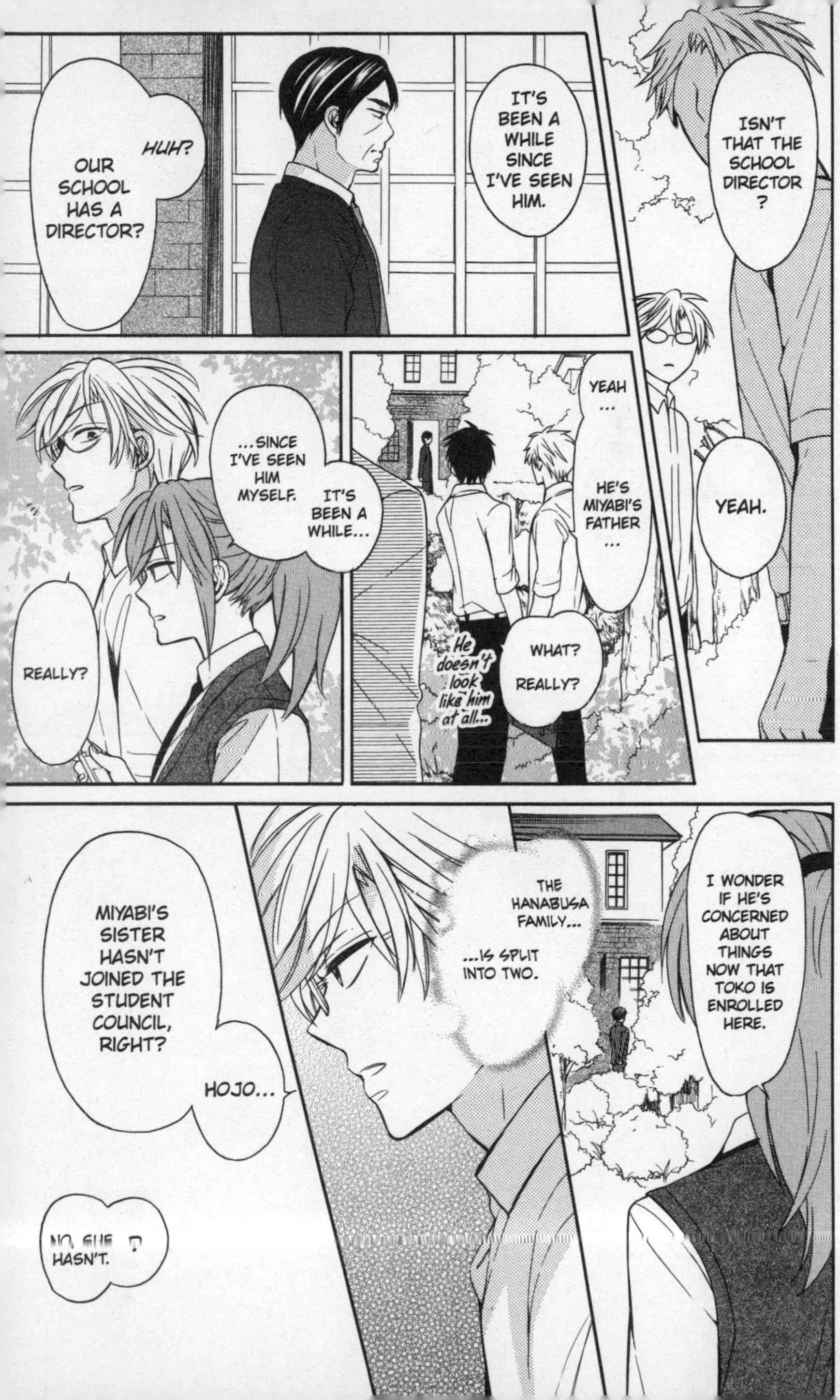
ISN'T THAT THE SCHOOL DIRECTOR?
YEAH.
IT'S BEEN A WHILE SINCE I'VE SEEN HIM.
HUH? OUR SCHOOL HAS A DIRECTOR?
YEAH... HE'S MIYABI'S FATHER...
WHAT? REALLY?
He doesn't look like him at all...
IT'S BEEN A WHILE...
...SINCE I'VE SEEN HIM MYSELF.
REALLY?
I WONDER IF HE'S CONCERNED ABOUT THINGS NOW THAT TOKO IS ENROLLED HERE.
THE HANABUSA FAMILY...
...IS SPLIT INTO TWO.
HOJO...
MIYABI'S SISTER HASN'T JOINED THE STUDENT COUNCIL, RIGHT?
NO, SHE HASN'T.

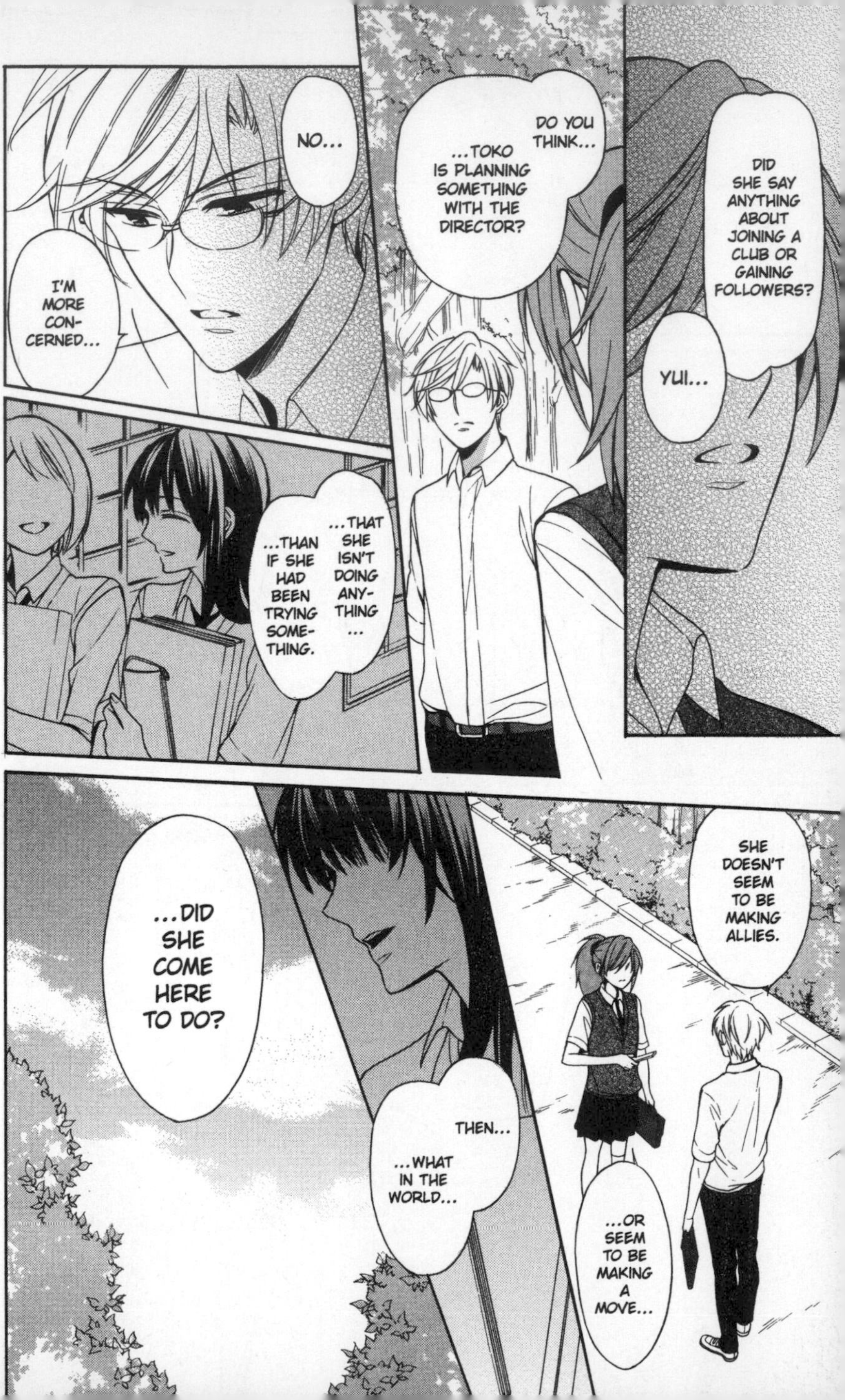
DID SHE SAY ANYTHING ABOUT JOINING A CLUB OR GAINING FOLLOWERS?
YUI...
DO YOU THINK...
...TOKO IS PLANNING SOMETHING WITH THE DIRECTOR?
NO...
I'M MORE CON-CERNED...
...THAT SHE ISN'T DOING ANY-THING...
...THAN IF SHE HAD BEEN TRYING SOME-THING.
SHE DOESN'T SEEM TO BE MAKING ALLIES.
...OR SEEM TO BE MAKING A MOVE...
THEN...
...WHAT IN THE WORLD...
...DID SHE COME HERE TO DO?

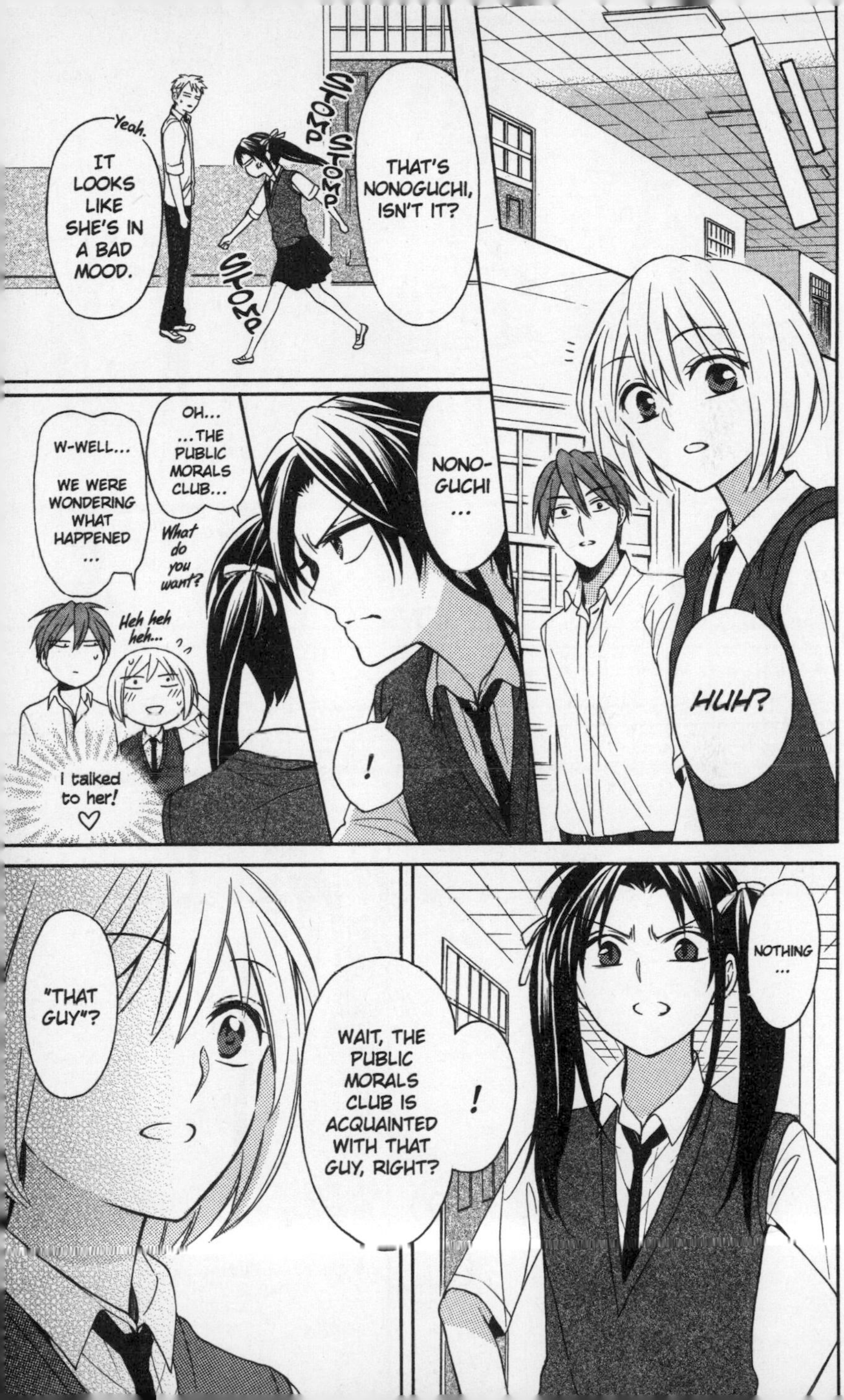
HUH?
STOMP STOMP STOMP STOMP
THAT'S NONOGUCHI, ISN'T IT?
Yeah.
IT LOOKS LIKE SHE'S IN A BAD MOOD.
NONO-GUCHI ...
!
OH... ...THE PUBLIC MORALS CLUB...
What do you want?
W-WELL... WE WERE WONDERING WHAT HAPPENED ...
Heh heh heh...
I talked to her! ♡
NOTHING ...
!
WAIT, THE PUBLIC MORALS CLUB IS ACQUAINTED WITH THAT GUY, RIGHT?
"THAT GUY"?

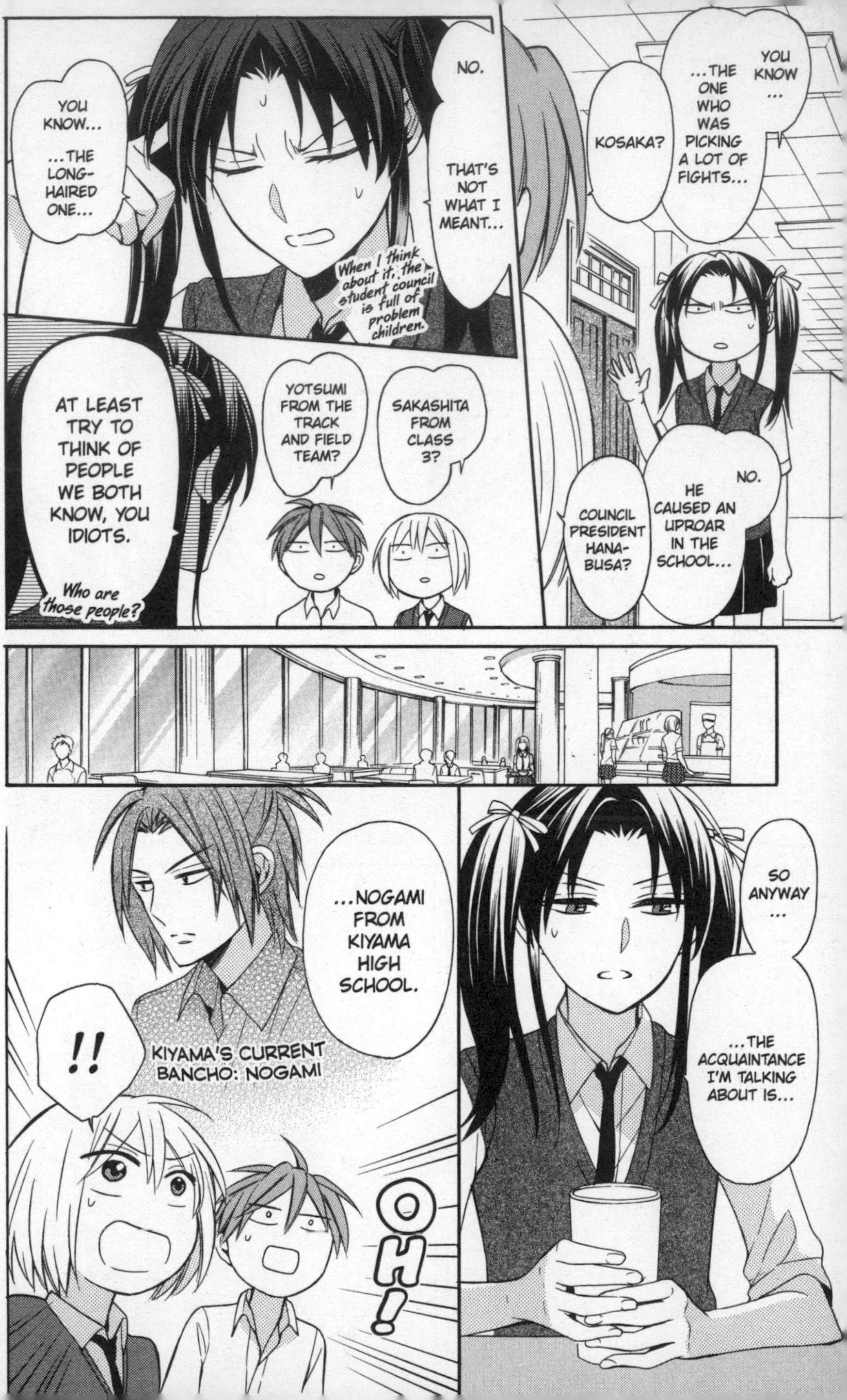
YOU KNOW...
...THE ONE WHO WAS PICKING A LOT OF FIGHTS...
KOSAKA?
NO.
HE CAUSED AN UPROAR IN THE SCHOOL...
COUNCIL PRESIDENT HANABUSA?
NO.
THAT'S NOT WHAT I MEANT...
When I think about it, the student council is full of problem children.
YOU KNOW...
...THE LONG-HAIRED ONE...
SAKASHITA FROM CLASS 3?
YOTSUMI FROM THE TRACK AND FIELD TEAM?
AT LEAST TRY TO THINK OF PEOPLE WE BOTH KNOW, YOU IDIOTS.
Who are those people?
SO ANYWAY...
...THE ACQUAINTANCE I'M TALKING ABOUT IS...
...NOGAMI FROM KIYAMA HIGH SCHOOL.
!!
KIYAMA'S CURRENT BANCHO: NOGAMI
OH!

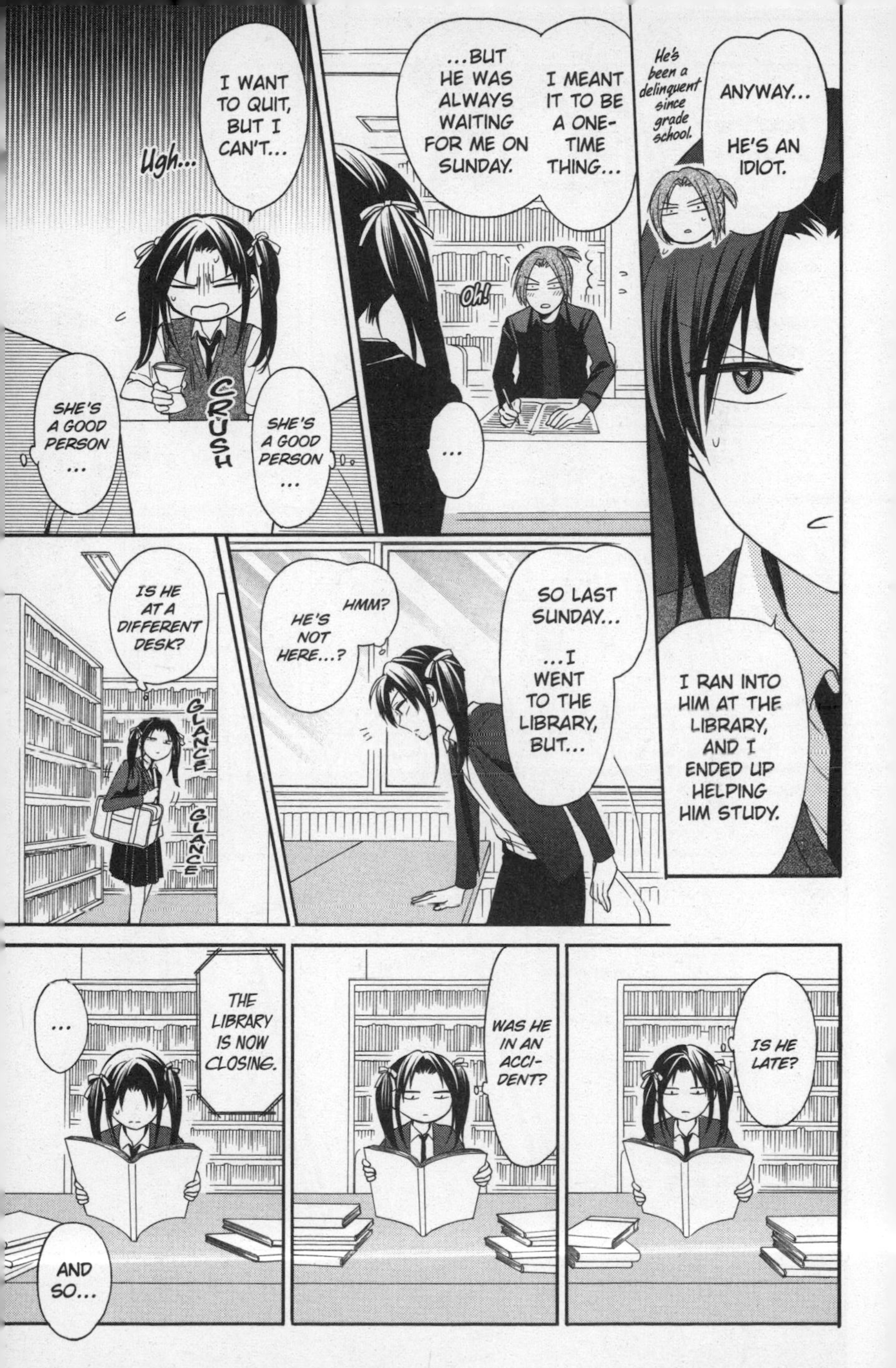
ANYWAY...
HE'S AN IDIOT.
He's been a delinquent since grade school.
I RAN INTO HIM AT THE LIBRARY, AND I ENDED UP HELPING HIM STUDY.
I MEANT IT TO BE A ONE-TIME THING...
...BUT HE WAS ALWAYS WAITING FOR ME ON SUNDAY.
Oh!
...
I WANT TO QUIT, BUT I CAN'T...
Ugh...
CRUSH
SHE'S A GOOD PERSON...
SHE'S A GOOD PERSON...
SO LAST SUNDAY...
...I WENT TO THE LIBRARY, BUT...
HMM?
HE'S NOT HERE...?
IS HE AT A DIFFERENT DESK?
GLANCE
GLANCE
IS HE LATE?
WAS HE IN AN ACCIDENT?
THE LIBRARY IS NOW CLOSING.
...
AND SO...

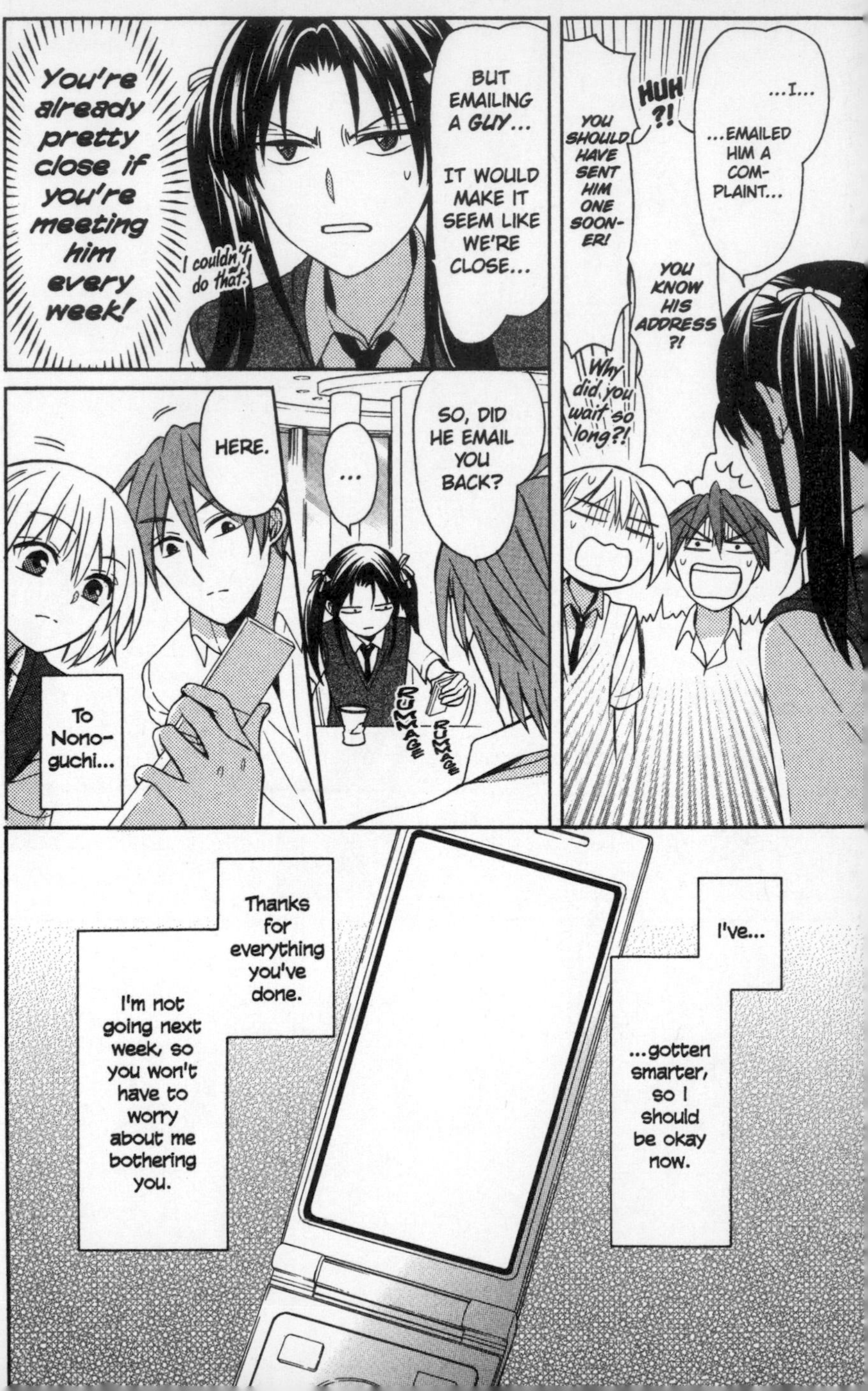
...I...
...EMAILED HIM A COM-PLAINT...
HUH ?!
YOU SHOULD HAVE SENT HIM ONE SOONER!
YOU KNOW HIS ADDRESS ?!
Why did you wait so long?!
BUT EMAILING A GUY...
IT WOULD MAKE IT SEEM LIKE WE'RE CLOSE...
I couldn't do that.
You're already pretty close if you're meeting him every week!
SO, DID HE EMAIL YOU BACK?
...
HERE.
RUMMAGE RUMMAGE
To Nonoguchi...
I've...
...gotten smarter, so I should be okay now.
Thanks for everything you've done.
I'm not going next week, so you won't have to worry about me bothering you.

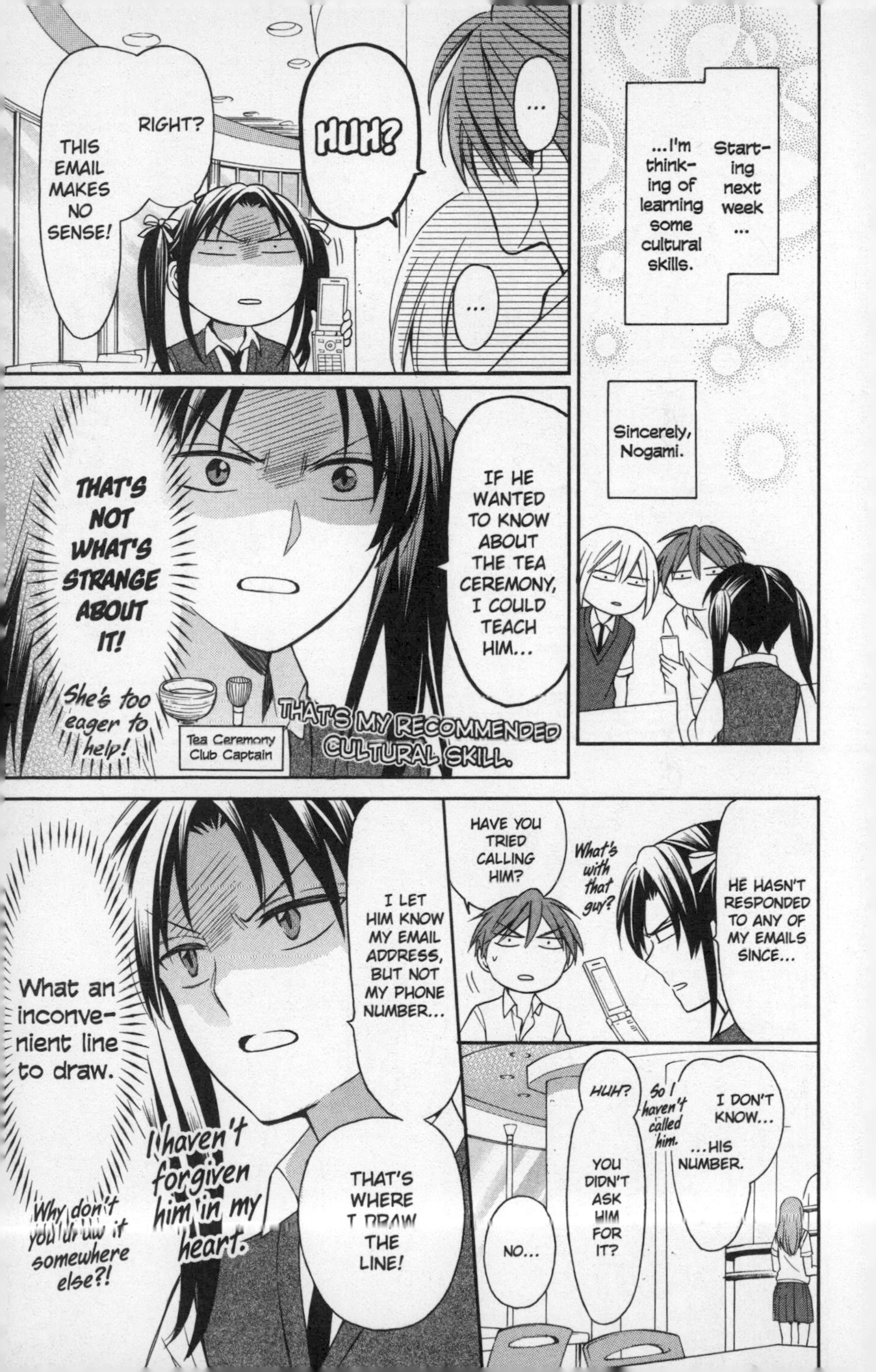
Starting next week...
...I'm thinking of learning some cultural skills.
Sincerely, Nogami.
...
...
HUH?
RIGHT?
THIS EMAIL MAKES NO SENSE!
IF HE WANTED TO KNOW ABOUT THE TEA CEREMONY, I COULD TEACH HIM...
THAT'S MY RECOMMENDED CULTURAL SKILL.
Tea Ceremony Club Captain
THAT'S NOT WHAT'S STRANGE ABOUT IT!
She's too eager to help!
HE HASN'T RESPONDED TO ANY OF MY EMAILS SINCE...
What's with that guy?
HAVE YOU TRIED CALLING HIM?
I LET HIM KNOW MY EMAIL ADDRESS, BUT NOT MY PHONE NUMBER...
I DON'T KNOW... ...HIS NUMBER.
So I haven't called him.
HUH?
YOU DIDN'T ASK HIM FOR IT?
NO...
THAT'S WHERE I DRAW THE LINE!
I haven't forgiven him in my heart.
What an inconvenient line to draw.
Why don't you draw it somewhere else?!

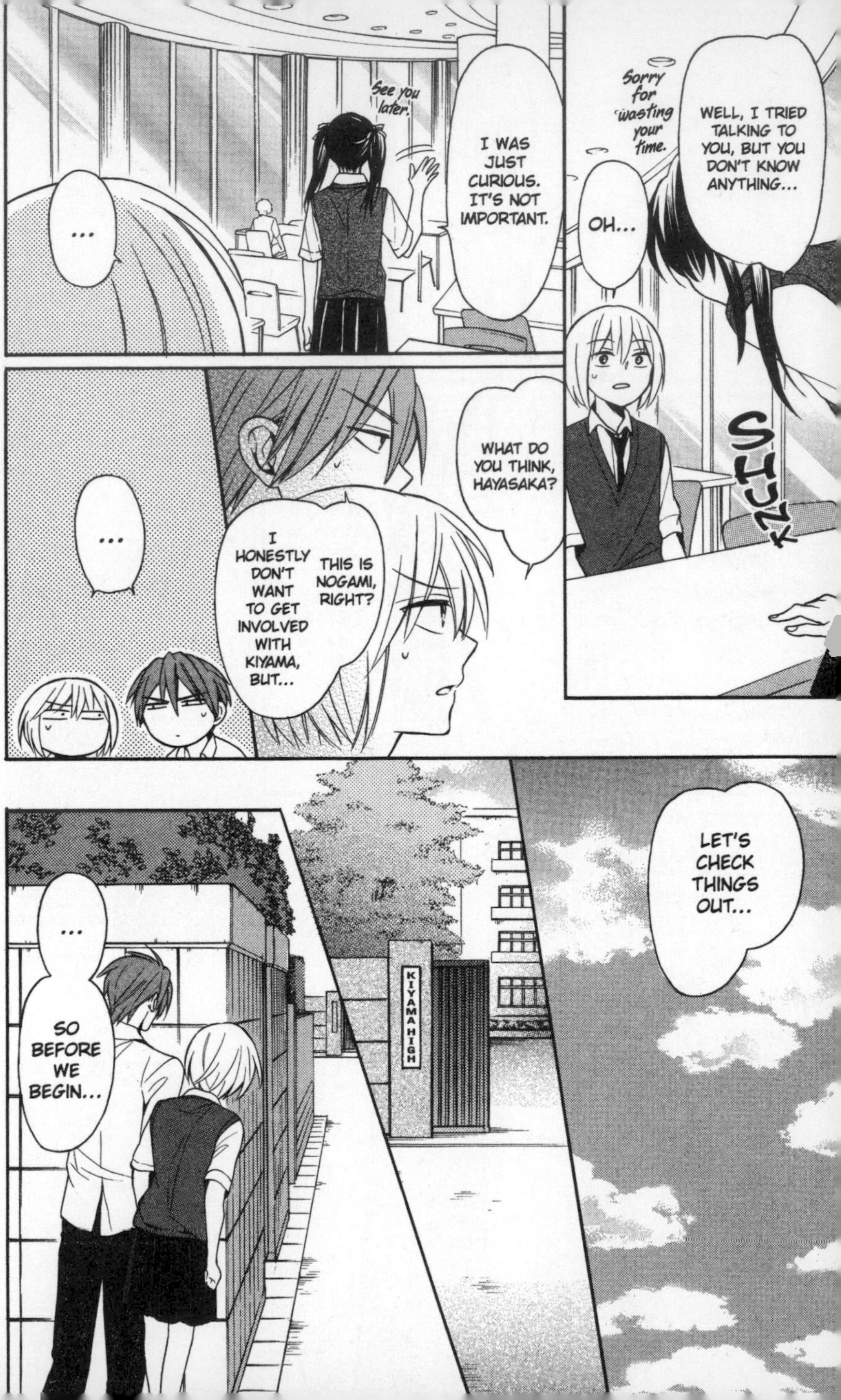
WELL, I TRIED TALKING TO YOU, BUT YOU DON'T KNOW ANYTHING...
Sorry for wasting your time.
OH...
SHUNK
I WAS JUST CURIOUS. IT'S NOT IMPORTANT.
See you later.
...
WHAT DO YOU THINK, HAYASAKA?
THIS IS NOGAMI, RIGHT?
I HONESTLY DON'T WANT TO GET INVOLVED WITH KIYAMA, BUT...
...
LET'S CHECK THINGS OUT...
KIYAMA HIGH
...
SO BEFORE WE BEGIN...

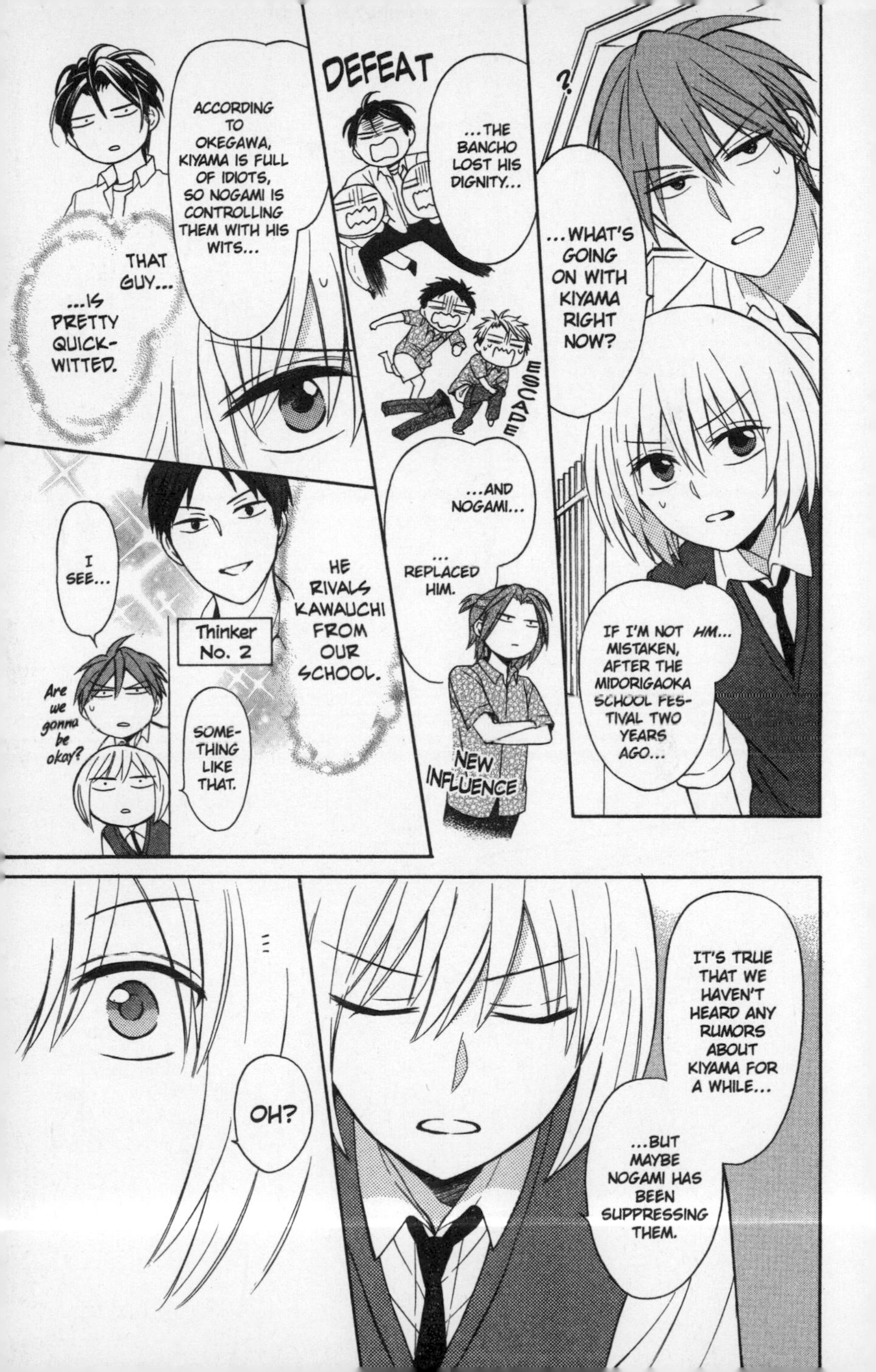
?
...WHAT'S GOING ON WITH KIYAMA RIGHT NOW?
HM...
IF I'M NOT MISTAKEN, AFTER THE MIDORIGAOKA SCHOOL FESTIVAL TWO YEARS AGO...
DEFEAT
...THE BANCHO LOST HIS DIGNITY...
ESCAPE
...AND NOGAMI...
...REPLACED HIM.
NEW INFLUENCE
ACCORDING TO OKEGAWA, KIYAMA IS FULL OF IDIOTS, SO NOGAMI IS CONTROLLING THEM WITH HIS WITS...
THAT GUY...
...IS PRETTY QUICK-WITTED.
HE RIVALS KAWAUCHI FROM OUR SCHOOL.
Thinker No. 2
I SEE...
SOMETHING LIKE THAT.
Are we gonna be okay?
IT'S TRUE THAT WE HAVEN'T HEARD ANY RUMORS ABOUT KIYAMA FOR A WHILE...
...BUT MAYBE NOGAMI HAS BEEN SUPPRESSING THEM.
OH?

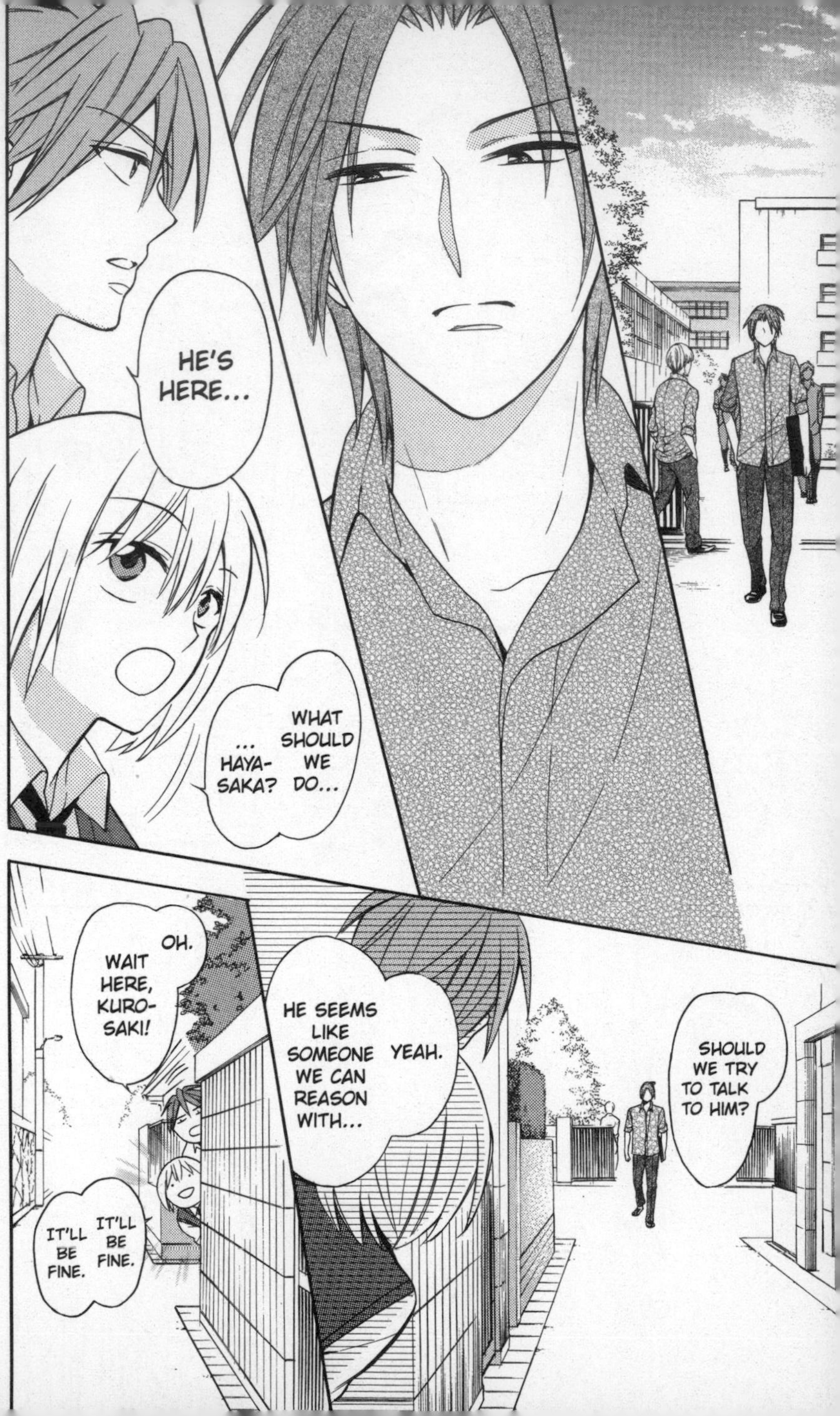
HE'S HERE...
WHAT SHOULD WE DO... ...HAYA-SAKA?
SHOULD WE TRY TO TALK TO HIM?
YEAH.
HE SEEMS LIKE SOMEONE WE CAN REASON WITH...
OH. WAIT HERE, KURO-SAKI!
IT'LL BE FINE. IT'LL BE FINE.

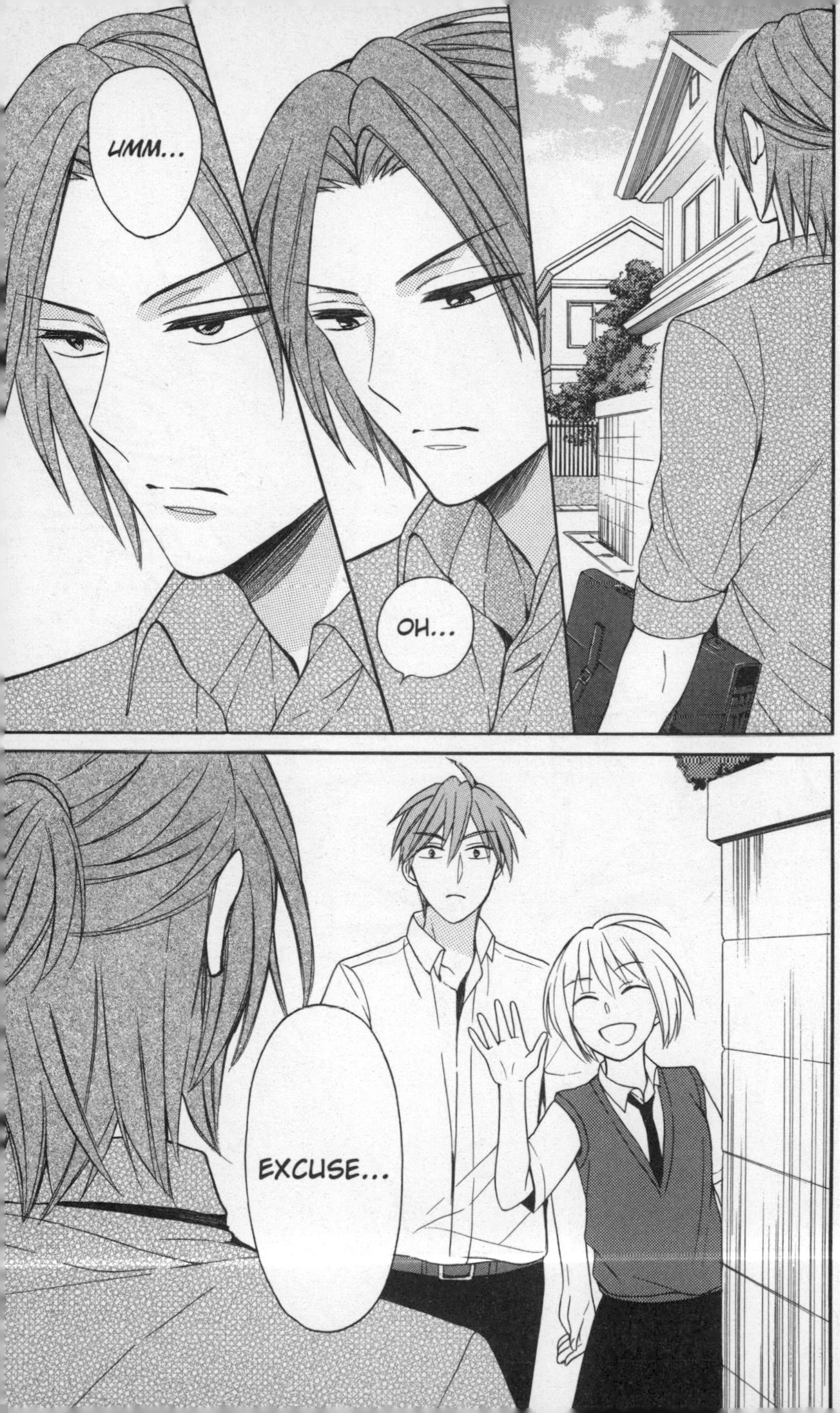
OH...
UMM...
EXCUSE...

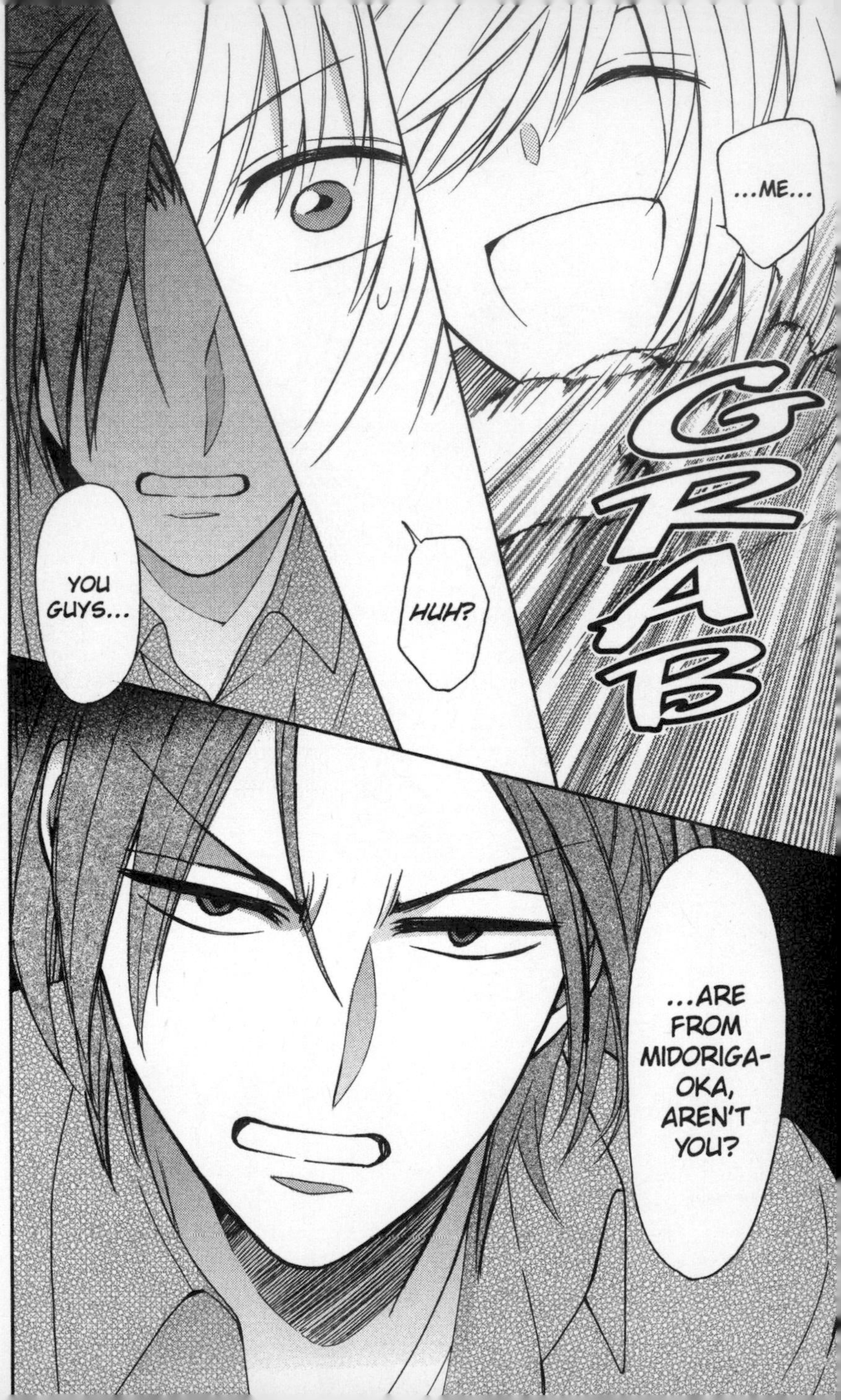
...ME...
GRAB
HUH?
YOU GUYS...
...ARE FROM MIDORIGA-OKA, AREN'T YOU?

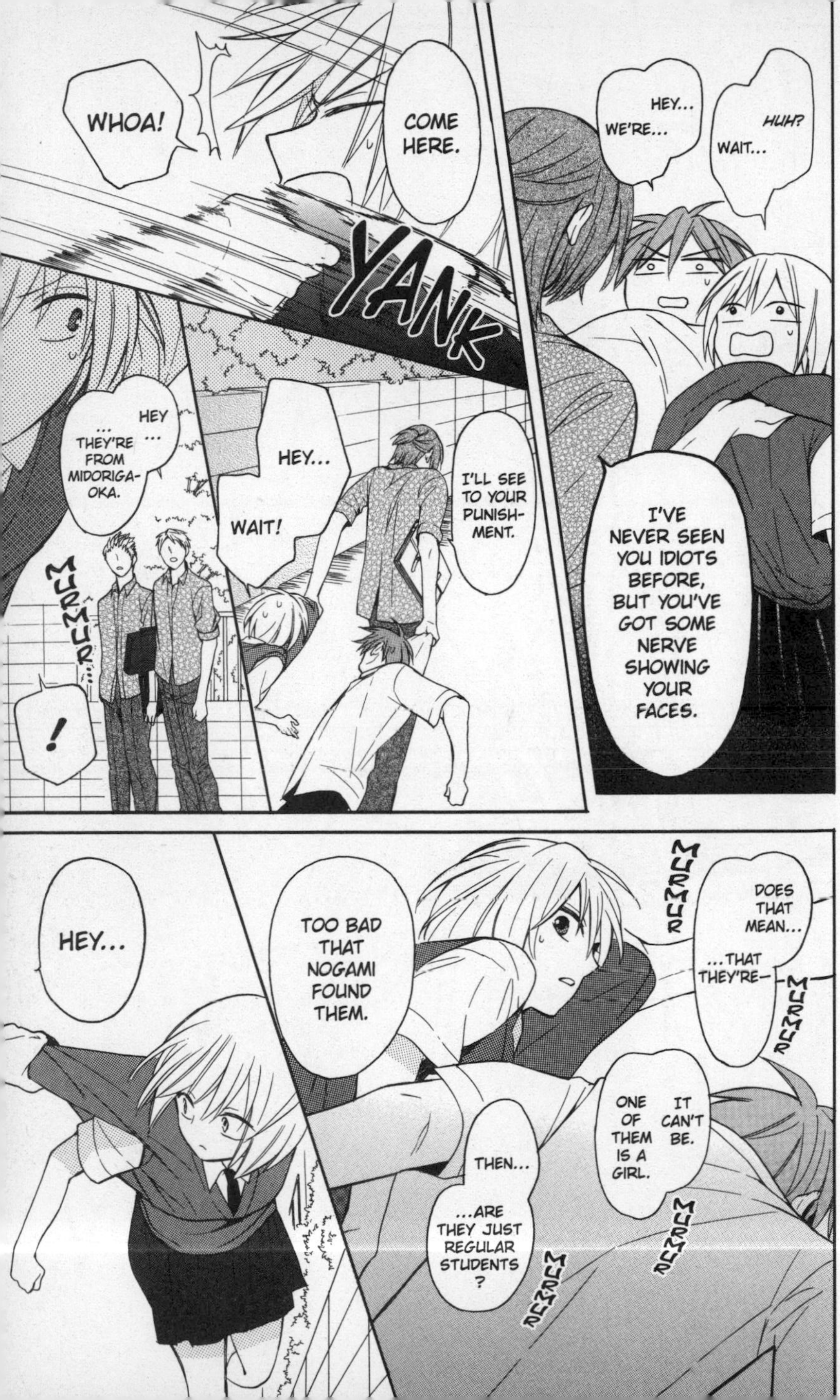
HUH? WAIT...
HEY... WE'RE...
I'VE NEVER SEEN YOU IDIOTS BEFORE, BUT YOU'VE GOT SOME NERVE SHOWING YOUR FACES.
COME HERE.
WHOA!
YANK
I'LL SEE TO YOUR PUNISHMENT.
HEY... WAIT!
HEY... ...THEY'RE FROM MIDORIGA-OKA.
MURMUR...
!
MURMUR
DOES THAT MEAN... ...THAT THEY'RE—
MURMUR
IT CAN'T BE. ONE OF THEM IS A GIRL.
MURMUR
THEN... ...ARE THEY JUST REGULAR STUDENTS?
MURMUR
TOO BAD THAT NOGAMI FOUND THEM.
HEY...

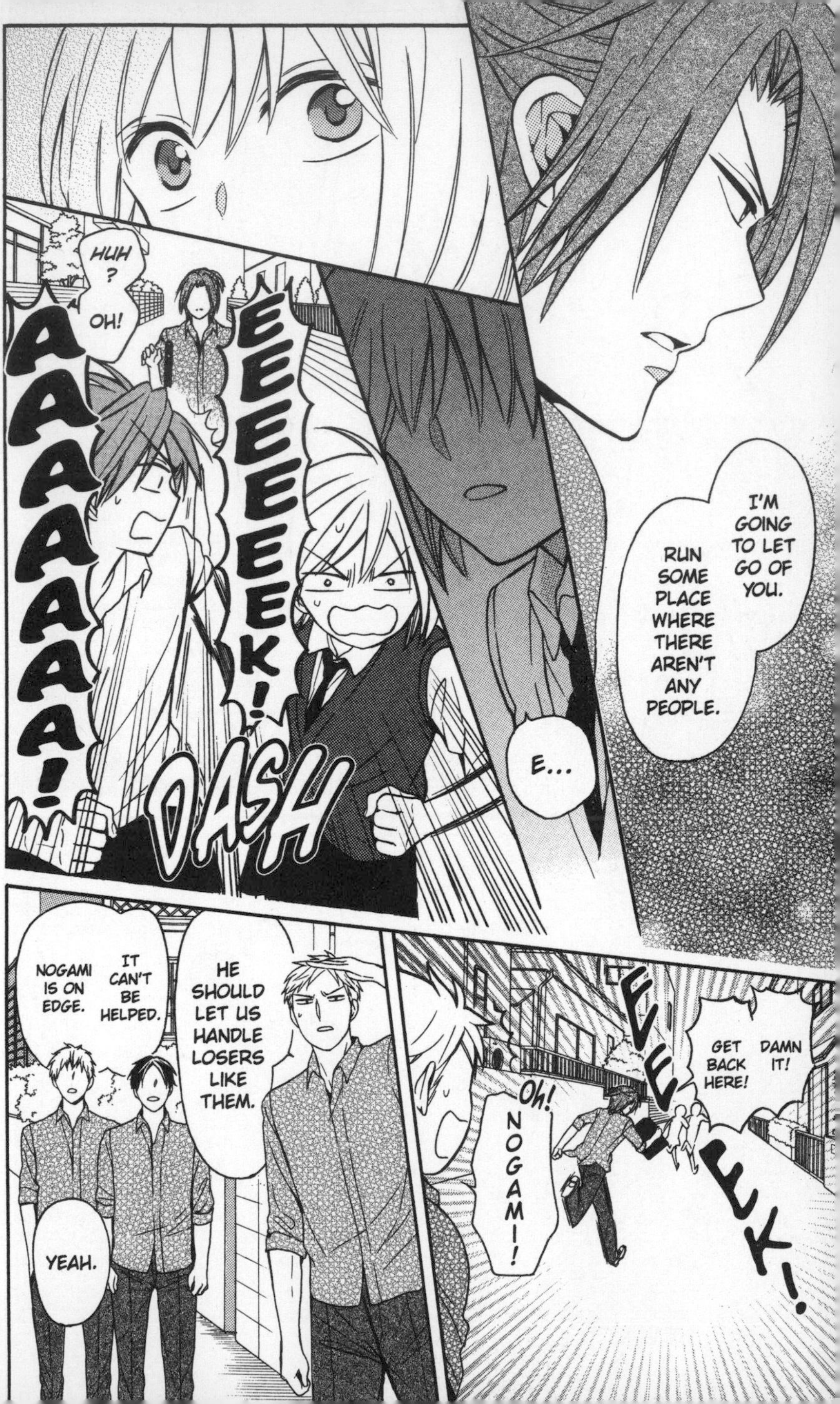
I'M GOING TO LET GO OF YOU.
RUN SOME PLACE WHERE THERE AREN'T ANY PEOPLE.
E...
HUH? OH!
AAAAAAAAI!
EEEEEEEEK!
DASH
DAMN IT!
GET BACK HERE!
EEEEK!
Oh! NOGAMI!
HE SHOULD LET US HANDLE LOSERS LIKE THEM.
IT CAN'T BE HELPED.
NOGAMI IS ON EDGE.
YEAH.

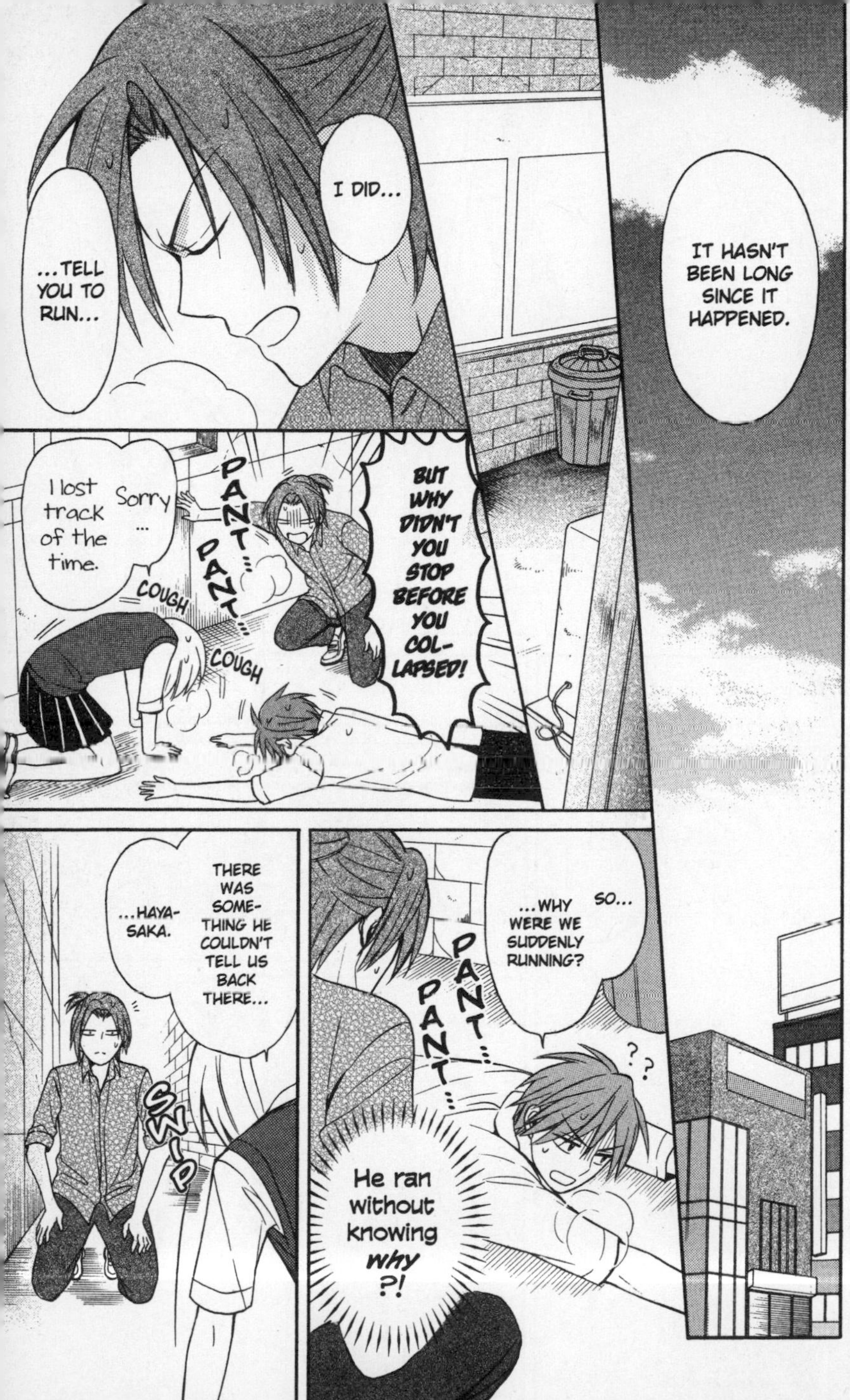
IT HASN'T BEEN LONG SINCE IT HAPPENED.
I DID...
...TELL YOU TO RUN...
BUT WHY DIDN'T YOU STOP BEFORE YOU COL-LAPSED!
PANT... PANT...
Sorry...
I lost track of the time.
COUGH
COUGH
SO...
...WHY WERE WE SUDDENLY RUNNING?
PANT... PANT...
??
He ran without knowing why?!
...HAYA-SAKA.
THERE WAS SOME-THING HE COULDN'T TELL US BACK THERE...
SWIP

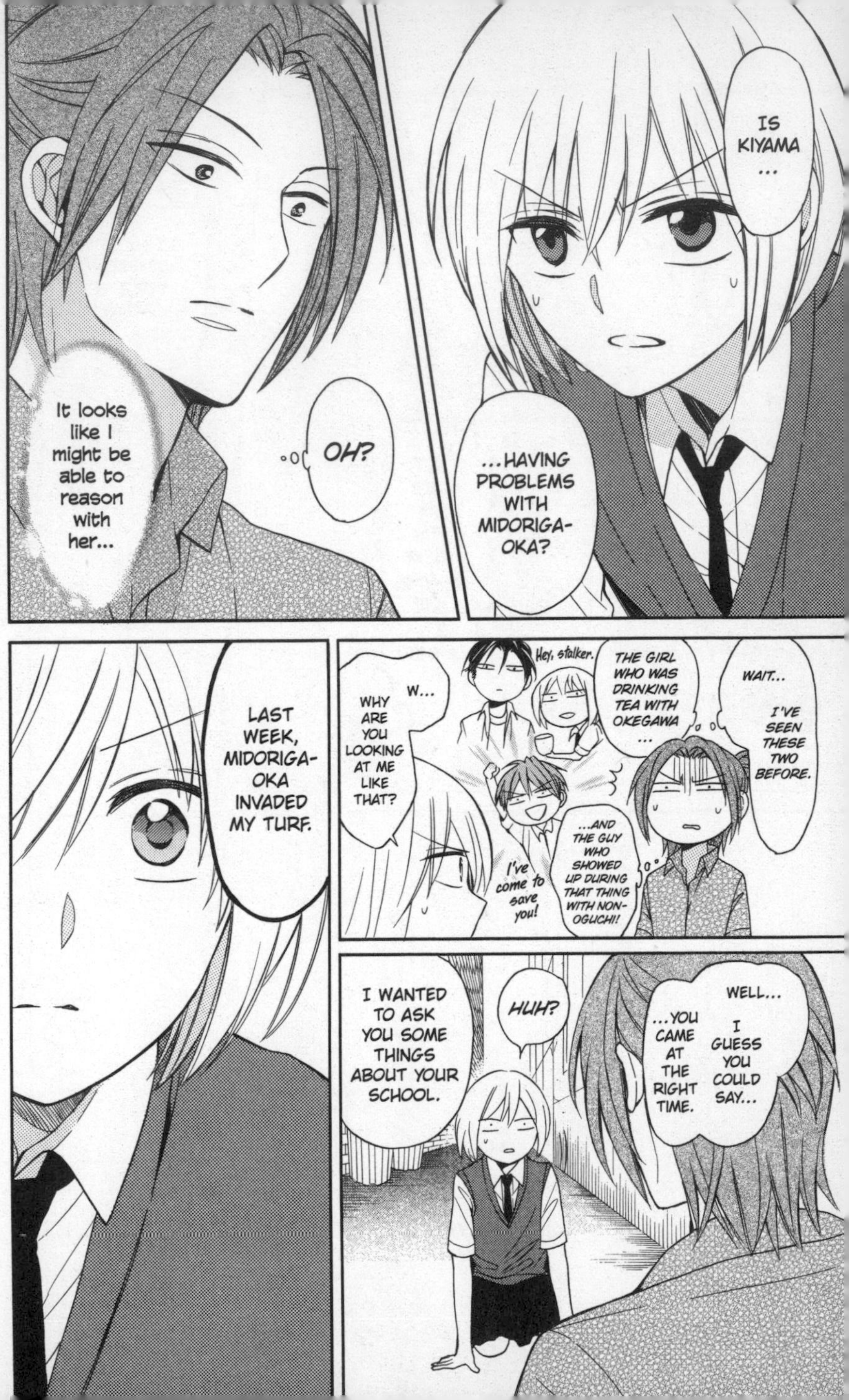
IS KIYAMA ...
...HAVING PROBLEMS WITH MIDORIGA-OKA?
OH?
It looks like I might be able to reason with her...
WAIT... I'VE SEEN THESE TWO BEFORE.
THE GIRL WHO WAS DRINKING TEA WITH OKEGAWA ...
Hey, stalker.
...AND THE GUY WHO SHOWED UP DURING THAT THING WITH NON-OGUCHI!
I've come to save you!
W... WHY ARE YOU LOOKING AT ME LIKE THAT?
WELL... I GUESS YOU COULD SAY...
...YOU CAME AT THE RIGHT TIME.
HUH?
I WANTED TO ASK YOU SOME THINGS ABOUT YOUR SCHOOL.
LAST WEEK, MIDORIGA-OKA INVADED MY TURF.

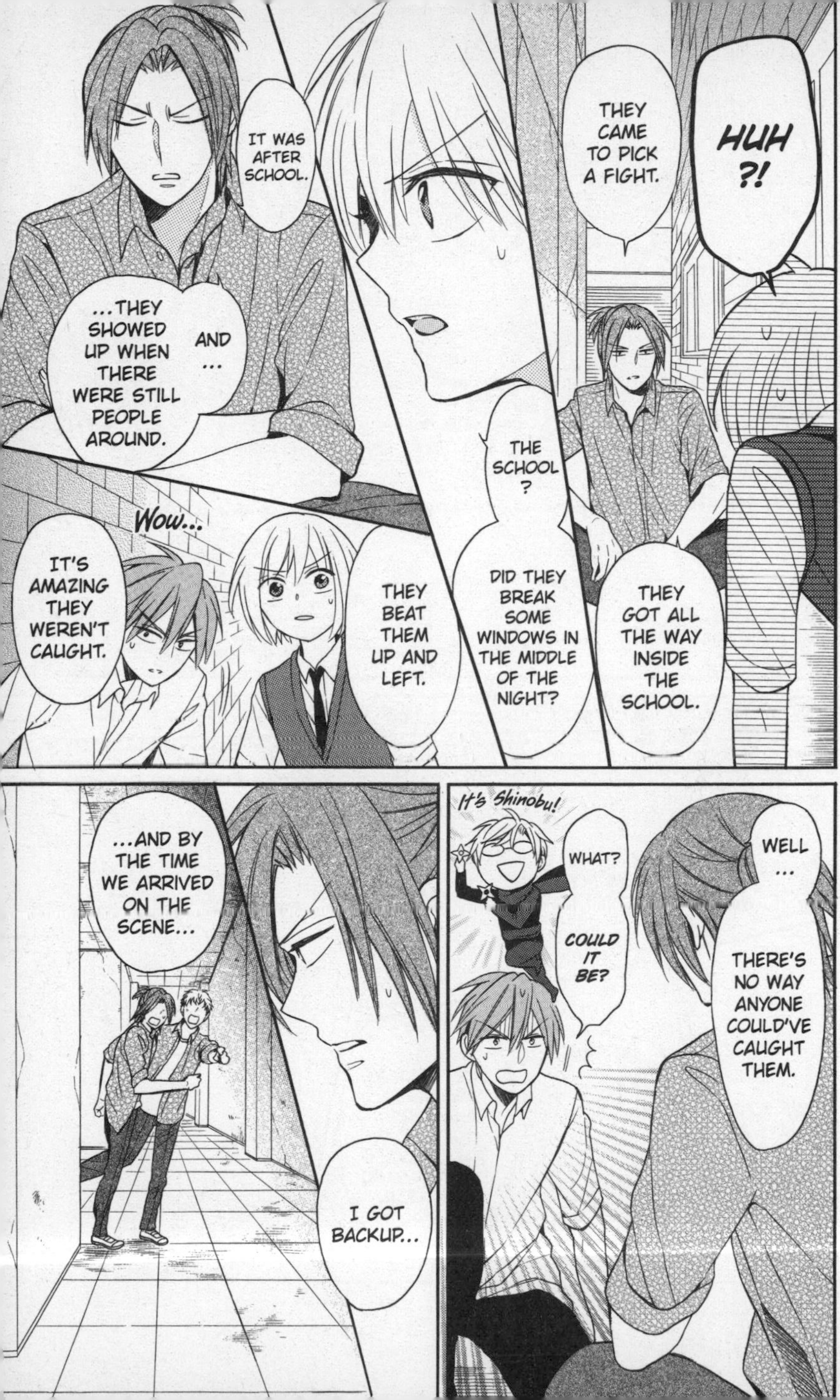
HUH ?!
THEY CAME TO PICK A FIGHT.
THEY GOT ALL THE WAY INSIDE THE SCHOOL.
THE SCHOOL ?
DID THEY BREAK SOME WINDOWS IN THE MIDDLE OF THE NIGHT?
IT WAS AFTER SCHOOL.
AND...
...THEY SHOWED UP WHEN THERE WERE STILL PEOPLE AROUND.
THEY BEAT THEM UP AND LEFT.
Wow...
IT'S AMAZING THEY WEREN'T CAUGHT.
WELL...
THERE'S NO WAY ANYONE COULD'VE CAUGHT THEM.
WHAT?
COULD IT BE?
It's Shinobu!
I GOT BACKUP...
...AND BY THE TIME WE ARRIVED ON THE SCENE...

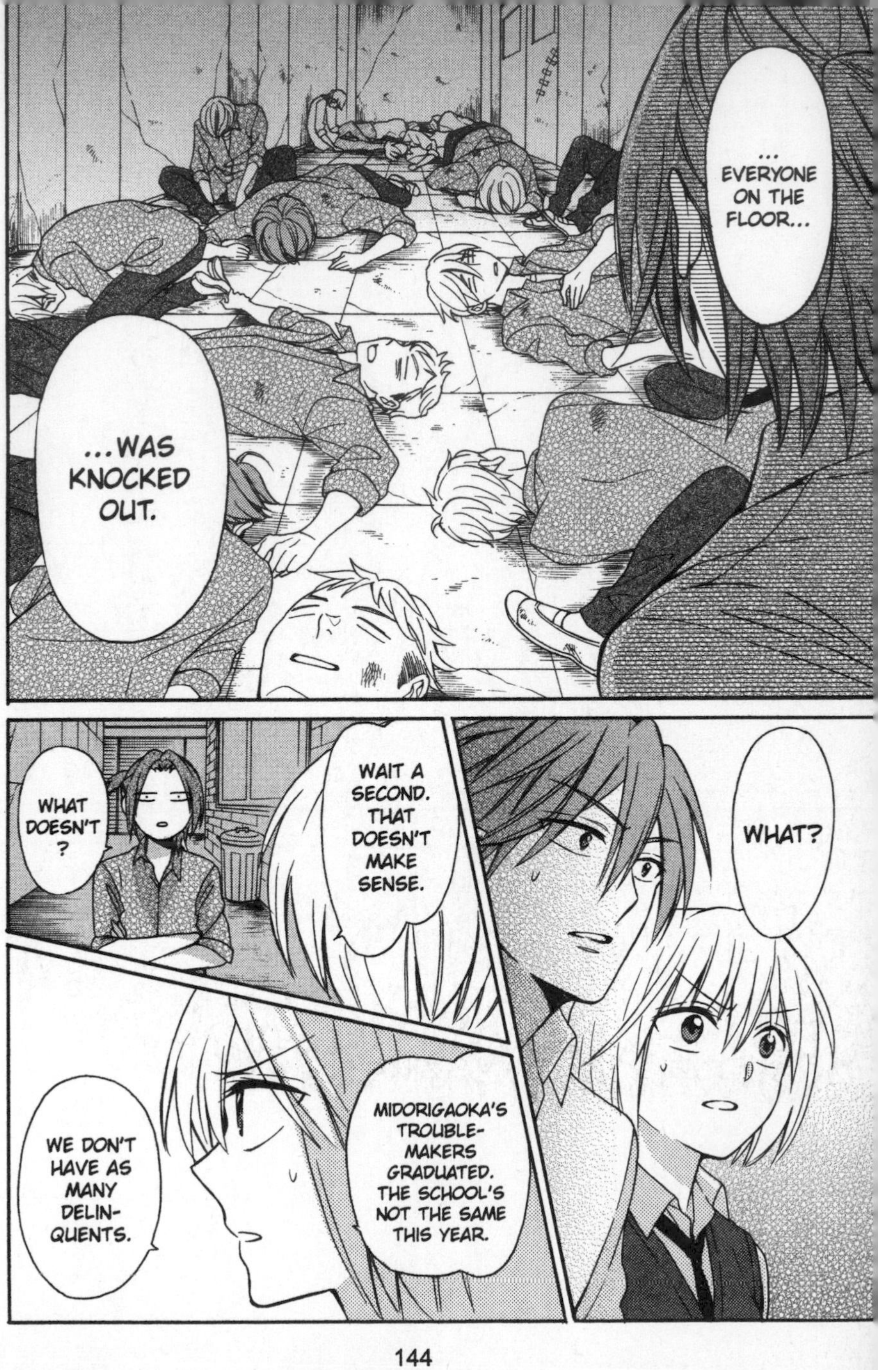
...EVERYONE ON THE FLOOR...
...WAS KNOCKED OUT.
WHAT?
WAIT A SECOND. THAT DOESN'T MAKE SENSE.
WHAT DOESN'T?
MIDORIGAOKA'S TROUBLE-MAKERS GRADUATED. THE SCHOOL'S NOT THE SAME THIS YEAR.
WE DON'T HAVE AS MANY DELIN-QUENTS.

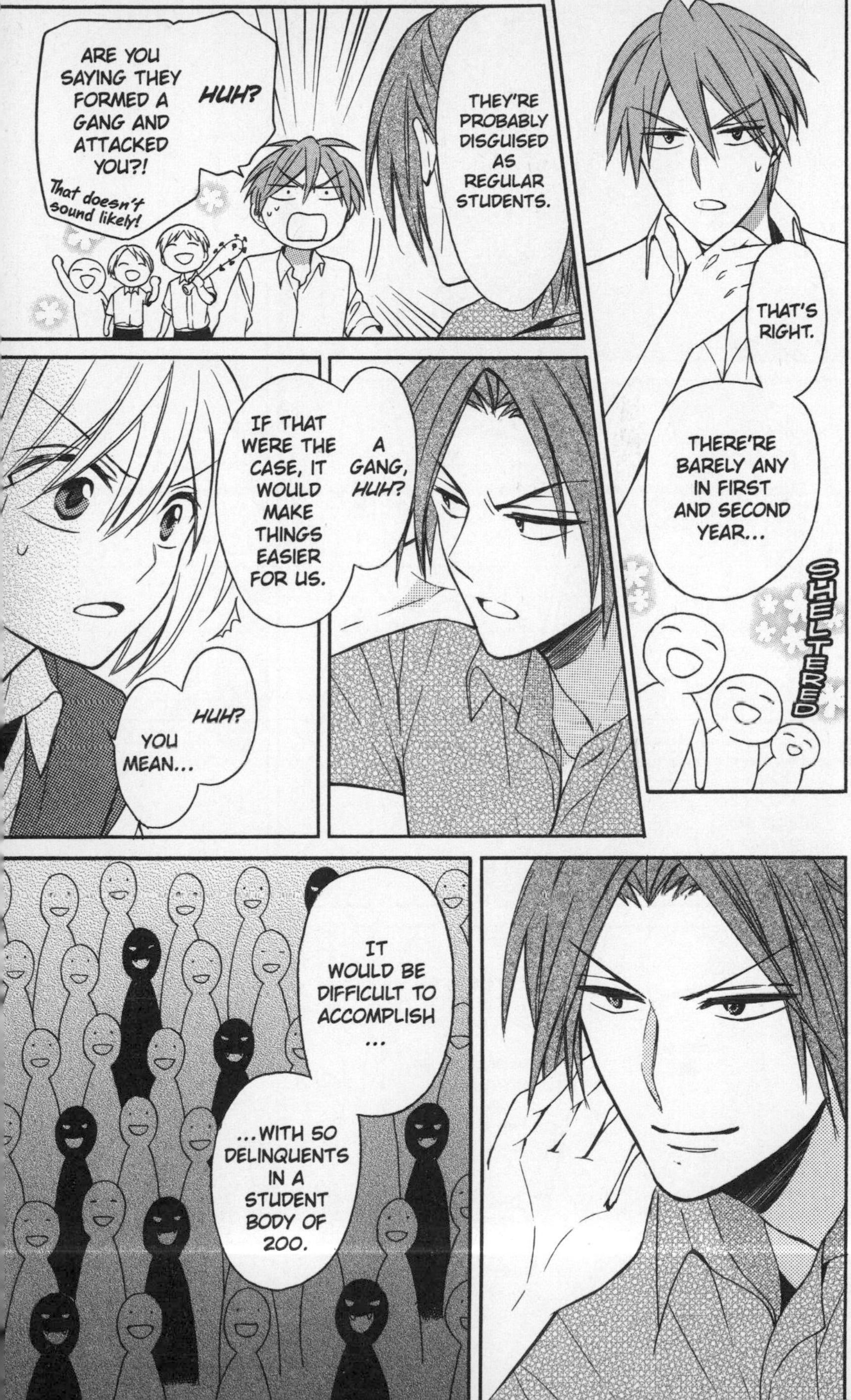
THAT'S RIGHT.
THERE'RE BARELY ANY IN FIRST AND SECOND YEAR...
SHELTERED
THEY'RE PROBABLY DISGUISED AS REGULAR STUDENTS.
HUH?
ARE YOU SAYING THEY FORMED A GANG AND ATTACKED YOU?!
That doesn't sound likely!
A GANG, HUH?
IF THAT WERE THE CASE, IT WOULD MAKE THINGS EASIER FOR US.
HUH? YOU MEAN...
IT WOULD BE DIFFICULT TO ACCOMPLISH ...
...WITH 50 DELINQUENTS IN A STUDENT BODY OF 200.

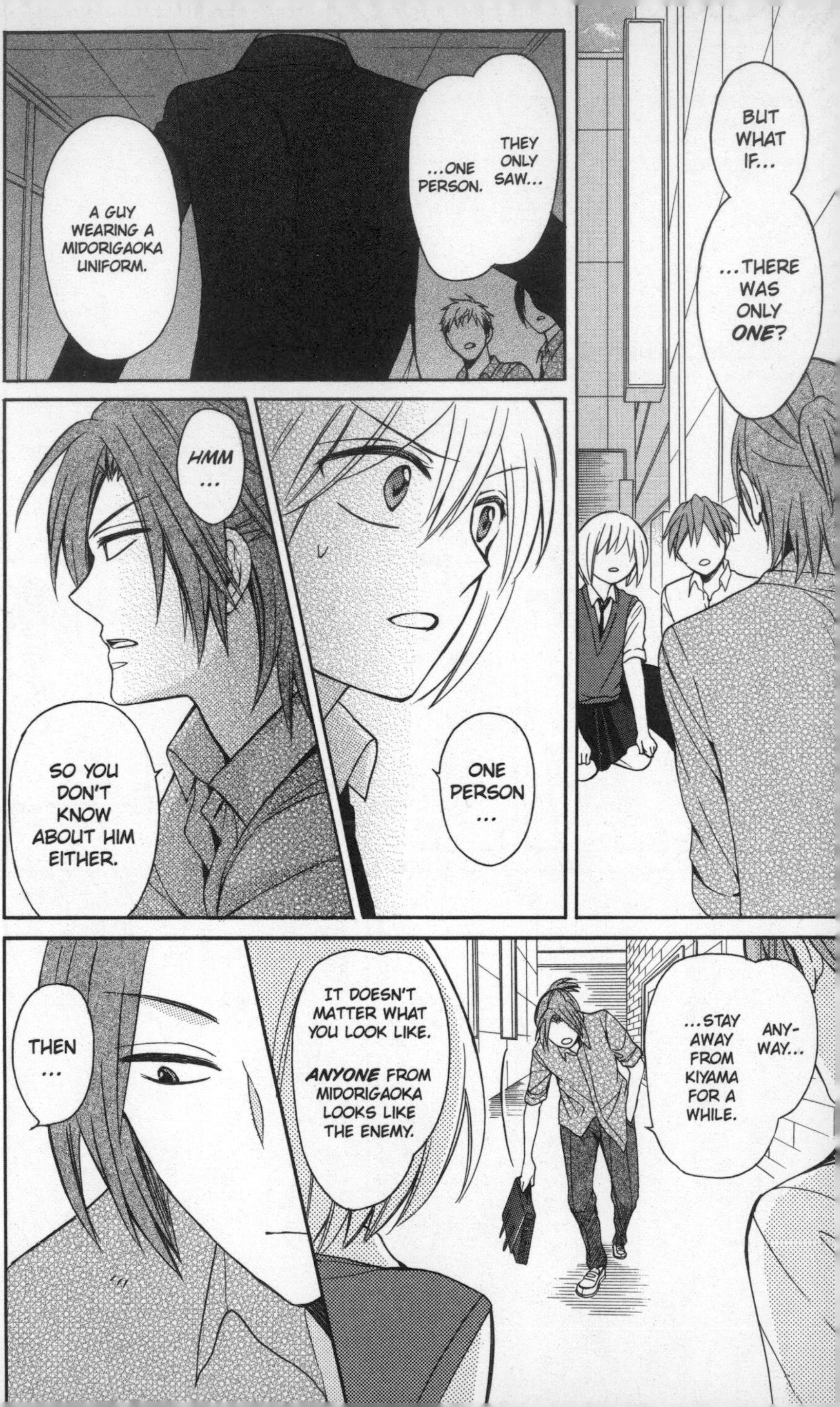

BUT WHAT IF...
...THERE WAS ONLY ONE?
THEY ONLY SAW...
...ONE PERSON.
A GUY WEARING A MIDORIGAOKA UNIFORM.
ONE PERSON...
HMM...
SO YOU DON'T KNOW ABOUT HIM EITHER.
ANY-WAY...
...STAY AWAY FROM KIYAMA FOR A WHILE.
IT DOESN'T MATTER WHAT YOU LOOK LIKE.
ANYONE FROM MIDORIGAOKA LOOKS LIKE THE ENEMY.
THEN...

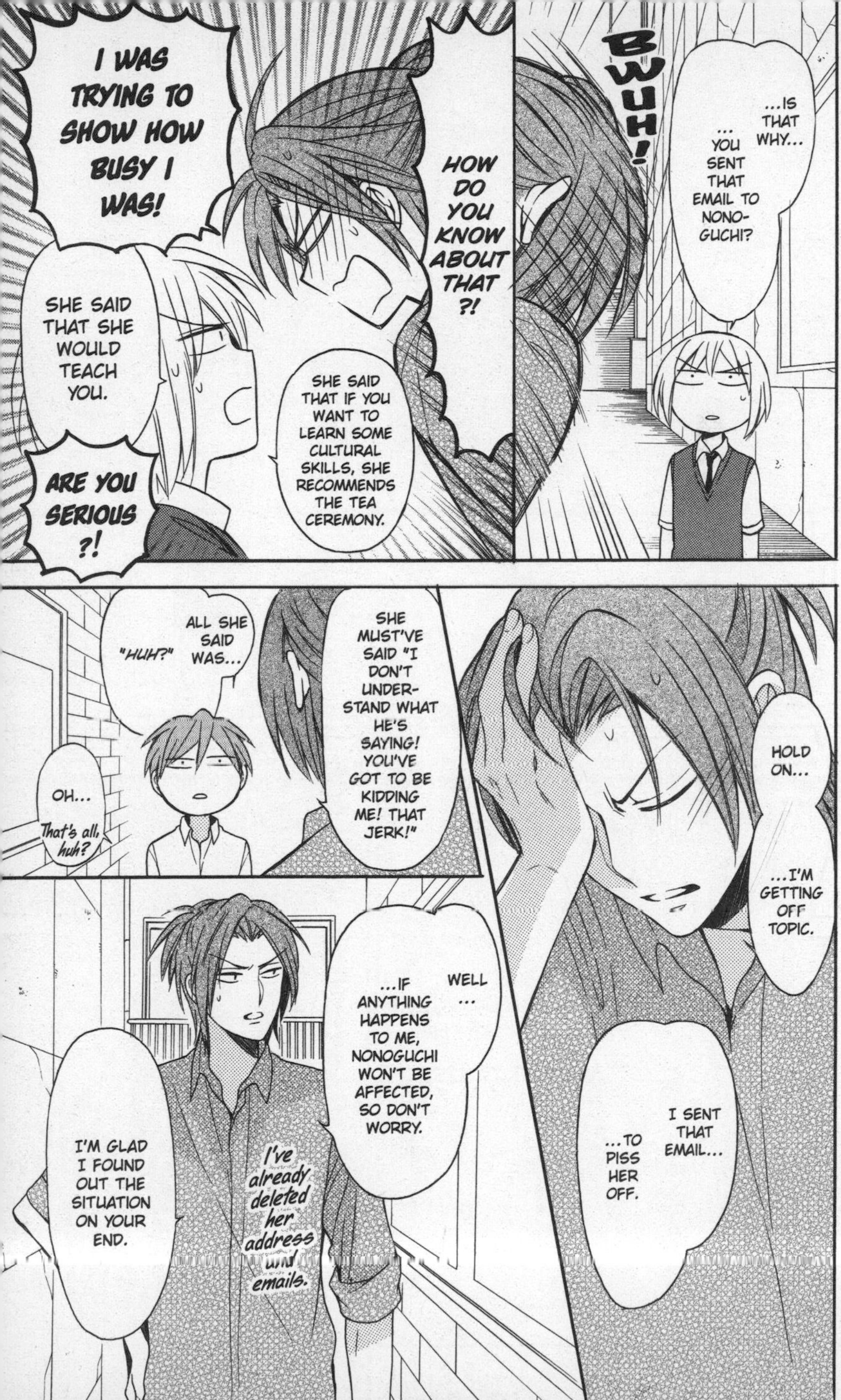
BWUH!
...IS THAT WHY...
...YOU SENT THAT EMAIL TO NONO-GUCHI?
HOW DO YOU KNOW ABOUT THAT?!
I WAS TRYING TO SHOW HOW BUSY I WAS!
SHE SAID THAT SHE WOULD TEACH YOU.
SHE SAID THAT IF YOU WANT TO LEARN SOME CULTURAL SKILLS, SHE RECOMMENDS THE TEA CEREMONY.
ARE YOU SERIOUS?!
HOLD ON...
...I'M GETTING OFF TOPIC.
I SENT THAT EMAIL...
...TO PISS HER OFF.
SHE MUST'VE SAID "I DON'T UNDER-STAND WHAT HE'S SAYING! YOU'VE GOT TO BE KIDDING ME! THAT JERK!"
ALL SHE SAID WAS...
"HUH?"
OH...
That's all, huh?
WELL...
...IF ANYTHING HAPPENS TO ME, NONOGUCHI WON'T BE AFFECTED, SO DON'T WORRY.
I've already deleted her address and emails.
I'M GLAD I FOUND OUT THE SITUATION ON YOUR END.

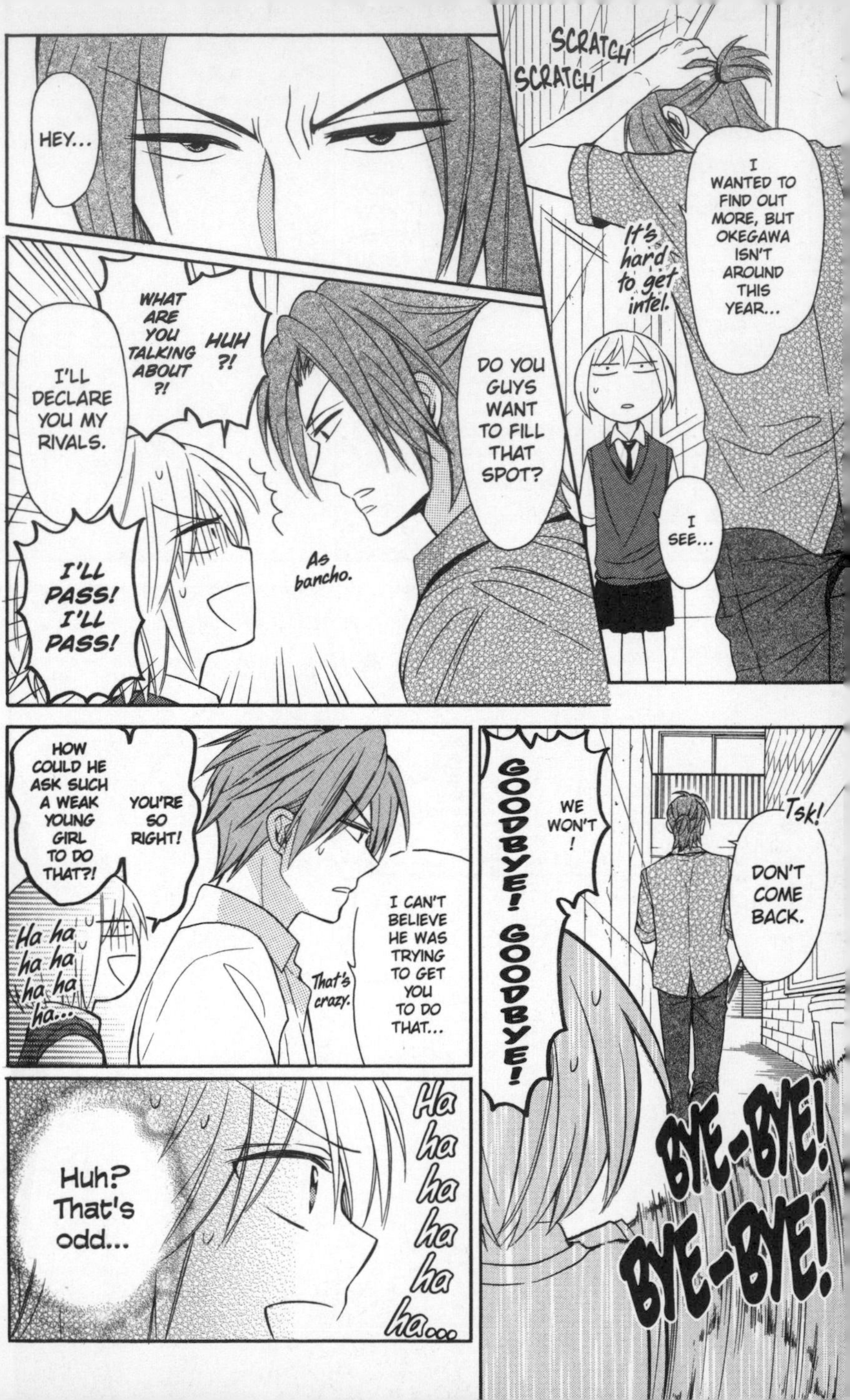
SCRATCH SCRATCH
I WANTED TO FIND OUT MORE, BUT OKEGAWA ISN'T AROUND THIS YEAR...
It's hard to get intel.
DO YOU GUYS WANT TO FILL THAT SPOT?
I SEE...
HEY...
I'LL DECLARE YOU MY RIVALS.
HUH ?!
WHAT ARE YOU TALKING ABOUT ?!
As bancho.
I'LL PASS! I'LL PASS!
Tsk!
DON'T COME BACK.
WE WON'T !
GOODBYE! GOOODBYE!
BYE-BYE! BYE-BYE!
HOW COULD HE ASK SUCH A WEAK YOUNG GIRL TO DO THAT?!
YOU'RE SO RIGHT!
I CAN'T BELIEVE HE WAS TRYING TO GET YOU TO DO THAT...
That's crazy.
Ha ha ha ha ha ha ha...
Ha ha ha ha ha ha ha...
Huh? That's odd...

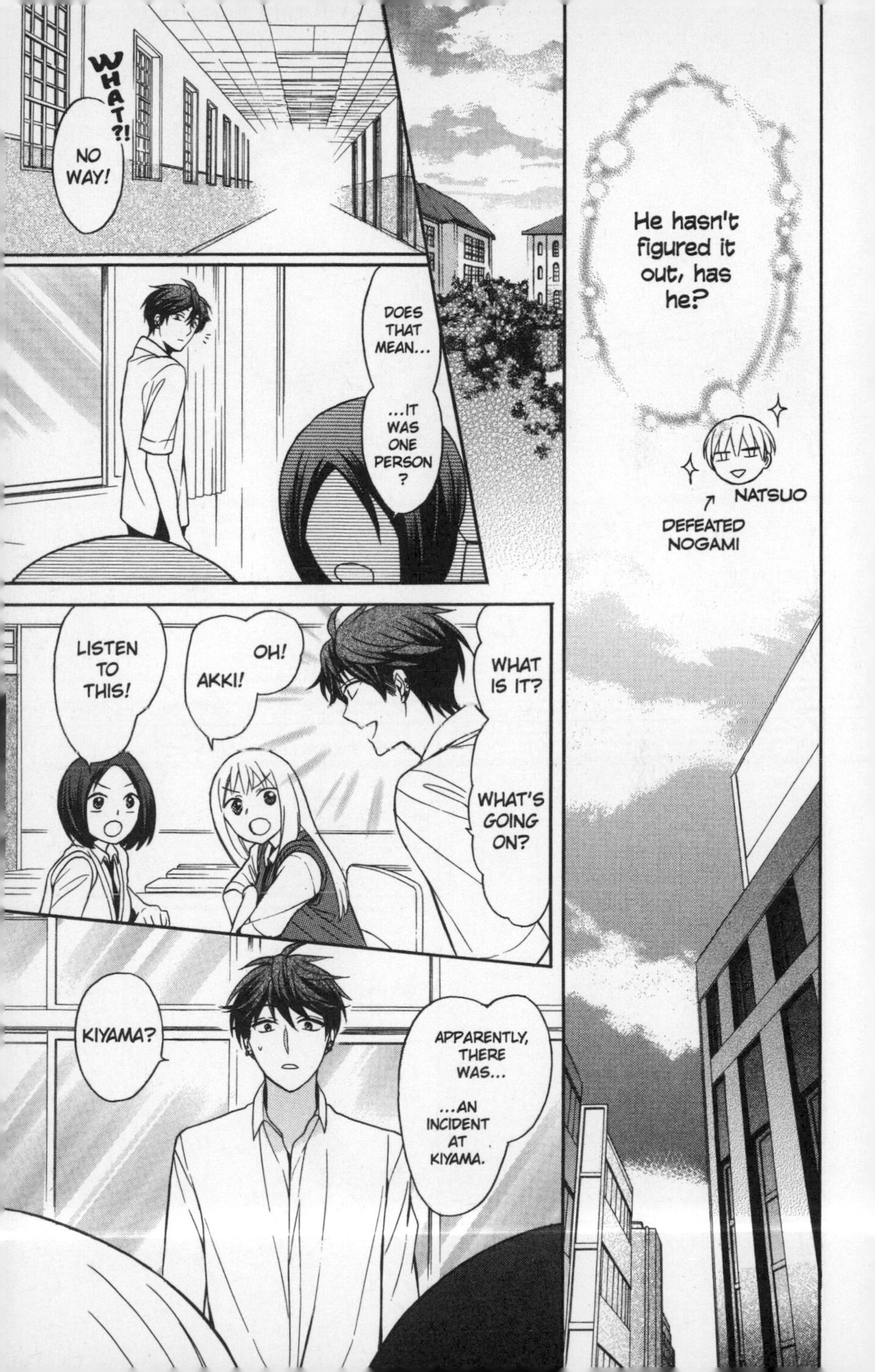
He hasn't figured it out, has he?
NATSUO
DEFEATED NOGAMI
WHAT?!
NO WAY!
DOES THAT MEAN...
...IT WAS ONE PERSON?
WHAT IS IT?
WHAT'S GOING ON?
OH!
AKKI!
LISTEN TO THIS!
APPARENTLY, THERE WAS...
...AN INCIDENT AT KIYAMA.
KIYAMA?

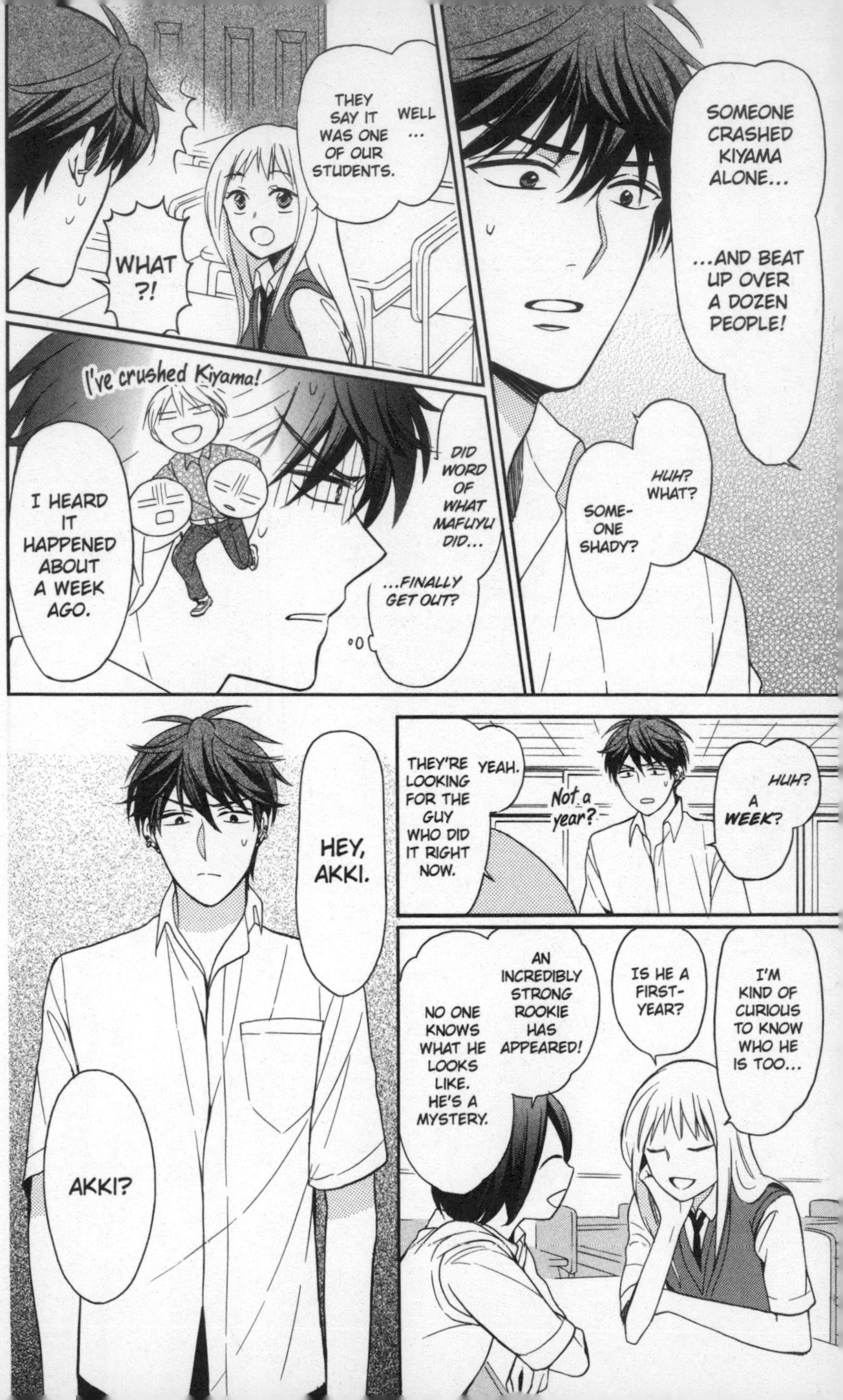
SOMEONE CRASHED KIYAMA ALONE...
...AND BEAT UP OVER A DOZEN PEOPLE!
HUH? WHAT?
SOME-ONE SHADY?
WELL...
THEY SAY IT WAS ONE OF OUR STUDENTS.
WHAT?!
DID WORD OF WHAT MAFUYU DID...
...FINALLY GET OUT?
I've crushed Kiyama!
I HEARD IT HAPPENED ABOUT A WEEK AGO.
HUH? A WEEK?
Not a year?
YEAH.
THEY'RE LOOKING FOR THE GUY WHO DID IT RIGHT NOW.
I'M KIND OF CURIOUS TO KNOW WHO HE IS TOO...
IS HE A FIRST-YEAR?
AN INCREDIBLY STRONG ROOKIE HAS APPEARED!
NO ONE KNOWS WHAT HE LOOKS LIKE. HE'S A MYSTERY.
HEY, AKKI.
AKKI?

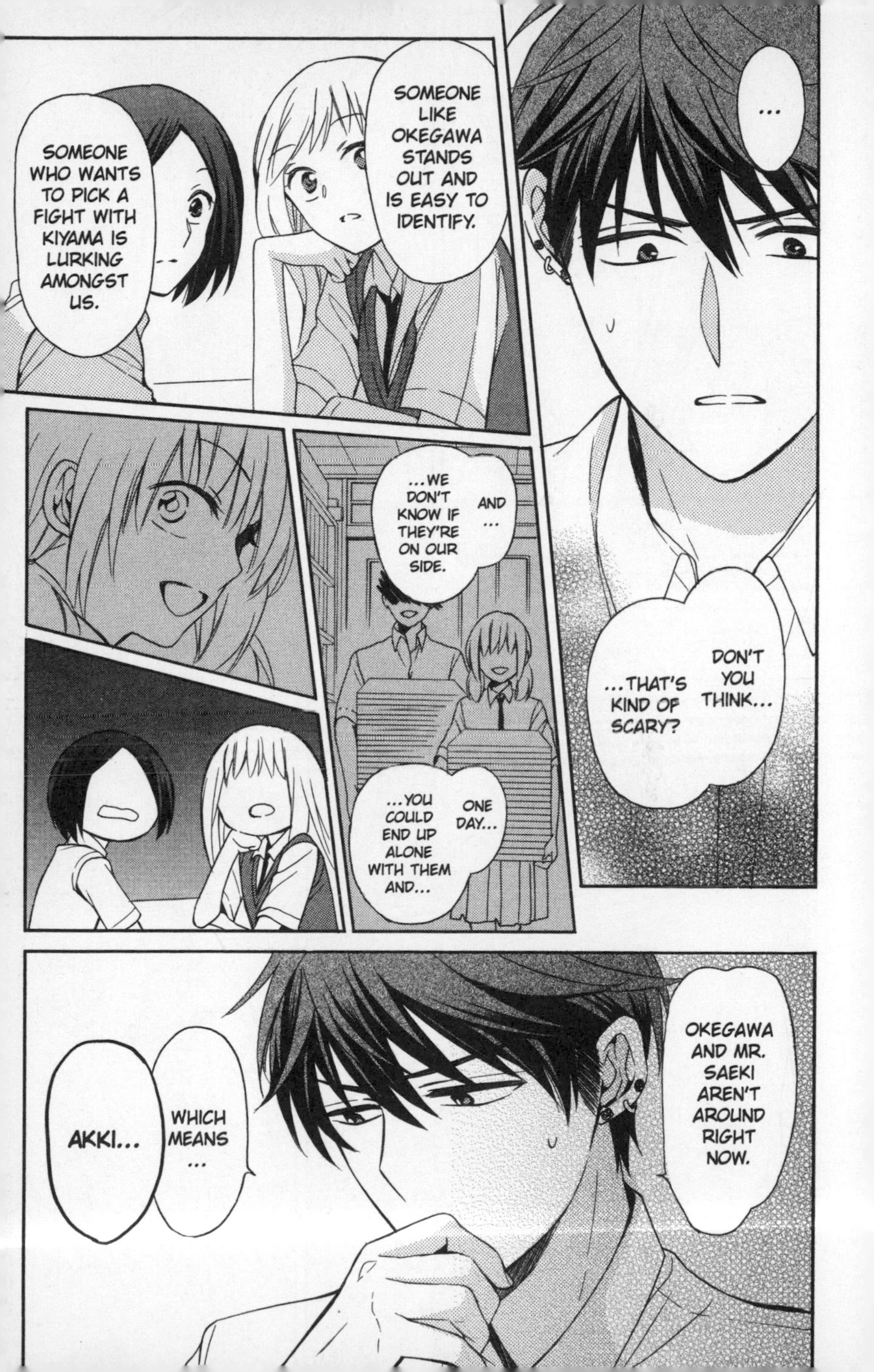
...
DON'T YOU THINK...
...THAT'S KIND OF SCARY?
SOMEONE LIKE OKEGAWA STANDS OUT AND IS EASY TO IDENTIFY.
SOMEONE WHO WANTS TO PICK A FIGHT WITH KIYAMA IS LURKING AMONGST US.
AND...
...WE DON'T KNOW IF THEY'RE ON OUR SIDE.
ONE DAY...
...YOU COULD END UP ALONE WITH THEM AND...
OKEGAWA AND MR. SAEKI AREN'T AROUND RIGHT NOW.
WHICH MEANS...
AKKI...

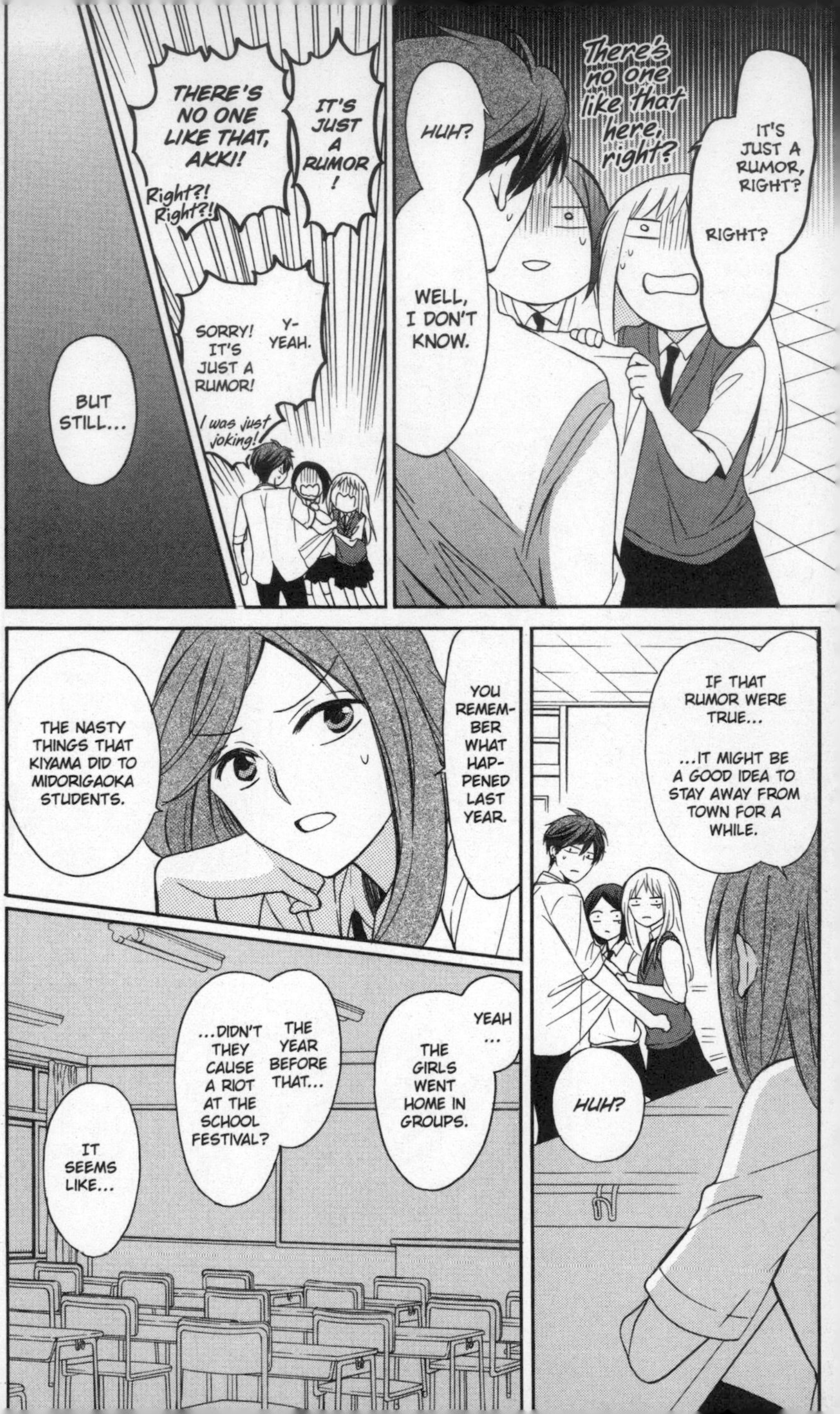
There's no one like that here, right?
IT'S JUST A RUMOR, RIGHT?
RIGHT?
HUH?
WELL, I DON'T KNOW.
IT'S JUST A RUMOR!
THERE'S NO ONE LIKE THAT, AKKI!
Right?! Right?!
Y-YEAH.
SORRY! IT'S JUST A RUMOR!
I was just joking!
BUT STILL...
IF THAT RUMOR WERE TRUE...
...IT MIGHT BE A GOOD IDEA TO STAY AWAY FROM TOWN FOR A WHILE.
HUH?
YOU REMEMBER WHAT HAPPENED LAST YEAR.
THE NASTY THINGS THAT KIYAMA DID TO MIDORIGAOKA STUDENTS.
YEAH...
THE GIRLS WENT HOME IN GROUPS.
THE YEAR BEFORE THAT...
...DIDN'T THEY CAUSE A RIOT AT THE SCHOOL FESTIVAL?
IT SEEMS LIKE...

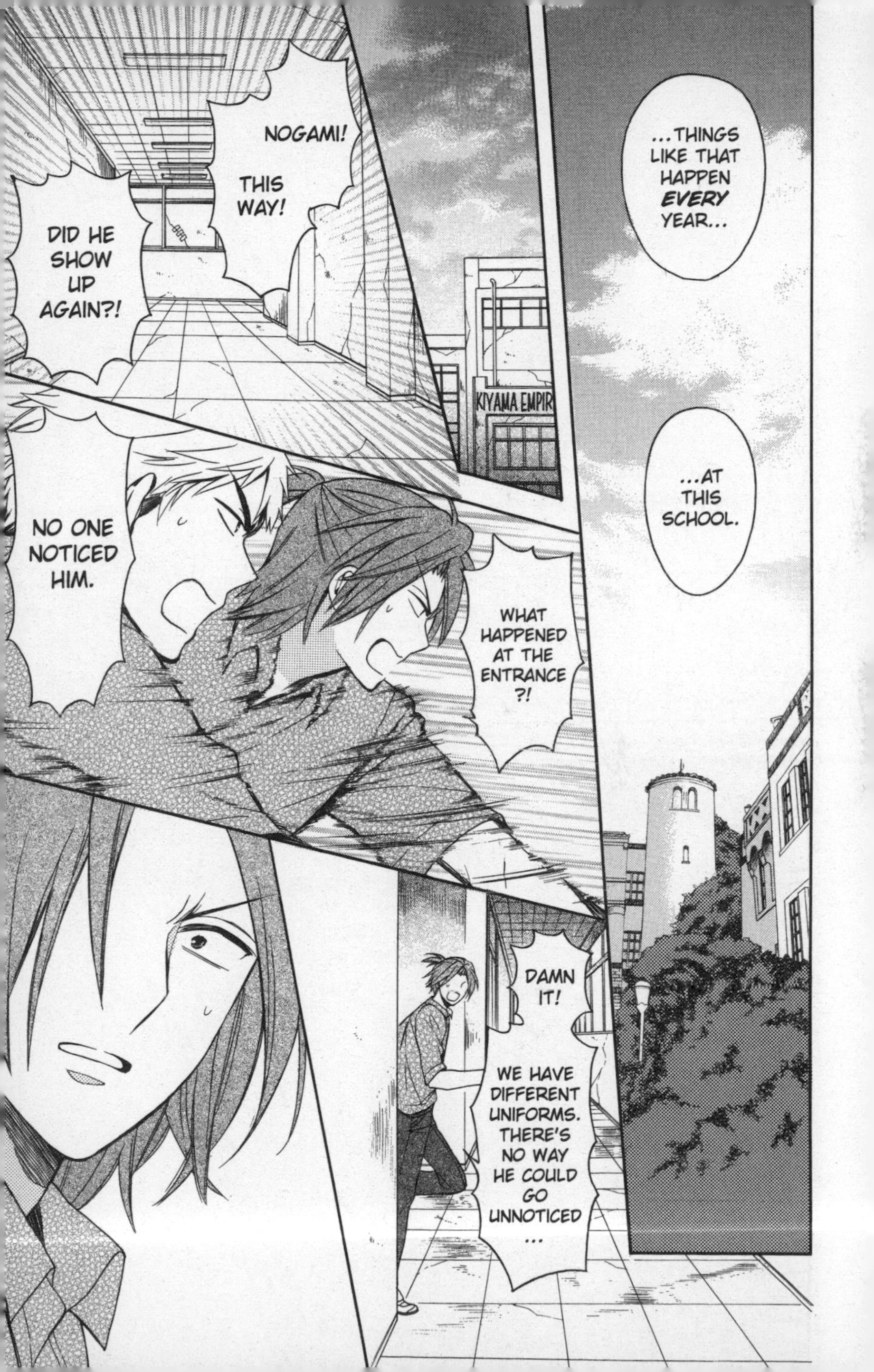
...THINGS LIKE THAT HAPPEN EVERY YEAR...
...AT THIS SCHOOL.
KIYAMA EMPIR
NOGAMI!
THIS WAY!
DID HE SHOW UP AGAIN?!
WHAT HAPPENED AT THE ENTRANCE ?!
NO ONE NOTICED HIM.
DAMN IT!
WE HAVE DIFFERENT UNIFORMS. THERE'S NO WAY HE COULD GO UNNOTICED ...

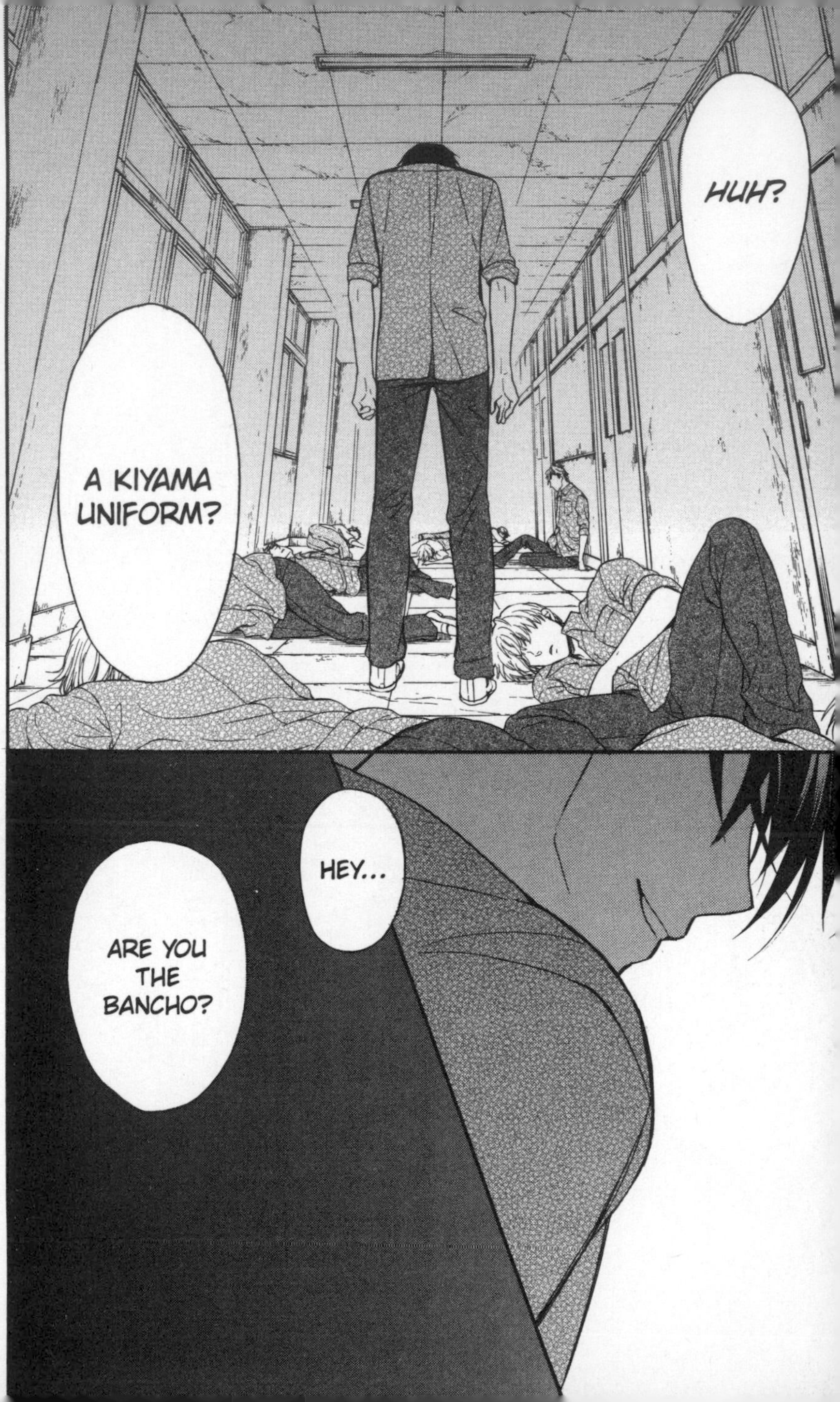
HUH?
A KIYAMA UNIFORM?
HEY...
ARE YOU THE BANCHO?

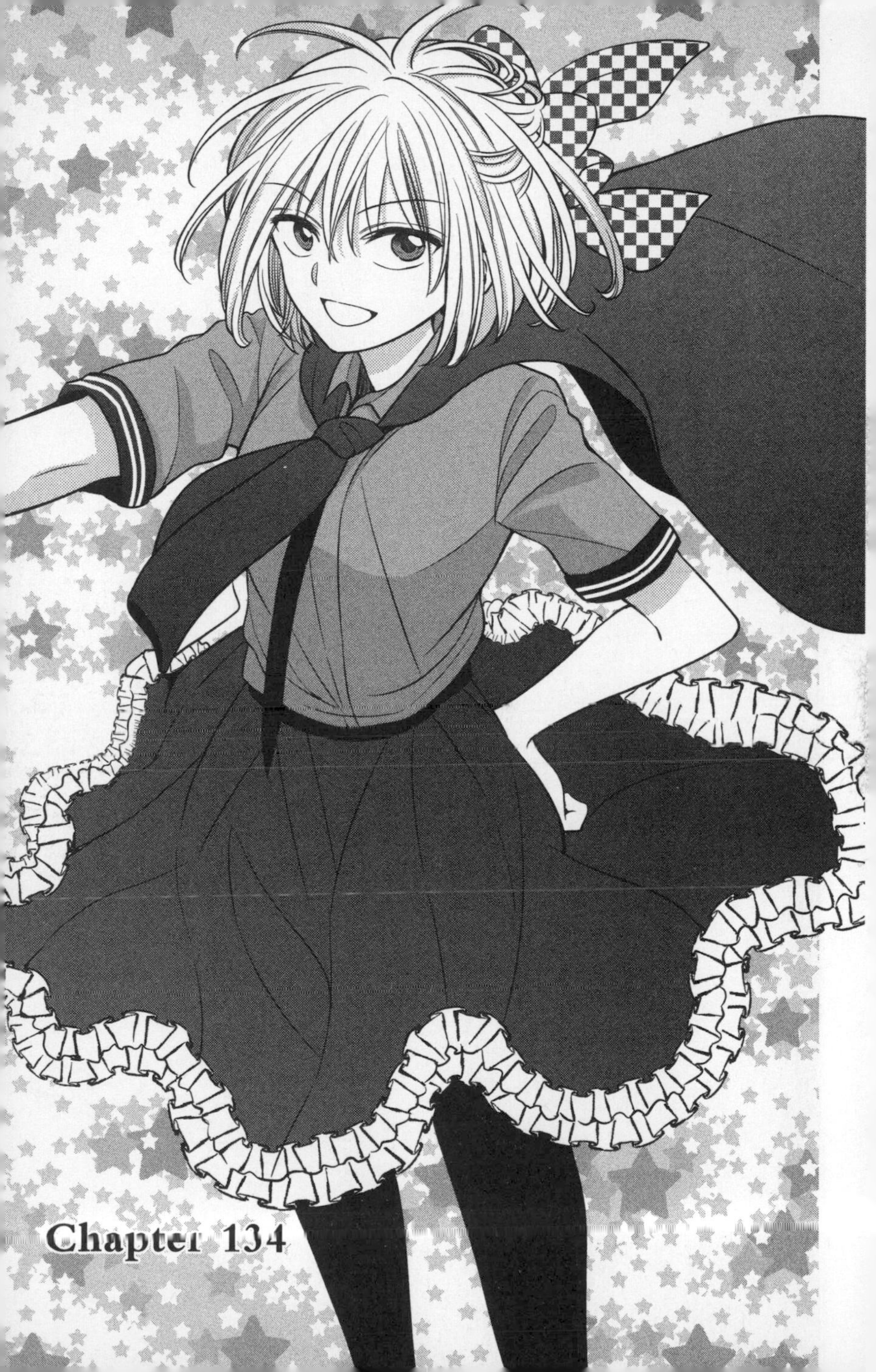

Chapter 134

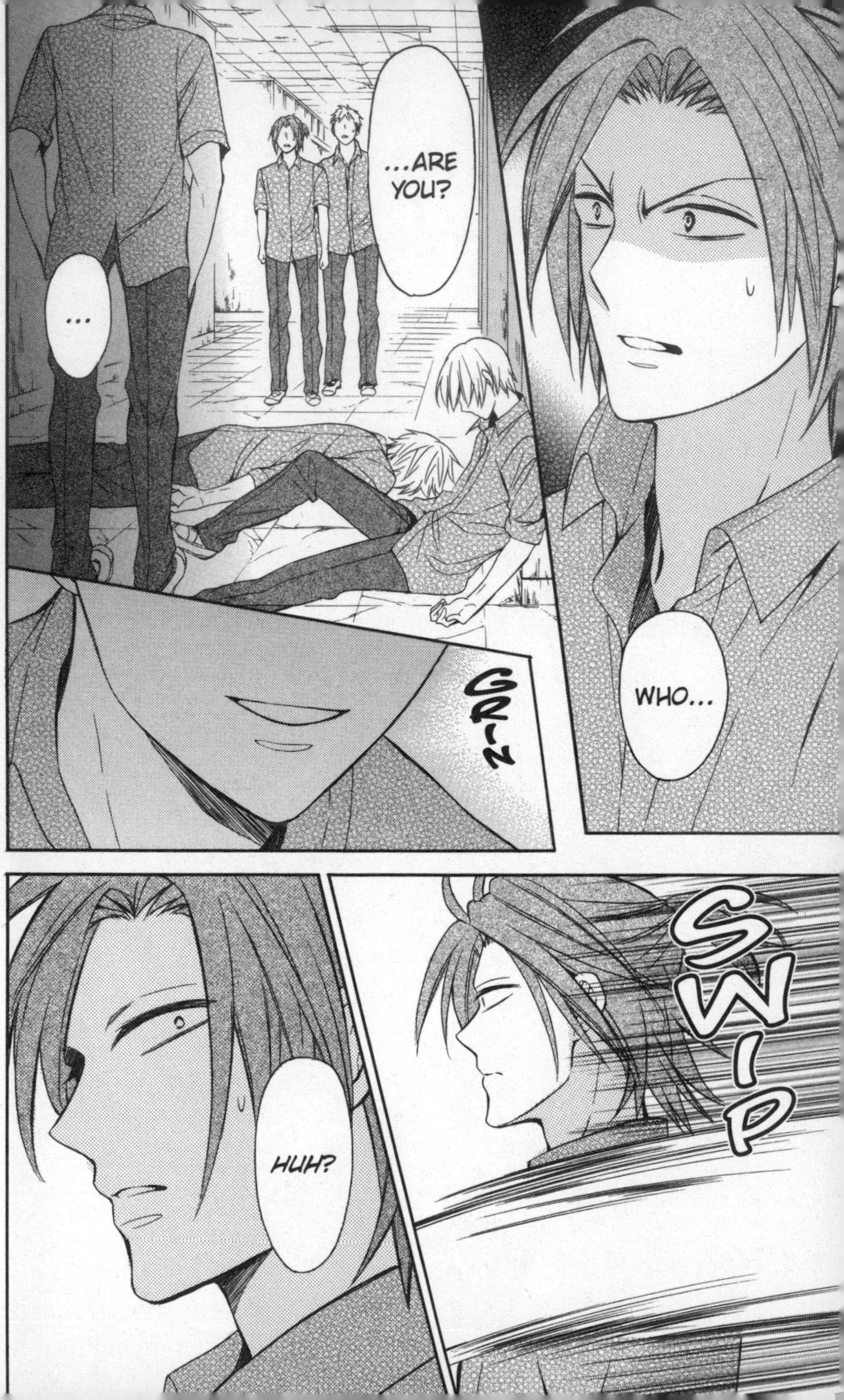
WHO...
...ARE YOU?
...
GRIN
SWIP
HUH?

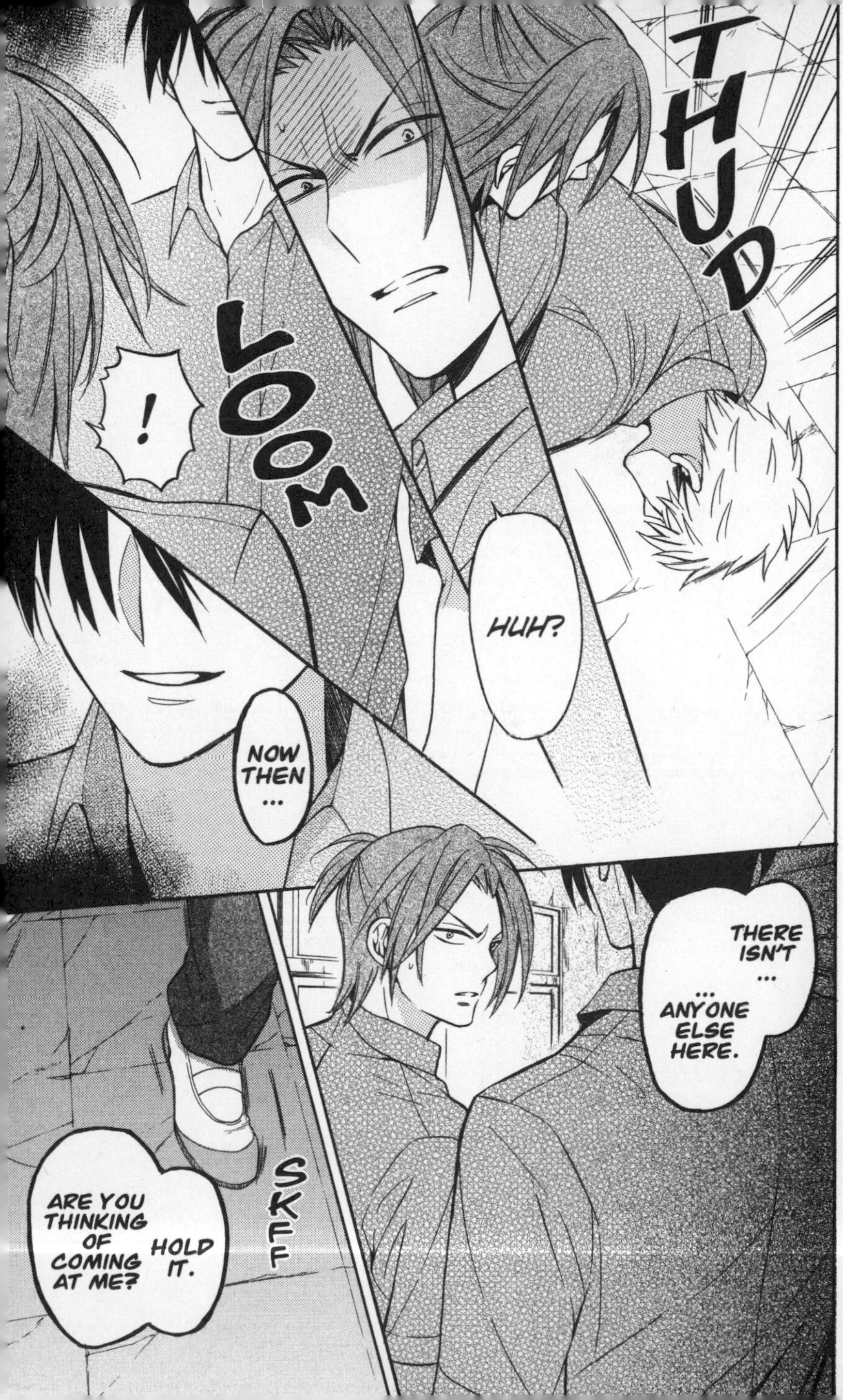
THUD
HUH?
LOOM
!
NOW THEN ...
THERE ISN'T ... ... ANYONE ELSE HERE.
SKFF
HOLD IT.
ARE YOU THINKING OF COMING AT ME?

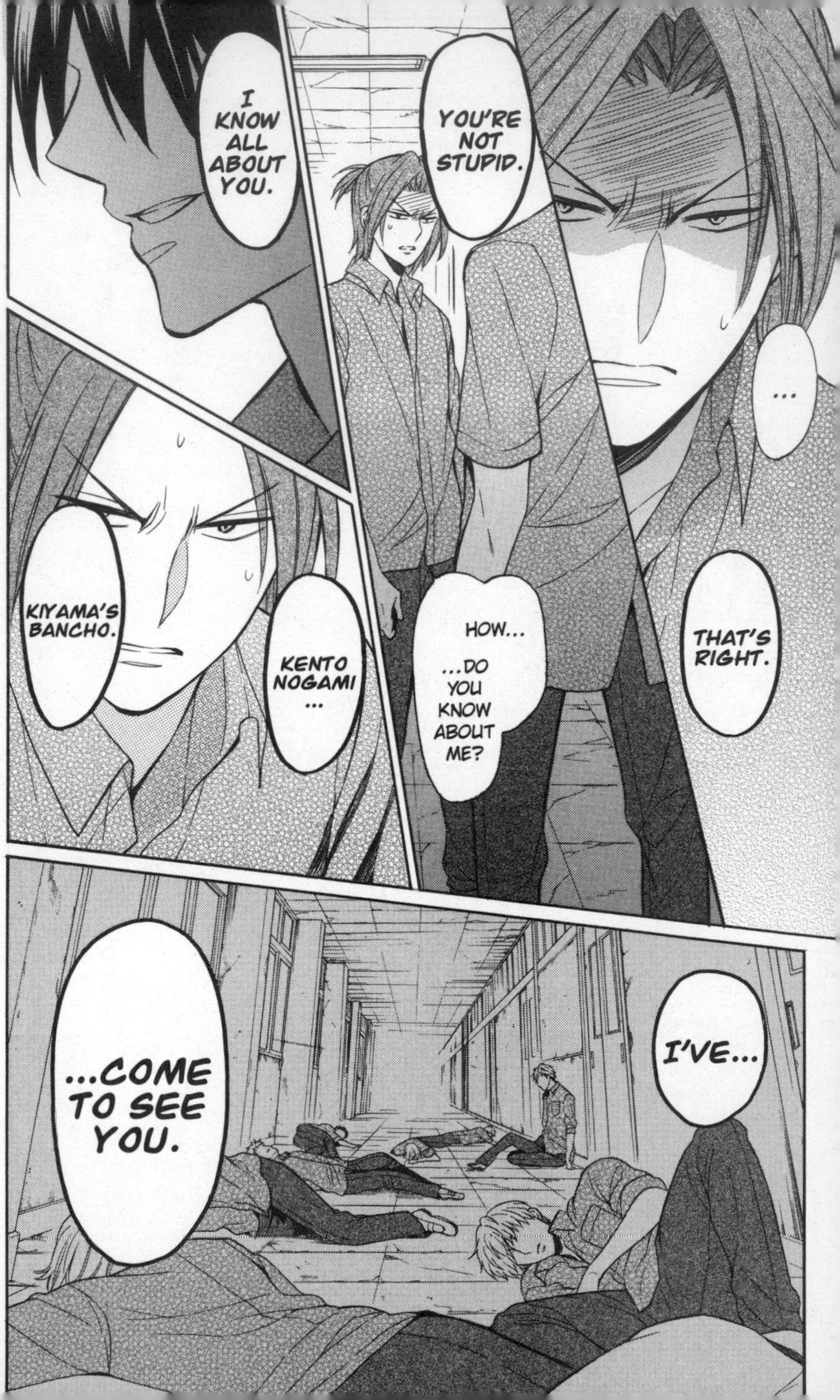
YOU'RE NOT STUPID.
...
THAT'S RIGHT.
HOW...
...DO YOU KNOW ABOUT ME?
I KNOW ALL ABOUT YOU.
KENTO NOGAMI...
KIYAMA'S BANCHO.
I'VE...
...COME TO SEE YOU.

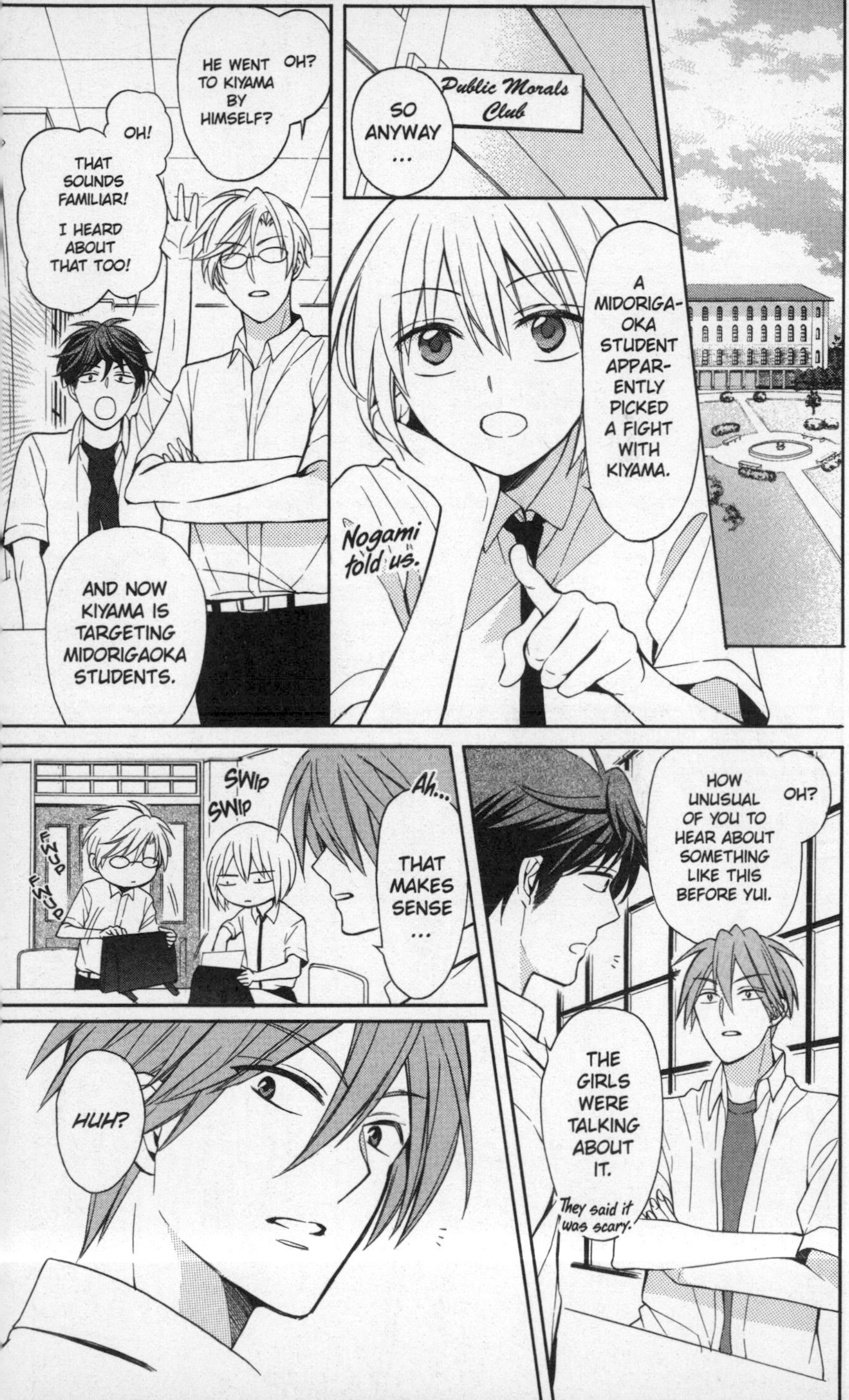
Public Morals Club
SO ANYWAY ...
A MIDORIGA-OKA STUDENT APPAR-ENTLY PICKED A FIGHT WITH KIYAMA.
Nogami told us.
OH?
HE WENT TO KIYAMA BY HIMSELF?
OH!
THAT SOUNDS FAMILIAR!
I HEARD ABOUT THAT TOO!
AND NOW KIYAMA IS TARGETING MIDORIGAOKA STUDENTS.
OH?
HOW UNUSUAL OF YOU TO HEAR ABOUT SOMETHING LIKE THIS BEFORE YUI.
THE GIRLS WERE TALKING ABOUT IT.
They said it was scary.
Ah...
THAT MAKES SENSE ...
SWIP SWIP
FWUP FWUP
HUH?

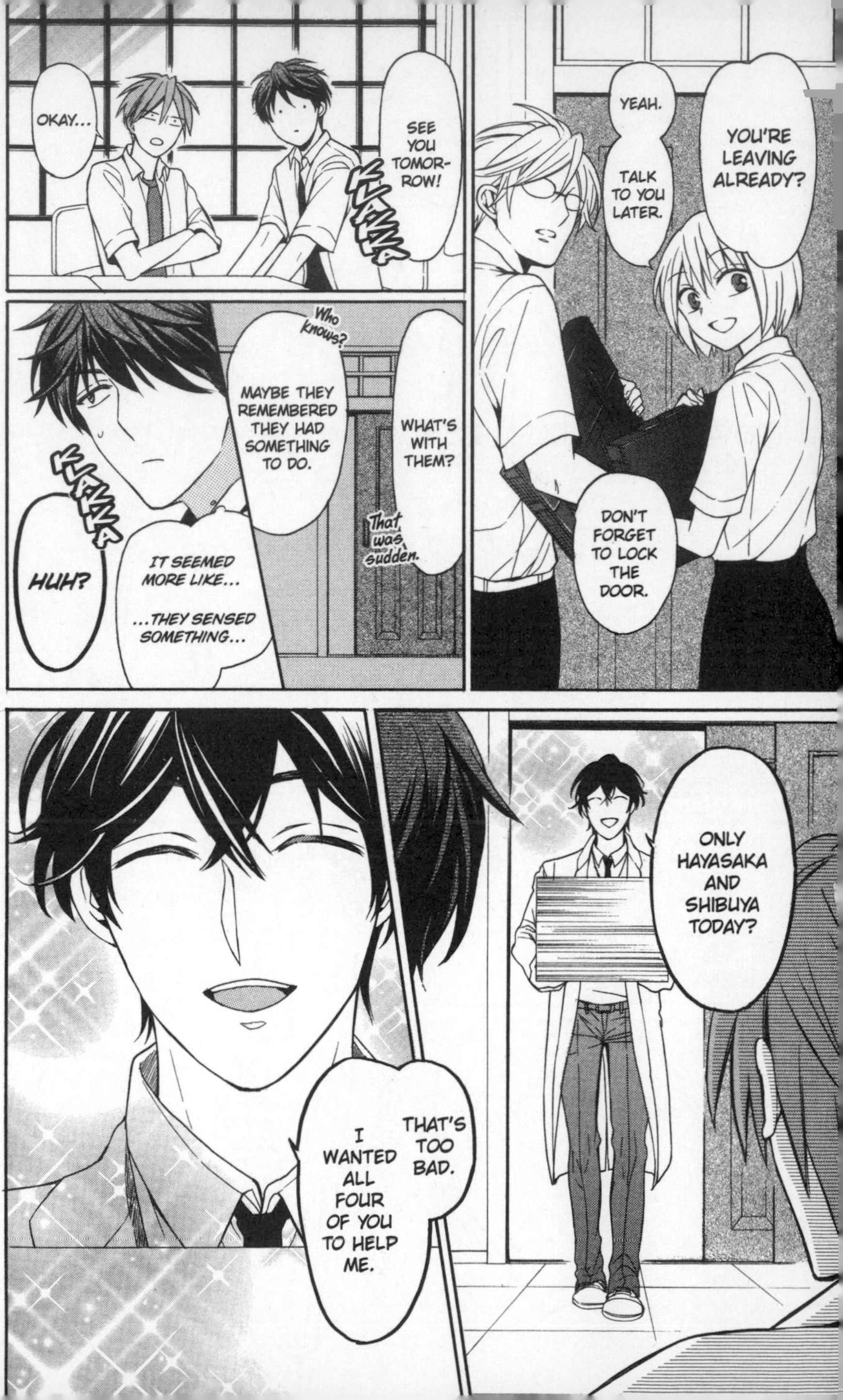
YOU'RE LEAVING ALREADY?
YEAH.
TALK TO YOU LATER.
DON'T FORGET TO LOCK THE DOOR.
SEE YOU TOMORROW!
OKAY...
WHAT'S WITH THEM?
That was sudden.
MAYBE THEY REMEMBERED THEY HAD SOMETHING TO DO.
Who knows?
IT SEEMED MORE LIKE...
...THEY SENSED SOMETHING...
HUH?
ONLY HAYASAKA AND SHIBUYA TODAY?
THAT'S TOO BAD.
I WANTED ALL FOUR OF YOU TO HELP ME.

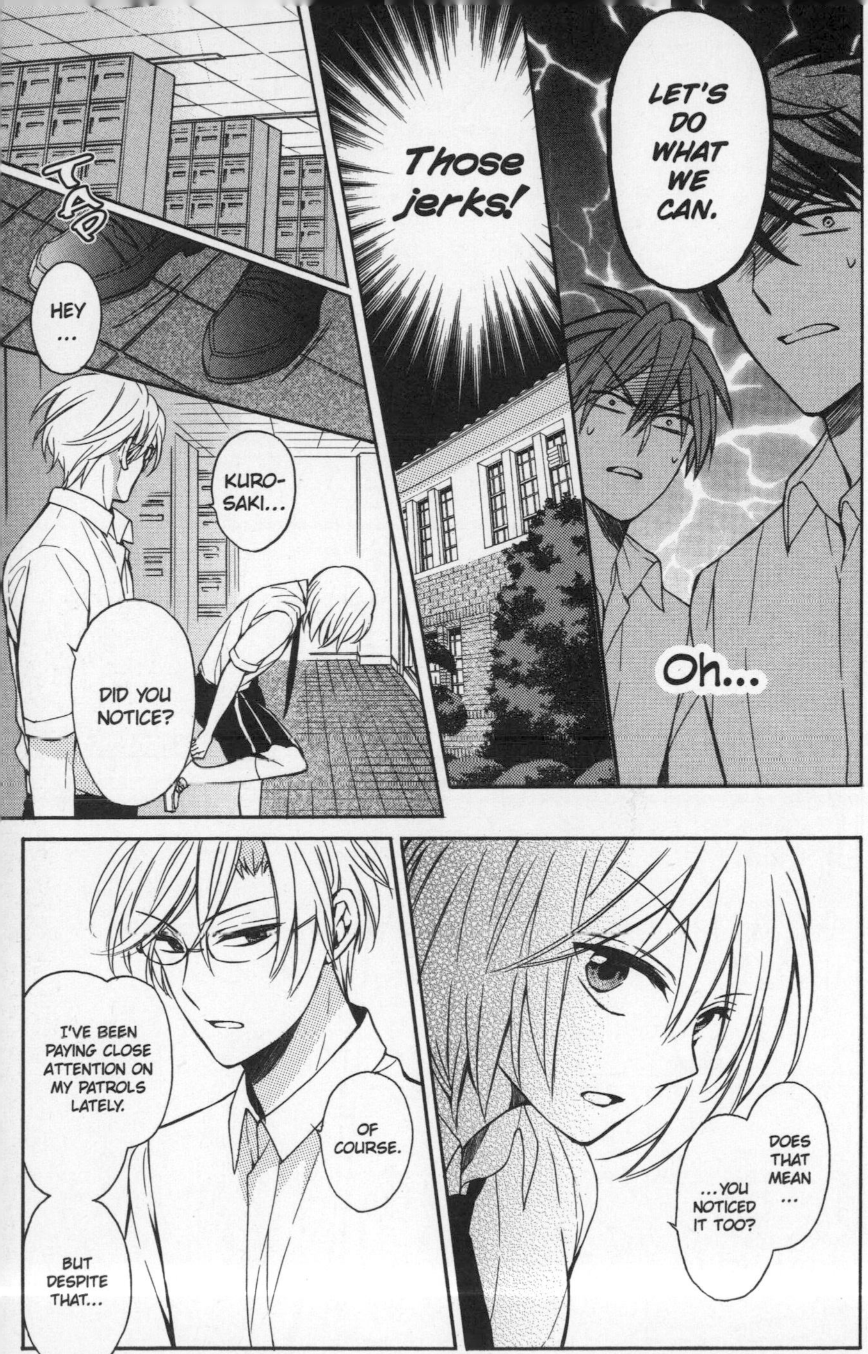
LET'S DO WHAT WE CAN.
Oh...
Those jerks!
TAP
HEY...
KURO-SAKI...
DID YOU NOTICE?
DOES THAT MEAN...
...YOU NOTICED IT TOO?
OF COURSE.
I'VE BEEN PAYING CLOSE ATTENTION ON MY PATROLS LATELY.
BUT DESPITE THAT...

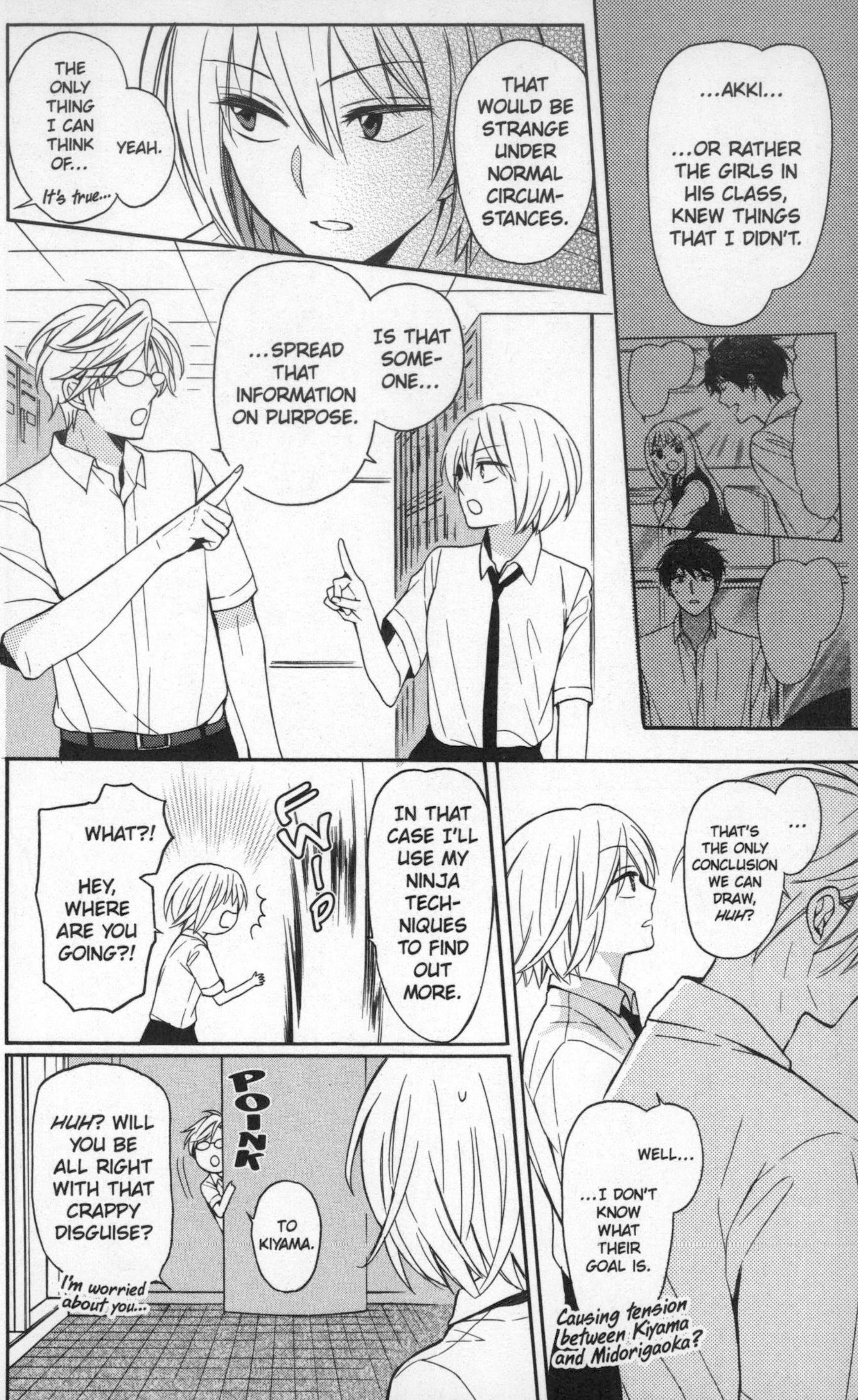
...AKKI...
...OR RATHER THE GIRLS IN HIS CLASS, KNEW THINGS THAT I DIDN'T.
THAT WOULD BE STRANGE UNDER NORMAL CIRCUM-STANCES.
YEAH.
THE ONLY THING I CAN THINK OF...
It's true...
IS THAT SOME-ONE...
...SPREAD THAT INFORMATION ON PURPOSE.
...
THAT'S THE ONLY CONCLUSION WE CAN DRAW, HUH?
WELL...
...I DON'T KNOW WHAT THEIR GOAL IS.
Causing tension between Kiyama and Midorigaoka?
IN THAT CASE I'LL USE MY NINJA TECH-NIQUES TO FIND OUT MORE.
FWIP
WHAT?!
HEY, WHERE ARE YOU GOING?!
POINK
TO KIYAMA.
HUH? WILL YOU BE ALL RIGHT WITH THAT CRAPPY DISGUISE?
I'm worried about you...

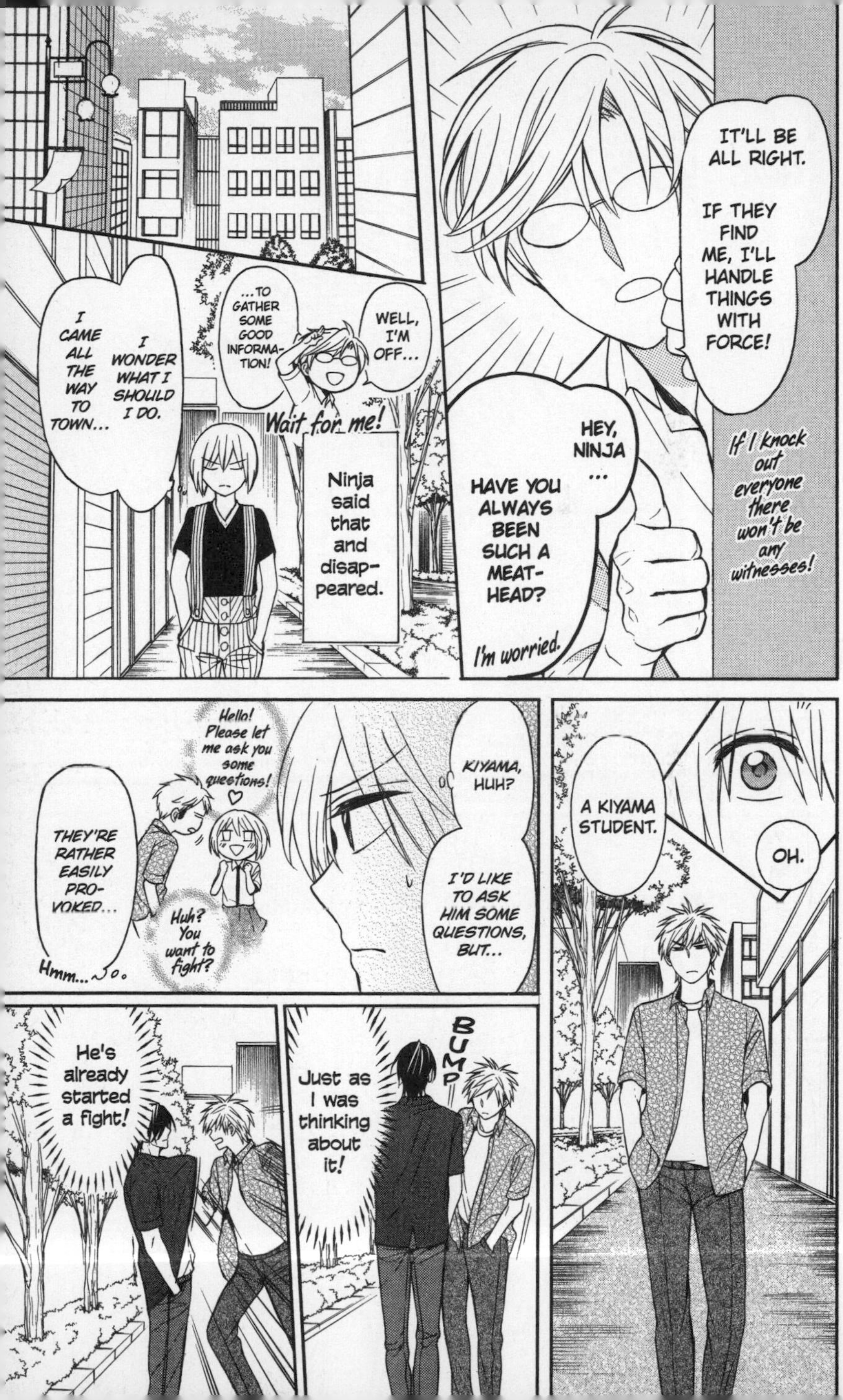
IT'LL BE ALL RIGHT.
IF THEY FIND ME, I'LL HANDLE THINGS WITH FORCE!
If I knock out everyone there won't be any witnesses!
HEY, NINJA...
HAVE YOU ALWAYS BEEN SUCH A MEAT-HEAD?
I'm worried.
WELL, I'M OFF...
...TO GATHER SOME GOOD INFORMATION!
Wait for me!
Ninja said that and disappeared.
I CAME ALL THE WAY TO TOWN...
I WONDER WHAT I SHOULD DO.
OH.
A KIYAMA STUDENT.
KIYAMA, HUH?
I'D LIKE TO ASK HIM SOME QUESTIONS, BUT...
Hello! Please let me ask you some questions! ♡
Huh? You want to fight?
THEY'RE RATHER EASILY PRO-VOKED...
Hmm...
BUMP
Just as I was thinking about it!
He's already started a fight!

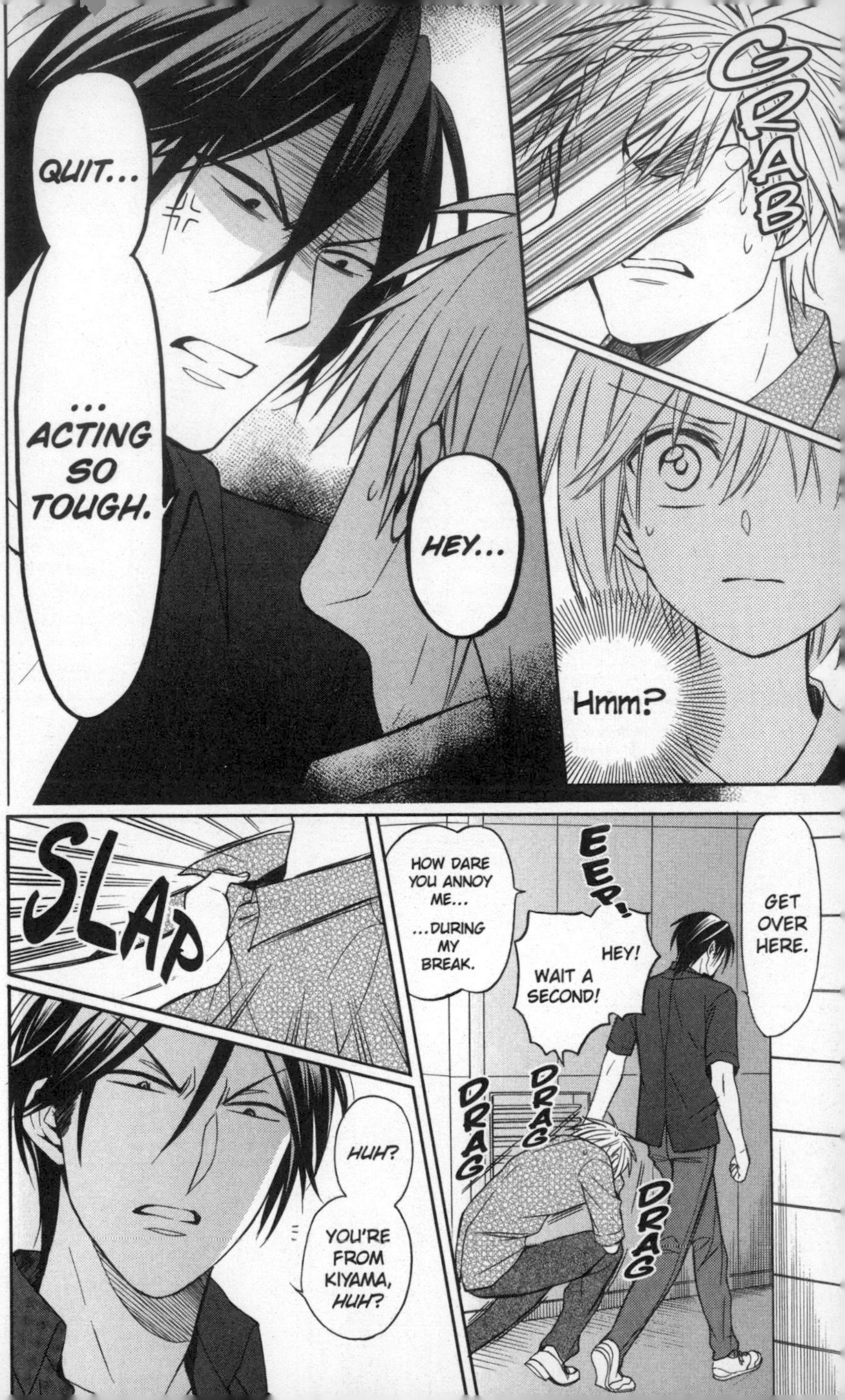
GRAB
Hmm?
QUIT...
...ACTING SO TOUGH.
HEY...
GET OVER HERE.
EEP!
HEY!
WAIT A SECOND!
HOW DARE YOU ANNOY ME...
...DURING MY BREAK.
DRAG
DRAG
DRAG
DRAG
SLAP
HUH?
YOU'RE FROM KIYAMA, HUH?

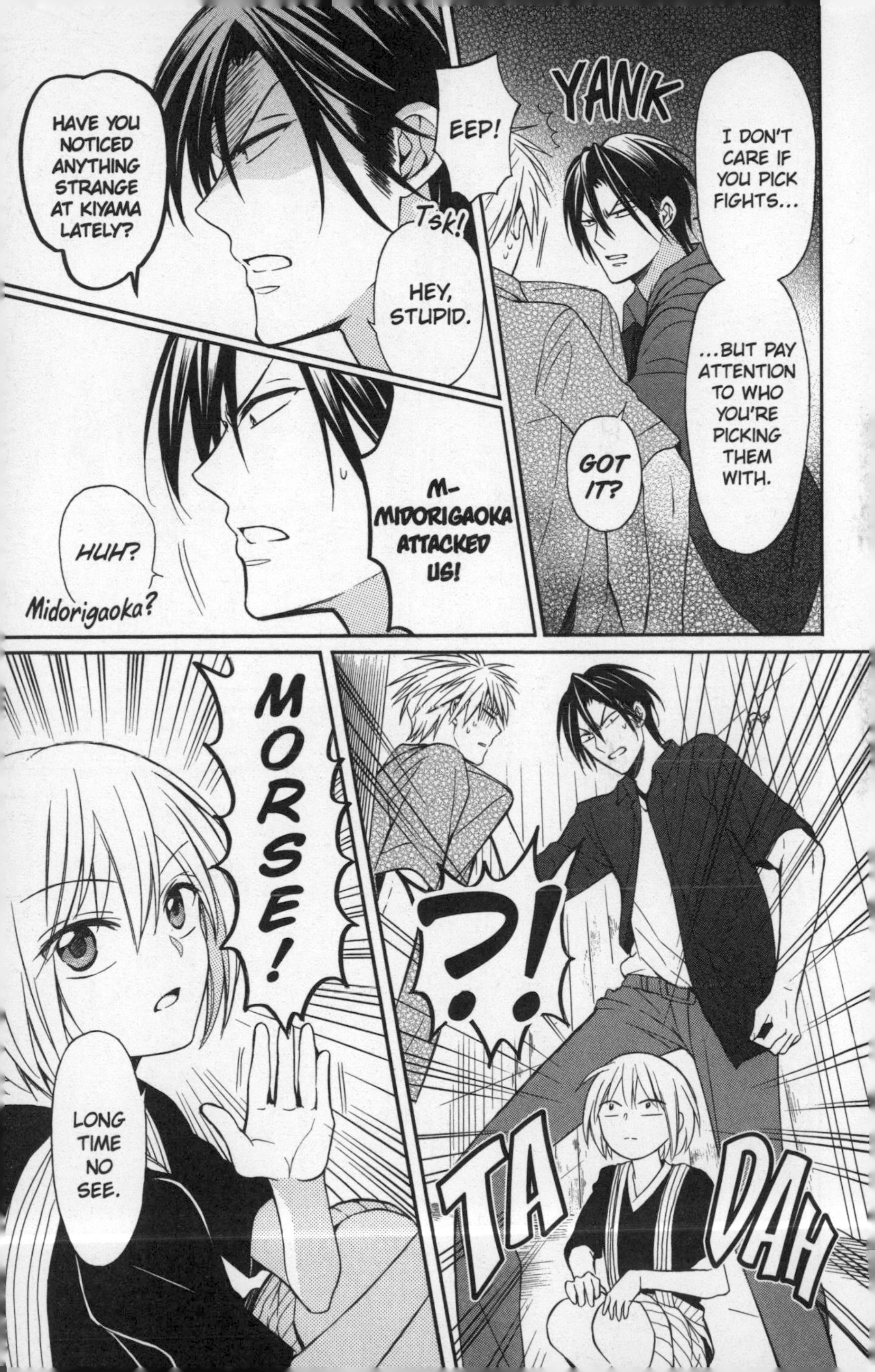
YANK
EEP!
I DON'T CARE IF YOU PICK FIGHTS...
...BUT PAY ATTENTION TO WHO YOU'RE PICKING THEM WITH.
GOT IT?
Tsk!
HEY, STUPID.
HAVE YOU NOTICED ANYTHING STRANGE AT KIYAMA LATELY?
M-MIDORIGAOKA ATTACKED US!
HUH?
Midorigaoka?
?!
TA DAH
MORSE!
LONG TIME NO SEE.

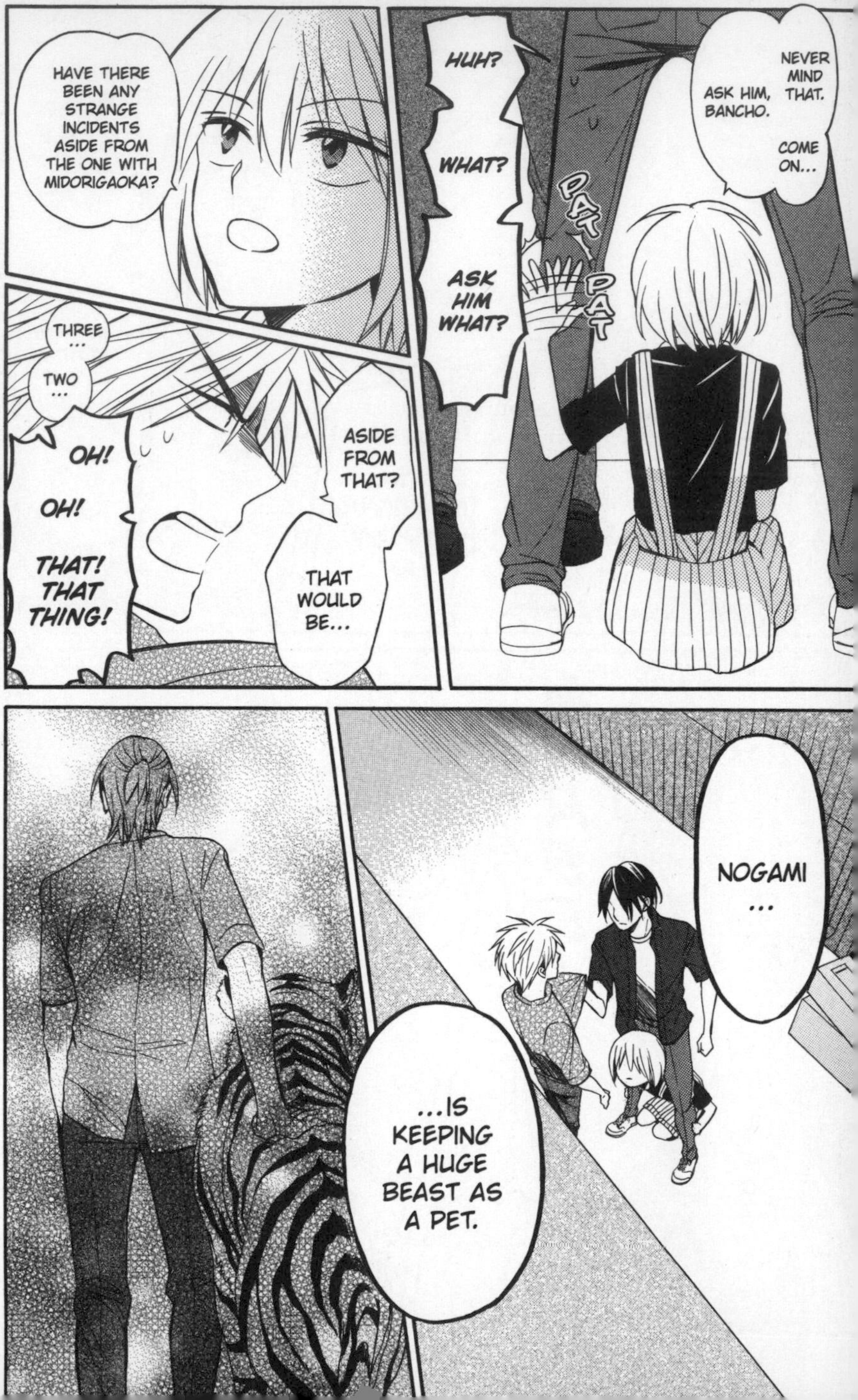
NEVER MIND THAT.
ASK HIM, BANCHO.
COME ON...
HUH?
WHAT?
ASK HIM WHAT?
PAT PAT
HAVE THERE BEEN ANY STRANGE INCIDENTS ASIDE FROM THE ONE WITH MIDORIGAOKA?
ASIDE FROM THAT?
THAT WOULD BE...
THREE...
TWO...
OH!
OH!
THAT! THAT THING!
NOGAMI...
...IS KEEPING A HUGE BEAST AS A PET.

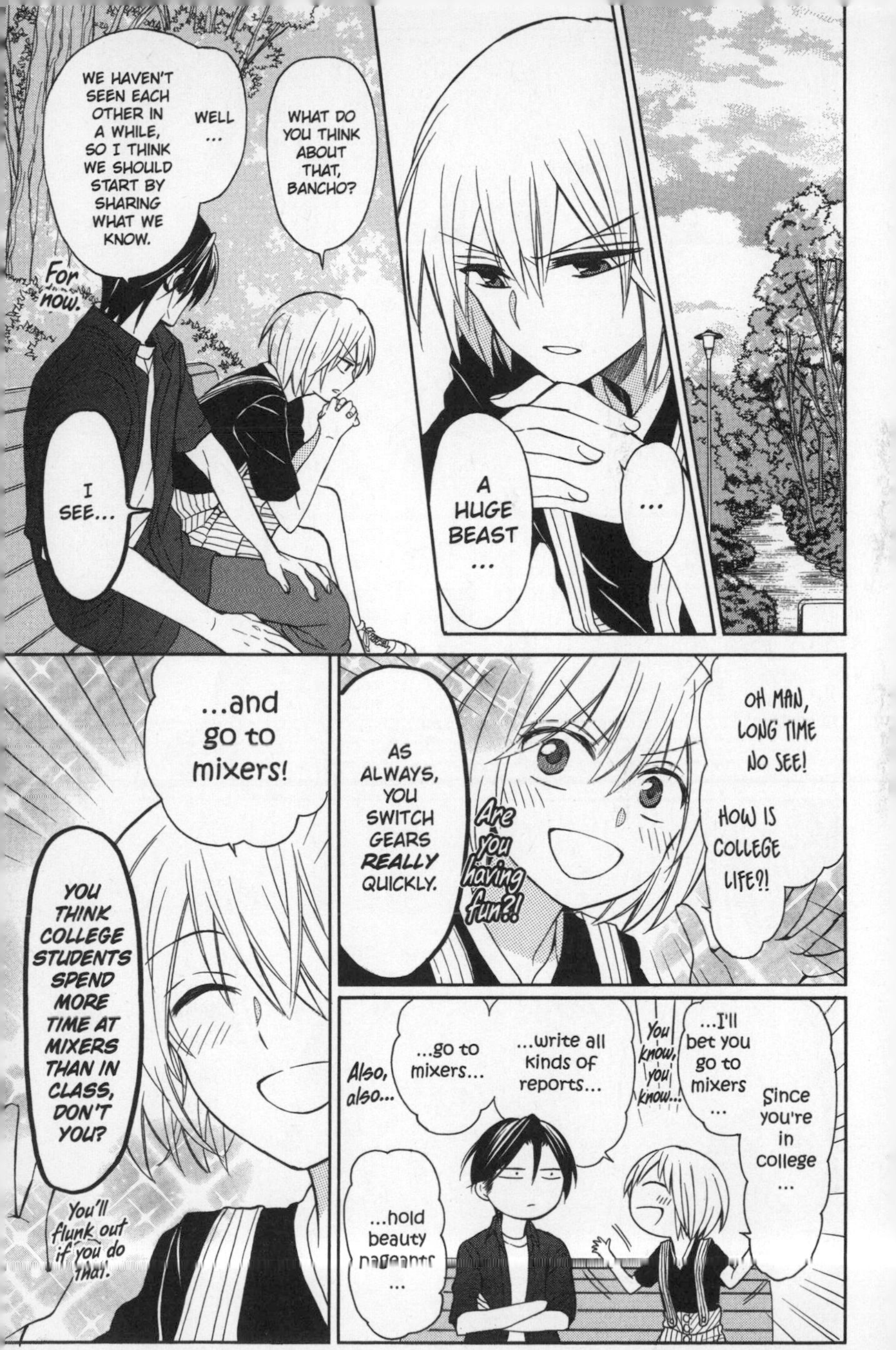
...
A HUGE BEAST ...
WHAT DO YOU THINK ABOUT THAT, BANCHO?
WELL ...
WE HAVEN'T SEEN EACH OTHER IN A WHILE, SO I THINK WE SHOULD START BY SHARING WHAT WE KNOW.
For now.
I SEE...
OH MAN, LONG TIME NO SEE!
HOW IS COLLEGE LIFE?!
Are you having fun?!
AS ALWAYS, YOU SWITCH GEARS REALLY QUICKLY.
...I'll bet you go to mixers ...
Since you're in college ...
You know, you know...
...write all kinds of reports...
...go to mixers...
Also, also...
...hold beauty pageants ...
...and go to mixers!
YOU THINK COLLEGE STUDENTS SPEND MORE TIME AT MIXERS THAN IN CLASS, DON'T YOU?
You'll flunk out if you do that.

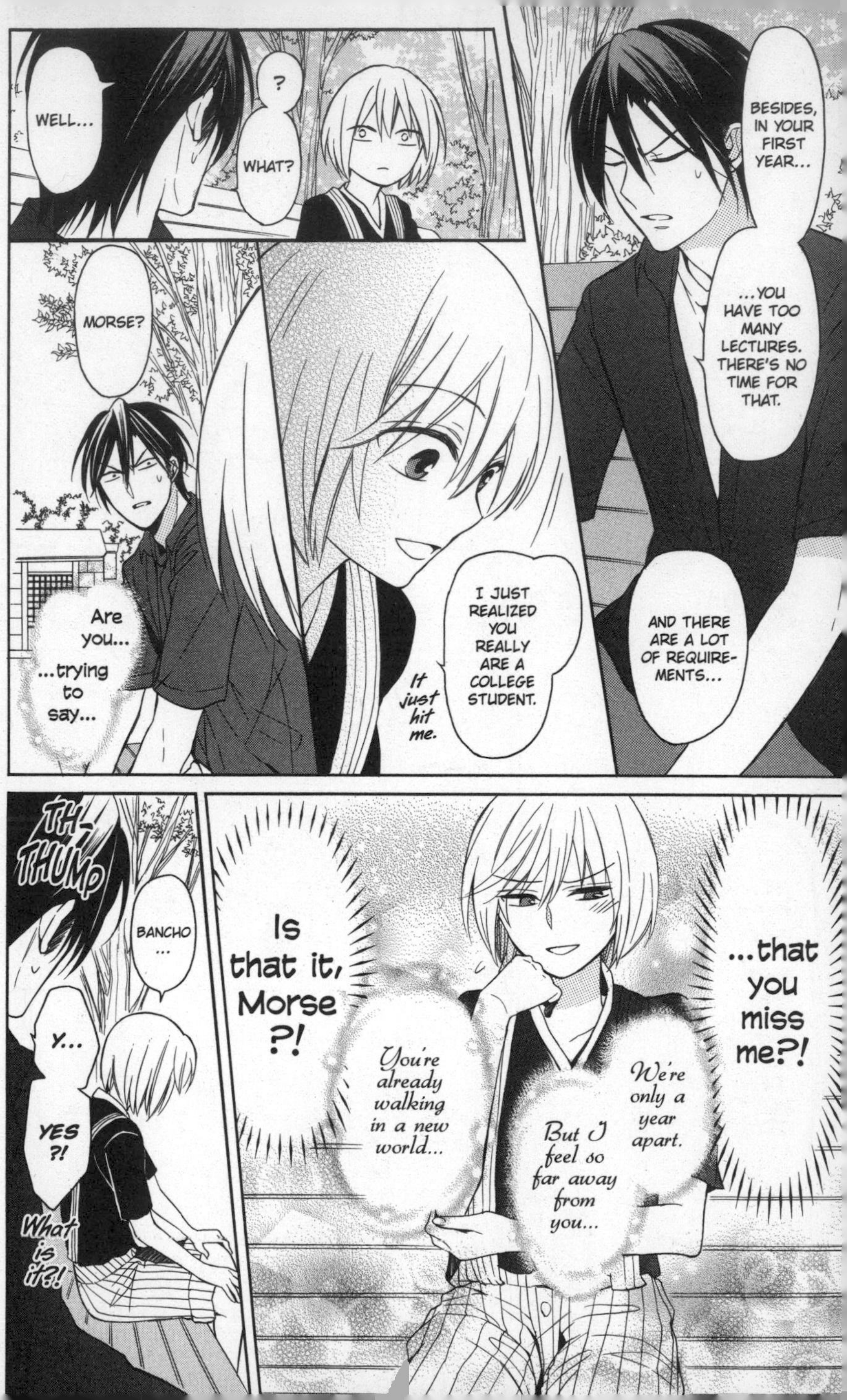
BESIDES, IN YOUR FIRST YEAR...
...YOU HAVE TOO MANY LECTURES. THERE'S NO TIME FOR THAT.
AND THERE ARE A LOT OF REQUIREMENTS...
?
WHAT?
WELL...
MORSE?
I JUST REALIZED YOU REALLY ARE A COLLEGE STUDENT.
It just hit me.
Are you...
...trying to say...
...that you miss me?!
We're only a year apart.
But I feel so far away from you...
You're already walking in a new world...
Is that it, Morse?!
TH-THUMP
BANCHO...
Y...
YES?!
What is it?!

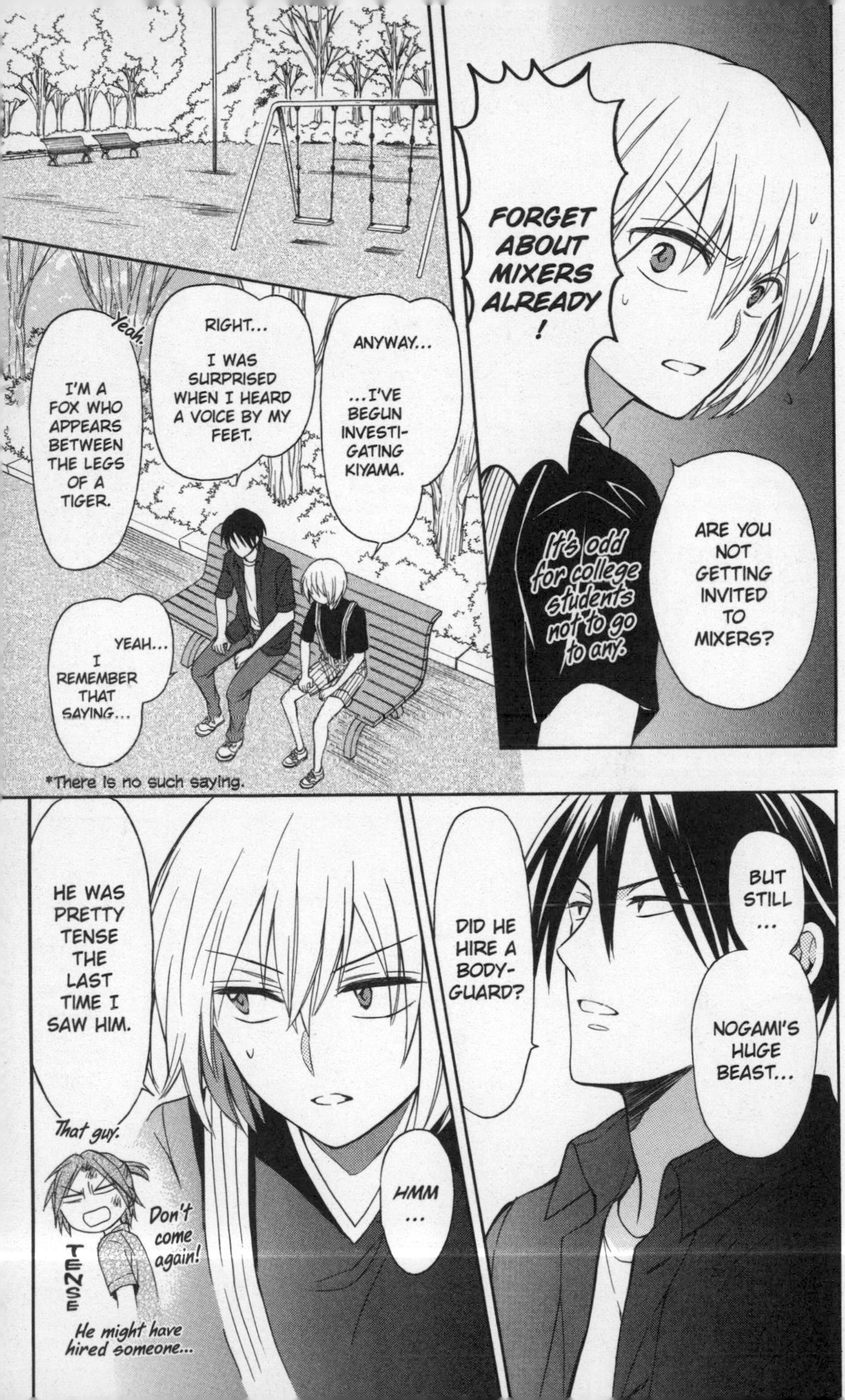
ARE YOU NOT GETTING INVITED TO MIXERS?
It's odd for college students not to go to any.
FORGET ABOUT MIXERS ALREADY!
ANYWAY... ...I'VE BEGUN INVESTIGATING KIYAMA.
RIGHT... I WAS SURPRISED WHEN I HEARD A VOICE BY MY FEET.
Yeah.
I'M A FOX WHO APPEARS BETWEEN THE LEGS OF A TIGER.
YEAH... I REMEMBER THAT SAYING...
*There is no such saying.
BUT STILL...
NOGAMI'S HUGE BEAST...
DID HE HIRE A BODYGUARD?
HMM...
HE WAS PRETTY TENSE THE LAST TIME I SAW HIM.
That guy.
Don't come again!
TENSE
He might have hired someone...

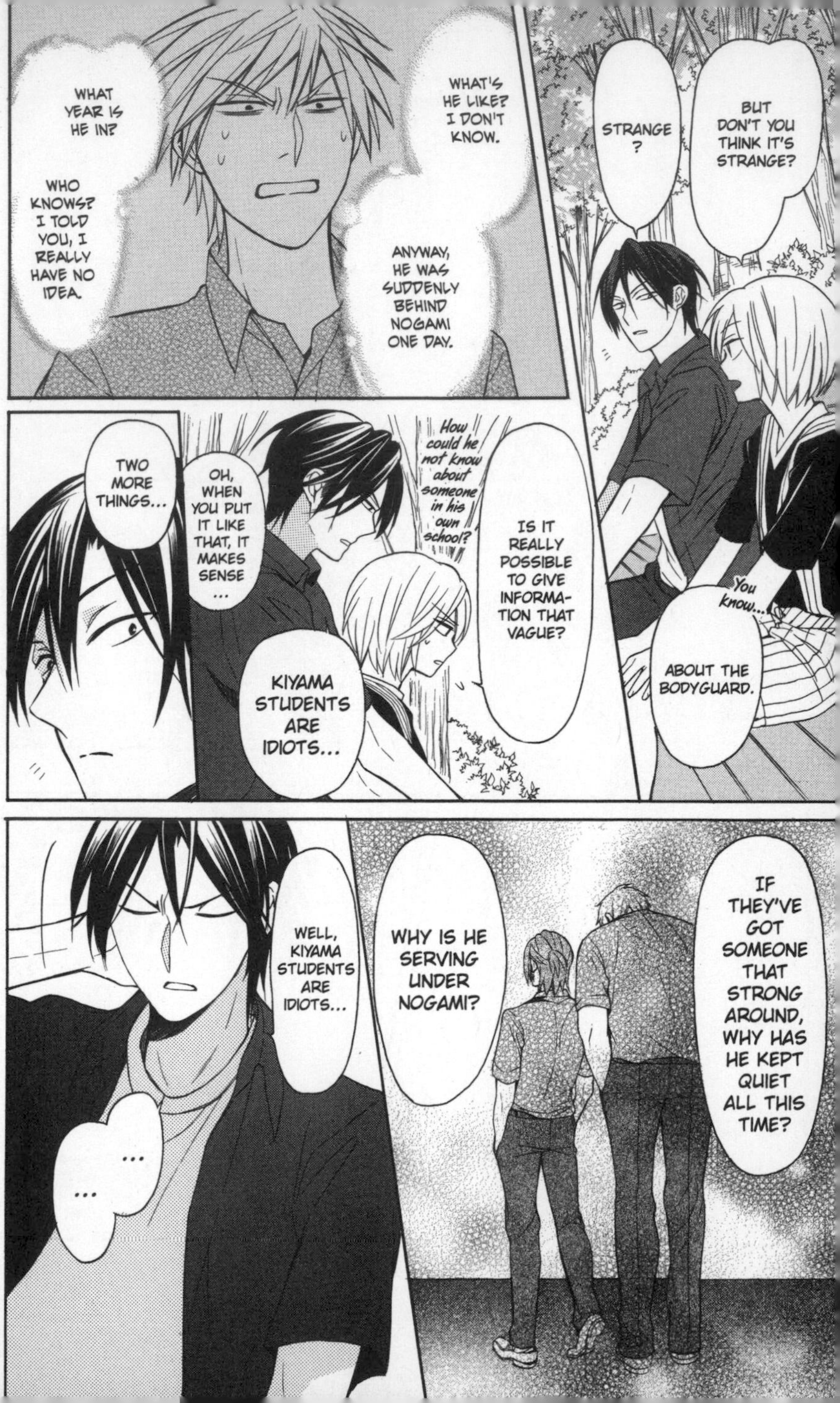
BUT DON'T YOU THINK IT'S STRANGE?
STRANGE?
You know...
ABOUT THE BODYGUARD.
WHAT'S HE LIKE? I DON'T KNOW.
WHAT YEAR IS HE IN?
ANYWAY, HE WAS SUDDENLY BEHIND NOGAMI ONE DAY.
WHO KNOWS? I TOLD YOU, I REALLY HAVE NO IDEA.
IS IT REALLY POSSIBLE TO GIVE INFORMATION THAT VAGUE?
How could he not know about someone in his own school?
OH, WHEN YOU PUT IT LIKE THAT, IT MAKES SENSE...
KIYAMA STUDENTS ARE IDIOTS...
TWO MORE THINGS...
IF THEY'VE GOT SOMEONE THAT STRONG AROUND, WHY HAS HE KEPT QUIET ALL THIS TIME?
WHY IS HE SERVING UNDER NOGAMI?
WELL, KIYAMA STUDENTS ARE IDIOTS...
... ...

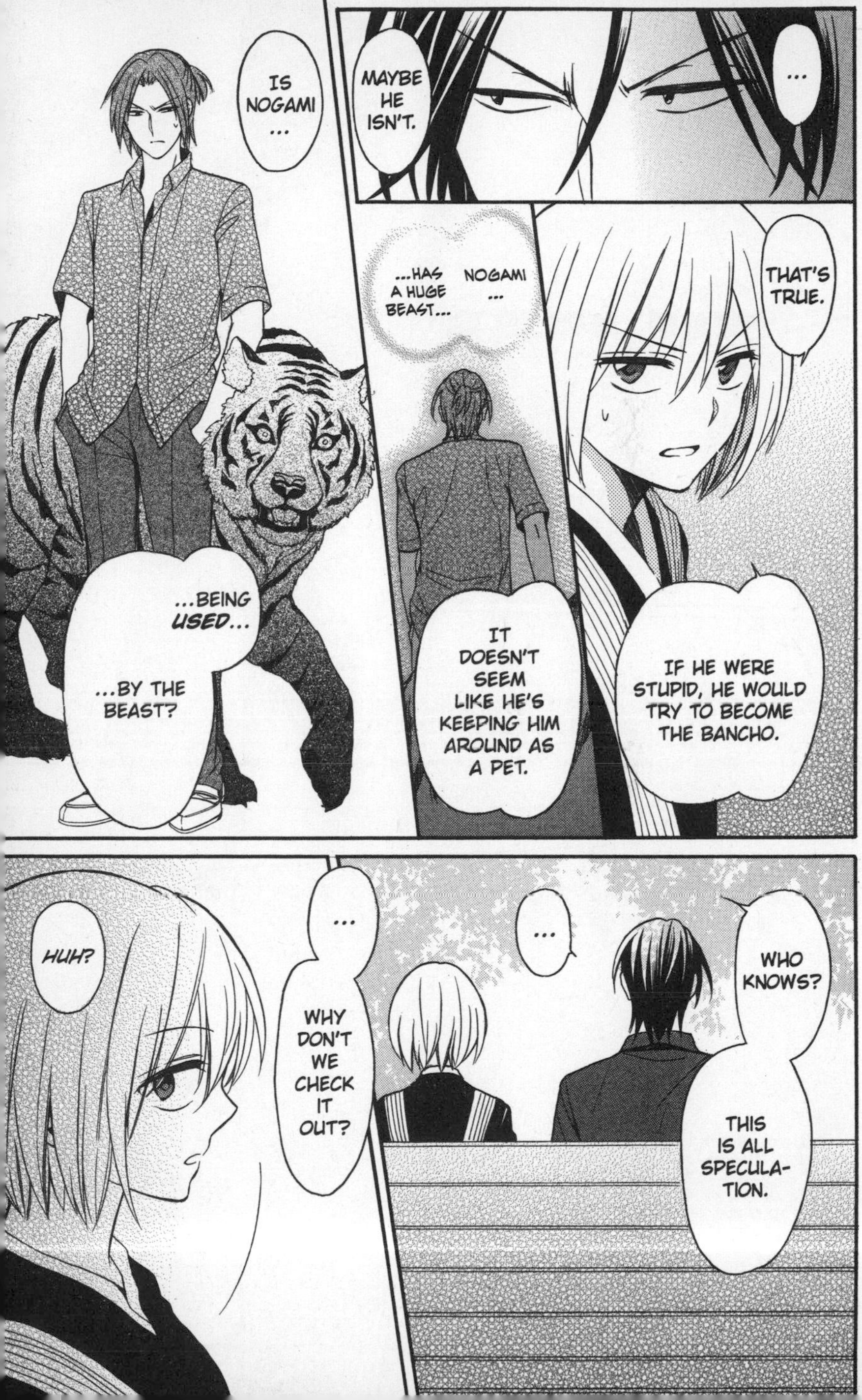
...
MAYBE HE ISN'T.
THAT'S TRUE.
IF HE WERE STUPID, HE WOULD TRY TO BECOME THE BANCHO.
NOGAMI ...
...HAS A HUGE BEAST...
IT DOESN'T SEEM LIKE HE'S KEEPING HIM AROUND AS A PET.
IS NOGAMI ...
...BEING *USED*...
...BY THE BEAST?
WHO KNOWS?
THIS IS ALL SPECULATION.
...
...
WHY DON'T WE CHECK IT OUT?
HUH?

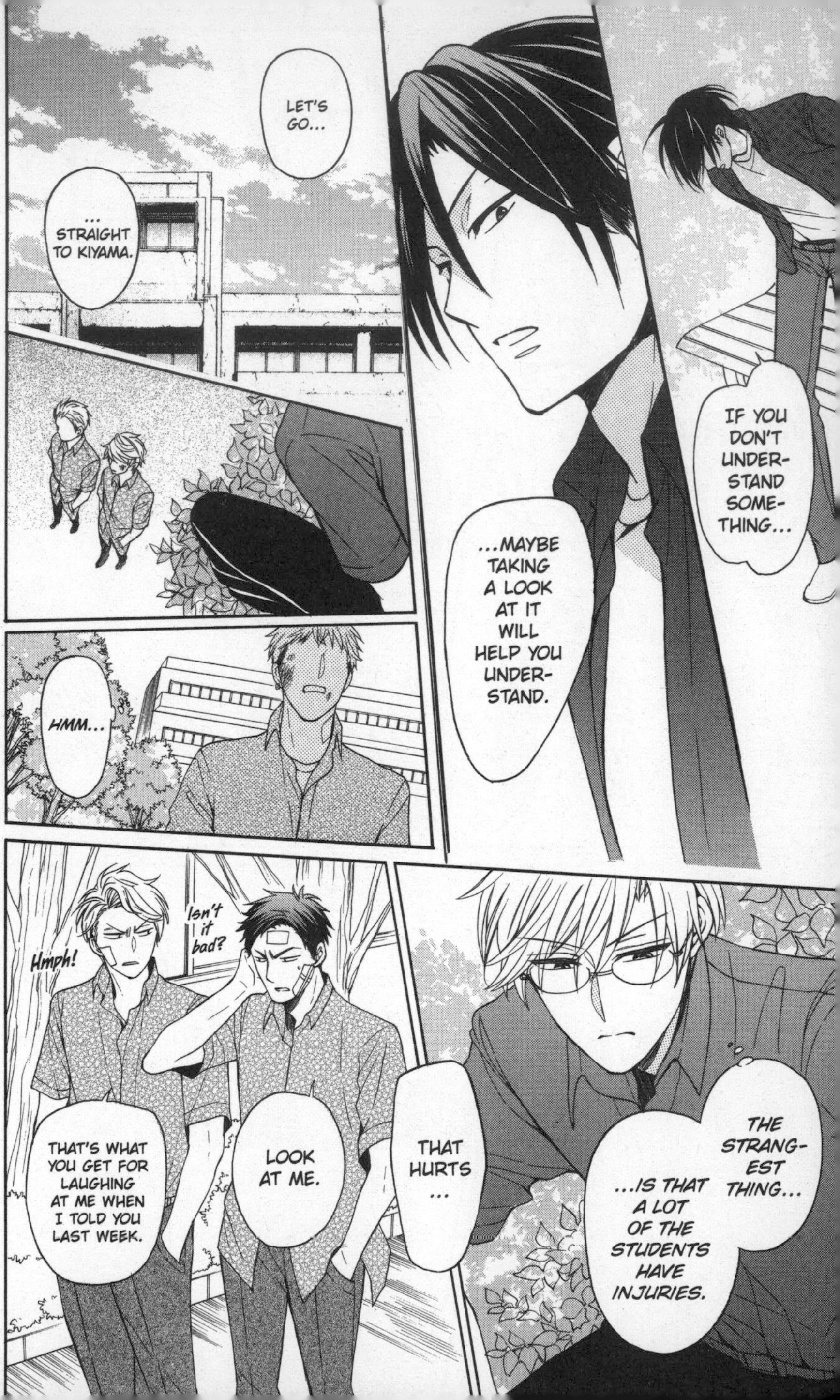
IF YOU DON'T UNDER-STAND SOME-THING...
...MAYBE TAKING A LOOK AT IT WILL HELP YOU UNDER-STAND.
LET'S GO...
...STRAIGHT TO KIYAMA.
HMM...
THE STRANG-EST THING...
...IS THAT A LOT OF THE STUDENTS HAVE INJURIES.
THAT HURTS...
Isn't it bad?
LOOK AT ME.
Hmph!
THAT'S WHAT YOU GET FOR LAUGHING AT ME WHEN I TOLD YOU LAST WEEK.

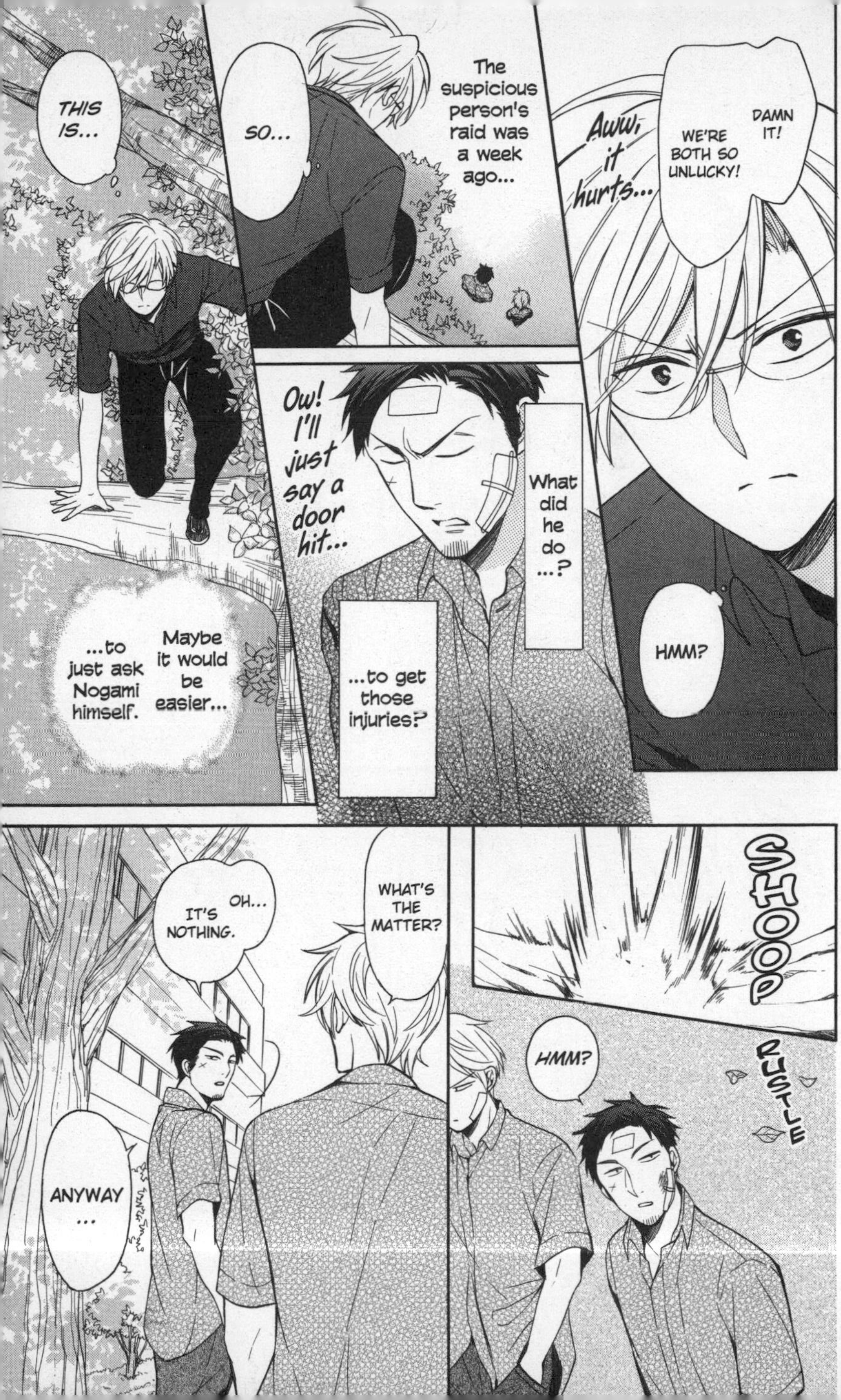
DAMN IT! WE'RE BOTH SO UNLUCKY!
Aww, it hurts...
HMM?
The suspicious person's raid was a week ago...
SO...
What did he do ...?
Ow! I'll just say a door hit...
...to get those injuries?
THIS IS...
Maybe it would be easier...
...to just ask Nogami himself.
SHOOP
RUSTLE
HMM?
WHAT'S THE MATTER?
OH... IT'S NOTHING.
ANYWAY ...

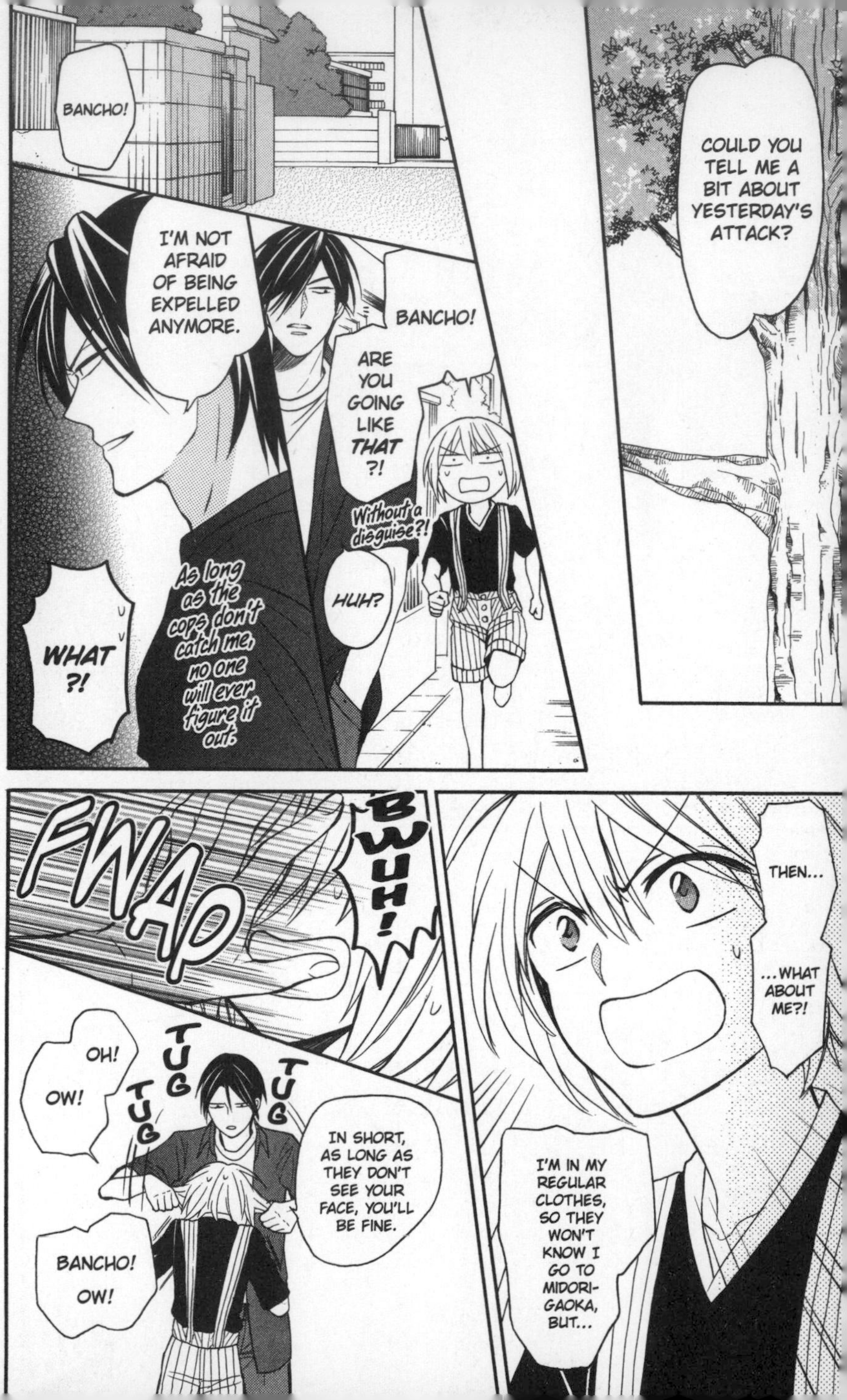
COULD YOU TELL ME A BIT ABOUT YESTERDAY'S ATTACK?
BANCHO!
I'M NOT AFRAID OF BEING EXPELLED ANYMORE.
BANCHO!
ARE YOU GOING LIKE THAT?!
Without a disguise?!
HUH?
As long as the cops don't catch me, no one will ever figure it out.
WHAT?!
THEN...
...WHAT ABOUT ME?!
I'M IN MY REGULAR CLOTHES, SO THEY WON'T KNOW I GO TO MIDORI-GAOKA, BUT...
BWUH!
FWAP
TUG
TUG
IN SHORT, AS LONG AS THEY DON'T SEE YOUR FACE, YOU'LL BE FINE.
OH!
OW!
TUG
TUG
BANCHO!
OW!

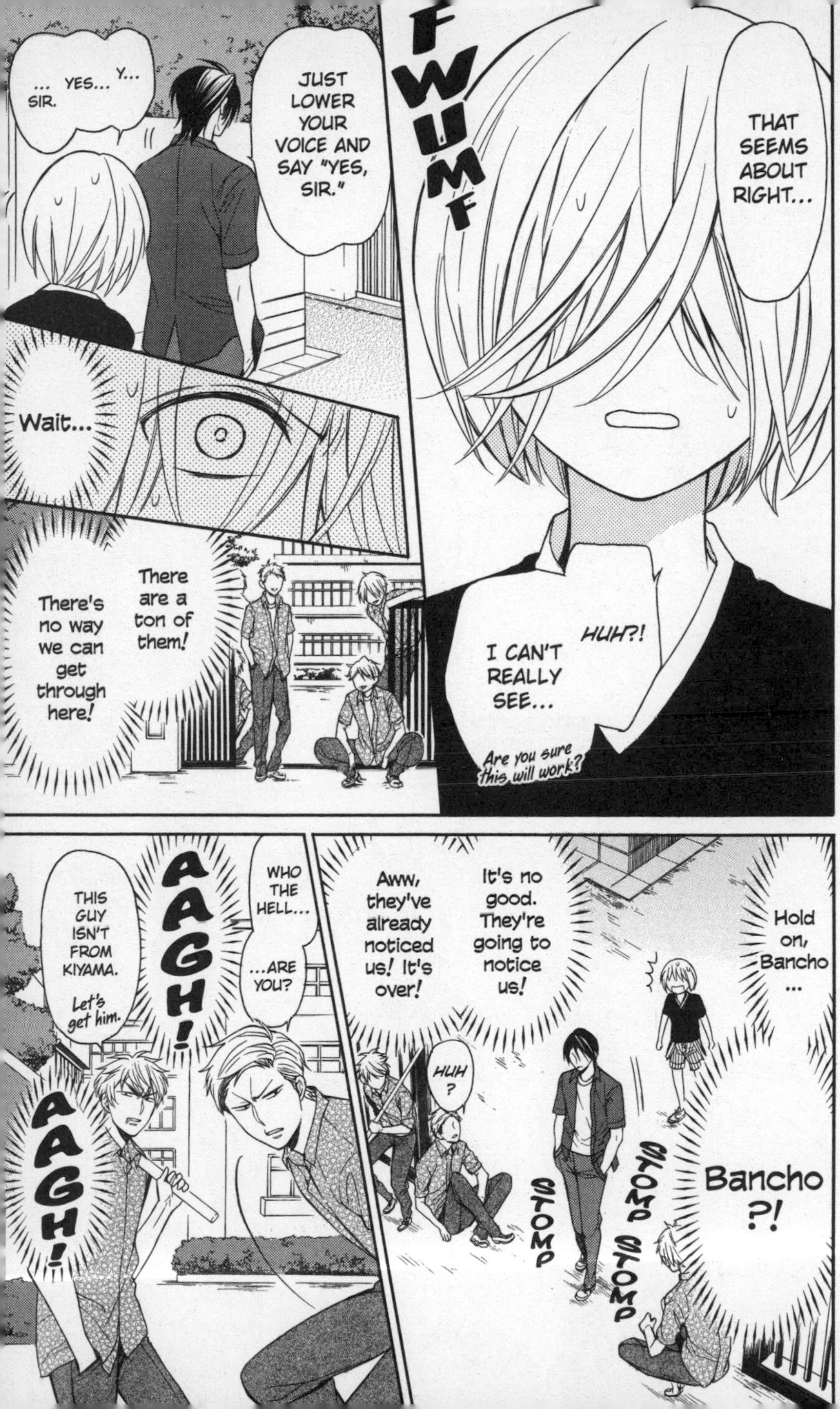
FWUMF
THAT SEEMS ABOUT RIGHT...
HUH?!
I CAN'T REALLY SEE...
Are you sure this will work?
JUST LOWER YOUR VOICE AND SAY "YES, SIR."
... YES... Y... SIR.
Wait...
There are a ton of them!
There's no way we can get through here!
Hold on, Bancho...
It's no good. They're going to notice us!
Aww, they've already noticed us! It's over!
HUH?
Bancho?!
STOMP STOMP
STOMP
STOMP
WHO THE HELL... ...ARE YOU?
AAGH!
THIS GUY ISN'T FROM KIYAMA.
Let's get him.
AAGH!

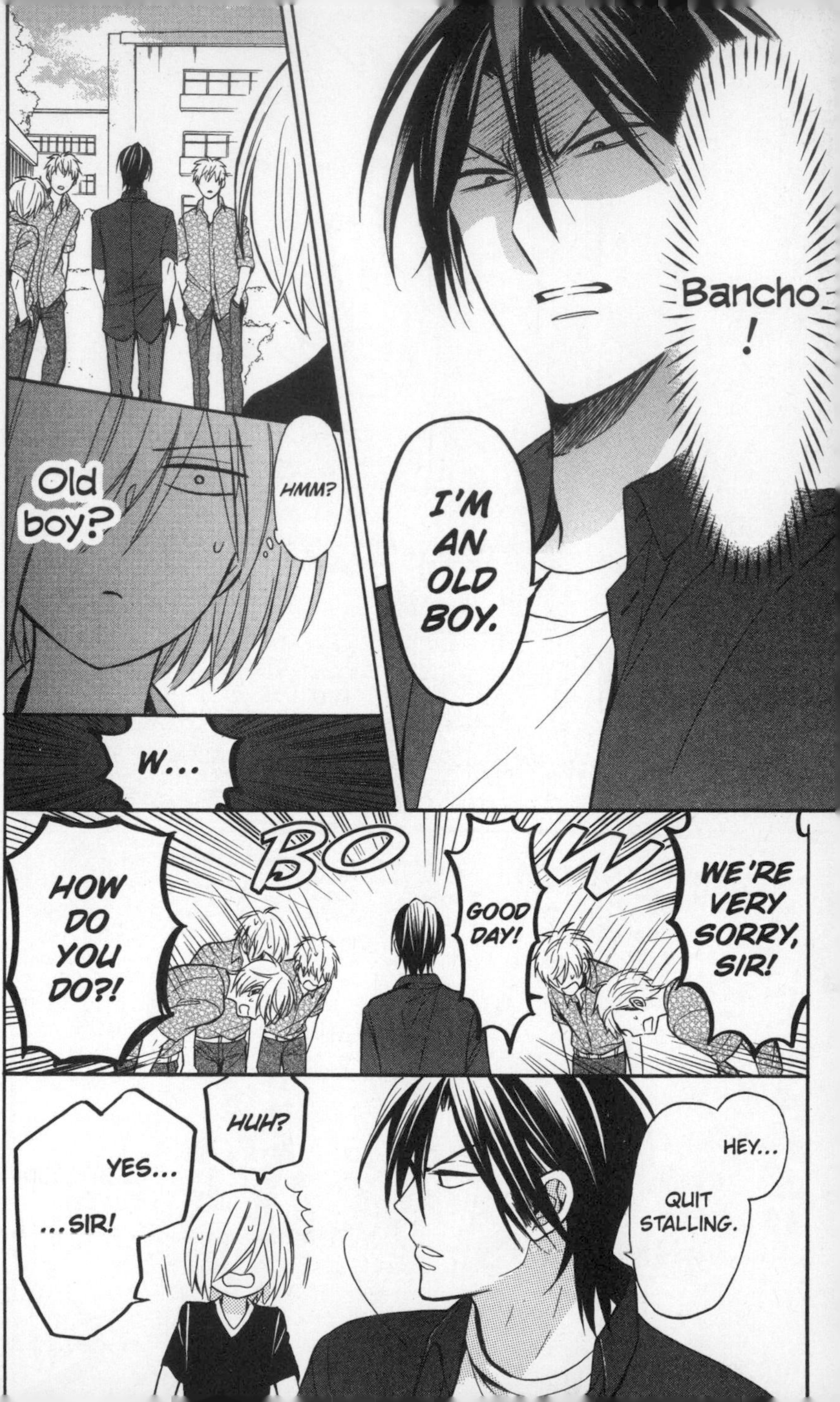
Bancho!
I'M AN OLD BOY.
HMM?
Old boy?
W...
WE'RE VERY SORRY, SIR!
BOW
GOOD DAY!
HOW DO YOU DO?!
HEY... QUIT STALLING.
HUH?
YES... ...SIR!

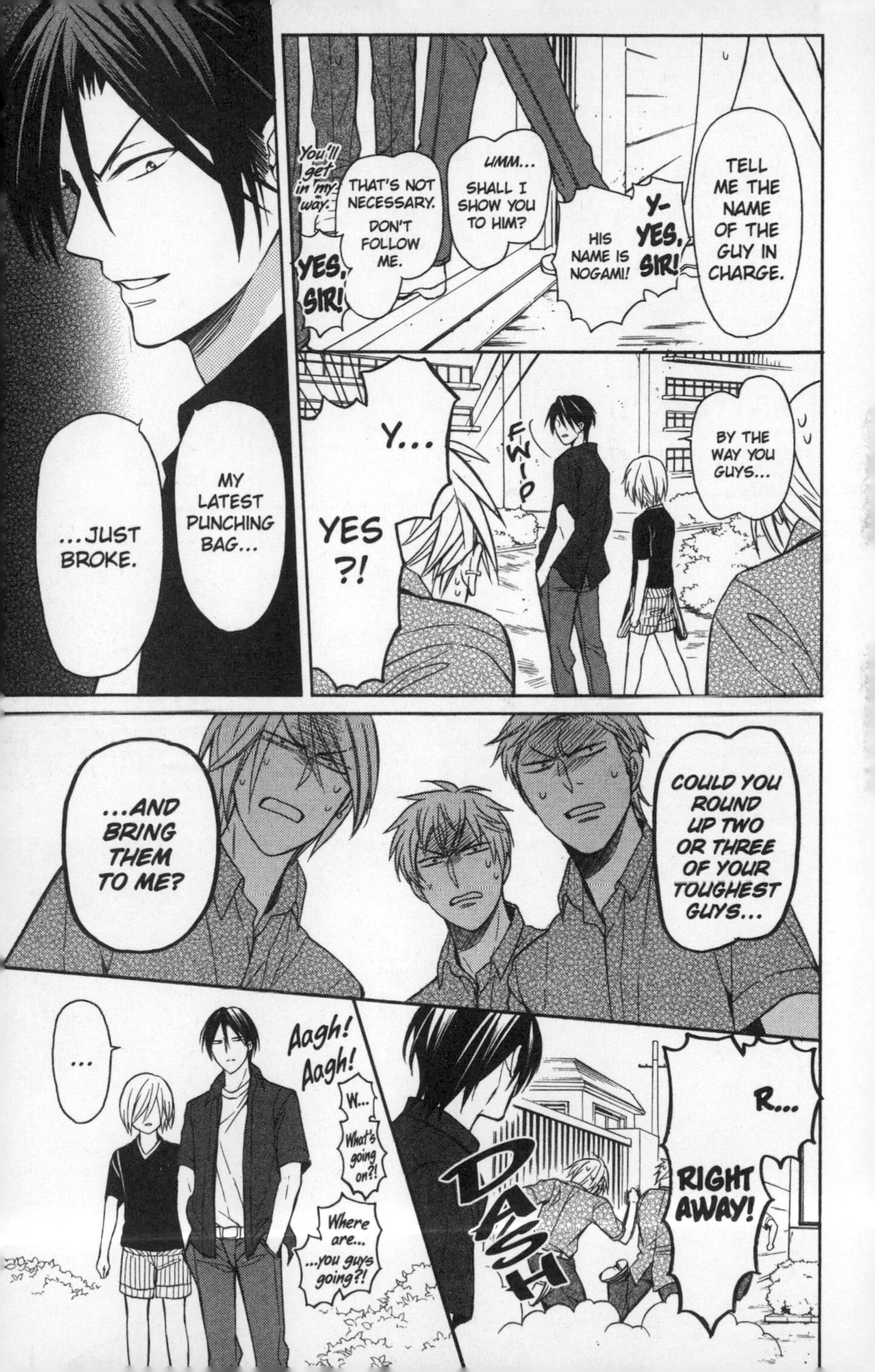
TELL ME THE NAME OF THE GUY IN CHARGE.
Y- YES, SIR!
HIS NAME IS NOGAMI!
UMM... SHALL I SHOW YOU TO HIM?
THAT'S NOT NECESSARY. DON'T FOLLOW ME.
You'll get in my way.
YES, SIR!
BY THE WAY YOU GUYS...
FWIP
Y...
YES?!
MY LATEST PUNCHING BAG...
...JUST BROKE.
COULD YOU ROUND UP TWO OR THREE OF YOUR TOUGHEST GUYS...
...AND BRING THEM TO ME?
R...
RIGHT AWAY!
DASH
Aagh! Aagh!
W... What's going on?!
Where are... ...you guys going?!
...

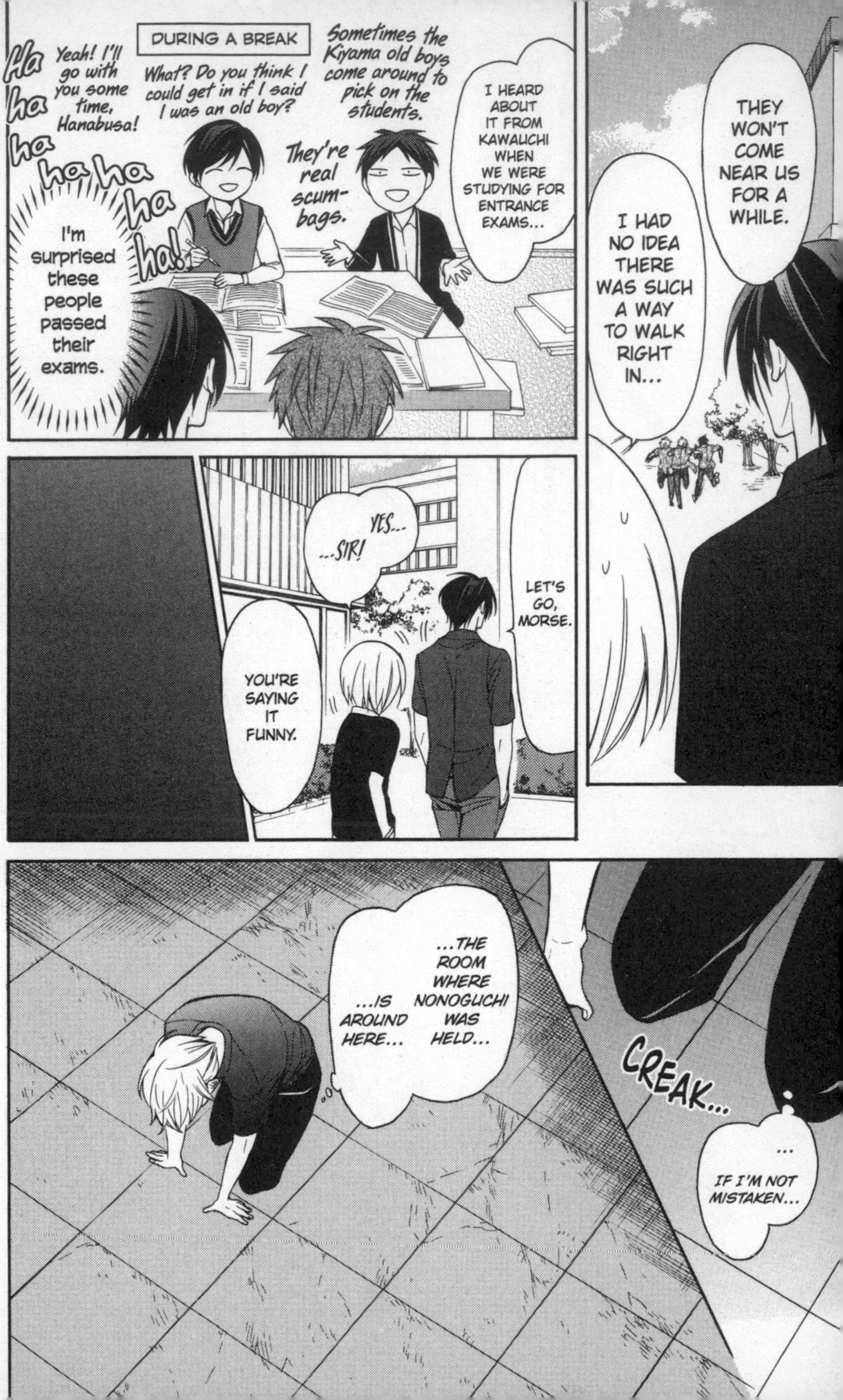
THEY WON'T COME NEAR US FOR A WHILE.
I HAD NO IDEA THERE WAS SUCH A WAY TO WALK RIGHT IN...
DURING A BREAK
I HEARD ABOUT IT FROM KAWAUCHI WHEN WE WERE STUDYING FOR ENTRANCE EXAMS...
Sometimes the Kiyama old boys come around to pick on the students.
They're real scum-bags.
What? Do you think I could get in if I said I was an old boy?
Yeah! I'll go with you some time, Hanabusa!
Ha ha ha ha ha ha ha!
I'm surprised these people passed their exams.
LET'S GO, MORSE.
YES... ...SIR!
YOU'RE SAYING IT FUNNY.
...THE ROOM WHERE NONOGUCHI WAS HELD...
...IS AROUND HERE...
CREAK...
... IF I'M NOT MISTAKEN...

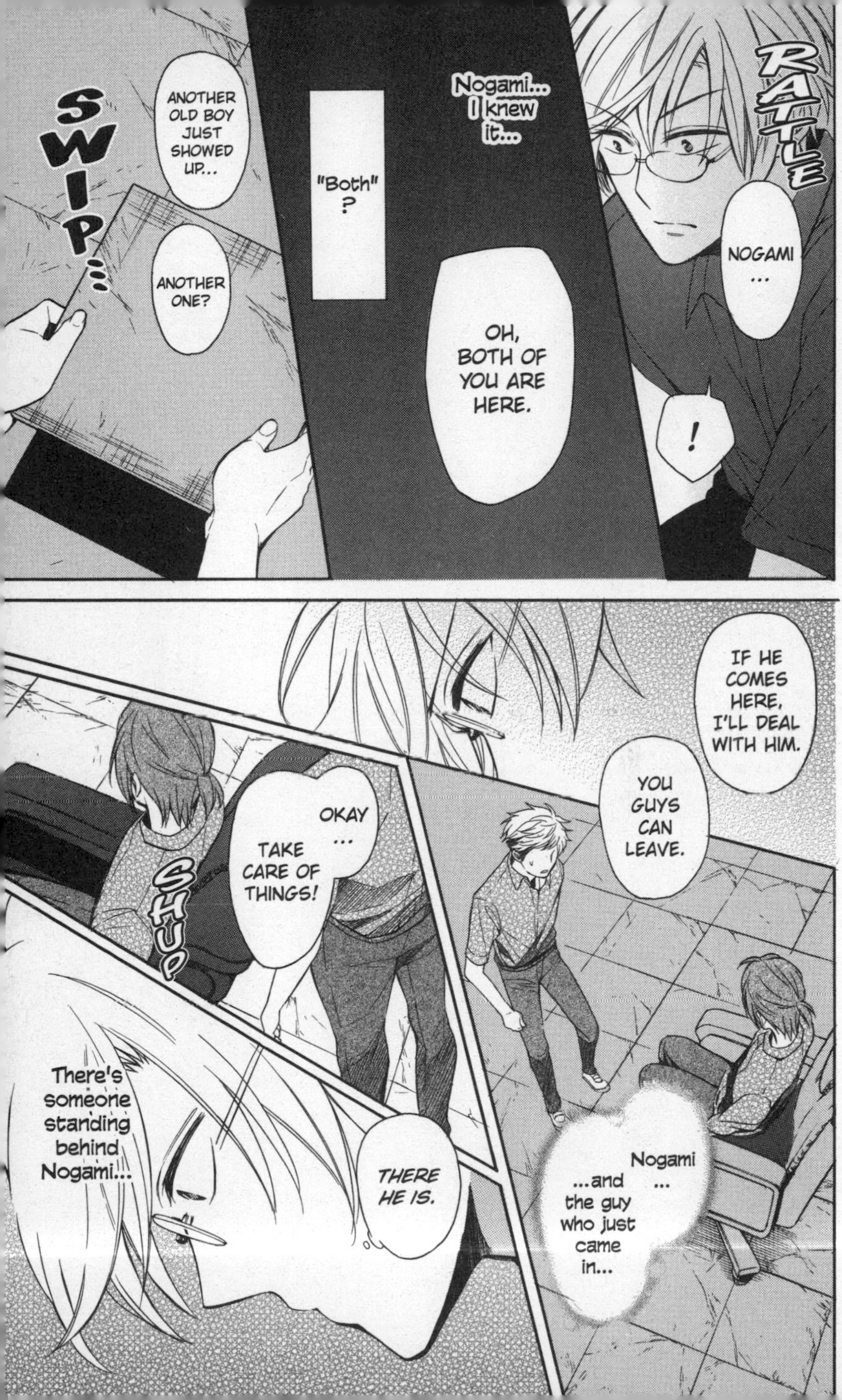
RATTLE
NOGAMI...
!
OH, BOTH OF YOU ARE HERE.
Nogami... I knew it...
"Both"?
SWIP...
ANOTHER OLD BOY JUST SHOWED UP...
ANOTHER ONE?
IF HE COMES HERE, I'LL DEAL WITH HIM.
YOU GUYS CAN LEAVE.
Nogami... ...and the guy who just came in...
OKAY... TAKE CARE OF THINGS!
SHUP
THERE HE IS.
There's someone standing behind Nogami...

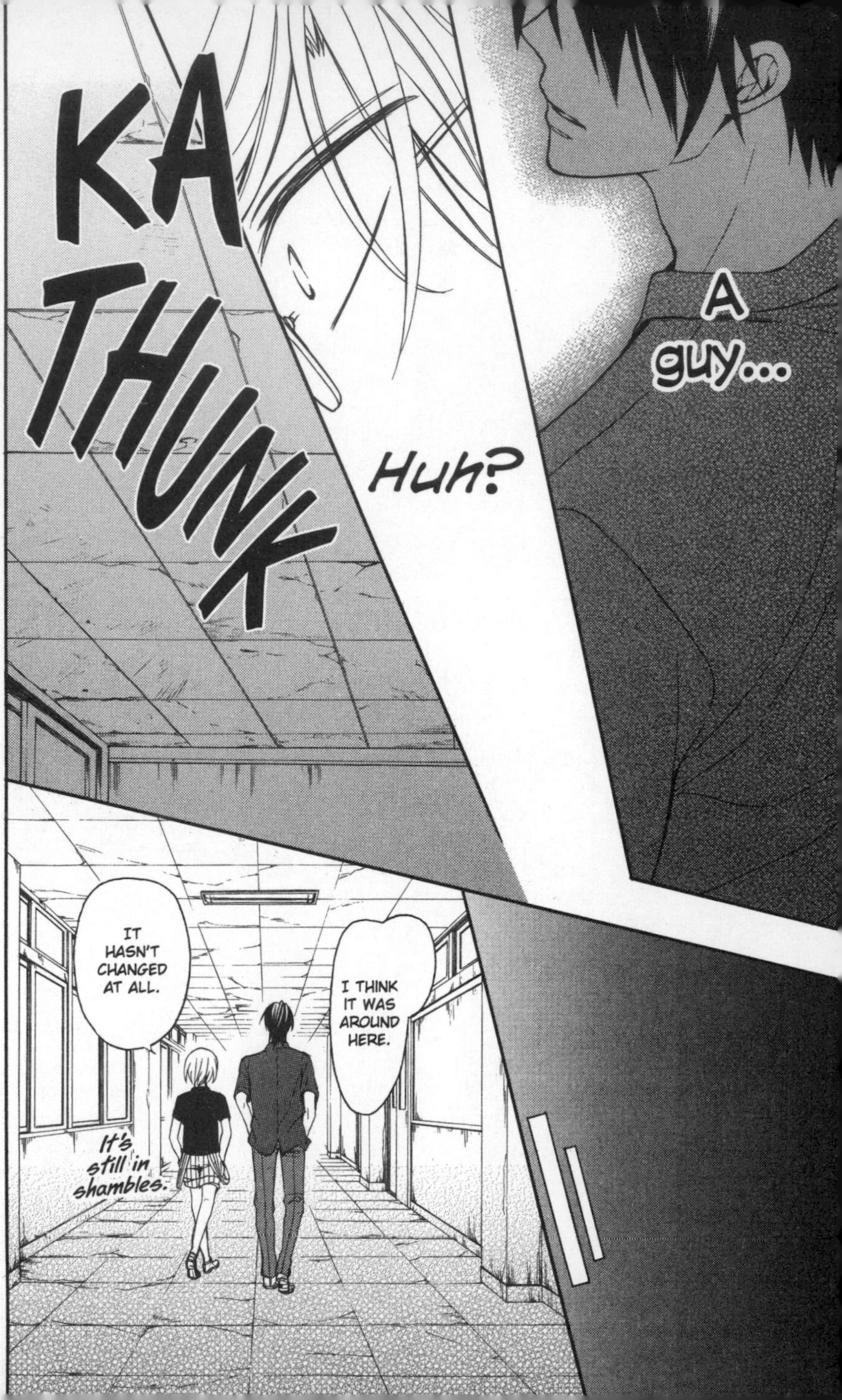
A guy...
Huh?
KA THUNK
I THINK IT WAS AROUND HERE.
IT HASN'T CHANGED AT ALL.
It's still in shambles.

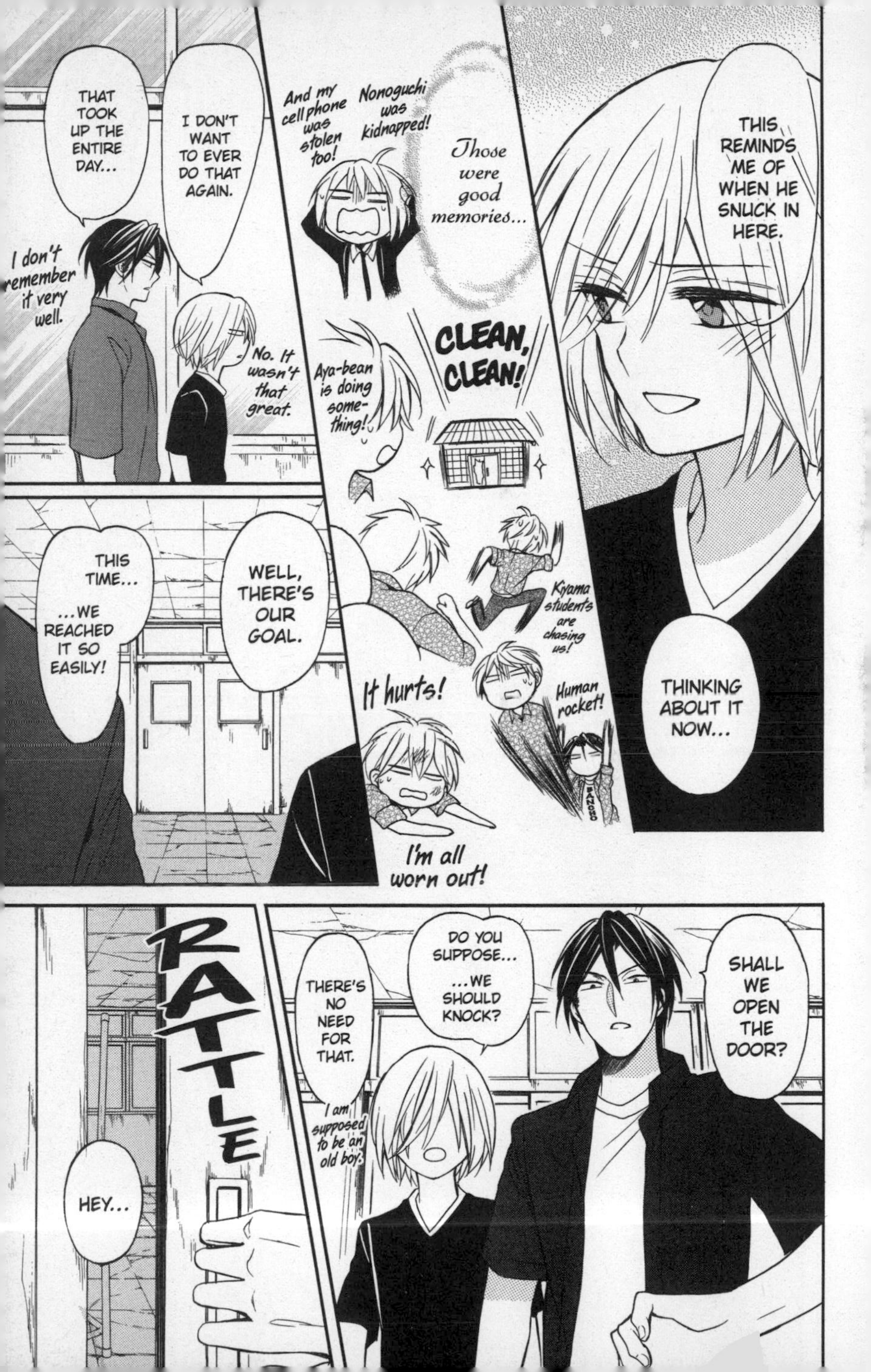
THIS REMINDS ME OF WHEN HE SNUCK IN HERE.
THINKING ABOUT IT NOW...
Nonoguchi was kidnapped!
And my cell phone was stolen too!
Those were good memories...
CLEAN, CLEAN!
Aya-bean is doing some-thing!
Kiyama students are chasing us!
Human rocket!
It hurts!
I'm all worn out!
I DON'T WANT TO EVER DO THAT AGAIN.
THAT TOOK UP THE ENTIRE DAY...
I don't remember it very well.
No. It wasn't that great.
WELL, THERE'S OUR GOAL.
THIS TIME...
...WE REACHED IT SO EASILY!
SHALL WE OPEN THE DOOR?
DO YOU SUPPOSE...
...WE SHOULD KNOCK?
THERE'S NO NEED FOR THAT.
I am supposed to be an old boy.
RATTLE
HEY...

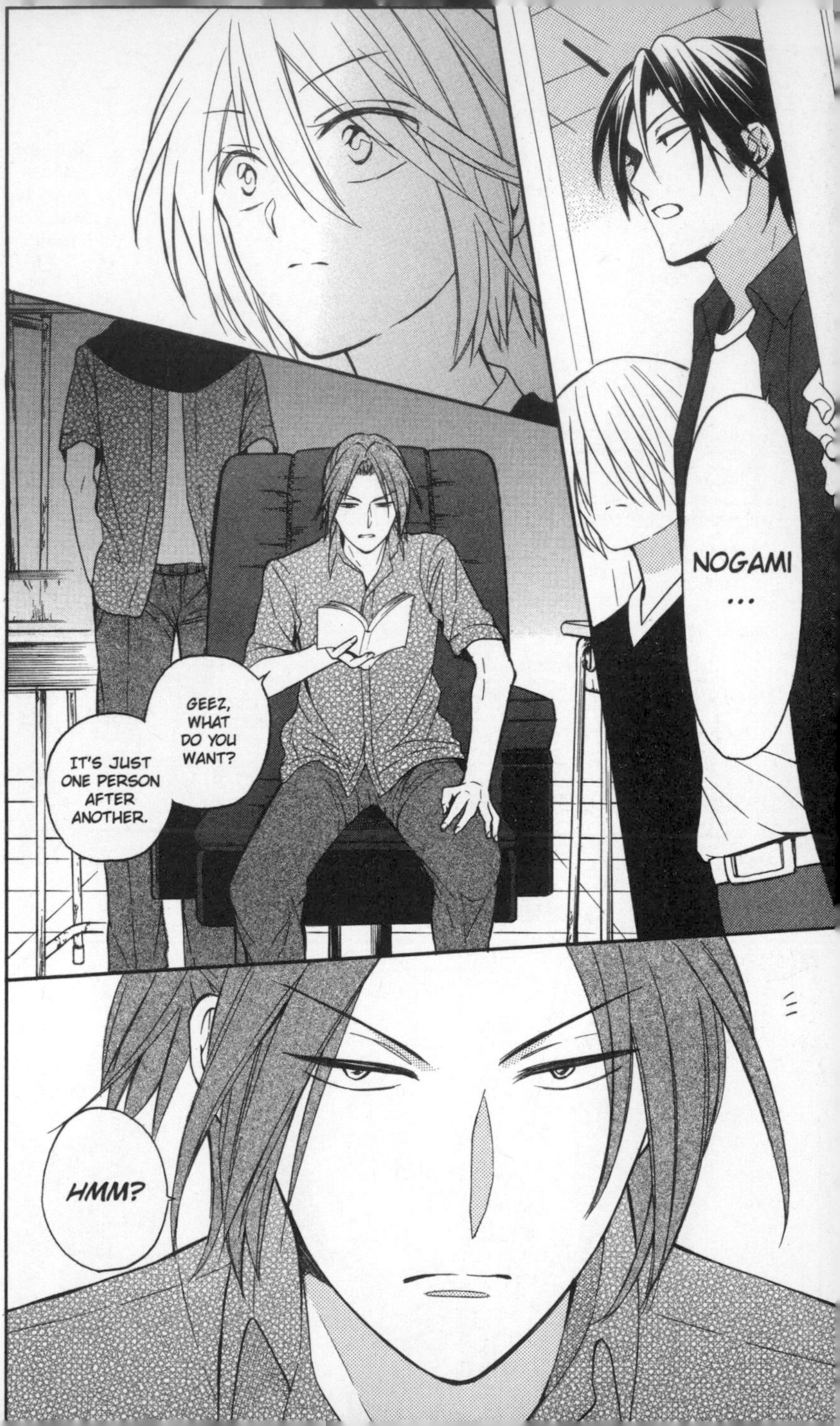

NOGAMI ...
GEEZ, WHAT DO YOU WANT?
IT'S JUST ONE PERSON AFTER ANOTHER.
HMM?

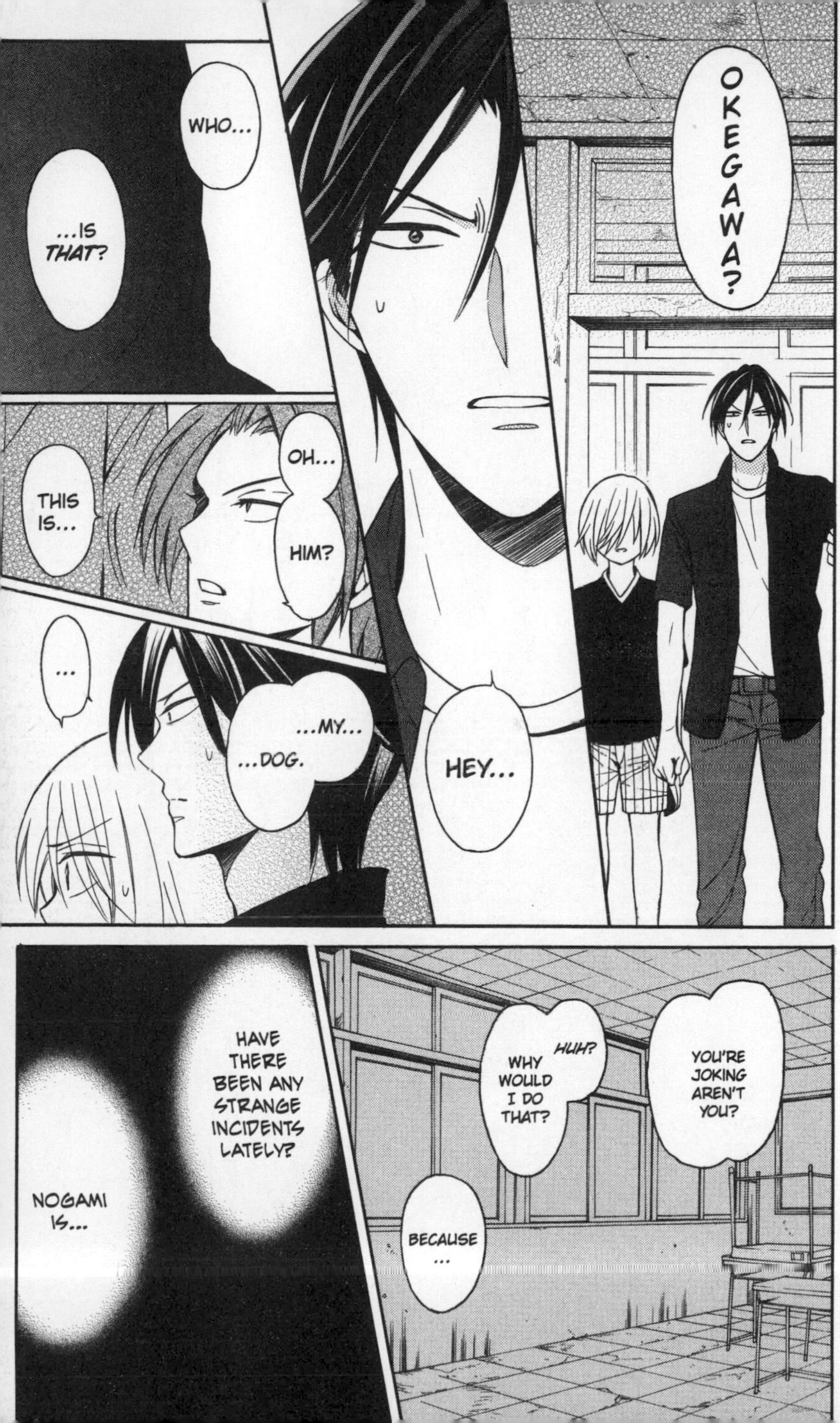
OKEGAWA?
HEY...
WHO...
...IS THAT?
OH... HIM?
THIS IS...
...MY... ...DOG.
...
YOU'RE JOKING AREN'T YOU?
HUH? WHY WOULD I DO THAT?
BECAUSE...
HAVE THERE BEEN ANY STRANGE INCIDENTS LATELY?
NOGAMI IS...

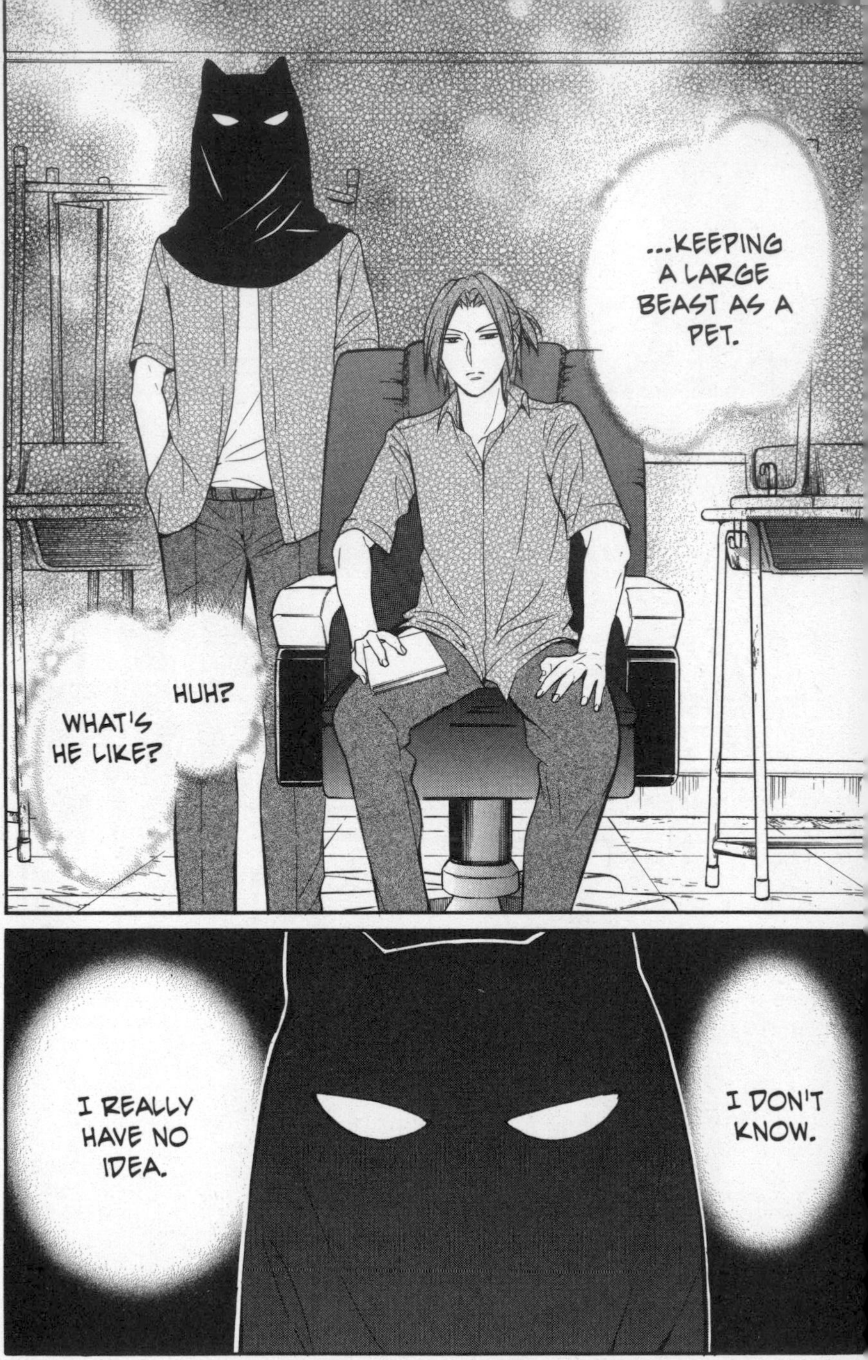
...KEEPING A LARGE BEAST AS A PET.
HUH?
WHAT'S HE LIKE?
I DON'T KNOW.
I REALLY HAVE NO IDEA.

HE'S ALREADY GRADUATED...

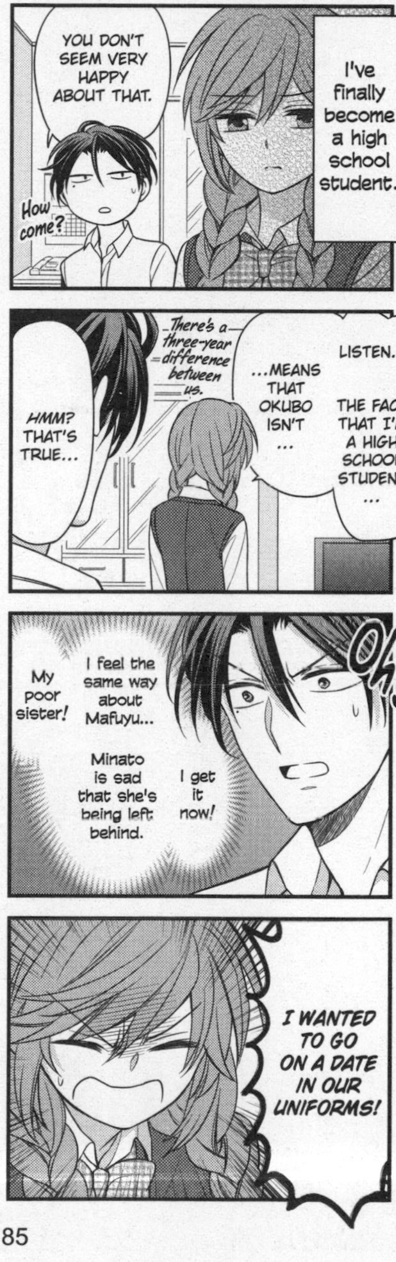
I've finally become a high school student.
YOU DON'T SEEM VERY HAPPY ABOUT THAT.
How come?
LISTEN...
THE FACT THAT I'M A HIGH SCHOOL STUDENT ...
...MEANS THAT OKUBO ISN'T ...
There's a three-year difference between us.
HMM? THAT'S TRUE...
OH!
I feel the same way about Mafuyu...
I get it now!
Minato is sad that she's being left behind.
My poor sister!
I WANTED TO GO ON A DATE IN OUR UNIFORMS!

THE WHEREABOUTS OF HIS UNIFORM

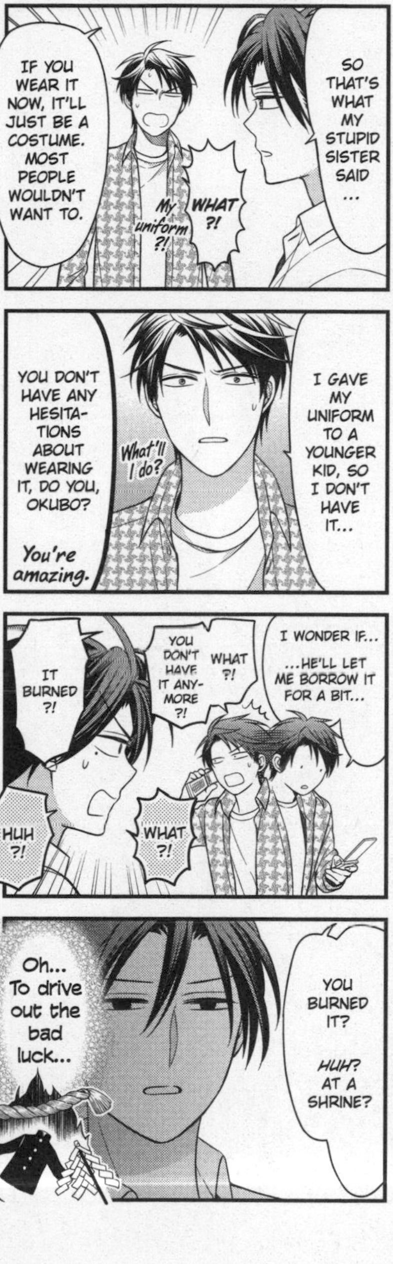
SO THAT'S WHAT MY STUPID SISTER SAID ...
WHAT ?!
My uniform ?!
IF YOU WEAR IT NOW, IT'LL JUST BE A COSTUME. MOST PEOPLE WOULDN'T WANT TO.
I GAVE MY UNIFORM TO A YOUNGER KID, SO I DON'T HAVE IT...
What'll I do?
YOU DON'T HAVE ANY HESITATIONS ABOUT WEARING IT, DO YOU, OKUBO?
You're amazing.
I WONDER IF...
...HE'LL LET ME BORROW IT FOR A BIT...
WHAT ?!
YOU DON'T HAVE IT ANYMORE ?!
WHAT ?!
IT BURNED ?!
HUH ?!
YOU BURNED IT?
HUH? AT A SHRINE?
Oh... To drive out the bad luck...

A KIND-HEARTED SOUTH HIGH STUDENT

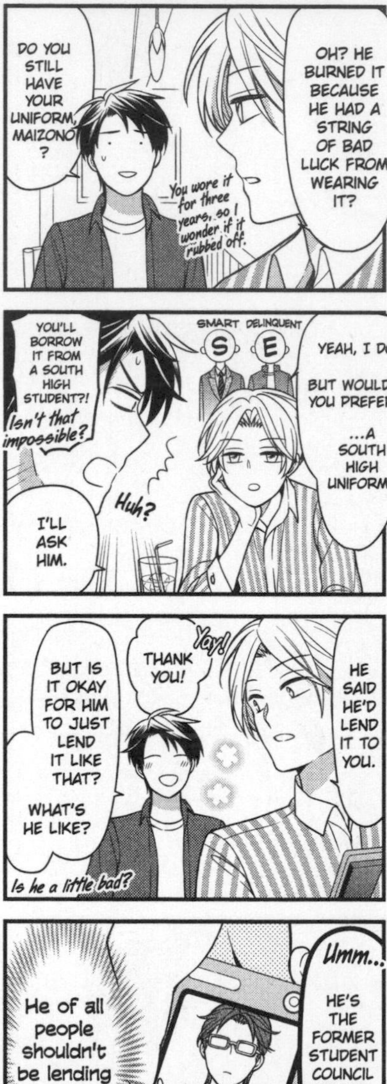
OH? HE BURNED IT BECAUSE HE HAD A STRING OF BAD LUCK FROM WEARING IT?
You wore it for three years, so I wonder if it rubbed off.
DO YOU STILL HAVE YOUR UNIFORM, MAIZONO?
YEAH, I DO. BUT WOULDN'T YOU PREFER... ...A SOUTH HIGH UNIFORM?
SMART
DELINQUENT
S
E
YOU'LL BORROW IT FROM A SOUTH HIGH STUDENT?!
Isn't that impossible?
Huh?
I'LL ASK HIM.
HE SAID HE'D LEND IT TO YOU.
Yay!
THANK YOU!
BUT IS IT OKAY FOR HIM TO JUST LEND IT LIKE THAT? WHAT'S HE LIKE?
Is he a little bad?
Umm...
HE'S THE FORMER STUDENT COUNCIL PRESIDENT.
He of all people shouldn't be lending out his uniform!

A SURPRISING TURN OF EVENTS

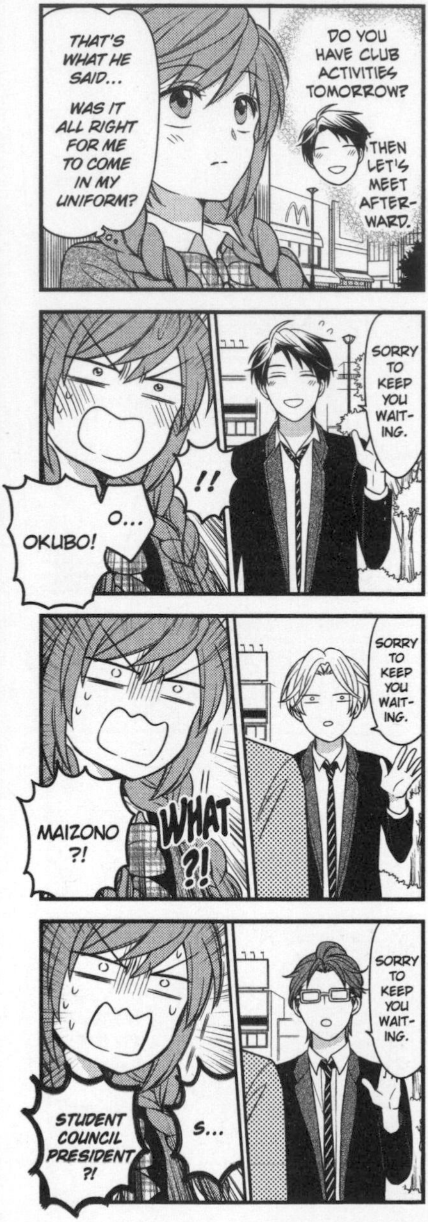
DO YOU HAVE CLUB ACTIVITIES TOMORROW?
THEN LET'S MEET AFTER-WARD.
THAT'S WHAT HE SAID... WAS IT ALL RIGHT FOR ME TO COME IN MY UNIFORM?
SORRY TO KEEP YOU WAIT-ING.
!!
O... OKUBO!
SORRY TO KEEP YOU WAIT-ING.
WHAT ?!
MAIZONO ?!
SORRY TO KEEP YOU WAIT-ING.
S... STUDENT COUNCIL PRESIDENT ?!

MYSTERY DATES

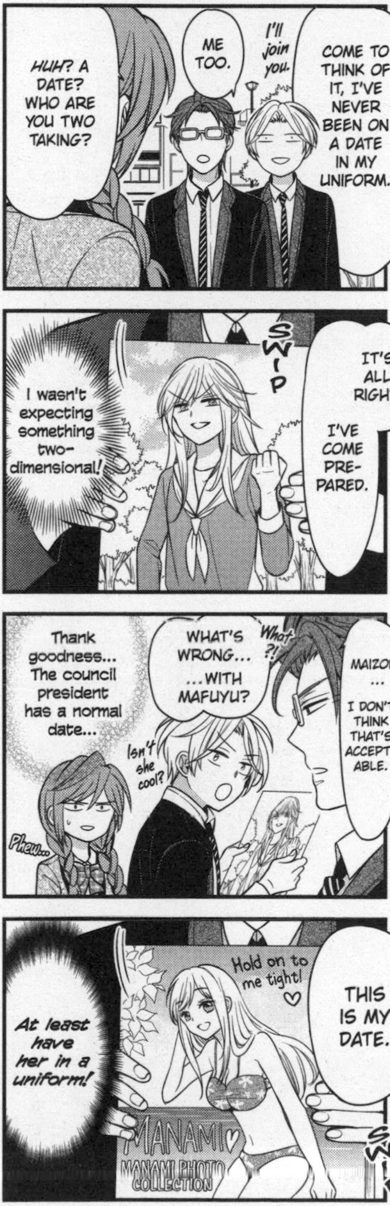
COME TO THINK OF IT, I'VE NEVER BEEN ON A DATE IN MY UNIFORM.
I'll join you.
ME TOO.
HUH? A DATE? WHO ARE YOU TWO TAKING?
IT'S ALL RIGHT. I'VE COME PREPARED.
SWIP
I wasn't expecting something two-dimensional!
MAIZONO... I DON'T THINK THAT'S ACCEPTABLE.
What?!
WHAT'S WRONG... ...WITH MAFUYU?
Isn't she cool?
Thank goodness... The council president has a normal date...
Phew...
THIS IS MY DATE.
Hold on to me tight! ♥
SWIP
At least have her in a uniform!
MANAMI ♥
MANAMI PHOTO COLLECTION

IF I THINK ABOUT IT LIKE THAT, I'LL MANAGE...

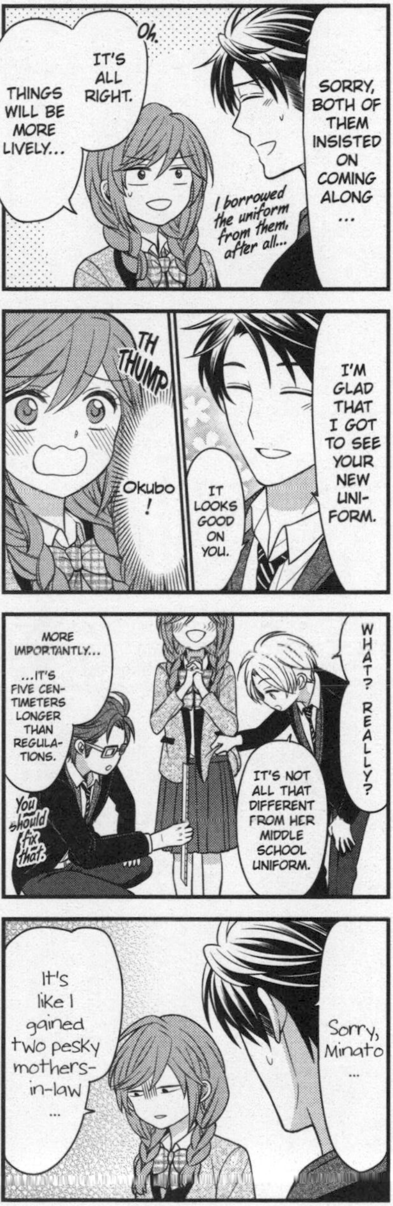
SORRY, BOTH OF THEM INSISTED ON COMING ALONG...
I borrowed the uniform from them, after all...
Oh.
IT'S ALL RIGHT.
THINGS WILL BE MORE LIVELY...
I'M GLAD THAT I GOT TO SEE YOUR NEW UNIFORM.
TH THUMP
IT LOOKS GOOD ON YOU.
Okubo!
WHAT? REALLY?
IT'S NOT ALL THAT DIFFERENT FROM HER MIDDLE SCHOOL UNIFORM.
MORE IMPORTANTLY... ...IT'S FIVE CENTIMETERS LONGER THAN REGULATIONS.
You should fix that.
Sorry, Minato...
It's like I gained two pesky mothers-in-law...

DELIVERING THE HIGHLIGHTS

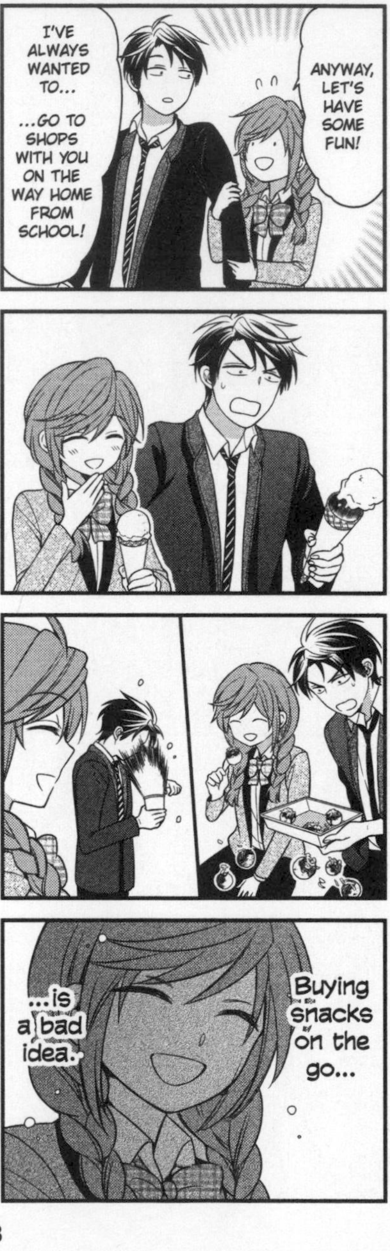

ANYWAY, LET'S HAVE SOME FUN!
I'VE ALWAYS WANTED TO...
...GO TO SHOPS WITH YOU ON THE WAY HOME FROM SCHOOL!
Buying snacks on the go...
...is a bad idea.

CUTE ANIMALS ♡

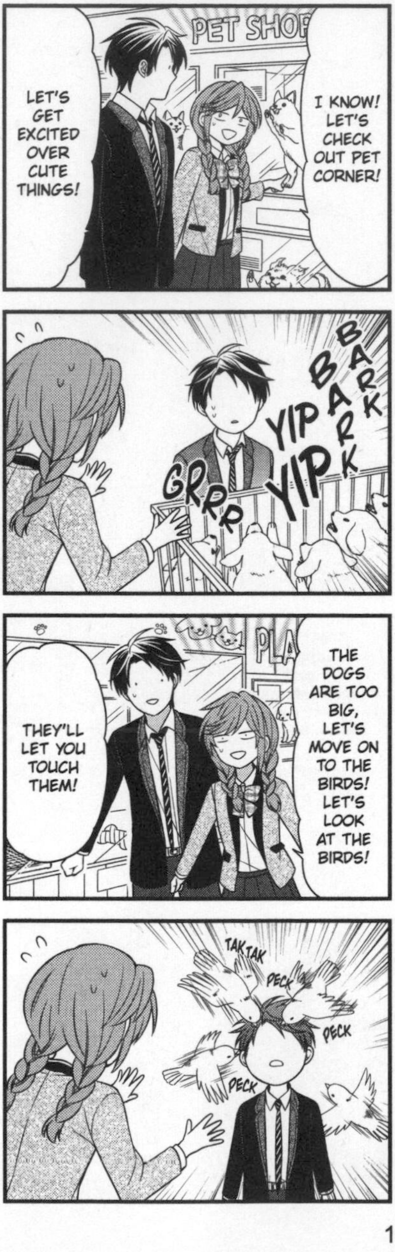

PET SHOP
I KNOW! LET'S CHECK OUT PET CORNER!
LET'S GET EXCITED OVER CUTE THINGS!
BARK BARK
YIP YIP
GRRR
PLA
THE DOGS ARE TOO BIG, LET'S MOVE ON TO THE BIRDS! LET'S LOOK AT THE BIRDS!
THEY'LL LET YOU TOUCH THEM!
TAK TAK
PECK
PECK
PECK

TWO EYESORES

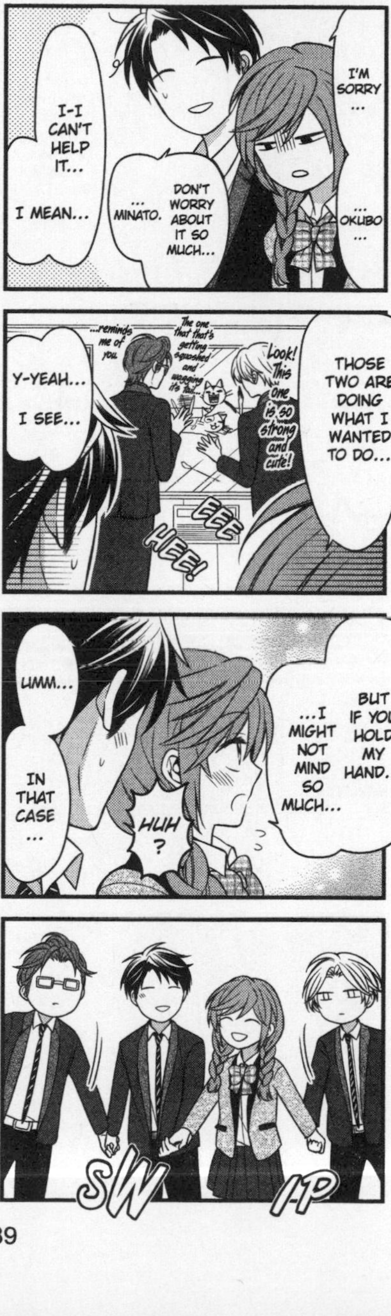
I'M SORRY...
...OKUBO...
DON'T WORRY ABOUT IT SO MUCH...
...MINATO.
I-I CAN'T HELP IT...
I MEAN...
THOSE TWO ARE DOING WHAT I WANTED TO DO...
Look! This one is so strong and cute!
EEE HEE!
The one that that's getting squashed and wagging its tail...
...reminds me of you.
Y-YEAH...
I SEE...
BUT IF YOU HOLD MY HAND...
...I MIGHT NOT MIND SO MUCH...
HUH?
UMM...
IN THAT CASE...
SW IP

IN THE WORDS OF THE FORMER STUDENT COUNCIL PRESIDENT

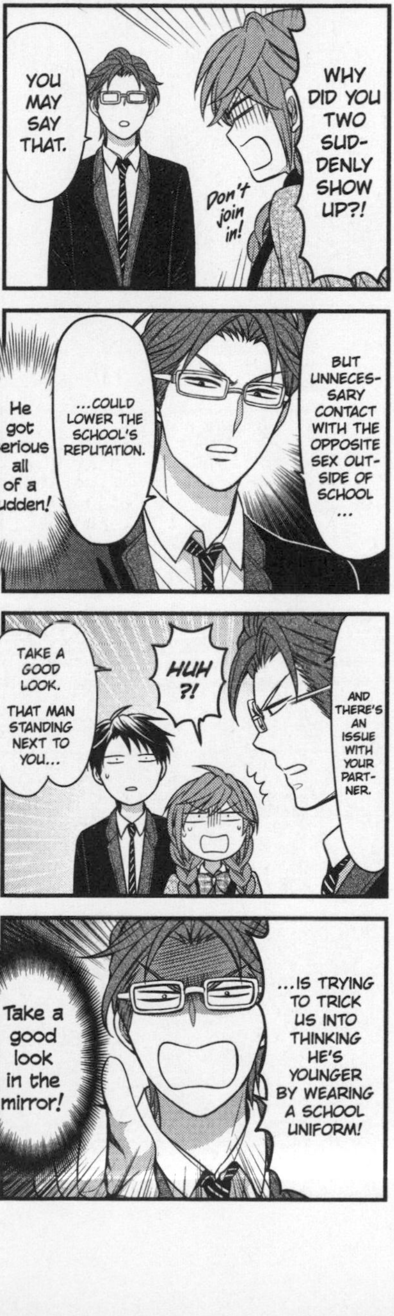
WHY DID YOU TWO SUDDENLY SHOW UP?!
Don't join in!
YOU MAY SAY THAT.
BUT UNNECESSARY CONTACT WITH THE OPPOSITE SEX OUTSIDE OF SCHOOL...
...COULD LOWER THE SCHOOL'S REPUTATION.
He got serious all of a sudden!
AND THERE'S AN ISSUE WITH YOUR PARTNER.
HUH?!
TAKE A GOOD LOOK.
THAT MAN STANDING NEXT TO YOU...
...IS TRYING TO TRICK US INTO THINKING HE'S YOUNGER BY WEARING A SCHOOL UNIFORM!
Take a good look in the mirror!

ENDLESS DESIRE

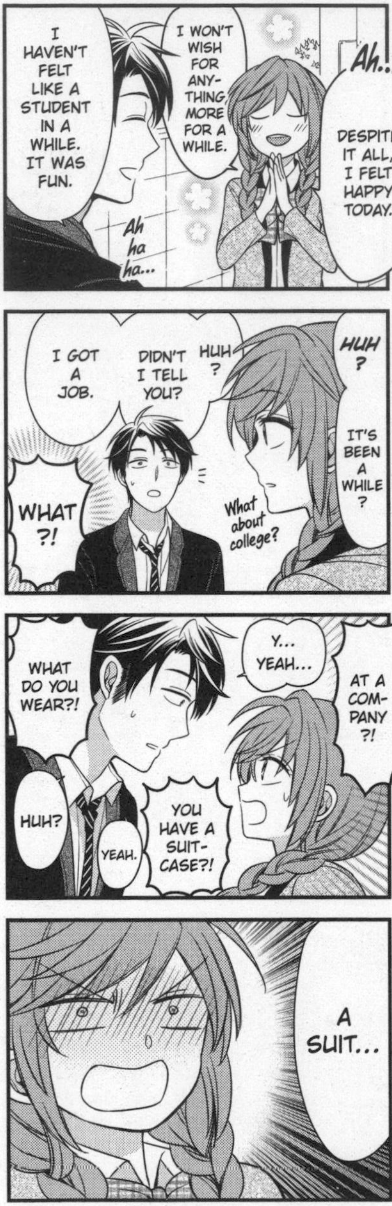
Ah...
DESPITE IT ALL, I FELT HAPPY TODAY.
I WON'T WISH FOR ANYTHING MORE FOR A WHILE.
I HAVEN'T FELT LIKE A STUDENT IN A WHILE. IT WAS FUN.
Ah ha ha...
HUH? IT'S BEEN A WHILE?
HUH?
DIDN'T I TELL YOU?
I GOT A JOB.
What about college?
WHAT?!
AT A COMPANY?!
Y... YEAH...
WHAT DO YOU WEAR?!
YOU HAVE A SUIT-CASE?!
YEAH.
HUH?
A SUIT...

WHAT DO YOU MEAN?

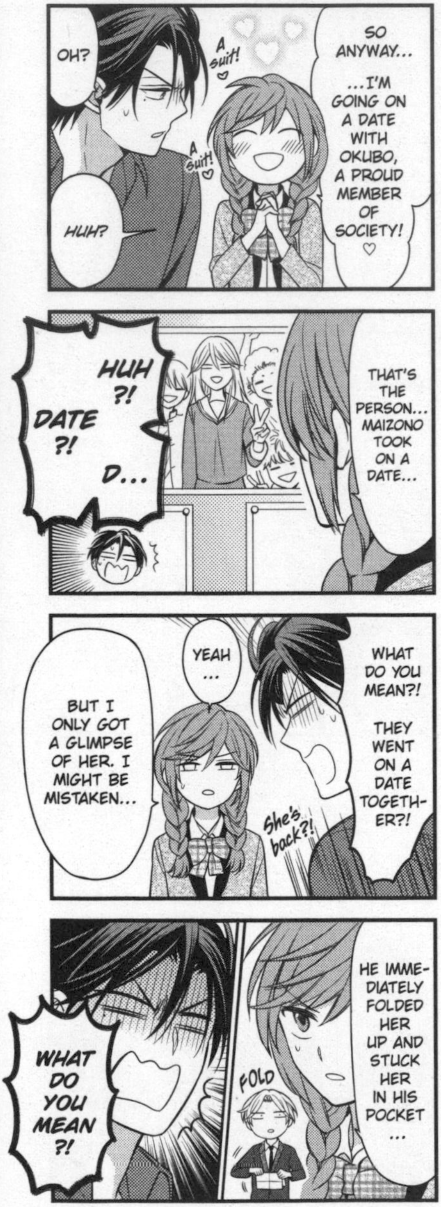
SO ANYWAY... ...I'M GOING ON A DATE WITH OKUBO, A PROUD MEMBER OF SOCIETY! ♡
A suit! ♡
A suit! ♡
OH?
HUH?
THAT'S THE PERSON... MAIZONO TOOK ON A DATE...
HUH?! DATE?! D...
WHAT DO YOU MEAN?! THEY WENT ON A DATE TOGETHER?!
YEAH...
She's back?!
BUT I ONLY GOT A GLIMPSE OF HER. I MIGHT BE MISTAKEN...
HE IMMEDIATELY FOLDED HER UP AND STUCK HER IN HIS POCKET...
FOLD
WHAT DO YOU MEAN?!

Starting this volume, we're seniors! Let's discuss our aspirations for our final year!

"Aspirations," *huh*? Well, I aim to be the strongest in the school!

Hold on, Hayasaka! That sounds like you're saying, "Now that those pesky seniors are out of the way, it's my time to shine. *Heh heh heh.*" Only a loser would say that!

Then I aim to become Miyabi's best ninja...

Miyabi's not around anymore! And you're the **only** ninja!

What about you, Kurosaki? Do you have any big goals?

Umm... D-Defeat Takaomi... I guess?

Impossible goals aren't aspirations. Rejected!

Izumi Tsubaki began drawing manga in her first year of high school. She was soon selected to be in the top ten of *Hana to Yume's* HMC (*Hana to Yume* Mangaka Course), and subsequently won *Hana to Yume's* Big Challenge contest. Her debut title, *Chijimete Distance* (Shrink the Distance), ran in 2002 in *Hana to Yume* magazine, issue 17. Her other works include *The Magic Touch* (*Oyayubi kara Romance*) and *Oresama Teacher*, which she is currently working on.

ORESAMA TEACHER
Vol. 23
Shojo Beat Edition

STORY AND ART BY
Izumi Tsubaki

English Translation & Adaptation/JN Productions
Touch-up Art & Lettering/Eric Erbes
Design/Yukiko Whitley
Editor/Pancha Diaz

ORESAMA TEACHER by Izumi Tsubaki © Izumi Tsubaki 2017
All rights reserved. First published in Japan in 2017 by HAKUSENSHA, Inc., Tokyo.
English language translation rights arranged with HAKUSENSHA, Inc., Tokyo.

Printed in the U.S.A.

Published by VIZ Media, LLC
P.O. Box 77010
San Francisco, CA 94107

10 9 8 7 6 5 4 3 2 1
First printing, February 2018

www.viz.com   www.shojobeat.com

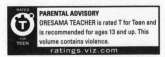